U.S. STAMP YEARBOOK 2000

A comprehensive record of technical data, design development and stories behind all of the stamps, stamped envelopes, postal cards and souvenir cards issued by the United States Postal Service in 2000.

By
George Amick

Published by *Linn's Stamp News*, the largest and most informative stamp newspaper in the world. *Linn's* is owned by Amos Press, 911 Vandemark Road, Sidney, Ohio 45365. Amos Press also publishes *Scott Stamp Monthly* and the Scott line of catalogs.

ISSN 0748-996X

ACKNOWLEDGMENTS

I am indebted to many people for their help in researching and writing *Linn's U.S. Stamp Yearbook* for 2000, a year when a new record was set for number of U.S. stamp varieties issued.

Foremost among them are Terrence McCaffrey, manager of stamp development for the U.S. Postal Service, and his art directors: Carl Herrman, Phil Jordan, Ethel Kessler, Derry Noyes, Howard Paine and Richard Sheaff. Their extraordinary generosity with their time and assistance makes the *Yearbook* possible.

Invaluable assistance has been provided by USPS officials Cathy Caggiano, Monica Hand, Don Smeraldi, Kelly Spinks, Frank Thomas, Robert Williams, and members of the Citizens' Stamp Advisory Committee. Louis Plummer, Sidney Brown and their associates at PhotoAssist are always available to answer my questions, no matter how trivial.

Thanks also to these artists and photographers for sharing their experiences in creating stamp art: Arnold Holeywell, Mike Summers, Bob Wickley, Robert Rodriguez, Michael Deas, Greg Berger, Patricia Fisher, William Sallaz, David Madison, Tom Till, Adam Grimm and Drew Struzan.

Others whose help has been essential are Cecilia Wertheimer of the Bureau of Engraving and Printing, Joe Sheeran of Ashton-Potter (USA) Ltd., Sandra Lane and Don Woo of Sennett Enterprises, Fernando Catta-Preta of Trace Holographic Art & Design, Phil Benoit and Susan Adrianne Tucker of Middlebury College, Brent Hyams of Ryman Auditorium and Walt Sturrock of the Walt Disney Studios.

I am grateful, of course, to my philatelic colleagues: Michael Laurence, Michael Schreiber, Charles Snee, Robert Dumaine, Stephen G. Esrati, Tom DeLuca, John Larson and Kim Johnson. I owe special thanks again to Veronica Schreiber, who was responsible for the layout of *Yearbook 2000*.

Finally, as always, my personal appreciation goes to my editor, Donna Houseman of *Linn's Stamp News*, whose knowledge, ability, organization and patience make her a joy to work with, and my wife, Donna Amick, for her tireless research assistance and infinite support.

George Amick

CONTENTS

Legend for Linn's Yearbook Specification Charts

The following is an explanation of the terminology used in the charts that appear at the beginning of each chapter in this *Yearbook*:

Date of Issue: The official first-day-sale date designated by the Postal Service.

Catalog Number: The number or numbers assigned to the stamp or other postal item by the Scott *Specialized Catalogue of United States Stamps and Covers*.

Colors: The color or colors in which the stamp is printed. A number in parentheses preceded by the letters PMS refers to the color's designation under the Pantone Matching System.

First-Day Cancel: The post office location that is identified in the official first-day cancellations.

FDCs Canceled: This figure represents the total number of first-day covers hand-canceled and machine-canceled for collectors and dealers by Stamp Fulfillment Services in Kansas City, Missouri. It does not include covers canceled at the first-day site on the day of issue.

Format: The number and arrangement of stamps in the panes and printing plates.

Perf: The number of teeth or holes per 2 centimeters, as measured with a perforation gauge, and the type of perforator used.

Selvage Inscriptions: Informational or promotional material printed in the selvage of certain sheet stamps.

Selvage Markings: Standard markings, other than plate numbers, of the kind found on most sheet stamps.

Cover Markings: Material printed on the inside and outside of booklet covers.

Designer: The artist commissioned by USPS to prepare the artwork for the stamp. In 1997, USPS began describing the artist as the "illustrator" and reserved the designation "designer" for the specialist who adapts the illustration to a stamp design.

Art Director: The USPS staff member or private-sector graphic arts specialist assigned to work with the illustrator and designer. Often the art director is also the designer.

Typographer: The specialist who selects and arranges the kind and size of type for the letters and numbers in the stamp design.

Engraver: Person who engraves the die for a stamp with an intaglio component.

Modeler: The specialist who takes the artwork and typography and makes any adaptations that are necessary to meet the requirements of the printing process. After completing this work, the modeler makes a stamp-size, full-color model of the design, which must be approved by USPS before production begins.

Stamp Manufacturing: The agency or company that manufactured the stamp, and the process by which it was made.

Quantity Ordered: The number of stamps or other postal items ordered by USPS.

Plate/Sleeve/Cylinder Number Detail: The number and location of plate, sleeve and/or cylinder numbers on the selvage of sheet stamps, on the peel-off strips, covers or stamps of booklet panes, and on coil stamps at constant intervals along the strip.

Plate/Cylinder Numbers Reported: The numbers or combinations of numbers of plates or cylinders used to print the stamp as reported and compiled by members of the United States Stamp Society.

Tagging: The method used to add phosphor to the stamp in order to activate automated mail-handling equipment in post offices.

1999 U.S. Stamp Yearbook Correction

The following correction should be made in the 1999 Yearbook: Page 439, paragraph 4. Ashton-Potter (USA) Ltd., which printed the Daffy Duck picture postal card, did not print the Daffy Duck stamp, as stated in this paragraph. The stamp was printed by Avery Dennison Security Printing Division.

INTRODUCTION

With a flurry of nondenominated rate-change stamps in December 2000, the Postal Service pushed the total number of new stamps and postal stationery items for the year to a record 221. The figure topped by six the previous high mark of 215 varieties issued in 1999.

A major factor in creating the record was the 49 postal cards produced during the year. The number of actual stamps issued in 2000, 167, was well below the 195 of 1999 and the 178 of 1998, the two top years for that category.

2000's most significant U.S. philatelic event was the appearance of the nation's first stamps containing holographic images. They were part of a set of 15 Space Achievement and Exploration stamps issued in five souvenir panes to salute World Stamp Expo 2000. The panes also included the first-ever U.S. circular and pentagon-shaped stamps. The previous use of holograms by USPS had been limited to stamped envelopes.

Still another U.S. first for 2000 was a "commemorative prestige booklet" containing five varieties, each with a different denomination, depicting historic submarines, with text and photos in addition to the stamps.

The Submarine and Space Achievement stamps were among 140 commemoratives issued during the year, many of them in panes containing multiple designs. The latter included two 15-stamp panes honoring the events, personalities and pop culture of the 1980s and 1990s. These brought to an end the Celebrate the Century series, at 150 stamps the longest commemorative series in U.S. postal history.

For the first time since 1962, when the first Christmas stamp was issued, there was no new stamp in this category. However, there was, for the first time, a set of Holiday picture postal cards. These incorporated the stylized deer images and four different background colors used on the four contemporary Christmas stamps of 1999.

Thirty-two definitives were issued in 2000, including the 18 nondenominated stamps issued December 15 in anticipation of the January 2001 rate change. The first definitive of 2000 was the 60¢ Grand Canyon international airmail-rate stamp with the correct caption: "Grand Canyon, Arizona." In 1999, USPS had ordered 100,750,000 specimens of the stamp destroyed at the printer's because the caption in the design had placed the canyon in Colorado.

However, the Postal Service's embarrassment over this jinxed design wasn't over. After the stamp was issued Jan. 20, it was discovered that the photographic transparency used to create its design had been flopped, or reversed, inadvertently when the printing plates were made. The image would have to be viewed in a mirror to be correct. This time, with the stamps already in circulation, USPS made no attempt to undo its mistake.

USPS announced in 2000 that there would be no more stamps in the

Great Americans series, the largest definitive series in U.S. postal history. The Great Americans' final count was 63 face-different varieties, issued over a 20-year period. It will be replaced by a similar series that USPS calls "Distinguished Americans." The two series prototypes that were issued in 2000 depicted Joseph W. Stilwell and Claude Pepper.

33¢ YEAR OF THE DRAGON
LUNAR NEW YEAR SERIES

Date of Issue: January 6, 2000

Catalog Number: Scott 3370

Colors: black, cyan, yellow, red (PMS 1805C)

First-Day Cancel: San Francisco, California

First-Day Cancellations: 155,586

Format: pane of 20, horizontal, 4 across, 5 down. Offset printing plates of 180 (12 across, 15 around).

Gum Type: water-activated

Overall Stamp Size: 1.56 by 0.99 inches; 39.62 by 25.17mm

Pane Size: 7.24 by 5.94 inches; 183.896 by 150.876mm

Perforations: 11¼ (Wista stroke perforator)

Selvage Markings: "©USPS/1999." ".33/x20/$6.60." "PLATE/POSITION" and diagram.

Designer and Illustrator: Clarence Lee of Honolulu, Hawaii

Art Director: Terrence McCaffrey (USPS)

Modeler: Joseph Sheeran of Ashton-Potter (USA) Ltd., Williamsville, New York

Stamp Manufacturing: Stamps printed for Ashton-Potter by Sterling Sommer of Tonawanda, New York, on Akiyama 628 offset press. Stamps finished by Ashton-Potter.

Quantity Ordered: 56,000,000

Plate Number Detail: 4 plate numbers preceded by the letter P in selvage above or below each corner stamp

Plate Number Combinations Reported: P1111, P2222

Paper Supplier: Tullis Russell

Tagging: phosphored paper

The Stamp

In 2000, for the fourth consecutive year, the U.S. Postal Service launched the year's stamp program with a commemorative stamp in its Lunar New Year Series. This one marked the Year of the Dragon in the modified lunar (lunisolar) calendar that is used in China and other parts of Asia. It was issued January 6 in San Francisco, California.

The stamp was the eighth in an annual sequence of stamps that feature the animals for which the lunar years are named. There are 12 animal symbols in the lunisolar calendar. The year 4698 was a Year of the Dragon, which is the fifth year of the 12-year cycle, and began February 5, 2000.

Many non-Asian countries now issue annual Lunar New Year stamps and souvenir sheets. The first such stamp from the U.S. Postal Service appeared late in 1992 and marked the forthcoming Year of the Rooster. It proved so popular with Asian-Americans and overseas buyers that USPS committed itself to a series. Subsequent stamps commemorated the years of the Dog, Boar, Rat, Ox, Tiger and Hare. Future stamps will be for the years of the Snake (2001), Horse (2002), Sheep (2003) and, completing the set, Monkey (2004).

Each design is the work of the same illustrator, Clarence Lee, a Chinese-American from Honolulu, Hawaii, who completed all 12 of them in the 1990s. Each bears a stylized image of the creature that gave its name to the year, along with the appropriate Chinese New Year inscription in Kanji characters and the words "HAPPY NEW YEAR!" in English.

The first stamp in the series was printed by American Bank Note Company by a combination of intaglio and offset. The next six were gravure-printed by Stamp Venturers or its successor firm, Sennett Security Products. The Year of the Dragon stamp, however, was printed by Sterling Sommer for Ashton Potter (USA) Ltd. of Williamsville, New York, and was the first to be produced by offset lithography. Like its predecessors, it was issued in panes of 20 and has conventional perforations and water-activated gum.

USPS ordered 56 million Year of the Dragon stamps. This represented an increase over the 51 million ordered for each of the two preceding stamps in the series, Year of the Tiger and Year of the Hare, but was little more than half the 105 million ordered for the first two, Year of the Rooster and Year of the Dog.

According to Chinese legend cited by the Postal Service, the order of the 12 signs of the zodiac was determined by Buddha when he invited all the animals in the kingdom to a meeting, and only 12 attended. The first animal was the talkative Rat, the second was the hard-working Ox, and these were followed by the aggressive Tiger and the cautious Hare. The outspoken Dragon, the philosophical Snake, the physically active Horse, the artistic Goat, the spirited Monkey and the showy Rooster joined the others. The last to attend were the watchful Dog and the meticulous Boar. Buddha gave each animal a year of its own, bestowing the nature and characteristics of each to those born in that animal's year.

The Lunar New Year, a time of celebration, renewal and hope for the future, is one of the most important holidays in the lunar calendar. A Year of the Dragon is regarded as an especially propitious year to make business deals, buy property and have a baby. A beneficent creature in Chinese tradition, the dragon is an auspicious symbol representing power and nobility. It is believed that a child born under its sign will grow up to be a brave, powerful leader. *The New York Times* reported early in 2000, based on information from hospitals and prenatal clinics, that pregnancies in the Asian-American community had increased significantly over the preceding year.

The New Year's celebration that inaugurates a new season also is known as the Spring Festival. Spring couplets, typically written on red paper and hung in windows and doors, wish good fortune to all. Oranges and tangerines, symbolizing abundance, and fresh flowers, such as plum blossoms and narcissus, enhance the festive atmosphere.

On New Year's Eve, families and friends congregate for celebratory dinners. New Year's festivities often include the performance of the traditional dragon dance. A dragon — sometimes more than 100 feet long and cast in many colors, including brilliant shades of gold, green, blue and red — is paraded through the streets to the sounds of pounding drums and crashing cymbals.

The Design

Clarence Lee, who has headed his own graphic design firm in Honolulu for more than three decades, depicts the featured animal on each Lunar New Year stamp in a way that suggests traditional Chinese cut-paper art. He cuts the figure from paper with an Exacto knife, then photographs the cutout and overlays the negative on an airbrushed background so the background color shows through the transparent parts of the figure.

The artist subcontracts the Kanji characters to Lau Bun, a professional calligrapher in Honolulu. Lau Bun is an elderly immigrant from China who comes from a long line of calligraphers. On the Year of the Dragon stamp, the character at the upper left signifies "dragon," and the character beneath it, which is common to all the stamps, signifies "year."

Like the previous stamps in the series, the dragon depicted on the stamp is shown in subtle tones of orange, yellow and green. It is silhouetted against a solid background of dark red, similar to the background of the second stamp in the series, for the Year of the Dog. In accordance with a plan developed by Lee and Terrence McCaffrey, head of stamp design for USPS and art director for the Lunar New Year series, the background colors of the first six stamps of the series proceeded through the darker portion of the spectrum, from bright red to blue-green, and the second six are following the same color sequence.

As the first Lunar New Year stamp to be printed by offset, the Year of the Dragon stamp also was the first to include microprinting in its design. Microprinting, which cannot be easily reproduced by photocopiers, is a

The microprinting on the Year of the Dragon stamp consists of the word "DRAG-ON" in the upper-left corner, just inside the dragon's green foreclaw. The word, in black against the dark red of the stamp's background, is virtually impossible to read, even with a strong magnifying glass.

security device that USPS customarily uses on its offset-printed stamps. On this one, it consists of the word "DRAGON" in the upper-left corner, just inside the dragon's green foreclaw. The word, in black against the dark red of the stamp's background, is virtually impossible to read, even with a strong magnifying glass.

First-day Facts

The Year of the Dragon stamp was the third in the Lunar New Year series to be issued in San Francisco, a city with a large Asian-American population. The others were the Year of the Rooster (the first in the series), in 1992, and the Year of the Rat, in 1996.

Clarence E. Lewis Jr., chief operating officer and executive vice president of USPS, dedicated the Year of the Dragon stamp in a ceremony at the Fairmont Hotel. Speakers included Claudine Cheng, past national president of the Organization of Chinese Americans, and Geomen Liu, president of the Chinese Chamber of Commerce. George Ong, national president of the Organization of Chinese Americans, gave the welcome. David Louie, a San Francisco television personality, presided. Scott Tucker, the Postal Service's San Francisco District manager for customer service and sales, introduced the distinguished guests, who included Clarence Lee, the stamp designer, and Jesse Durazo, vice president for Pacific Area operations of USPS.

The earliest-known use of a Year of the Dragon stamp was on a cover postmarked December 30, 1999, eight days before the official first day of issue.

33¢ 1980S (15 DESIGNS)
CELEBRATE THE CENTURY SERIES

Date of Issue: January 12, 2000

Catalog Numbers: Scott 3190, pane of 15; 3190a-3190o, stamps

Colors: black, cyan, magenta, yellow (offset); black (offset, back)

First-Day Cancel: Kennedy Space Center, Titusville, Florida. Stamps released nationally the same day.

First-Day Cancellations:

Format: Pane of 15, square, horizontal rows of 5, 5, 3, 2 at 8-degree angle. Printing plates of 4 panes (2 across, 2 around). Also sold in uncut sheets of 4 panes.

Gum Type: water-activated

Overall Stamp Size: 1.225 by 1.225 inches; 31.09 by 31.09mm

Pane Size: 7.5 by 9 inches; 190.36 by 228.43mm

Uncut Press Sheet Size: 16.4 by 19 inches

Perforations: 11½ (Ashton-Potter stroke perforator)

Selvage Inscription: "1980S/CELEBRATE THE CENTURY®." "Space Shuttle Launched,/Berlin Wall Falls." "The space shuttle *Columbia*, the first

13

reusable spacecraft,/was originally launched April 12, 1981. Sandra Day/O'Connor became the first female justice on the U.S./Supreme Court, and Sally Ride became the first American/woman in space. The Iran-Contra hearings made headlines./Several events signaled the easing of international tensions. In/December 1987 President Ronald Reagan and Soviet leader Mikhail/Gorbachev signed a nuclear arms reduction treaty. The fall of the/Berlin Wall in November 1989 presaged the end of the Cold War./The Vietnam Veterans Memorial was dedicated November 13,/1982. A new national holiday, Martin Luther King Day, was first/celebrated in January 1986./The growth of cable television, video games, and compact discs/had a major impact on home entertainment. *Dallas* and *The Cosby/Show* topped TV ratings. Hip-hop culture and music videos gained/popularity./New Words: yuppie, infomercial, biodiversity" "ART • SPORTS • HISTORICAL EVENTS • TECHNOLOGY • ENTERTAINMENT • SCIENCE • POLITICAL FIGURES • LIFESTYLE."

Back Markings: On selvage: "BACKGROUND PHOTO:/The space shuttle *Columbia* is launched June 27, 1982,/on its fourth mission. The shuttle's first mission in April 1981/inaugurated a new age of spaceflight." "CELEBRATE THE CENTURY® 1980S THIS SHEET IS NUMBER 9 IN A SERIES OF TEN SHEETS ©1999 USPS/CATS™ ©1981 RUG ltd. 'The Cosby Show' ©1999 The Carsey-Werner Company, LLC./'E.T. The Extra-Terrestrial' is a trademark and copyright of Universal City Studios, Inc. Licensed by Universal Studios, Licensing, Inc. All rights reserved."

On individual stamps:

"Figure skating gained/popularity during the 1980s/as fans eagerly followed/national and international/rivalries. Americans captured/nine World Championships,/and American men won/the gold medal in 1984/and 1988."

"On November 4, 1979,/Iranian militants seized the/U.S. embassy in Tehran,/taking hostages. Following/prolonged negotiations, the/hostage crisis came to an/end after 444 days."

"The San Francisco 49ers/were the most successful/football team of the 1980s./Led by their high-powered/'West Coast' offense, the/49ers won four Super Bowls/between 1982 and 1990."

"Based on children's poems/by T.S. Eliot, the Andrew/Lloyd Webber musical/'Cats' first appeared on/Broadway October 7, 1982./Wildly popular with people/of all ages, it has become/the longest-running show in/Broadway history."

"Space shuttles have/transformed U.S. space/exploration. These reusable/crafts can launch satellites/and house labs for scientific/experiments. *Columbia*, the/first space shuttle, was/launched April 12, 1981."

"Debuting in 1984, 'The/Cosby Show' became TV's/top-rated program the next/year, remaining at number/one for five straight seasons./The Huxtables were African-/American professionals who/used warmth and humor/to raise their five children."

"Homely and lovable,/Cabbage Patch Kids® were/the surprising toy success of/the 1983-84 holiday season/when they set off a shopping/frenzy. In an increasingly/electronic era, the low-tech/'adoptable' dolls were a/welcome change."

"First marketed in the U.S. in/1983, compact discs (CDs)/dramatically changed the/music industry. With features/such as durability,/convenience, and sound/quality, CDs outsold records/by the end of the decade."

"Designed by Maya Lin and/dedicated on November 13,/1982, the Vietnam/Veterans Memorial in/Washington, D.C., displays/the names of the more than/58,000 Americans who died/in the Vietnam War or are/listed as missing."

"The cable TV industry/expanded rapidly in the/1980s. Satellite transmission,/coupled with advancements/in cable technology,/allowed a wider variety of/programming, including/channels devoted specifically/to news, movies, or sports."

" 'E.T.' tells the story of a boy/who befriends a stranded/space alien and helps him/'phone home.' Winner of/four Academy Awards® and/one of the most beloved/films of all time, 'E.T.' held/the record as the top-/grossing film for 15 years."

"With the rise in popularity/of video games, Americans/spent more than 20 billion/quarters and countless/hours in arcades in 1981/alone. Home video games,/with consoles plugged into/TVs, turned living rooms into/personal arcades."

"Built in 1961 to prevent/citizens from fleeing/communist East Germany to/the West, the Berlin Wall/symbolized the Cold War./When travel restrictions were/suddenly lifted November 9,/1989, Germans celebrated/the end of Berlin's division."

"Created predominantly by/African-American and Latino/youths from the South Bronx,/hip-hop culture—including/rapping, break dancing,/ DJing, and graffiti—spread/across the U.S. and world,/influencing dance, music,language, and fashion."

"During the 1980s, personal/computers from companies/such as Tandy, Commodore,/Apple, and IBM/revolutionized desktops./Home and office users could/run business software,/play games, or even write/their own programs."

Each stamp also bears the inscription "CELEBRATE THE CENTURY—1980S."

Designer and Art Director: Carl Herrman of Carlsbad, California

---

Illustrator: Robert Rodriguez of Pasadena, California

Typographer: Tom Mann of Vancouver, Washington

Modeler: Joseph Sheeran of Ashton-Potter (USA) Ltd., Williamsville, New York

---

Stamp Manufacturing: Stamps printed by Ashton-Potter (USA) Ltd. on offset portion of Stevens Variable Size Security Documents webfed 6-color offset, 3-color intaglio press. Stamps processed by Ashton-Potter. Cardboard covers printed in red, yellow and blue (front) and black (back) by Partners Press, Buffalo, New York.

Quantity Ordered: 90,000,000

Plate Number Detail: no plate numbers

Paper Supplier: Westvaco/Ivex

Tagging: block tagging on stamps

The Stamps

In 1998, the Postal Service launched the longest and most ambitious commemorative stamp series in U.S. history. The Celebrate the Century series would consist of 150 stamps, to be issued over a period of a little more than two years, and would feature the events, prominent people, cultural phenomena and other aspects of the 20th century. The series would comprise 10 panes of 15 stamps each, each pane marking one of the century's decades.

The first four panes, for the 1900s, 1910s, 1920s and 1930s, were issued in 1998. The next four, for the 1940s, 1950s, 1960s and 1970s, appeared in 1999. The final two panes, for the 1980s and 1990s, were released in 2000.

For visual uniformity, USPS assigned the series to only two art directors, Carl Herrman and Howard Paine, who supervised the design process for alternating decades. Tom Mann was the typographer and computer-graphics specialist for the entire project. For diversity, the stamps on each pane were planned as a mix of new illustrations (with a different illustrator assigned to each decade), new and vintage photographs, and existing artwork.

All 10 panes are conventionally gummed and perforated, and were printed by Ashton-Potter (USA) Ltd. of Williamsville, New York, using a

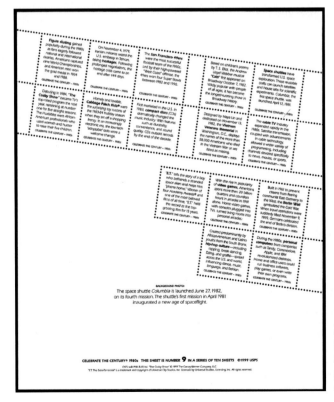

Each stamp bears a few words printed on the reverse, under the gum, describing the design subject.

common format. The stamps are square. Each has a few words printed on the reverse, under the gum, describing the design subject. They are arranged on the panes in four rows at an 8-degree angle from the horizontal. The selvage of each pane displays a large photograph representative of the decade, plus descriptive text that includes a short list of new words that came into use during the period.

The stamps were printed on Ashton-Potter's Stevens Variable Size Security Documents combination offset-intaglio press. The original plan, announced at the outset, was to print one stamp on each pane by single-color intaglio — a process preferred by many older stamp collectors — and the other 14 by offset lithography. The first eight panes were produced according to that plan. On the panes for the 1980s and 1990s, however, all 15 stamps were offset-printed. A USPS spokesman quoted by *Linn's Stamp News* explained that the agency's stamp design group decided the more contemporary designs representing the final two decades of the 20th century "worked better with full color treatment."

The 1980s and 1990s stamps, like their predecessors, were offered for sale to collectors in uncut press sheets of four panes each.

Azeezaly S. Jaffer, then the executive director of stamp services for USPS, conceived the idea for the series. Under his plan, the Citizens' Stamp Advisory Committee chose the subjects for the first five decades, and the public was invited to pick them for the 1950s through the 1990s, using lists nominated by CSAC.

Critics inside and outside the Postal Service warned that this arrangement would lead to the selection of some frivolous subjects and the omission of significant ones. Their fears turned out to be well-founded. The critics found it particularly inappropriate that children's votes should weigh so heavily in a process of selecting historically significant subjects. As Jaffer himself noted, in a June 24, 1999, speech, 60 percent of the participants in the balloting for the 1990s subjects took part through a USPS-sponsored classroom project and were aged 8 to 12.

Voting for subjects for the 1980s pane was held February 1-28, 1999, on official ballots distributed in post offices and on the Internet's World Wide Web. The ballots offered a total of 30 choices in five categories: People & Events (P&E), Arts & Entertainment (A&E), Sports (S), Science & Technology (S&T) and Lifestyle (L). As was the case with balloting for previous decades, participants could vote for no more than three nominated subjects in each category.

The top two vote-getters in each category, plus the next five highest vote-getters overall, were chosen for the 1980s pane. These were:

P&E: Fall of the Berlin Wall (265,147 votes), Vietnam Veterans Memorial (258,515), American Hostages Freed (182,784).

A&E: E.T. The Extra-Terrestrial (239,189), The Cosby Show (Hit Comedy) (194,517), Cats (169,357), Hip-Hop Culture (158,509).

S: Figure Skating (198,841), San Francisco 49ers (188,845).

S&T: Personal Computers (205,527), Compact Discs (199,925), Cable

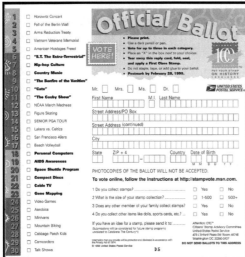

This is a copy of the ballot distributed to the public and listing the proposed subjects for the 1980s pane.

Television (190,533), Space Shuttle Program (177,138).

L: Video Games (268,746), Cabbage Patch Kids (207,505).

The also-ran subjects were:

P&E: Arms Reduction Treaty (94,928), Vladimir Horowitz Concert in the Soviet Union (64,563).

A&E: Country Music (120,977), The Bonfire of the Vanities (34,669).

S: Lakers vs. Celtics (158,075), NCAA March Madness (141,308), Beach Volleyball (126,687), Senior PGA Tour (58,475).

S&T: AIDS Awareness (144,824), Gene Mapping (55,411).

L: Mountain Biking (147,779), Talk Shows (127,283), Camcorders (114,950), Aerobics (77,904), Minivans (75,915).

Thus, Video Games led the overall balloting, defeating the Fall of the Berlin Wall as the decade's most significant subject by 3,599 votes. At the other end of the list of winners, Hip-Hop Culture captured the 15th spot on the pane by a mere 434 votes over the Los Angeles Lakers' and Boston Celtics' domination of the National Basketball Association during the 1980s. Trailing the entire field was the Tom Wolfe novel *The Bonfire of the Vanities*, which finished 20,742 votes behind the next-to-last topic, Gene Mapping.

The numbers of subjects in each voting category (five to seven) were more nearly equal on the 1980s ballot than they had been for previous decades. The 1960s and 1970s ballots each had four to eight subjects per category. Because voters could select only three subjects from each group, that imbalance in the earlier decades gave a strong statistical edge to subjects in the smaller categories.

The pane for the 1980s was issued nationwide on January 12, 2000, with a first-day ceremony in the visitors' complex at the Kennedy Space Center in Titusville, Florida. USPS originally planned to issue the stamps January 13, immediately following the launch of the space shuttle *Endeavour*. However, on December 16, 1999, USPS announced that the date would be changed because of Kennedy Space Center regulations that restrict access to the visitors' complex immediately prior to a launch. *Endeavour* had been scheduled to lift off from launch pad 39A on mission STS-99 at 7:18 a.m. January 13, but in mid-December the launch time was pushed back to the afternoon of the same day, which necessitated rescheduling the stamp ceremony.

The Postal Service ordered 90 million 1980s stamps (6 million panes) from Ashton-Potter. The print quantity was the same as for the 1970s pane and represented another reduction from the number ordered for the first stamps in the Celebrate the Century series. Of the first six panes (1900s to 1950s), 12.5 million each were printed. The order was reduced to 8 million for the 1960s pane.

SPACE SHUTTLE PROGRAM. After the Apollo moon landings, U.S. manned space flight entered a new phase with the use of reusable shuttles. The orbiting vehicles enabled astronauts to stay in space for prolonged periods, launch satellites, conduct experiments, retrieve and repair craft already in orbit and observe the Earth and solar system to unprecedented advantage. The National Aeronautics and Space Administration launched the first shuttle, *Columbia*, April 12, 1981. Next came *Challenger*, which made nine successful flights before coming to a tragic ending January 28, 1986, with an explosion 73 seconds after liftoff that killed its crew of seven. The program was grounded for 32 months while NASA made more than 400 modifications to its four ships. Since then, NASA has successfully launched

about six missions per year.

U.S. space shuttles appeared on nine U.S. stamps before this one, as well as three stamped envelopes. The first stamps to picture a shuttle were four of the eight stamps in the 18¢ Space Achievement issue of 1981 (Scott 1912-19).

MUSICAL SMASH. The longest-running show in Broadway history was *Cats*, a musical comedy with music by Andrew Lloyd Webber based on T.S. Eliot's little book of verse, *Old Possum's Book of Practical Cats*. With feline choreography by Gillian Lynne, furry costumes by John Napier and direction by Trevor Nunn, *Cats*, already a hit in London, opened at the Winter Garden Theater October 7, 1982, and ran for nearly 18 years, closing September 10, 2000. During its 7,485-performance run on Broadway, *Cats* grossed more than $400 million and became as much a tourist mecca as a musical. It was seen by an estimated 50 million people worldwide. Its score included the hit song *Memory*.

SAN FRANCISCO 49ERS. As the Green Bay Packers dominated the National Football League in the 1960s and the Pittsburgh Steelers in the 1970s, the San Francisco 49ers were the team of the 1980s. With quarterback Joe Montana passing to receivers Dwight Clark and Jerry Rice (Rice could "catch a BB in the dark," one coach said), and with running backs like Wendell Tyler and Roger Craig, the 49ers won four Super Bowls, in 1982, 1985 and 1989 under head coach Bill Walsh and in 1990 under Walsh's successor, George Seifert.

The 49ers stamp was the fifth in the CTC series to celebrate professional football. The Green Bay Packers and the first Super Bowl game were featured on the 1960s pane, while stamps on the 1970s pane commemorated the Pittsburgh Steelers and the advent of ABC-TV's *Monday Night Football*.

HOSTAGES COME HOME. For 444 days, from November 4, 1979, to January 20, 1981, Iran's revolutionary government under Ayatollah Ruholla Khomeini held captive 52 Americans who had been taken hostage when radical students seized the U.S. embassy in Tehran. The action was precipitated by President Jimmy Carter's decision to let Iran's exiled Shah Mohammad Reza Pahlavi enter the United States for medical treatment. The Americans' captivity persisted despite extensive diplomatic efforts

and a disastrous helicopter rescue attempt authorized by President Carter. Finally, as President-elect Ronald Reagan prepared to take office, the Iranians agreed to a deal to free the hostages in return for U.S. release of $8 billion in frozen Iranian assets.

FIGURE SKATING. From the first telecasts of the Winter Olympics in the 1960s, figure skating, a sport that demands athletic skill and balletic grace, won the highest viewership numbers. Dorothy Hamill's gold-medal performance at the 1976 Olympics at Innsbruck made fans of millions. By the early 1980s, competitive skating shifted from an exhibition of artistry to one of jumping prowess. The ability, aesthetic charm and competitive spirit of stars like Linda Fratianne, Elaine Zayak, Rosalynn Sumners, Katarina Witt and Debi Thomas, men competitors such as Brian Boitano and Brian Orser, and pairs such as Great Britain's Jayne Torvill and Christopher Dean and the Russians Ekaterina Gordeeva and Sergei Grinkov further increased the popularity of the sport.

Figure skating previously had been depicted on stamps for the Winter Olympics of 1976 (Scott 1698), 1984 (Scott 2067), 1992 (Scott 2612) and 1994 (Scott 2809), and for the Winter Special Olympics in 1985 (Scott 2142).

CABLE TV. Because television signals, unlike radio waves, travel in a straight line and stop when they hit an obstacle, early TV stations had a limited range. In rural areas, especially in the West, where few places were big enough to support their own TV station and where mountains blocked signals, cable was a solution. In Casper, Wyoming, for example, Bill Daniels took a signal from Laramie, 150 miles away, and delivered it to homes by cables for a $150 installation fee and $7.50 a month. Cable delivered a picture and sound of reliable quality, and, in the 1980s, the industry flourished everywhere, bringing over-the-air network shows as well as cable-only systems such as Ted Turner's Cable News Network (CNN) and the all-sports ESPN to millions of homes.

VIETNAM VETERANS MEMORIAL. In 1979, Jan Scruggs, a combat infantry veteran of

the Vietnam War, teamed up with lawyer and Air Force veteran Bob Doubek to found the Vietnam Veterans Memorial Fund. The next year Congress approved a bill to provide a site on the Mall in Washington, D.C. Out of a total of 1,421 designs submitted in a competition, judges chose a design by Maya Lin, 21, an architecture student at Yale University. Her concept was of two triangular sections of polished black granite set together in a wide angle and containing the carved names of the some 58,000 American servicemen dead or missing in the war. Two years after its November 11, 1982, dedication, a statue of three infantrymen, by sculptor Frederick E. Hart, was added. "The Wall" has become by far the most popular memorial in Washington.

USPS issued a 20¢ commemorative stamp picturing the memorial (Scott 2109) in 1984.

COMPACT DISCS. More than a century ago, Thomas Edison recreated recorded sound by dragging a stylus through a groove. That simple principle continued to be the basis of sound recording, from Edison's cylinders to 78rpm shellac discs to long-playing (LP) vinyl, until 1980, when Philips and Sony invented the compact disc, or CD. The CD, which hit the U.S. market three years later, is made of molded aluminum and plastic and is only 4.75 inches in diameter. It uses lasers and microprocessors to produce sound so clear and crisp it is almost indistinguishable from a studio master tape. It has a greater dynamic range than even the best LPs, it stores more music, and because only a laser beam touches the disc during playback, it suffers none of the kind of wear and tear that affects albums and tapes.

CABBAGE PATCH KIDS. By far the most popular toy of the 1983 holiday season, with nearly 3 million sold that year, was the Cabbage Patch Kid, a homely, runt-of-the-litter doll. Stores ran short, then ran out, as parents waited in line for hours and sometimes shoved, screamed and threatened as they sought to buy the coveted dolls for their children at prices of up to $150. The toy was a smaller adaptation of a batch of 22-inch handcrafted dolls created in 1976 by Xavier Roberts, a 21-year-old art student. Their hair color, dimples, freckles and other features were varied so that no two dolls were identical, and Coleco marketed them with birth certificates and individual adoption papers. Later made and sold by Mattel, Cabbage Patch Kids have remained a best-seller.

The Cabbage Patch Kids stamp was preceded in the CTC series by a stamp on the pane for the 1960s decade featuring the Barbie doll. Interestingly, both the Barbie and Cabbage Patch dolls had been omitted from a 1997 pane of stamps depicting 15 different classic American dolls because their inclusion would constitute plugs for a commercial product. All such concerns were abandoned for the CTC series.

HIT COMEDY. The most popular television series of the 1980s was NBC's *The Cosby Show*, named for its co-creator and star, comedian Bill Cosby. Cosby and Phylicia Rashad played Cliff and Clair Huxtable, a professional couple and parents of five children. The family was African-American, but its internal dynamics, its stresses and satisfactions and its adherence to positive family values had a universal appeal, as evidenced by the success of the series. *The Cosby Show* finished second in the ratings in its first season, 1984-85, and topped the charts, sometimes by huge margins, for the next four seasons.

Cosby was the second television sitcom to be featured on a stamp in the CTC series. *All in the Family* was the subject of a stamp on the 1970s pane.

Bill Cosby himself made an appearance on Rosie O'Donnell's televised talk show February 22, 2000, carrying an enlarged replica of the stamp, which he autographed and presented to O'Donnell as an item for her charitable auction for children. Four days later, the signed stamp image was sold by the Internet auction house eBay for $1,435.

FALL OF THE BERLIN WALL. Mikhail Gorbachev, who came to power in the Soviet Union in 1985, instituted a series of reforms — perestroika — including a declaration that "any nation has the right to decide its fate by itself." Former Soviet satellites opened their borders, and on the evening of November 9, 1989, the Berlin Wall, the most vivid physical symbol of the Cold War since 1961, began to crumble. A wave of East Germans overwhelmed a confused border patrol and fell into the welcoming arms of surprised West Berliners. East and West Germans alike spontaneously began tearing at the wall with hammers, pickaxes and chisels. Together they celebrated atop the 12-foot-high structure. Within 48 hours, 2 million East Germans visited the West; in less than two years, the two Germanys were reunited.

VIDEO GAMES. The first video game, Spacewar, was created on a mainframe computer at MIT by Steve Russell, an electrical-engineering student. As computers got faster and smaller, video games entered the mainstream with Atari's Pong, a crudely rendered coin-operated game of tennis with two white bars as electronic rackets, that launched the industry in bars and arcades in 1972. A home version of the game appeared in 1974. Midway Games' Space Invaders and Namco's Pac-Man helped usher in the golden age of video games, with both the arcade and home-console markets flourishing in the early 1980s. Home-use games were distributed on cartridges, floppy disks and CD-ROMs, as well as through telephone and cable TV lines.

"E.T. THE EXTRA-TERRESTRIAL." Opening in the summer of 1982, *E.T.: The Extra-Terrestrial* became one of the most beloved and lucrative films of all time. It was made at a cost of $10.5 million and by the end of the 1980s had generated more than $1 billion in movie theaters and $400 million in video sales. The film, about a lonely boy and a stranded space alien who was both a sage and a wide-eyed innocent, was directed by Steven Spielberg, starred 9-year-old Henry Thomas and a title character designed by Carlo Rambaldi, who reportedly modeled E.T.'s distinctive features on the faces of Albert Einstein and Carl Sandburg. The film won four Academy Awards, including one for its visual effects, and a Golden Globe for best picture.

PERSONAL COMPUTERS. The 1982 "Machine of the Year," as *Time* magazine named it, was the personal computer, which was small and inexpensive enough for individual ownership. In only a few short years, the PC would bring dramatic changes in the way people worked, played, shopped, banked, communicated — in short, the way they lived. One of the first affordable PCs was the Altair 8800, which came on the market in the mid-1970s. It was severely limited, lacking both a keyboard and a screen, but by owning and tinkering with Altair 8800s, two of the industry's founding pioneers were launched: Stephen Wozniak, who, with Steve Jobs, founded Apple Computer, and Bill Gates, who, with Paul Allen, started Microsoft. A landmark event was the unveiling in August 1981 of the IBM PC, which was equipped with Microsoft's MS-DOS operating system.

HIP-HOP CULTURE. The four cornerstones of what came to be called Hip-Hop Culture, a highly controversial product of the inner city, were graffiti, break dancing, rap music and boom boxes. Graffiti, or "tagging," consisted of messages and designs spray-painted onto public spaces, usually in defiance of the law. Break dancing was a kind of ground-level acrobatics, performed with great dexterity, that required no more than a patch of pavement and a beat. Rap music — the tuneless recitation in rhythm of a crudely poetic message, sometimes defiant or misogynistic — is a genre that has produced immense profits for its stars and marketers. The high-volume sound systems called boom boxes made rap highly portable, often to the distress of those who didn't wish to partake of it.

The Designs

To illustrate the stamps, art director Carl Herrman chose Robert Rodriguez of Pasadena, California. Rodriguez previously had painted the dancers who were shown on the 32¢ and 33¢ Cinco de Mayo holiday stamps of 1998-99, and the 3.50-peso stamp from Mexico issued jointly with the 32¢ U.S. Cinco de Mayo stamp.

For Rodriguez, a dividend of the assignment was that he taught himself to illustrate on a computer, using a tablet, electronic pen and Photoshop software. "I did my preliminary sketches on the computer, and it was a great way to learn to use it," he said. "I made 150 or so sketches, and since they were relatively loose, I didn't have to be all that proficient. When the time came to do the finished artwork, I knew how to do it. I use the computer all the time now for my work."

With acrylics and Prisma colored pencils, Rodriguez paints a picture in sections — the main figure, parts of the background — and scans each section into the computer. If he intends to model a painting closely on a photograph, he may photocopy the source photo, mount the copy on cardboard and paint over it before scanning in the resulting image. Then he assembles the elements of the illustration on the monitor screen, adjusts colors and touches up details to his liking. The end product is an electronic file that is used to make the color separations for printing.

"The nice thing about this system is that if any changes are needed, I don't have to totally repaint," he said. "I can repaint the specific section and scan that in. If [postal officials] look at an illustration and say, 'Can you move that figure up just a little bit, and keep the background where it is,' I can do it, because I have everything separated into different layers."

SPACE SHUTTLE PROGRAM. The stamp depicts a shuttle craft and its booster rocket in the launch position, with an illuminated gantry standing nearby. A portion of a giant American flag provides the backdrop for

25

the spacecraft; the flag's dark tones contrast with the white of the shuttle and booster. The artwork was based on two photographs of the shuttle *Columbia* in the period before its maiden launch in 1981, taken by freelance photographer Ken Sherman of Lewisburg, West Virginia. Although the shuttle is shown at night, *Columbia*'s actual mission began in the daytime.

Rodriguez's original concept sketch showed a shuttle lifting off in a blaze of rocket exhaust, but the scene was felt to be too similar to the $10.75 Express Mail stamp of 1995 — and too similar, in fact, to the launch photograph shown in the pane's selvage. Adding the flag "gave it a fresh look, a real patriotic look," said Carl Herrman.

MUSICAL SMASH. The face of one of the actors in *Cats*, painted in tones of orange and brown, fills the square stamp frame. Superimposed on the top half of the stamp is the word CATS in yellow hand-lettering as it appears on the show's signs and posters.

The image is based on a photograph of actor Terrence Mann, the production's original Rum Tum Tugger, that appears in the book *Cats, the Book of the Musical*. The photo is by John

This is the photograph of actor Terrence Mann, who originated the role of Rum Tum Tugger in Cats, on which Rodriguez based his illustration.

These are alternative design ideas for the Musical Smash stamp using photographs of actors and actresses from Cats.

26

Napier, who designed the show. For the final artwork, Rodriguez broadened the face and features, but the actor in his role remains recognizable.

The chosen design was deemed much stronger than alternative design concepts using photographs of other cat-actors and actresses from the musical. "It's one of my favorite stamps," Carl Herrman said. "It's so graphic looking."

The design was unveiled January 12, 2000, at New York's Winter Garden Theater, where the show played during its nearly 18-year run.

SAN FRANCISCO 49ERS. Because this was the fifth CTC stamp to illustrate a professional football subject, the design team was hard pressed to come up with an original idea. One preliminary sketch by Rodriguez showed a 49ers' helmet upside down in the grass with a taped hand holding the face mask, "as if a player sitting on the bench just got a break and put his helmet down," Herrman said. However, a helmet close-up had been used in 1999 for the Pittsburgh Steelers stamp design.

Rodriguez settled on a painting depicting a red-jerseyed player leaping exultantly into the arms of another player, in celebration of a victory. The hard-edged action picture is set off against a blurred, soft-color background showing a stadium crowd. According to PhotoAssist, the stamp art combined elements of two PhotoAssist photographs that used models Derrick Mashore of Arlington, Virginia, and Ralph (Latae) Allsopp of Lanham, Maryland, plus a photo-agency photograph taken at a 49ers game in 1989. None of the three photos could be obtained for reproduction in the *Yearbook*.

On the action photograph, and on Rodriguez's first version of the stamp art, the player holding his teammate has what appears to be his left index finger raised in the "we're number one" gesture. Officials worried that some people would think the finger was the middle one, and asked Rodriguez to lower the digit on his final artwork.

"I did the crowd as a separate painting," Rodriguez said. "I painted it fairly loosely, and then made it out of focus using Photoshop. It wound up looking really photographic."

Scott Tucker, USPS San Francisco district manager for customer service and sales, unveiled the stamp December 12, 1999, during halftime ceremonies at a 49ers game at 3COM Park, San Francisco. Bill Walsh, vice president and general manager of the team, and Roger Craig, Bill Ring and Keena Turner, three 49ers of the 1980s, participated.

Rodriguez's original concept sketch for the San Francisco 49ers stamp showed an upside-down helmet in the grass with its owner's gloved hand holding it by the face mask.

27

These two preliminary designs prepared for the Hostages Come Home stamp were based on contemporary newspaper headlines.

HOSTAGES COME HOME. Carl Herrman considered using a photograph of ex-hostages leaving their plane after being flown to freedom or, alternatively, a photo of an ex-hostage being hugged by a relative, but the faces were recognizable, and altering the features didn't seem to make sense for this subject. He then created some designs based on headlines telling of the hostages' liberation and return. He found his ultimate solution in a *Washington Post* photograph depicting the returnees, in a motorcade led by Vice President George H.W. Bush, being driven through the streets of Washington, D.C., January 27, 1981, on their way to a private reception hosted by President and Mrs. Ronald Reagan. "The hostages were riding in buses, so you couldn't recognize their faces, which solved that problem," Herrman said. "There were people along the way waving American flags, and there was the U.S. Capitol in the background. It was just perfect. We did a little retouching, with some minor rearrangements to improve the photo. With the caption, 'Hostages Come Home,' it told the whole story." The stamp appears to be printed in black and white, like the newspaper picture, but all four process colors were used in its production, "which makes it a lot richer in appearance," Herrman said.

FIGURE SKATING. Rodriguez's painting is a study in lines, angles and curves. A female skater in a purple and gold costume glides across the ice on her right skate, her left leg and left arm extended behind her, her right arm in front. The left leg and left arm are parallel to each other; the right leg and right arm are parallel to two edges of the stamp image. The skater is tightly cropped, so that her left hand and left foot are outside the illustration. The circles, arcs and lines of the school figures that are required in skating competition stand out in white on the ice, which is shown in dark and light shades of lavender to suggest the play of spotlight beams.

Rodriguez based his artwork on photographs of well-known female skaters. "Bob did alter the images extensively," Herrman said. "We went through level after level, 'change the hair, change the face more, change the hair color more, change the costume,' until we had done enough that we felt the picture couldn't be connected with anyone who was a skating superstar."

In an earlier version, the artist superimposed a stylized snowflake on the illustration. CSAC felt that the snowflake was an unnecessary element

28

This earlier version of the Figure Skating illustration shows the skater centered in the stamp frame, without the tight cropping of the final version, and includes a stylized snowflake superimposed over the lower-left corner that isn't in the final.

and asked that it be removed.

CABLE TV. The painted illustration shows a field of satellite dishes. Three dishes are visible in profile against a background of trees, while a portion of one large concave dish dominates the lower half of the design. "When you think of cable TV you don't think of dishes, but this is what the cable TV companies have. It's how they get their signals in and out," Herrman said. "So this was the correct way to deal with the subject. It's a nice composition, and suggests an abstract piece of art."

VIETNAM VETERANS MEMORIAL. The illustration shows a close-up of a section of the wall, with the carved names of Americans killed in the war clearly legible. In the foreground, seen from behind, is a veteran in camouflage jacket and floppy hat, his head bowed, his right hand pressed against the wall, as if overcome by the memory of fallen comrades.

The image combines a photograph of the wall by PhotoAssist, the Postal Service's research firm, with a drawing by Rodriguez based on a photo of the veteran by Peter Marlow, supplied by Magnum Photos. Rodriguez included the hand of another person resting on the veteran's shoulder in a comforting way. "The CSAC design subcommittee felt that the additional arm from the second person was distracting when cropped so tight, so they asked that it be removed," said Terrence McCaffrey. The artist made the man's hair longer than it appears in the source photograph.

One alternative illustration was based on the tradition of loved ones and friends of persons named on the wall leaving miniature shrines to their memory. Rodriguez depicted a rose and a small American flag at the base of the wall. Another illustration showed a veteran in fatigues squatting by

In Rodriguez's first version of the design chosen for the stamp, a companion's hand rests supportively on the shoulder of the veteran at the wall. CSAC felt the hand was distracting and asked the artist to remove it.

Two alternative designs for the Vietnam Memorial stamp showed an American flag and a rose that had been left at the base of the wall in memory of one of the persons honored, and a veteran reading the names of fallen comrades.

the memorial with flowers in his hand.

The final image "is really a strong one," said Carl Herrman. "It's about as fine a stamp as you could ever have done on a subject like this. It has emotion and style."

Several months after the pane was issued, Herrman received a telephone call from Charles Darden, the brother of Otis Darden, whose name appears on the stamp two rows above the veteran's fingertips. Charles Darden, an internationally known musician, wrote from St. Barthelemy in the French West Indies, where he was playing piano in a cabaret. "He was very moved," Herrman said. "He was astonished that of 58,000 names on the wall, his brother's name should be one of the few that can be read on the stamp. I made some blowups of the design for him and sent them to him to be shared by his family. The whole family was very touched by this. We did the appropriate thing when we chose this design, obviously."

The design was unveiled January 11, 2000, at the Vietnam Veterans Memorial.

COMPACT DISCS. An early concept design combined photographs of a silver-coated compact disc and a seascape. The illustration that was chosen combines a photo of a CD with a painted treble clef and staff that are visible through a transparent portion of the disc. The curves of the clef complement the curve of the disc's outer circumference. An orange background has a texture that suggests parchment.

"Illustrating this subject was about as much 'fun' as illustrating the VCR [for the 1970s pane], but because of Robert's magic, he was able to make it work by not being too literal," Herrman said.

An early concept sketch for the Compact Discs stamp combined photos of a CD and a seascape.

CABBAGE PATCH KIDS. For this stamp, Herrman adapted a tightly cropped photograph of a green-eyed Cabbage Patch Kid with vermilion hair, white hair ribbons and a yellow knit short-sleeved dress. The photo, made by PhotoAssist, is of "Trista Lara," a Cabbage Patch Kid owned by a collector, Leah Salt of Mississauga, Ontario, Canada.

The design was unveiled January 10, 2000, at Babyland General Hospital in Cleveland, Georgia.

HIT COMEDY. For the second time in the CTC series, USPS was confronted with the problem of honoring a television situation comedy without depicting any of the featured actors. For *The Cosby Show*, official chose the same solution they had hit on for the *All in the Family* stamp on the 1970s pane: They showed a view of the familiar living-room set where much of the sitcom's action took place. With a sofa, tables and chairs in the foreground and a banistered staircase at the rear, the Huxtable family's living room resembled Archie and Edith Bunker's living room as Kazuhiko Sano had painted it for the *All in the Family* stamp.

This time, a photograph provided by the Carsey-Werner Company of Studio City, California, the holder of rights to the series, was used for the design, with the show's signature logotype, THE COSBY SHOW, superimposed in capitals in an off-white color. Using the name of a living person, Bill Cosby, prominently in the stamp design was unusual, but not unprecedented. The USPS rule "No living person shall be honored by portrayal on U.S. postage" has been interpreted in recent years to allow the names of living individuals to be printed in the text on the reverse of stamps, on such accessories as booklet covers, and even as part of the stamp design itself.

"I first tried the logo quite large, in white," Herrman said. "Then CSAC suggested that we add a tint to the logo so it wouldn't have that white neon glowing look to it against the pastel-colored background. It made everything more subtle."

PhotoAssist was unable to identify the painting on the wall on the left side of the set. Because officials were afraid the artist might turn up and complain that his work had been depicted without his permission, the "C" of "COSBY" was placed in such a way as to conceal the picture. In the final version, however, most of the painting is visible. No problem has developed as a result.

FALL OF THE BERLIN WALL. Robert Rodriguez's dramatic illustration shows a Berliner in the foreground about to swing a sledgehammer at the Berlin Wall, while in the background is the graffiti-covered wall itself with East German soldiers standing impassively on top against a yellow sky. The artist added a wide brown transparent border to frame the image.

Rodriguez used as reference material several photographs, one of a man with a hammer attacking the wall, others of groups of soldiers atop it. Rather than base his painting of the foreground figure on an unknown individual who might later come forward and identify himself, he created his own hammer wielder, in several steps.

An early design concept for the Fall of the Berlin Wall stamp showed a sledgehammer against a breach in the graffiti-covered wall.

PhotoAssist's president, Louis Plummer, posed for this photograph for Robert Rodriguez to use in illustrating the Fall of the Berlin Wall stamp. Rodriguez modeled the features of the man in the stamp's foreground on Plummer, but based the body on a photograph of himself, wearing a leather jacket.

He began with a photo supplied by PhotoAssist of the company's president, Louis Plummer, posing with a sledgehammer. "I didn't like the lighting," Rodriguez said, "and I wanted the pose to be a little more heroic — I had WPA-style art in mind — so I had someone photograph me in the pose I wanted. I wore a leather jacket, because in photos I had seen of the Berlin Wall coming down, everyone seemed to be wearing leather jackets.

"I scanned in the head and face of the photo they had sent me, and scanned in the photo of myself, and put them together on the computer. I made a printout and then painted on top of the print. Then I scanned the painting back into the computer and composed it with about three different paintings that made up the background."

Although Rodriguez said he changed the face on the Louis Plummer photograph "quite a bit," Plummer's features remain recognizable (see photo).

"I'm absolutely thrilled with the illustration," Carl Herrman said. "I think it made a great stamp."

VIDEO GAMES. Rodriguez's painting shows a boy and a girl lying on their stomachs in front of a video monitor, playing a game called Defender that is visible on the screen. The boy clutches a joystick of the kind players use to control the video action.

One early sketch by the artist showed a boy by himself in front of a monitor; another showed a boy and girl, but from a different angle. CSAC wanted the stamp to depict two children rather than one, but felt the latter sketch didn't immediately convey the idea of video games. "There was too much emphasis on the kids, and you could hardly tell that they were playing with a joystick," said Terrence McCaffrey. "The committee asked that a new piece of art be created with a better angle, and more emphasis on

One early sketch for the Video Games illustration showed a boy playing a game alone; another showed a boy and girl, but from a different angle than the pair shown on the finished stamp.

the screen, to show they were playing a video game, not watching a regular television show."

The painting of the video game monitor was based on a photograph obtained by PhotoAssist of an Atari VCS 2600 owned by Keith Feinstein of New Providence, New Jersey.

Ensuring that all the elements in the design were contemporaneous was a difficult job, Carl Herrman said. "At points we had three different vintages in one picture," he said. "Ultimately, we got ourselves to where all the experts agreed we had the right game, the right TV and the right stick."

"E.T. THE EXTRA-TERRESTRIAL." This illustration, which Rodriguez calls his favorite of the 12 that he made and were used on the 1980s pane, features a portrait of E.T. against a backdrop of a magnified moon with the cratered surface clearly visible. The alien's right index finger is extended, its tip glowing.

On Rodriguez's initial submission, the moon was not shown and a geometric diagram was superimposed on the picture, with the Earth at E.T.'s fingertip and circular bodies in orbit around it. "Steven Spielberg's group immediately asked that we drop that," Terrence McCaffrey said. "It was never part of the film, and they felt it was misleading. The CSAC design subcommittee had also expressed concerns about it and felt it should be eliminated."

Rodriguez's next version showed E.T. with the lower part of his face lit by the glow of his finger. Spielberg himself asked that the light's reflection on the face be taken out and that E.T. be given more of a smile. The artist complied.

On his first version of the E.T. illustration, Rodriguez superimposed a geometric diagram with the Earth shown at E.T.'s fingertip and circular bodies in orbit around it. Representatives of the film's creator, Steven Spielberg, asked that the diagram be removed.

33

PERSONAL COMPUTERS. Rodriguez's original sketch had shown a child doing homework using a computer. "We felt that this particular situation didn't reflect the total impact of the personal computer on our society," said Terrence McCaffrey. "The committee asked that a new illustration be done to reflect an office situation, which better defined the computer's overall societal impact."

The final artwork depicted a woman at a PC, using a word-processing function and referring to a yellow pad on the table beside her. "We were trying to be so ethnic in all these illustrations," said Carl Herrman, "and we had kind of left Asians out, so we made her Asian-American."

Through PhotoAssist, the design team verified how a PC of 1980s vintage would look, while taking care not to show an identifiable brand. "We learned a lot of little things," Herrman said. "For instance, there's a little green light above the three buttons on the monitor, and if the computer is on that green light is on. Originally it wasn't on in the painting, so we lit it up."

Herrman pointed out the unusual color scheme of the illustration, with a solid yellow background and a reflected purple light on the back of the woman's head and jacket. "Those were colors you ordinarily wouldn't put into a picture like this, but Bob Rodriguez made it work," he said. "Bob saved us with a lot of these difficult subjects, pulling them out with good art, good composition, good thinking. He deserves a lot of credit for the way he solved these problems."

HIP-HOP CULTURE. In this illustration, a young man in blue warm-up suit, white sneakers and a blue cap with the bill turned to the rear break-dances on a sunlit pavement while a boom box plays behind him. At the rear are several spectators, shown out of focus in a soft reddish-gold color.

Rodriguez originally submitted two other illustrations using scanned-in

34

reference photographs in order to get CSAC's guidance on the process. Neither one satisfied the committee. The finished artwork was based on a photograph made by PhotoAssist of Earl Williams of Annandale, Virginia.

The design was unveiled January 11, 2000, at the Rock 'n' Roll Hall of Fame and Museum in Cleveland, Ohio.

As it had done for the 1950s, 1960s and 1970s panes, USPS at the outset authorized the creation of designs for most of the subjects nominated for the 1980s pane, even though only 15 of them would be used on stamps. This was done to save time once the results of the balloting were in.

LAKERS VS. CELTICS. Two teams, the Los Angeles Lakers and the Boston Celtics, dominated the National Basketball Association in the 1980s. In each year of that decade, at least one of the two teams was in the finals, and in three of those years, 1984, 1985 and 1987, the teams played each other for the championship. The Lakers, led by Earvin "Magic" Johnson, won five NBA titles in the 1980s, while the Celtics, starring Larry Bird, won three.

Rodriguez developed several alternative illustrations for this stamp, each dominated by a tightly cropped image of a Lakers player holding the ball as if ready to pass, dribble or shoot. The player wears the team's distinctive gold and purple uniform; his features and uniform numbers are concealed so no actual player's identity can be inferred. One version showed the player alone, while in another he confronts a defender wearing the green of the Celtics. In two other versions, smaller figures in action are shown in the foreground.

MOUNTAIN BIKING. This sport, invented in California in the 1970s, involves races over rugged terrain and requires sturdy equipment and participants able to take bone-jarring impacts and frequent spills. Mountain bikes also became popular for transportation as well as competition. Rodriguez based his artwork for this stamp on a combination of photographs showing a helmeted biker with his bike's front wheel in the air and a rock-covered hillside awash in light and shadow filling the frame in the background.

AIDS AWARENESS. AIDS awareness previously was publicized by a U.S. commemorative stamp of 1993, issued in sheet and booklet form (Scott 2806-06a), which depicted the looped red ribbon symbolic of the effort to prevent and cure the disease. For the proposed CTC stamp on the subject, Carl Herrman adapted a poster depicting an octagonal red stop sign with the word AIDS in place of STOP. The poster was designed by Steff Geissbuhler of New York,

New York, and is included in a book of AIDS posters titled *Images for Survival*, created by Charles Helmpin. "A lot of the posters weren't simple enough to be usable, but this one was so clear, so simple, it made an outstanding design," Herrman said.

NCAA MARCH MADNESS. The National Collegiate Athletic Association's annual Division I-A men's basketball tournament, held over two weeks in March with the "Final Four" meeting to crown a champion on the final weekend, became a major television spectacle in the 1980s. For this subject, Rodriguez created a photo montage, with upraised hands in the foreground giving the "We're number one" sign. At the rear, a player on the winning team is triumphantly cutting the net from the hoop. "It got to only the first stage, which is basically a photo montage," Herrman said. "If he had gone deeper, the next stage would have looked more and more like a painting. The player's number already was covered by one of the hands, and we would have figured out how to make his face look generic."

TALK SHOWS. Audience-participation talk shows on daytime television, emceed by articulate hosts like Phil Donahue and Oprah Winfrey, became highly popular in the 1980s. Working with photographs of scenes staged by PhotoAssist, Rodriguez developed alternative illustrations, each featuring a woman standing and speaking into a microphone held by a man whose face and body are cropped out of the picture, while audience members look on.

BEACH VOLLEYBALL. Using a photograph from PhotoAssist as the basis, Rodriguez created a painting of a woman in a two-piece red bathing suit using a fists-together stroke to set up a volleyball for an unseen teammate to spike. Her wraparound sunglasses and visored cap shield her eyes from the sun. Palm branches hang from the upper-left corner; sylized waves are shown in the lower right. "It would have made a spectacular stamp," Herrman said.

"She's on a diagonal, and the ball is just disappearing off the edge of the design. It's another example of Bob's ability to compose his subject matter and achieve terrific lighting effects. I can imagine him doing a great series of Olympics stamps."

COUNTRY MUSIC. Some of America's best-known Country and Western music performers were depicted on a set of four stamps in the Legends of American Music series issued in 1993: Hank Williams, the Carter Family, Patsy Cline and Bob Wills. For the proposed CTC stamp saluting Country Music, Herrman and Rodriguez decided to depict a generic woman singer. Rodriguez developed several paintings, each based on a photograph furnished by PhotoAssist. The one the design team liked best showed a woman with long, curly hair, wearing a spangled outfit and a broad-brimmed hat, playing a guitar and singing into a microphone. The image is tightly cropped and dramatically illuminated. "It's a beautiful illustration," Herrman said. "Unfortunately, the people who voted didn't know what it would have looked like, or maybe they would have picked the subject."

CAMCORDERS. Home video cameras became affordable and popular in the 1980s. Rodriguez's proposed way to illustrate the subject was to show a child at his birthday party, complete with birthday cake and framed by the lines and dots of a video camera viewfinder. This design progressed no farther than the photograph stage.

ARMS REDUCTION TREATY. The subject was the treaty signed December 8, 1987, by U.S. President Ronald Reagan and Soviet General Secretary Mikhail Gorbachev. "We had some really bad solutions to this one that everyone hated equally well," Herrman said. One approach that was worked up into a design was based on a photograph showing several missiles lying on the ground to be dismantled, "spread out like fingers pointing toward you," he said. "It looked like a junkyard." The design problem was tricky, the art director added, "because anything we showed could have been perceived as the reverse of what was intended. If we had rockets going up, it would have suggested that 'this treaty didn't work,' or 'this is what would have happened without the treaty.' We kept looking for other solutions, but then they announced the winning subjects in the voting and arms reduction wasn't one of them."

AEROBICS. Aerobics is a system of physical conditioning based on sustained activity that is designed to increase the efficiency of the body's intake of oxygen. Organized aerobic exercise programs became popular in the 1980s. For this might-have-been stamp, Rodriguez made several sketches based on photographs of exercise participants. His final version depicted a smiling man and woman in a typical aerobic maneuver, bending far to their right, holding their right ankles in their right hands while holding their left arms aloft. The direction of their bodies was emphasized by radiating lines on a golden background.

MINIVANS. For this subject, Rodriguez scanned in a photograph of a parked Dodge minivan with a mother and her daughter beside it spreading the contents of a picnic basket on a blanket, and then created several variations, each featuring a father in the foreground in a different activity: fishing in a stream, carrying a bedroll, and holding a life jacket, life preservers and snorkeling gear. If one of the compositions had been turned into a finished piece of art, the appearance of the van would have been altered to conceal its make and model. "Bob had it in mind that the purpose of the minivan was to load a lot of stuff in, and that's what he was trying to show," Herrman said.

VLADIMIR HOROWITZ CONCERT. In 1986, 61 years after he had left the Soviet Union to make his home in the West, world-renowned pianist Vladimir Horowitz returned in triumph to his homeland to play concerts in Moscow and Leningrad. Horowitz died in 1989 at the age of 85, and thus was eligible to be shown on a U.S. stamp issued in 2000 under the Postal Service's 10-years-deceased rule. Rodriguez's painting showed a profile view of Horowitz from the waist up, bent over the keyboard, his right hand raised in

a flourish. The artist provided two different backgrounds, one plain, the other with the faint outline of a musical score. "The colors are pastel, and the lighting, coming from one side, is very dramatic," Herrman said. "The picture is cropped to perfectly fit the space." Rodriguez himself called the Horowitz painting his personal favorite among the subjects that weren't used. "It's one of the best things in my portfolio," he said.

SENIOR PGA TOUR. The Professional Golfers' Association tour for its former youthful stars began in 1980 with two events and total prize money of $250,000, and has developed into an extended program with prizes totaling in the tens of millions of dollars. Rodriguez's finished art-

work shows a senior PGA player, in red shirt, khaki slacks and a white billed cap, following through on his tee shot, while spectators watch from behind a rope. A pattern of numbers, suggesting a golf-course leader board, is in the background. "We used an actual photograph and then Bob changed the golfer's appearance so people wouldn't speculate on who it was," Herrman said.

GENE MAPPING. In the 1980s, genetic engineering — the application of biochemical and genetic techniques to alter the chromosomal material, the basic genetic substance of cells — made major advances. The design chosen by Herrman for the proposed stamp incorporated a highly magnified color photograph of a DNA (deoxyribonucleic acid) molecule, which consists of two molecular chains wound spirally around each other in a structure called a double helix. "It looks like a surrealistic paint-

ing — like two big floating flounders against a marbleized background," Herrman said. "It would have been outstanding if only for the abstract quality of it."

THE BONFIRE OF THE VANITIES. Because the design team believed there was little chance that Tom Wolfe's best-selling novel of 1987 would be chosen as a stamp subject, no artwork was prepared for it.

MUSIC TELEVISION. Although this subject was discussed by CSAC, it wasn't included in the final list of 30 subjects placed on the ballot for the public's consideration. Nevertheless, Herrman developed a design for an MTV stamp, using the network's logo: a green block M with the letters TV in red superimposed. The background color shaded from yellow to pink. "I know it broke all our rules about not using logos, but what else could you do?" Herrman asked. "If

The design team's original plan was to use a photograph of President Ronald Reagan speaking at the 1984 Republican National Convention in the pane selvage. In the end, this photo was replaced by one showing the space shuttle Columbia *during a 1982 launch.*

you pick one show on MTV, you're doing a stamp for that show, not for the network."

For its selvage photo, the design team originally planned to use a photograph of the dominant American political figure of the 1980s, President Ronald Reagan. The photo selected showed Reagan at the podium of the 1984 Republican National Convention, at which he was nominated to run for a second term.

"The committee felt the image did not convey a specific theme for the decade, other than the Reagan presidency," Terrence McCaffrey said. "They asked that Carl [Herrman] pursue the space theme instead." Although it apparently wasn't a factor in the decision, the use of Reagan's picture in the selvage would have marked the first time that a specific living person would have been postally depicted in such a way.

The final choice for the spot was a NASA photo showing the *Columbia* — the same shuttle that is depicted on the first stamp on the pane — blasting off from Cape Canaveral on its fourth mission June 27, 1982. The selvage image was printed in multicolors; previous CTC selvage photos had been monochromatic. "The color was subtle, and so it didn't detract from the stamp images," said Herrman. "The photograph was good to us in that it allowed the rising space shuttle to exactly fill that little notch in the bottom block of stamps on the pane. Photographs don't always help you out that way, but this one worked out perfectly."

The space shuttle "bumped" Reagan from the headline over the selvage text block, as well. The first version of the headline read: "Peace and the

Reagan Legacy." The headline as it appeared on the pane read: "Space Shuttle Launched, Berlin Wall Falls."

Interestingly, the original draft of the text block included this sentence: "In the Iran-Contra scandal, Reagan's administration illegally armed a guerrilla group and exchanged weapons for hostages." In the finished version, the statement had been diluted to a noncontroversial: "The Iran-Contra hearings made headlines."

First-day Facts

Viki M. Brennan, manager of the Postal Service's Central Florida District, dedicated the 1980s stamps in a ceremony at the Universe Theater in the Kennedy Space Center's visitors' complex. Speakers were U.S. Representative Dave Weldon, Republican of Florida's 15th Congressional District, and Richard Linnehan, a NASA shuttle astronaut. Steve Hooks, manager of post office operations for the USPS Central Florida District, opened the ceremony. Honored guests were introduced by Roy D. Bridges Jr., director of the Kennedy Space Center. The guests included Rick Abramson, president of the space center's visitors' complex, and Ed Link, Titusville, Florida, postmaster.

33¢ PATRICIA ROBERTS HARRIS
BLACK HERITAGE SERIES

Date of Issue: January 27, 2000

Catalog Number: Scott 3371

Colors: black, cyan, magenta, yellow

First-Day Cancel: Washington, D.C.

First-Day Cancellations: 82,211

Format: Self-adhesive pane of 20, vertical, 5 across, 4 down. Offset printing plates of 180 (15 across, 12 around).

Gum Type: self-adhesive

Overall Stamp Size: 0.99 by 1.56 inches; 25.16 by 39.62mm

Pane Size: 5.90 by 7.26 inches; 149.860 by 184.404mm

Perforations: 11½ by 11¼ (die-cut simulated perforations) (Arpeco die cutter)

Selvage Markings: "©USPS/1999." ".33/x20/$6.60." "PLATE/POSITION" and diagram.

Photographer: David Valdez, U.S. Department of Housing and Urban Development

Designer and Art Director: Howard Paine of Delaplane, Virginia

Typographer: Thomas Mann of Vancouver, Washington

Modeler: Joseph Sheeran of Ashton-Potter (USA) Ltd., Williamsville, New York

Stamp Manufacturing: Stamps printed by Ashton-Potter (USA) Ltd. on offset portion of Stevens Variable Size Security Documents webfed 6-color offset, 3-color intaglio press. Stamps finished by Ashton-Potter.

Quantity Ordered: 150,000,000

Plate Number Detail: 4 plate numbers preceded by the letter P in selvage above or below each corner stamp

Plate Number Combinations Reported: P1111, P2222, P3333, P4444

Paper Supplier: Fasson/Glatfelter

Tagging: phosphored paper

The Stamp

The 23rd stamp in the Black Heritage series honored Patricia Roberts Harris, the first African-American woman to serve as an ambassador and the first to be a member of a presidential Cabinet. It was issued January 27 in Washington, D.C.

Harris was the seventh woman to be pictured on a Black Heritage stamp, following Harriet Tubman, Mary McLeod Bethune, Sojourner Truth, Ida B. Wells, Bessie Coleman and Madam C.J. Walker.

The stamp is a self-adhesive and was printed by the offset process and sold in panes of 20. Like all the stamps in the series, it is commemorative size, vertically arranged. It is the fifth consecutive Black Heritage stamp with a design based on a photograph, and the first to be printed by Ashton-Potter (USA) Ltd. The previous four, also offset-printed, were produced by Banknote Corporation of America.

The choice of Harris stemmed from an effort by the Citizens' Stamp Advisory Committee to include a larger number of contemporary personalities in the Black Heritage series, such as Malcolm X, the 1999 subject. "We've done a lot of historical figures," said Terrence McCaffrey, head of stamp design for USPS. "Even Madame C.J. Walker, whose stamp was a runaway best-seller, was from the early part of the century.

"So the committee said, 'Let's try to get more contemporary.' The committee also has been making a concentrated effort to honor more women; the series has been dominated by men up to now. Those factors caused Patricia Roberts Harris to be moved to the top of the list."

Harris was born May 31, 1924, in Mattoon, Illinois, the daughter of Bert Roberts, a Pullman car waiter, and his wife Hildren. She graduated summa cum laude from Howard University in 1945, and served as a director of the Chicago YWCA (1946-49) and of the American Council on Human Rights in Washington (1949-53).

She became the first executive director of the Delta Sigma Theta sorority in 1953. She began attending law school shortly after her marriage to attorney William Harris in 1955. In 1960 she received her law degree from George Washington University, graduating at the top of her class.

After a stint as a trial attorney for the Department of Justice, Harris was named to the faculty of Howard University School of Law in 1961. She met Attorney General Robert F. Kennedy and soon thereafter was appointed co-chairwoman of the National Women's Committee for Civil Rights, established by President John F. Kennedy in 1963.

When President Lyndon B. Johnson sought election in 1964, he asked Harris to deliver a seconding speech for his nomination at the Democratic National Convention. The following year he named her ambassador to Luxembourg.

Appointed dean of the Howard University School of Law in 1969, Harris remained active in national politics, serving on several commissions dealing with problems of civil rights, federal law and education. In 1971 she was named a director of IBM. She also was active at the 1972 Democratic National Convention.

She left Howard University and practiced law in Washington for several years until President Jimmy Carter chose her to be secretary of Housing and Urban Development in 1977. Two years later, he asked her to head the Department of Health, Education and Welfare. When the department was divided into the Department of Education and the Department of Health and Human Services in 1980, Harris headed the latter until the Republican Party regained the White House in 1981.

Harris ran unsuccessfully for mayor of Washington in 1982, losing the Democratic nomination to incumbent Marion Berry. She served as a professor at the George Washington University National Law Center from 1982 until her death from cancer March 23, 1985, at the age of 60.

The Design

From 1994 to 1999, Richard Sheaff was art director for the Black Heritage stamps, and the series was redesigned under his direction. Elements that had been standard on the early stamps were abandoned, including the Clarendon typeface and a miniature illustration beside the portrait that suggested some aspect of the subject's life. Since 1996, the designs have featured monochrome photographs of the honored individuals.

For the 2000 stamp, Terrence McCaffrey assigned the art director's job to Howard Paine. "In some cases, we try to keep the creative juices flowing by allowing other art directors to design one stamp in a series," McCaffrey explained.

PhotoAssist, the Postal Service's research firm, obtained numerous photographs of Patricia Roberts Harris, and from them Paine developed a selection of designs with a variety of type treatments. Two of the photos show Harris at news conferences, facing batteries of microphones. In one of these, she is wearing large glasses, and CSAC rejected it as unflattering. However, the committee liked the other photo, of a smiling Harris without the glasses. It was a black-and-white print, supplied by the National Archives, of a color photo made by David Valdez, a Department of Housing and Urban Development staff photographer. Paine cropped out the microphones and retouched the photo to eliminate a chain necklace.

A solid background grades from dark at the bottom to light at the top. Across the top of the stamp, in block sans-serif capitals, are the words "BLACK HERITAGE." Across the bottom, in dropped-out white uppercase and lowercase letters, is "Patricia Roberts Harris," with "USA 33" just above in the lower-right corner. The apparent color of the stamp is

The photograph of a bespectacled Harris at a news conference in these two proposed designs was deemed unflattering by CSAC. Both incorporate the Clarendon typeface that had been standard on early Black Heritage stamps but was abandoned in 1994 when the series was redesigned.

This proposed design features the David Valdez photograph that was used on the finished stamp, but it has been reversed so that Harris looks to the right rather than to the left. For the final image, designer Howard Paine oriented the photo correctly, eliminated the microphones and the chain necklace Harris is wearing, and revised the typography.

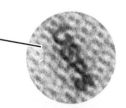

The microprinted letters "USPS" can be found just to the right of Harris' head.

purple, although all four process colors — black, cyan, magenta and yellow — were used to create a richer effect.

Because the stamp is printed by offset, microprinting is included in the design as a security measure. It consists of the letters "USPS" just to the right of Harris' head.

First-day Facts

LeGree S. Daniels of the USPS Board of Governors dedicated the stamp in a ceremony at Crampton Auditorium on the Howard University campus. She was introduced by James C. Tolbert Jr., USPS executive director of stamp services.

Sharon Pratt Kelly, former mayor of the District of Columbia, was the principal speaker. Tributes to Patricia Roberts Harris were given by Donna E. Shalala, U.S. secretary of health and human services, and Marcia L. Fudge, national president of Delta Sigma Theta sorority. Susan Kidd read a message from former President Jimmy Carter, under whom Harris served. The audience was welcomed by Anthony A. Williams, mayor of the District of Columbia, and Dr. H. Patrick Swygert, president of Howard University.

The earliest-known use of a Harris stamp was on a cover bearing an Albuquerque, New Mexico, postmark dated January 5, 22 days before the official first day of issue. The mailer informed *Linn's Stamp News* that he had bought two panes of Harris stamps January 3 at a post office in Albuquerque.

U.S. NAVY SUBMARINES PRESTIGE BOOKLET
(5 DENOMINATIONS, 5 DESIGNS)

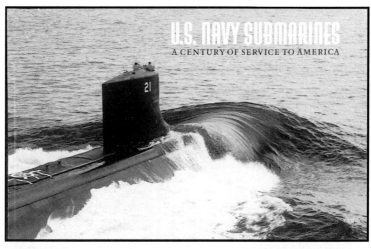

Date of Issue: March 27, 2000

Catalog Numbers: 22¢, Scott 3373; 33¢, Scott 3374; 55¢, Scott 3375; 60¢, Scott 3376; $3.20, Scott 3377; 3377a, booklet pane of 5

Colors: yellow, magenta, cyan, black, gray (selvage background)

First-Day Cancel: Groton, Connecticut

First-Day Cancellations: 265,226 (includes 33¢ stamp issued separately)

Format: Booklet containing 2 panes, each containing 5 stamps, 1 of each variety, in 3 horizontal rows of 2, 1 and 2 stamps, plus pages of text and pictures. Offset printing plates of 18 panes, 3 across by 6 around.

Gum: water activated

Overall Stamp Size: 1.56 by 0.99 inches or 39.62 by 25.15mm, 22¢, 33¢, 55¢, 60¢ stamps; 3.12 by 0.99 inches or 146.05 by 88.90mm, $3.20 stamp

Pane Size: 5.50 by 3.50 inches; 139.70 by 88.90mm

Booklet Size: 5.75 by 3.50 inches; 146.05 by 88.90mm

Perforations: 11 (Wista BP 9700 stroke perforator)

Selvage Markings: On first pane: "THE DOLPHIN PIN/The U.S. Navy Submarine Force/insignia is a pin featuring a pair/of dolphins flanking a sub with/its bow planes rigged for diving./The pin is gold plated for/officers, silver plated for enlisted/personnel. Training prepares/submariners not only for/day-to-day responsibilities such/as navigation and depth control,/but also for the most extreme/situations, from floods and fires/to fighting the enemy. Only after/the ability to handle these/difficult scenarios has been/confirmed can a candidate finally/wear the coveted 'dolphins.' " On second pane: "THE SUBMARINE STAMPS/U.S. Navy Submarines/A Century of Service to America/USS Holland, the U.S. Navy's/first submarine, was/purchased in 1900./S-class submarines/were designed during WWI./Gato class submarines/played a key role in/the destruction of Japanese/maritime power in the/Pacific during WWII./Los Angeles class/attack submarines, armed with/"smart" torpedoes and cruise/missiles, are nuclear powered./Ohio class submarines — also/nuclear powered — carry more/than half of America's strategic/weapons, making them a vital part/of America's nuclear deterrence."

Cover Markings: On front: "U.S. NAVY SUBMARINES/A CENTURY OF SERVICE TO AMERICA." On back: "AIC 092/Prestige booklet with/ten U.S. postage stamps/sold at face value of/$9.80." "© USPS 1999." USPS logo and Universal Product Code (UPC) "990200."

Stamp Illustrator: James Griffiths of Glenview, Illinois

Designer, Art Director and Typographer: Carl Herrman of Carlsbad, California

Stamp Manufacturing: Stamps printed by Banknote Corporation of America, Browns Summit, North Carolina, on Goebel 670 offset press. Covers and text printed by Greensboro Printing Company, Greensboro, North Carolina, on Komori Lithrone 640p offset press. Stamps and booklets processed by Greensboro Printing Company.

Quantity Ordered: 1,500,000 booklets (15,000,000 stamps)

Plate Number Detail: no plate numbers

Paper Supplier: Paper Corporation of the United States/Spinnaker Coatings (stamps); Vintage 91 (cover and text)

Tagging: block tagging over stamps

Introduction

The first submarine in the U.S. Navy was named after her inventor, John Philip Holland, and accepted for service April 11, 1900. Our second submarine inventor was Simon Lake, a contemporary of Holland. In 1983 submarine number 709 was named after Hyman G. Rickover, who led the development of the nuclear-powered submarine. Our early submarines served in World War I, but World War II showed the tremendous combat potential of our big diesel-powered fleet boats. During World War II our Submarine Force, 1.6 percent of our Navy, sank a third of Japan's navy and nearly two-thirds of her merchant marine. These losses effectively eliminated Japan's ability to continue the war. Following WWII our nuclear-powered submarines served as a strategic challenge to the Soviet Union, and they are still our best deterrent to nuclear warfare. The end of the Cold War ushered in a new era for our Submarine Force. Increasingly sophisticated in design, submarines are today one of the most vital components of our Navy.

Edward L. Beach, Captain, U.S. Navy (Ret.)
Commanding, USS *Triton*, 1959–1962

Cover photo: USS *Seawolf*

USS *HOLLAND*: FIRST U.S. NAVY SUBMARINE

As a ship she was no sweetheart—short, slow, and awkward-looking. But the 54-foot *Holland* fulfilled an ancient dream: a vessel that could swim underwater like a fish. USS *Holland* was our first practical submarine. Her inventor, Irish-born John P. Holland, designed her as a warship, driven by an internal combustion engine on the surface, switching to a battery-powered electric motor as she opened ballast tanks to take on water and dive. Holland equipped her with a bow torpedo tube and two pneumatic guns.

Holland's final trial run impressed the U.S. Navy. Officials

saw her submerge in twelve seconds, then run a straight course, holding her depth, for ten minutes at a respectable six knots. She reversed course as required, returned toward the starting point, and surfaced.

USS Holland was the Navy's first submarine. With a crew of six plus the skipper, she served from 1900 to 1910.

The Navy purchased *Holland* on April 11, 1900. So was born our elite submarine service.

EARLY UNDERWATER WARFARE

Early in our Revolution a Connecticut Yankee, David Bushnell, built a barrel-like vessel, aptly named *Turtle.* Her operator, controlling her with cranks and pedals, was to bob along like a bit of flotsam, submerge near a British ship, screw a mine against the hull, and crank madly away. Although efforts to attach the mine failed, *Turtle* took her

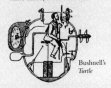

Bushnell's Turtle

place in history as the first combat submarine.

Some 25 years later Robert Fulton came up with *Nautilus*, a hand-cranked, four-man submarine that could sail on the surface, then fold her mast and submerge. Fulton showed her off in France, then at war with Britain. *Nautilus* interested Napoleon, but no sale. Fulton took his plan to Britain, but some admirals were horrified

H. L. Hunley was the first submarine in history to sink an operational warship. In 1864 she sent USS Housatonic to the bottom.

by the very idea. Again, no sale.

H.L. Hunley, built by the Confederacy during the Civil War, was the first submarine to sink an operational warship. Fashioned from a boiler and hand-cranked by eight men, she sank USS *Housatonic* in a surface attack. But for unknown reasons *Hunley* sank, too, on her way back to Charleston. Recently discovered, *Hunley* will be carefully salvaged.

Nearly 1,200 people died—including more than 120 Americans—when a German U-boat torpedoed RMS Lusitania off the southern coast of Ireland on May 7, 1915.

WORLD WAR I INSPIRES NEW DESIGNS

Our early submarines quickly improved, growing longer, more capable, and—with new diesel engines for surface use—safer. The older boats were largely relegated to guarding harbors, mostly in the Philippines. The newer, longer-range boats were used in both oceans. During World War I the German *Unterseeboot*, or U-boat, proved that the submarine could be a devastating weapon. Small and dangerous to serve in, U-boats made fierce attacks on merchant ships and warships, and almost cut Britain's maritime lifeline.

A U-boat sank the British passenger liner RMS *Lusitania* in 1915. The loss of civilian lives, some of them American, helped push us into the Great War two years later. By then our Navy had some 50 subs, including 153-foot K-boats and 165-foot L-boats. During and after the war we continued to develop sub classes on up the alphabet (except for P, Q, and—obviously—U) to V. The V-class submarines were designed to be "fleet boats"—able to speed on the surface at some 20 knots, and so keep up with a fleet. In World War II at least 33 surviving S-boats made war patrols, and one old veteran, S-44, even sank a Japanese cruiser.

S-class: S-49
Length: 240'

THE FIGHTING SUBS OF WORLD WAR II

Stern view, WWII-era submarine

The attack on Pearl Harbor so damaged our Pacific Fleet that submariners suddenly found themselves carrying the burden of the fight. At first faulty torpedoes frustrated them. But after solving this problem well into the war, our capable submarine fleet tore into Japanese shipping.

Life aboard a sub was cramped and rigorous, water for bathing limited, ventilation poor. Men slept alongside greased torpedoes and above huge, often overheated storage batteries. But crews were chosen for unflappable personalities as well as proficient skills. In action, teamwork erased grumbles. "Take her down!" "Clear the bridge!" "Dive! Dive!" Orders like these sparked a controlled explosion: sailors slithering through hatches and watertight doors, racing to battle stations.

A DESIGN FOR WAR, A TIME FOR HEROES

After Pearl Harbor, sub design froze with *Gato, Balao,* and *Tench.* Those classes – just over 300 feet long, with six torpedo tubes forward and four astern – built legends. USS *Growler's* skipper Howard Gilmore, posthumously awarded the first Medal of Honor for the Silent Service, was badly hurt on the bridge when *Growler* collided with a Japanese ship that then opened fire. "Take her down!" Gilmore

ordered; saving his sub, losing his life. USS *Harder,* skippered by Sam Dealey, sank or damaged five destroyers in less than a week. Dealey also received a posthumous Medal of Honor. Lawson "Red" Ramage received a Medal of Honor after his sub and one other intercepted a Japanese convoy and cut loose like gunfighters at the O.K. Corral, sinking five ships. Eugene Fluckey and George Street were awarded

Medals of Honor for entering enemy harbors at night, in shallow water where they could not dive, and sinking several important ships.

Our wartime subs – 1.6 percent of the Navy – caused 55 percent of Japan's maritime losses. They sank warships as well as freighters, ferried raiders to hostile shores, and rescued 380 downed Navy fliers and many Army pilots – often under fire.

Gato class: USS Harder
Length: 307'

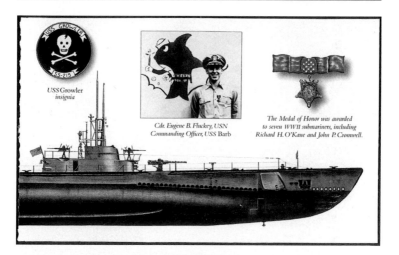

USS Growler
insignia

Cdr. Eugene B. Fluckey, USN
Commanding Officer, USS Barb

The Medal of Honor was awarded
to seven WWII submariners, including
Richard H. O'Kane and John P. Cromwell.

COLD WAR INSPIRES A GIANT STEP FOR SUBS

Peace brought new designs. Underwater speed shot up when USS *Albacore* appeared in the early 1950s with a hydrodynamic hull that gave her more than 25 knots – an unbelievable 28.8 mph – *underwater!* If only she'd had more staying power....

That came in January 1955, when USS *Nautilus* signaled, "Underway on nuclear power."

It was a long-sought dream. The Navy's controversial Adm. Hyman Rickover, packing in his small, thin body energy best described as atomic, drove the nuclear sub program. Now, with reserve power galore, range was almost unlimited. A "nuke" could

With sail planes at vertical to break
through 18 inches of ice, USS Pogy
surfaces near the North Pole.

Adm. Hyman G. Rickover

run CO_2 scrubbers and generate oxygen to keep air fresh. Moving like a shark at great depth, it could remain submerged indefinitely. The frozen Arctic Ocean was no longer a forbidden wasteland. Nukes could go anywhere under ice, even surface at the North Pole!

Los Angeles class: USS Jefferson City
Length: 362'

ATTACK SUBMARINES: SAILING BELOW EVERY SEA

Planesmen "fly" USS Memphis underwater at speeds exceeding 25 knots.

In 1960 the nuke USS *Triton* circled the globe submerged— 26,723 nautical miles in 61 days. Logging a grand total of 35,979 nautical miles in 83 days, *Triton's* epic underwater voyage pointed the way to the future. In the mid-1970s attack subs of the *Los Angeles* class began prowling far below waves and weather— round-nosed sea monsters, shadowing possible foes, ready to use "smart" torpedoes and cruise missiles. The latest attack sub classes, employing cutting- edge technology, will enable the U.S. to continue to maintain undersea dominance well into the 21st century.

Seawolf class: USS Seawolf
Length: 353'

THE ULTIMATE DETERRENT: TRIDENT "BOOMERS"

Here's a sea monster, nearly two football fields long, carrying 24 Trident ballistic missiles with nuclear warheads. "Boomer" they call her. Yet, like an attack sub, she depends on silence to steal anywhere under the world's oceans. Inside her dark, whalelike hull, lights glow as her crew move quietly about their tasks—holding depth and angle with airplane-like controls, monitoring sonar that sifts ocean murmurs for a man-made sound. For some two months the crew live and work in an undersea town, with space to study, pump iron, and jog on a treadmill in their spare time. They enjoy movies and the best food in the Navy. Always they're ready with only a moment's notice to launch missiles that can blast from the sea and destroy targets thousands of miles away. In one century the submarine has become a weapon that, to quote one sub captain, "has made future world wars unthinkable."

Ohio class: USS *Maryland*
Length: 560'

THE SUBMARINE STAMPS

U.S. Navy Submarines
A Century of Service to America

USS *Holland*, the U.S. Navy's first submarine, was purchased in 1900.

S-class submarines were designed during WWI.

***Gato* class** submarines played a key role in the destruction of Japanese maritime power in the Pacific during WWII.

***Los Angeles* class** attack submarines, armed with "smart" torpedoes and cruise missiles, are nuclear powered.

***Ohio* class** submarines—also nuclear powered—carry more than half of America's strategic weapons, making them a vital part of America's nuclear deterrence.

Acknowledgments

We are especially grateful to Capt. Edward L. Beach, USN (Ret.), and Professor Carl Boyd, Old Dominion University, for reviewing the stamp art and providing expert advice and guidance during preparation of the booklet, and to Ron Martini for reviewing the stamp art. We would also like to thank the following individuals and organizations for their generous assistance: Capt. David S. Cooper, USN (Ret.); Charles R. Hinman, John Anderson, and Daniel Del Monte, USS Bowfin Submarine Museum & Park; Erve Easton, Neil Ruenzel, and Dave Tela, Electric Boat Corporation.

Photo and Illustration Credits

Front cover: Jim Brennan/Electric Boat Corporation
Page 1: Brown Brothers
Page 2: *bottom left,* Culver Pictures/PNI
top right, Painting by Conrad Wise Chapman/Courtesy Corbis
Page 3: © 1997 Ken Marschall, from *Lost Liners,* a Hyperion/Madison Press Book
Page 4: National Archives/Courtesy PhotoAssist, Inc.
Page 5: Painting by Jim Griffiths
Pages 6-7: *bottom,* Original Prismacolor rendering by Michael W. Wooten
Page 7: *top left,* Original Prismacolor rendering by Michael W. Wooten
top center, U.S. Naval Historical Center
top right, Original Prismacolor rendering by Michael W. Wooten
Page 8: *center,* U.S. Navy photo by Steven H. Vanderwerff
top right, Archive Photos/PNI
Page 9: U.S. Navy photo by Matthew Hostetler
Pages 10-11: Jim Brennan/Electric Boat Corporation
Page 12: Walter P. Calahan
Stamp page 1: © 1993 Steve and Yogi Kaufman

Production

Stamp Illustrator: Jim Griffiths
Art Director, Designer: Carl Herrman
Creative Director: Terry McCaffrey
Text: Edwards Park
Captions: Andy Park
Stamp Art Research; Picture Research; Rights & Permissions; Text Research & Editing: PhotoAssist, Inc.
Production & Typography: John Boyd

Conversions

1 nautical mile = 1 minute of latitude or longitude at the Equator, or 1.15078 statute miles
1 knot = 1 nautical mile per hour

AIC 092

Prestige booklet with
ten U.S. postage stamps
sold at face value of
$9⁸⁰

UNITED STATES
POSTAL SERVICE®

0 990200 2

33¢ LOS ANGELES CLASS SUBMARINE

Date of Issue: March 27, 2000

Catalog Number: Scott 3372

Colors: black, cyan, magenta, yellow

First-Day Cancel: Groton, Connecticut

First-Day Cancellations: 265,226 (includes prestige booklet stamps)

Format: Pane of 20, horizontal, 4 across, 5 down. Offset printing plates of 180 subjects, 12 across, 15 around.

Gum: water activated

Overall Stamp Size: 1.56 by 0.99 inches; 39.62 by 25.15mm

Pane Size: 7.26 by 5.94 inches; 184.4 by 150.88mm

Perforations: 11 (Wista BPA stroke perforator)

Selvage Markings: "©/USPS/1999." ".33/x20/$6.60." "PANE/POSITION" and diagram. Universal Product Code (UPC) "450100."

Illustrator: James Griffiths of Glenview, Illinois

Designer, Art Director and Typographer: Carl Herrman of Carlsbad, California

Stamp Manufacturing: Stamps printed by Banknote Corporation of America, Browns Summit, North Carolina, on Goebel 670 offset press. Stamps processed by BCA.

Quantity Ordered: 65,150,000

Plate Number Detail: 1 set of 4 plate numbers preceded by the letter B in selvage above or below each corner stamp.

Plate Number Combination Reported: B1111

Paper Supplier: Paper Corporation of the United States/Ivex

Tagging: phosphored paper

The Stamps

On March 27, the Postal Service issued five commemorative stamps in an unprecedented format. The stamps, honoring the U.S. Navy Submarine

Force on its 100th anniversary, are of five different denominations and are contained in what USPS calls a "commemorative prestige booklet" containing text and pictures in addition to the stamps.

The booklet contains 12 pages plus front and back covers of a stiffer stock. Bound in the back of the booklet are two panes of stamps, conventionally gummed and perforated. Each pane contains a se-tenant block containing all five varieties.

Submarine booklet intact.

These varieties and the submarines shown on them are arranged chronologically on the pane. They are:

• 60¢, *USS Holland*, the first U.S. Navy submarine, 54 feet in length, diminutive by today's standards. The date of *Holland*'s formal commissioning, October 12, 1900, is now officially recognized as the birth date of the U.S. Submarine Force.

• 22¢, a submarine of the S Class, developed in World War I.

• $3.20, a Gato Class sub, used in the Pacific Theater in World War II.

• 33¢, a nuclear-powered Los Angeles Class attack submarine of the Cold War period. This stamp also was issued separately in panes of 20.

• 55¢, a nuclear-powered Ohio Class sub, designed to carry ballistic missiles. At 560 feet, Ohio-class submarines are more than 10 times longer than their pioneering forebear, *USS Holland*.

A total of 1.5 million booklets (15 million stamps) was printed.

The combination of denominations was chosen so the booklet could be sold at its stamps' face value — $9.80 — and still cover the cost of its manufacture, on the assumption that a significant number of the stamps would be retained rather than used as postage.

"Many prestige booklets done by foreign countries carry different denominations," said Terrence McCaffrey, head of stamp design for USPS. "This was our first time out of the blocks with this kind of product, and we knew it would be very costly to produce. We needed to recoup our costs. So it was determined that we would cover different postal rates.

"Cathy Caggiano [manager of stamp acquisition and distribution] and her staff determined which rates were most frequently used, and what combination of number of stamps plus denominations would yield a good

round-number total that we could work with. Stamp customers like round numbers."

The rates met by each stamp were: 33¢, first ounce, first-class mail; 22¢, second ounce; 55¢, two ounces; 60¢, international airmail to destinations other than Canada and Mexico; and $3.20, basic Priority Mail.

It is rare for the United States to issue stamps of different denominations in a se-tenant arrangement. Past examples have been souvenir panes or booklet panes, but the latter have been for vending-machine booklets in which an even-number face value was necessary. In 1977, a $1 booklet was issued with a pane containing one 9¢ Right to Assemble stamp (Scott 1590) and seven 13¢ Flag Over Capitol stamps (Scott 1623). Four years later, a $1.20 booklet contained a pane with two 6¢ Ring of Stars stamps (Scott 1892) and six 18¢ Purple Mountain Majesties stamps (Scott 1893).

The two panes of Submarines stamps in each prestige booklet carry different selvage text. The first pane's text describes the dolphin pin that is worn by members of the Submarine Force; the second offers a brief description of the submarines shown on each of the stamps. Although many collectors would consider the two panes collectible varieties, the Scott *Specialized Catalogue of U.S. Stamps & Covers* doesn't give them separate listings, but merely notes that the pane "was issued with two types of text in the selvage."

The stamps were printed by the offset method by Banknote Corporation of America (BCA). The covers and text pages of the booklet were printed by the Greensboro Printing Company of Greensboro, North Carolina, which also cut, collated and bound the booklets with the stamp panes inside. A total of 1.5 million booklets (15 million stamps) was ordered.

The additional variety of the 33¢ Los Angeles Class Submarine stamp also was printed by BCA. It was issued to satisfy the demand of Navy

The 33¢ Los Angeles Class Submarine stamp from the prestige book-let (top) has no microprinting. The version of the stamp sold in panes of 20 (below) has the letters "USPS" microprinted directly below the submarine's horizontal diving plane.

officials and other advocates for a stamp that would be widely used in the mail. The extra stamp was sold in regular post office panes of 20 and was issued in a quantity of 65,150,000, compared to only 3 million of its book-let counterpart.

The pane-of-20 version differs from the booklet version in several ways. First, it includes in its design the microprinted letters USPS at the base of the submarine's sail, or conning tower. There is no microprinting on the booklet stamp. The stamp from the booklet is block tagged, while the stamp from the pane of 20 is printed on phosphored paper. A stamp from the booklet may have traces of gray on the perf tips at the left or bot-tom from the background color of the adjacent selvage.

Finally, as one alert *Linn's Stamp News* reader, Dick Celler, pointed out, the booklet variety of the 33¢ stamp shows a tiny bit of extra illustration at the top, most noticeable when one looks at the ocean waves in the upper-left corner. A measurement of the vertical height of the design images shows the booklet variety to be about one-half millimeter taller, which would account for the extra design detail visible on the stamp, Celler wrote.

The 20-stamp pane incorporated a new kind of selvage marking: a bar code in the lower-left corner, for scanning by postal clerks. Bar codes have been printed on U.S. stamp booklets and convertible booklets for years — one can be found on the back cover of the prestige booklet — but this was the first time that a regular pane of stamps contained such a marking.

The five stamps in the prestige booklet are horizontally arranged. Four of them are commemorative size. The fifth, the $3.20 Gato Class stamp, is twice the width of the other four, and is located in the center of the block of five, with two of the smaller stamps above it and two below.

At 3.12 inches, the Gato Class stamp is the widest U.S. stamp ever produced for regular postage. The $3 Mars Pathfinder commemorative of 1997 is 3 inches wide; however, its depth — 1.5 inches — is greater than the 0.99 inches of the Gato stamp, giving the Mars stamp a greater overall area.

The Submarines booklet came about because of a strong push by influential Navy officials and their friends for a stamp or stamps to mark the 100th anniversary of the Submarine Force. The Citizens' Stamp Advisory Committee at first resisted because it was convinced that to approve postal honors for a subdivision of one of the Armed Forces would open the door to demands for similar recognition by other branches.

"But there was so much pressure," recalled Carl Herrman, one of the Postal Service's part-time art directors. "There were letters from people like former President Jimmy Carter [who had served in the Submarine Force], the secretary of the Navy ... the pack of letters was very powerful. It was that pressure that made the committee tell me 'Go ahead, see what you can develop.'"

Herrman's subsequent research and graphic experiments generated so many different design possibilities (see below) that CSAC, which at first had turned down the idea of even one stamp, began thinking in terms of multiple stamps. From that, it was just a short jump to the decision to create a "prestige booklet."

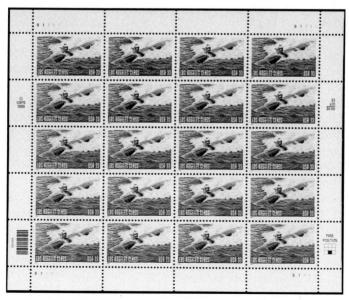

The 33¢ Los Angeles Class Submarine stamp pane of 20 was the first U.S. stamp issued in sheet form to carry a Universal Product Code (UPC) in its selvage.

"We had talked about doing a prestige booklet for a long time," said Terrence McCaffrey, head of stamp design for USPS. "Carl showed us there was such a wealth of graphic material here, so many different types of submarines and so much fascinating information to be learned from them, that maybe the time had come to do it."

Although prestige booklets — oversized booklets containing stamps and other printed matter, tied to a specific topic — were new to the United States, several other countries had issued them, including Australia, Canada, Denmark, Guernsey, Ireland, Norfolk Island, the Philippines, San Marino and Tonga. The concept had originated in Great Britain in 1969, with a booklet titled "Stamps for Cooks" that contained recipes printed on the interleaving between panes of Queen Elizabeth II stamps.

McCaffrey and his art directors invited a presentation on the subject from Barry Switzer and Joseph Sheeran, executives of Ashton-Potter (USA) Ltd., a company that produces stamps for USPS and had created prestige booklets for other countries. Later, the Ashton-Potter executives spoke to CSAC.

"They made a real sales pitch to us to do a prestige booklet," McCaffrey said. "They informed us about prestige booklets, what you can and can't do with them, how they work and how they sell. We talked it over, and decided this would be the time to try the format."

As part of their promotion campaign, the Ashton-Potter executives prepared and submitted to USPS a sample Submarines prestige booklet, complete with four panes of eight stamps each, numerous color pictures, and elaborate touches that included embossed gold and silver replicas of the Submarine Force's dolphin pin. Ironically, in the end USPS awarded the contract to produce the booklet not to Ashton-Potter, but to another printer, BCA.

The decision of CSAC and USPS officials to produce the Submarines stamps as a prestige booklet greatly expanded the task of research, fact verification, picture procurement and rights acquisition that is normally involved in creating a stamp, and added the need for skilled writing and editing. The responsibility for much of the added burden fell on PhotoAssist, the Postal Service's research firm. Carl Herrman, the designated designer and art director for the stamps, was given the extra duty of designing the prestige booklet, and Terrence McCaffrey assumed overall creative direction of the project.

For consultation and writing, a team of accomplished individuals was assembled. The principal expert was Captain Edward L. Beach, a retired Navy officer, historian and novelist. Beach was a submariner in the Pacific during World War II, and in 1960 commanded the nuclear-powered *USS Triton* when it circled the globe submerged, logging 26,723 nautical miles in 61 days. He also served as naval aide to President Dwight D. Eisenhower. His 1955 novel about submarine warfare, *Run Silent, Run Deep*, was made into a 1958 film starring Clark Gable and Burt Lancaster. Among his highly praised works of nonfiction is *The United States Navy:*

Submarines

Thirty-two U.S. commemorative stamps $10.56

The word smaller U.S. submarines that fought in WW II were decendents from the unlikely cockleshell craft that made the first undersea attack over 160 years before.

During the Civil War the Confederacy built more than a dozen submarines in it's effort to break the Union blockade of Southern seaports. The first U.S. Navy submarine was the Holland named after John Holland an Irish immigrant and onetime schoolteacher, turned submarine designer. The Navy

bought the Holland and with six similar boats formed the U.S. Submarine Force in 1903.

The Submarine Force has been dubbed the Silent Service. Historically the submariners have used stealth and silence to overpower their enemies. Today's modern Trident submarines are nuclear powered and can stay underwater for over 90 days.

Their armament includes up to 26 long range ballistic missiles capable of reaching targets thousands of miles away.

This is a sample submarine caption. It will increase the cognitive exchange between the audience's vision system.

The Silent Service Pin is awarded to submariners who complete the rigorous training program.

Here is the cover and a page from a sample prestige booklet on submarines, with dummy copy, prepared for USPS by Ashton-Potter (USA) Ltd. to show the possibilities of such a format. One of the elaborate details included by the printer was a replica of the Submarine Service's Dolphin pin, embossed in gold.

200 Years, published in 1986, and an autobiography, *Salt and Steel: Reflections of a Submariner* (1999).

Another key consultant was Carl Boyd, a professor of history at Old Dominion University and author of *Hitler's Japanese Confidante* (1993), an account of the breaking of the Japanese diplomatic code by the United States during World War II. The prestige booklet's text, as well as the selvage text on the stamp panes, was written by Edwards Park, a founding editor of *Smithsonian* magazine, author of the magazine's monthly "Around the Mall and Beyond" column, and author also of the book *Treasures of the Smithsonian*. Park, like Beach, was a combat veteran of World War II. The Postal Service turned for additional advice to officials of the *USS Bowfin* Submarine Museum and to the Electric Boat Corporation, a long-time manufacturer of submarines for the Navy.

Complicating the process, however, was the necessity to clear the pictures and text of the booklet with various Navy officials. "It was a can of worms," Terrence McCaffrey said. "It had to go through that whole bureaucracy. They all had to look at the layout, look at the photos, read the text, and they all had to agree that the photos were OK, the text was OK. They all had to satisfy themselves that their portion [of the subject] had been covered. It took a long time.

"We [the Postal Service] have learned some lessons. We still want to do prestige booklets, but we will do them on subjects that are not specific to a proponent or group that has so much influence. We'll do something that's more generic."

USPS originally announced that the Navy Submarines booklet would be available only at philatelic centers and postal stores in selected post offices, and by mail through the USPS mail-order center in Kansas City, Missouri. Among critics of this limited distribution policy was Michael Laurence, editor-publisher of *Linn's Stamp News*.

"Instead of hiding the Submarine booklets behind inaccessible philatelic windows, USPS should send them out to post offices along with all the other commemorative stamps," Laurence wrote. "These booklets should be offered in every post office nationwide, and they should be enthusiastically promoted with colorful lobby posters showing potential customers what the booklet contains. Limited distribution does nothing to promote stamp collecting, which is the objective USPS uses to justify such products."

Later, the Postal Service expanded distribution of the booklets. It announced in the June 15 issue of the *Postal Bulletin* that the booklets could henceforth be sold through all local post offices.

Even so, USPS officials admitted to being disappointed at the public's lukewarm response to the booklet, which remained on sale through Stamp Fulfillment Services until September 30, 2001. Terrence McCaffrey, for his part, appeared to agree in retrospect with Michael Laurence's assessment.

"It was our first prestige booklet, and it was hard to know what to do," McCaffrey said. "We printed 1.5 million, which is a small number for a country this size. We were hoping to sell out. Obviously, we didn't. We learned that we need to put it out there so it's more accessible.

"In the postal stores, it was on display, but in post offices, if you didn't see it you didn't know it existed. The clerks were not about to pull it out of the drawer — or even put it in the drawer, which was the bigger problem. The post offices weren't buying it. It only sold where clerks were pushing it.

"I think we printed too many, and we need better distribution. We'll keep that in mind in the future."

Another criticism from the collecting community focused on the high cost of the booklet. After the initial announcement by the Postal Service, Peter P. McCann, president of the American Philatelic Society, wrote to Azeezaly S. Jaffer, then the director of stamp services. "We recognize that new formats and new technology require higher face values to both cover costs and assure a reasonable profit," he wrote. "But issues such as these have a tremendous potential to hook the interest of new adherents to the

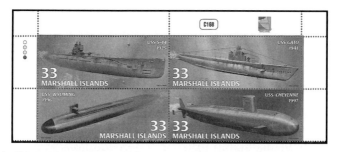

The Marshall Islands, a former U.S. trust territory, often issues stamps with U.S. themes to appeal to collectors in this country. This block of four stamps was issued October 12, 2000, the official centennial date of the U.S. Navy Submarine Force. The designs reproduce paintings by Dean Ellis.

hobby, and the high face values will discourage that."

Shortly after the prestige booklet was issued, *Linn's* readers began reporting freak specimens in which either one of the two panes of stamps was omitted, which shortchanged the customer, or an extra pane of stamps was included, providing a bonus. One reader reported opening her booklet and finding the contents of two complete booklets, stamps, text pages and all, between one set of covers.

U.S. submarines had made two previous appearances on U.S. stamps. *USS Nautilus*, the world's first nuclear-powered sub and the first to cross the North Pole under the ice, was depicted on the 4¢ Arctic Explorations commemorative of 1959 (Scott 1128). A view inside a sub in combat was shown on a 29¢ stamp on the World War II pane marking the events of 1944 with the caption "Submarines shorten war in Pacific, 1944" (Scott 2838e).

The Marshall Islands, a former U.S. trust territory that often issues stamps with U.S. themes to appeal to collectors in this country, issued a block of four stamps depicting U.S. Navy submarines on October 12, 2000, the official centennial date of the Submarine Force.

The Designs

When CSAC and Terrence McCaffrey asked Carl Herrman to explore the possibilities of a stamp or stamps to commemorate the Submarine Force, they had in mind a conventional 20-stamp pane. Herrman acquired an assortment of existing illustrations and photographs and began laying them out in various designs and combinations.

Included in his layouts was a stamp depicting the reason for the commemoration: the Holland submarine that was acquired in 1900 by the U.S. Navy. Herrman inserted into some of the layouts an extra-wide horizontal stamp bearing an image of the *USS Harder*, a Gato-type submarine of World War II, based on a painting by Michael W. Wooten; he had ordered a print of the picture from an ad in a historical magazine. CSAC and McCaffrey were intrigued by this combination of normal-size commemorative stamps with an oversized stamp, and ultimately would decide to create such a combination in the finished product. (In the end, the Wooten painting wasn't used on a stamp, but was displayed on pages 6 and 7 of the prestige booklet.)

Even before the decision was made to issue the stamps in a booklet, the number of varieties was set at five, with the subjects to be the *USS Holland*, a submarine from each of the two World Wars and two types of nuclear sub from the Cold War era.

Herrman found his stamp artist in a serendipitous way. "I was in a hobby store and came across some plastic ship model kits, one of which was of a German U-boat, and the illustration on the box was just spectacular," he said. "The submarine was blasting out torpedoes and bubbles were flying and a ship was burning on the surface. It was everything I was looking for."

From the kit manufacturer, the Revell company, PhotoAssist obtained the name of one of its artists, Jim Griffiths of Glenview, Illinois. Griffiths turned out to be a well-known painter of maritime subjects who works in watercolors and gouache. Herrman signed him up for the stamp project.

Each of Griffiths' sketches and finished paintings was reviewed by the Postal Service's consultants, who suggested changes that would make the pictures more accurate. For example, the artist, working from his reference photograph of the Los Angeles Class submarine, faithfully reproduced two sets of white marks and metal cleats on the aft deck. Then Captain Beach informed the design team that the marks and cleats would be used only during a sea test, to indicate where a rescue device should be attached in case the vessel ran into trouble. "Because we decided we wanted to show really operating subs and not just test runs, Jim removed them from his painting," Herrman said. In the source photos for the Los Angeles and Ohio Class subs, the ships' hulls were a rusty red color, but after learning from Beach that the paint turned black after a period of time, Griffiths painted them black.

The design team originally intended to label the submarines on the stamps in a descriptive way, e.g. "World War Two Submarine," "Attack Submarine" and "Ballistic Missile Submarine." Ultimately, however, it was decided to identify each sub other than the *Holland* by its class, even though that form of identification would be less meaningful to the lay observer.

60¢ USS HOLLAND. The photograph on which Griffiths based his painting is similar to one included in the text-and-pictures section of the prestige booklet. The booklet photo, taken in 1898, shows the sub on the surface with two men on the deck. Griffiths' painting shows three men. He originally painted the submarine facing right, "but when we put the five stamps together, all the other subs were facing left," Herrman said. "It was as if the *Holland* were being attacked by the other four. We had him repaint it so we would have all five submarines going in the same direction."

Jim Griffiths' original sketch for the USS Holland stamp showed the pioneering Navy submarine with its bow on the right, stern on the left. He was asked to repaint it facing left, to conform to the direction of the other four submarines in the booklet.

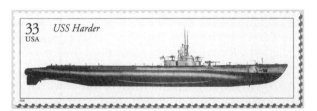

Carl Herrman obtained a print of a painting by Michael W. Wooten of the USS Harder, a Gato Class submarine of World War II, from an advertisement in a magazine of history, and developed it into an ultra-long stamp design. He later used the image in the prestige booklet, spread across pages 6 and 7.

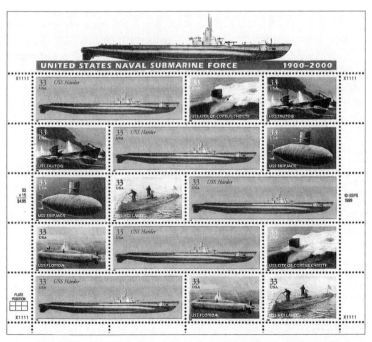

This is an early layout created by Carl Herrman of a pane of 15 Submarines stamps, using images from various sources, including Michael Wooten's painting of the USS Harder both on a double-width stamp and in the header.

These two alternative versions of the Gato Class stamp are in normal commemorative size, but CSAC wanted a double-width design as part of the pane of stamps. In these illustrations, Griffiths included several sharks escorting the submarine, but CSAC decided the fish were an unnecessary element in the design, and the artist eliminated them.

22¢ S CLASS. Griffiths' painting depicts the World War I vintage submarine on the surface, with sunlit clouds of early morning or late afternoon on the horizon. Eight sailors stand on the deck fore and aft of the conning tower.

$3.20 GATO CLASS. The extra-long stamp in the middle of the block shows a World War II submarine, submerged in a blue-green ocean, firing a torpedo from one of its port tubes. Griffiths originally had painted a large bubble cloud in the torpedo's wake, but reduced its size after learning from Beach that the vessels' equipment included suppressors in the torpedo tubes to help limit the bubbles that might betray the sub's location. Griffiths also made alternative paintings of a Gato Class submarine that Herrman worked up into stamp designs of normal commemorative size, but CSAC preferred the double-width design.

33¢ LOS ANGELES CLASS. The illustration shows the attack submarine under way at high speed on the surface, with three officers in the conning tower or sail, and the U.S. flag flying behind them. The sub bears the number 709, identifying it as the *USS Hyman G. Rickover*. "We purposely included the number, just to see if anyone would notice," Herrman said. "Every submariner in the world knows what Admiral Rickover contributed" — the late admiral was the driving force behind the Navy's nuclear-powered submarine program — "and we did this out of respect for him."

55¢ OHIO CLASS. For this stamp, Griffiths painted a sub launching a

An alternative painting by Griffiths of the Los Angeles Class attack submarine, showing the vessel submerged.

Shown here are two alternative versions of the Ohio Class submarine design, including one in which ice floats on the surface above the sub. The ice was removed from the picture after one of the Postal Service's consultants said a submarine commander wouldn't launch a missile through ice.

missile from beneath a dark blue ocean. The missile has just cleared the vessel's hull and is heading straight up, trailing a cloud of bubbles. In one of his earlier versions, the sub is shown in Arctic waters with patches of ice floating above and dramatic shafts of light penetrating the water. "One of our consultants said a submarine commander would never fire a missile through ice," Herrman recalled. "It could easily explode right on top of the sub if it hit the ice. So we had Jim remove the ice. We opted for accuracy over artistic effect."

In an early layout of the prestige booklet, Herrman included a dramatic painting of the sinking of the British liner *Lusitania* by a German U-boat in 1915. However, the painting was found to have been an Allied propaganda picture that inaccurately showed the U-boat crew firing their deck guns at survivors in lifeboats. Herrman replaced the picture with another *Lusitania* painting made by Ken Marschall and published in the 1997 book *Lost Liners*.

This painting of the sinking of the Lusitania *in 1915 was included in an early layout of the prestige booklet, but was found to have been an Allied propaganda picture that inaccurately showed the crew of the German U-boat training its deck guns on survivors in lifeboats. The* Lusitania *painting that replaced it in the booklet was made by Ken Marschall and published in the 1997 book* Lost Liners.

The illustration on the booklet cover is a photograph by Jim Brennan of the attack submarine *USS Seawolf*, while another Brennan photo of the *Seawolf* is shown on page 11 of the booklet. Herrman made extensive use of one of his favorite typefaces, Huxley Vertical, which appears on the stamps, in dropout white capitals; in the headings on the selvage text, in black; on the booklet cover, in white; and in the inside section headings, in black.

First-day Facts

Einar V. Dyhrkopp, chairman of the USPS Board of Governors, dedicated the Submarine stamps in a ceremony at the Dealey Center Theater at the Submarine Base New London in Groton, Connecticut.

Speakers were Connecticut's two U.S. senators, Christopher J. Dodd and Joseph I. Lieberman; U.S. Representative Sam Gejdenson; Vice Admiral Edmund P. Giambastiani Jr., commander of the U.S. Atlantic Fleet's Submarine Force; and Andy Feindt, chief electrician's mate, retired, who was Connecticut state commander of the Submarine Veterans of World War II. Jo Saunders, USPS district manager for the Connecticut District, presided, and Captain H.A. Lincoln Jr., commanding officer of the Submarine Base New London, gave the welcome.

Honored guests included John F. Walsh of the USPS Board of Governors; Admiral Frank L. Bowman, director, naval nuclear propulsion, NAVSEA-08; Admiral Richard W. Mies, commander in chief, U.S. Strategic Command; Rear Admiral John B. Padgett, commander of Navy Region Northeast and of Submarine Group Two; Dee Hauber, mayor of the town of Groton; Dennis Popp, mayor of the city of Groton; Jon M. Steele, vice president, area operations, for the USPS Northeast Area; and Michael W. Toner, president of Electric Boat.

Groton has long been associated with the Navy and with submarines. In 1868 a Navy yard was established there, and during World War I it was commissioned as the first U.S. submarine base. The Electric Boat Corporation of Groton delivered 74 diesel subs to the Navy in World War II. In 1954 the *USS Nautilus*, the world's first nuclear-powered submarine, was launched at Groton. The historic vessel now is berthed permanently near Groton's submarine base. Groton also is home to the Submarine Force Library and Museum.

Because the Submarines booklet pane contains a 22¢ stamp, the Postal Service announced that all covers submitted to the postmaster at Groton for first-day cancellations must either be in five-cover complete sets, with each cover including one of the five stamps on the pane, or have a minimum of 33¢ postage to cover the first-class rate. Single covers franked with the 22¢ stamp alone would be returned to the sender without a first-day cancel, USPS said.

33¢ PACIFIC COAST RAIN FOREST (10 DESIGNS)
NATURE OF AMERICA SERIES

Date of Issue: March 29, 2000

Catalog Number: Scott 3378, pane of 10; 3378a-3378j, stamps

Colors: magenta, cyan, yellow, black, special green

First-Day Cancel: Seattle, Washington

First-Day Cancellations: 435,549

Format: Pane of 10, vertical and horizontal. Offset printing plates of 60 subjects (2 panes across, 3 panes around). Also sold in uncut sheets of 6 panes, 2 panes across, 3 panes down.

Gum Type: self-adhesive

Stamp Size: 1.56 by 1.23 inches; 39.62 by 31.24mm

Pane Size: 9.13 by 6.75 inches; 231.90 by 171.45mm

Uncut Press Sheet Size: 18.25 by 20.5 inches

Perforations: vertical stamps: 11¼ by 11½, horizontal stamps: 11½ (die-cut simulated perforations) (rotary die cutter)

Selvage Inscription: "PACIFIC COAST RAIN FOREST/SECOND IN A SERIES" "NATURE OF AMERICA"

Liner Back Markings: "PACIFIC COAST RAIN FOREST/Temperate rain forest stretches along the Pacific coast/from northern California to the Gulf of Alaska./Characterized by the occurrence of Sitka spruce, this/ecosystem typically occupies a relatively narrow strip/between the ocean and the mountains. The climate/is mild and very wet — average annual precipitation/ranges from 80 to 160 inches. Summer fogs are com-/mon, and intense winter storms bring large amounts/of rain and strong winds./Immense old-growth conifers form a canopy over a/luxuriant understory of ferns, mosses, herbs, and/shrubs. This ecosystem supports the greatest accumu-/lation of organic material per square mile in the/world. The rain forest is home to many bird and/mammal species; some populations have been seri-/ously reduced in size. Numerous streams and rivers/abound with fish and amphibians./©USPS 1999/NATURE OF AMERICA/THIS SERIES OF STAMPS FEATURES THE BEAUTY AND COMPLEXITY OF PLANT AND ANIMAL COMMU-NITIES IN NORTH AMERICA." Universal Product Code (UPC). Numbered illustration. "1. Western Hemlock/Tsuga heterophylla/2. Common Raven/Corvus corax/3. Roosevelt Elk/Cervus elaphus roosevelti/4. Vine Maple/Acer circinatum/5. Sitka Spruce/Picea sitchensis/6. Harlequin Duck/Histrionicus histrionicus/7. Western Sword Fern/Polystichum muni-tum/8. Deer Fern/Blechnum spicant/9. Varied Thrush/Ixoreus naevius/10. Douglas Squirrel/Tamiasciurus douglasii/11. Dwarf Oregongrape/-Berberis nervosa/12. Winter Wren/Troglodytes troglodytes/13. Oregon Oxalis/Oxalis oregana/14. Red Huckleberry/Vaccinium parvifolium/15. American Dipper/Cinclus mexicanus/16. Pacific Giant/Salamander/-Dicamptodon tenebrosus/17. Western Tiger Swallowtail/Pterourus rutu-lus/18. Foliose Lichen/Lobaria oregana/19. Banana Slug/Ariolimax columbianus/20. Chinook Salmon parr/Oncorhynchus tshawytscha/21. Cutthroat Trout/Oncorhynchus clarki/22. Rough-skinned Newt/Taricha granulosa/23. Tailed Frog/Ascaphus truei/24. Caddisfly larvae/Lim-nephilus sp./25. Stair-step Moss/Hylocomium splendens/26. Snail-eating Ground Beetle/Scaphinotus angusticollis"

Illustrator: John Dawson of Hilo, Hawaii

Designer, Typographer and Art Director: Ethel Kessler of Bethesda, Maryland

Stamp Manufacturing: Stamps printed by Banknote Corporation of America, Browns Summit, North Carolina, on Goebel 670 offset press. Stamps finished by BCA.

Quantity Ordered: 100,000,000 stamps

Plate Number Detail: no plate number

Paper Supplier: Paper Corporation of the United States/Spinnaker Coatings

Tagging: block tagging on individual stamps

The Stamps

On March 29, the Postal Service issued the second in a planned series of 10-stamp panes called "Nature of America." The series, according to USPS, will consist of six "educational stamp panes designed to promote our appreciation of the North American biomes." A biome is a major ecological community.

The first pane appeared in 1999 and depicts creatures and plants of the Sonoran Desert of the southwestern United States and northwestern Mexico. The second one features the wildlife of the Pacific Coast Rain Forest, including some that are beneath the surface of a stream. Like its predecessor, the new pane displays a colorful murallike picture, with 10 self-adhesive stamps that peel off from within the mural.

The stamps are laid out in a staggered fashion to correspond to the location of their design subjects in the overall illustration. Each stamp has a self-contained design that depicts at least one identifiable plant or animal native to the Pacific Coast Rain Forest, and each stamp touches at least one other.

The stamps are semijumbo in size. Seven are vertically oriented, and three are horizontal. At no point does the die cutting run to the edges of the pane, and there are no cuts in the backing paper, which makes it difficult to extract individual stamps from the pane without tearing through the selvage.

To ensure uniformity, it was decided that all the panes in the series would be created by the same design team: John Dawson of Hilo, Hawaii, as illustrator, and Ethel Kessler, a Postal Service art director, as designer and typographer. Like the Sonoran Desert pane, the Pacific Coast Rain Forest pane was offset-printed by Banknote Corporation of America

(BCA). There are no plate numbers in the selvage.

The paper used is unphosphored, and the phosphorescent tagging needed to activate post office facer-canceler machines was applied on press, over the printed image. However, the tagging on the Pacific Coast Rain Forest pane differs from that on the Sonoran Desert pane in two ways.

The 10 Sonoran Desert stamps are coated with one large, irregularly shaped block of tagging that covers every stamp from edge to edge

Viewed under ultraviolet light, the phosphor tagging on the 1999 Sonoran Desert stamps (top) and on the 2000 Pacific Coast Rain Forest stamps (bottom) look quite different.

and even extends slightly beyond the die-cut outer edges of each stamp. On the new pane, each stamp is individually tagged with a phosphor block that covers most of the stamp's printed surface, but does not quite extend to the die-cut edges (see illustration).

Linn's Stamp News quoted officials of USPS and Banknote Corporation of America explaining why the tagging process was changed. "We have learned that perforating or die-cutting through the phoshor, which is actually a heavy metal, lessens the die life," the officials said. "The abrasive nature of the phosphor dulls the pins and cutting edges of the perforating die and die-cutting plate. By stopping the phosphor inside the die-cut shape, we extend the life of the die."

The second tagging change came about because BCA used a screen during the application of the phosphor tagging on the Pacific Coast Rain Forest pane. Under ultraviolet light, the yellow-green glow of the phosphor-tagging block on the Sonoran Desert stamps is very smooth, solid and uniform across the pane. On the new pane, the phosphor application on each stamp shows a conspicuous diagonal crisscrossing textured pattern, as if the stamp were printed on woven fabric instead of smooth paper.

Use of a screen enabled BCA to reduce the overall amount of phosphor needed for the print run, while still providing on each stamp the level of

The tagging applied to Sonoran Desert stamps looks smooth (left), while the tagging on the Pacific Coast Rain Forest stamps is printed with a diagonal screening (center). The pattern left by the screening process can be seen more easily in the close-up view at right.

phosphorescence required by USPS specifications.

The tagging applied to both panes is a zinc orthosilicate compound, with special additives to apply the phosphor to the paper. BCA representatives told *Linn's* that because the inks they used are cured by ultraviolet light, the phosphor is applied using a UV-curable varnish as a carrier.

On the back of the liner to which the stamps are attached is an outline drawing reproducing the scene on the pane, with numbers corresponding to those on an accompanying list of the plants and animals depicted. A total of 26 species are identifiable. For a list of the species with their scientific names, see the technical information at the head of this chapter.

As was the case with the Sonoran Desert pane, some of the plants and

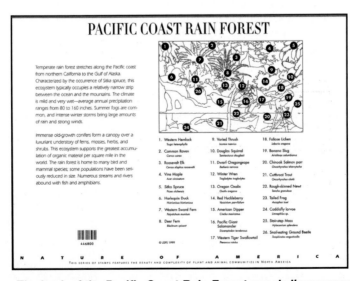

The back of the Pacific Coast Rain Forest pane's liner paper contains descriptive text and a key to the plant and animal life shown on the front of the pane.

A large amount of John Dawson's illustration remains after the 10 stamps are removed from the pane.

creatures depicted in Dawson's painting are outside the borders of the 10 stamps. After the stamps are extracted, these species remain behind in the large selvage, which covers a total area of approximately 43 square inches, more than twice the approximately 19 square inches accounted for by the stamps.

In 1999, Terrence McCaffrey, head of stamp design for USPS, discussed the Sonoran Desert pane, which has the same ratio of stamps to selvage, a ratio that presumably will remain constant throughout the Nature of America series. He acknowledged that there is "waste within the illustration area, but we felt it was a good tradeoff." The alternative, he said, would have been to create five more stamps within the mural for a total of 15. Holding the number of stamps on the pane to 10 keeps a large annual stamp program from becoming even larger.

The stamps of the Pacific Rain Forest pane and the species shown on them are: 1, harlequin duck and small portions of Western hemlock and Western sword fern; 2, dwarf oregongrape and snail-eating ground beetle; 3, American dipper and Oregon oxalis; 4, cutthroat trout; 5, Roosevelt elk; 6, winter wren and deer fern; 7, Pacific giant salamander and rough-skinned newt; 8, Western tiger swallowtail and red huckleberry; 9, Douglas squirrel, Sitka spruce and foliose lichen; and 10, banana slug, tailed frog and stair-step moss.

Among the identifiable species that appear on the selvage but not on stamps is the varied thrush, near the right center of the pane; two common ravens in flight; caddisfly larvae; vine maple; and Chinook salmon parr, one of which is about to become a meal for the cutthroat trout on an adjacent stamp. In addition, there are some small fauna, such as an ant just to the right of the Douglas squirrel and a small aquatic creature immediately above the trout, that are not numbered and identified on the outline drawing on the back of the liner paper.

In choosing the species to be illustrated, Dawson relied on the advice of two University of Washington faculty members enlisted by PhotoAssist, which does research for USPS under contract. Jerry Franklin, professor of ecosystems analysis, suggested the list of animals and plants, and Gordon Orians, professor of zoology, concurred.

The artist and the consultants made certain that all the depicted species could logically be found in the same time period. Thus they excluded, for example, the Northern spotted owl, which lives in the Pacific Coast rain forest and is on the federal government's list of endangered and threatened species but is primarily nocturnal and normally would not be seen during the day.

Asked by the design team to justify including the banana slug in the illustration, Jerry Franklin wrote: "I definitely think it should be included. It is one of the very most characteristic species in the temperate rain forest — one that you invariably encounter during a walk in such forests. Indeed, the distinctiveness of this organism as an indicator of these forests is demonstrated by the way that hundreds of carvings of this animal are sold in gift and tourist shops in the region. If there is one animal symbol of the Northwestern forests, it is the banana slug."

The six biomes that have been or will be featured in the Nature of America series came from a list prepared by PhotoAssist, the Postal Service's research firm, also after consultation with experts. The remaining four panes will feature the Great Plains prairie, the longleaf pine forest, and, reportedly, the taiga or tundra (as in Alaska) and the tropical rain for-

est (as in Hawaii).

Officials at first intended that the panes be conventionally gummed and perforated, but this posed a problem. A special perforating die would have to be created to form the stamps within the mural. Once the configuration of the die had been established for the first pane, practical economics would have dictated that it be used for all the subsequent panes, which would have put the illustrator in an artistic straitjacket. He would have had to accommodate his paintings to the perforation pattern, rather than vice versa.

The answer, it turned out, was to make the stamps self-adhesive. The die-cutting mechanism used for self-adhesives easily could be altered to fit any stamp layout and orientation.

Collectors experienced difficulty soaking used specimens of Pacific Rain Forest stamps from their envelopes; the same problem had turned up with the Sonoran Desert stamps. *Linn's Stamp News* found that it takes up to four hours in water at room temperature for the water to permeate the stamps and allow removal. *Stamp Collector* said it obtained the best results by using naptha-based lighter fluid, with the stamp and cover fragment sandwiched between glass plates to limit evaporation and ensure that the fluid penetrated the stamp well.

The stamps, when they do separate from their envelope paper, curl tightly and require careful flattening before they dry. This curling process sometimes causes the inked image that covers the stamp to crack slightly.

USPS had offered the Sonoran Desert stamps to collectors in uncut press sheets of six panes at face value ($19.80), and did the same with the Pacific Rain Forest stamps. Their sale in this form was limited to five sheets per customer.

Frequently, collectors who obtain uncut press sheets of U.S. stamps extract from them blocks and pairs that span the gutters separating individual panes. Such multiples fit in stamp albums, and their gutters are evidence that they came from the larger sheets. The Nature of America sheets, however, don't lend themselves to such a breakdown. The Scott *Specialized Catalogue of U.S. Stamps & Covers*, which normally lists collectible gutter pairs and blocks from uncut sheets, makes no attempt to do so for the Nature of America series.

In addition to the stamps, panes and sheets, Stamp Fulfillment Services offered large posters with 10 stamps affixed for $9, and matted panes suitable for framing for $12.95.

The rain forest of the Pacific Northwest is

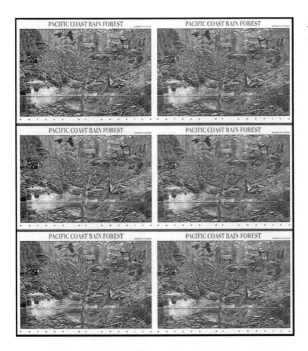

An uncut press sheet of six Pacific Rain Forest panes.

one of the largest remaining temperate rain forests in the world. High levels of precipitation, 80 to 160 inches per year, provide the water necessary to support the forest's giant conifers, many of them taller than 200 feet with bases up to 7 feet wide. Trees in the forest have normal lifespans ranging from 400 to 700 years. Living plants occupy almost all the available space in the rain forest, which is said to contain the greatest accumulation of organic material per square mile in the world.

The Designs

John Dawson is a veteran wildlife and nature artist who had worked with another USPS art director, Howard Paine, during Paine's days as a graphics editor at *National Geographic* magazine. His previous U.S. stamp credits, besides the Sonoran Desert stamps, include the Cats block of four of 1988, the Idaho Statehood commemorative of 1990 and the four Flowering Trees of 1997.

Of necessity, Dawson's acrylic paintings for the Nature of America panes involve crowding a lot of detail into a relatively small (8¾- by 5⅝-inch) space. The need to include large animals, such as deer, and small to very small ones, such as fish, birds and insects, requires the artist to position the small creatures in the foreground and the large ones in the distance, making their apparent size the same.

Some of the details in the Pacific Rain Forest illustration are subtle and reward close examination. For example, Dawson included evidence of human interaction with the landscape, such as a cut log in the stream that

77

At the beginning of the Nature of America project, John Dawson made quick pencil sketches of each of the biomes that would be included in the series. This is his sketch of the Pacific Coast Rain Forest. The general layout of the illustration is the same as on the finished pane, but the details differ extensively.

Before creating his painting, Dawson made this detailed pencil sketch.

might have washed down from an old logging camp and lodged along the bank, and a fishing fly hooked over a stick on the stream bed. Dawson had an artistic reason to add the cut end of the log in his final version, as well, art director Ethel Kessler pointed out. It was to help confine the picture on the right side and prevent the viewer from "meandering off the image."

To ensure that the wildlife was accurately depicted, Dawson prepared a detailed color sketch that PhotoAssist submitted to the project consultants, Gordon Orians and Jerry Franklin, for their review. The artist then made the revisions they suggested.

For example, he changed the butterfly at the right center of the illustration from a red admiral, with predominantly red and black coloration, to a Western tiger swallowtail, whose yellow and black wings appeared much brighter in the picture. The butterfly was included to provide color, even though the professors noted that the primary forest in which the scene is set has no food source for butterflies. "Both the red admiral and the Western tiger swallowtail would live and be found in disturbed areas in the forest," the consultants wrote. "They do occasionally enter the primary forest, and no one will hit the roof if you add [a butterfly], but it really isn't characteristic."

The consultants suggested the inclusion of "the most conspicuous insect in the forest," the snail-eating ground beetle, and Dawson made it his final addition to the scene.

Other recommendations relayed by PhotoAssist and acted upon by the artist included these:

"Vine maple. The leaf could look more realistic. Samples submitted for John to work from.

"Deer fern. The artwork currently contains only one of the two frond types that make up the fern, vegetative fronds. John should add the spore-bearing fronds, which stand up and are a brown color.

"Varied thrush. The orange wing bars extend too far dorsally. Recommendation to shorten the coloration a bit, because the bars continue up a bit too far toward the top of the back of the bird.

"Douglas squirrel. The belly appears off-white. It should have an orange tint.

"Oregon grape. Be careful that the yellow of the flowers be accurate. In the color photocopy, they are not as yellow as they should be.

"Winter wren. The bird is very small and compact. The one in the art looks 'fluffed up.' It is primarily shades of brown, with some very obscure light brown banding. There should not be any white showing. The stripe below the eye should be omitted. The bird's tail is very turned up and narrow, not spread widely as portrayed in the artwork. The wings are almost always folded in against the body when the animal is sitting on a branch.

"Red huckleberry. Stems should be bright green, a definitive characteristic of the species.

"Foliose lichen. The lichen is an epiphyte and grows in the tree canopy. Recommendation to modify the artwork so that it is clear that this lichen is not growing on the ground, but rather has fallen from the canopy or is attached to a fallen branch.

"Banana slug. The color of the slug should be changed from orange to an olive green. It can either be solid olive, or some black blotches can be added.

"Rough-skinned newt. The skin should be rough or 'pebbly.' In the artwork it appears smooth, like a salamander. The underside of the animal is orange. If John rolled the animal over, you could see this coloration."

On the pane, Dawson's illustration is surrounded by a narrow white border. All the wording is in capitals. Across the top is a bar of green and, beneath it, the words "PACIFIC COAST RAIN FOREST" in a typeface called Didot. Across the bottom, also in green, are the words "NATURE OF AMERICA" in a font called Eras. The inscription "SECOND IN A SERIES," in small gray Eras lettering, is above the upper-right corner of the illustration. The "USA 33," dropped out of each stamp, is also in Eras type.

First-day Facts

Katherine Nash, postmaster of Seattle, Washington, dedicated the stamps at Seattle's Woodland Park Zoo. The ceremony took place at the Elk Overlook, located within the zoo's Northern Trail Exhibit.

John Bierlein, manager of planning and interpretive exhibits at Woodland Park Zoo, was the speaker. Mike Waller, director of the zoo, gave the welcome. Richard Wilson, Postal Service manager of marketing, presided, and Dale Zinser, Seattle District manager for customer service and sales for USPS, was an honored guest.

In the Spring 2000 edition of its *USA Philatelic* mail-order catalog, USPS had listed Olympia, Washington, as the first-day site for the stamps. The new location, Seattle, was announced in mid-February.

The earliest-known use of Pacific Coast Rain Forest stamps was on a Priority Mail envelope franked with an entire 10-stamp pane and tied by four March 22 double-outline circular datestamps from the South Lake Tahoe, California, post office. The March 22 date was one week prior to the official first day of issue. A *Linn's Stamp News* reader who submitted the cover to the newspaper said he obtained the pane at a California business. The reader said a representative of the business informed him that one of the clerks at a local post office sometimes sold stamps before their official issue date so the business could obtain them before they were sold out.

33¢ LOUISE NEVELSON (5 DESIGNS)

Date of Issue: April 6, 2000

Catalog Number: Scott 3379-3383, stamps; 3383a, strip of 5

Colors: black, cyan, magenta, yellow

First-Day Cancel: New York, New York

First-Day Cancellations: 389,200

Format: Panes of 20, vertical, 5 across, 4 down. Offset printing plates of 80 subjects (8 across, 10 around).

Gum Type: water-activated

Overall Stamp Size: 1.222 by 1.560 inches; 31.04 by 39.62mm

Pane Size: 9.5000 by 7.0312 inches; 241.30 by 178.59mm

Perforations: 11 by 11¼

Selvage Inscription: "LOUISE NEVELSON/SCULPTOR/1899-1988/My work is delicate;/it may look strong, but it is delicate./True strength is delicate./My whole life is in it. ..." "DETAILS OF SCULPTURES: SILENT MUSIC I ROYAL TIDE I BLACK CHORD NIGHTSPHERE-LIGHT DAWN'S WEDDING CHAPEL I."

Selvage Markings: "©USPS/1999." ".33/x20/$6.60." "PLATE/POSITION" and diagram.

Photographers: The Pace Gallery, Jerry L. Thompson, Whitney Gallery of Art, Arnold Newman

Designer, Typographer and Art Director: Ethel Kessler of Bethesda, Maryland

Modeler: Joseph Sheeran, Ashton-Potter (USA) Ltd., Williamsville, New York

Stamp Manufacturing: Stamps printed by Ashton-Potter on offset portion of Stevens Variable Size Security Documents 6-color offset, 3-color intaglio press. Stamps finished by Ashton-Potter.

Quantity Ordered: 55,000,000

Plate Number Detail: 1 set of 4 plate numbers preceded by the letter P in selvage next to each corner stamp

Plate Number Combinations Reported: P1111, P2222

Paper Supplier: Tullis Russell

Tagging: block tagging

The Stamps

On April 6, the Postal Service issued five stamps featuring the work of sculptor Louise Nevelson. Each stamp depicted a detail from one of Nevelson's sculptures, which often took the form of expansive, three-dimensional walls of stacked wooden boxes containing carved or recycled wood objects painted black, white or gold.

The Nevelson stamps were the latest of many issued over the years to depict the work of Americans in the graphic arts. Several of these, in the 1960s and 1970s, comprised an informal series called "American Artists." The more recent ones, such as the 1996 stamp reproducing a Georgia O'Keeffe painting and the 1998 set of five stamps illustrating the stabiles and mobiles of Alexander Calder, have had no series designation.

Like the O'Keeffe and Calder panes, the pane of Nevelson stamps has a wide decorative selvage on one side bearing a photograph of the artist. This format, which also has been used for stamps in the Legends of Hollywood series, was devised by Carl Burcham, former head of stamp and product marketing for USPS, as a way to entice collectors to buy entire panes rather than single stamps.

The Nevelson stamps are vertical semijumbos and are arranged in horizontal se-tenant strips of five on a pane of 20. As was the case with the Calder pane, the horizontal rows contain all five stamp varieties, while the vertical rows comprise stamps of the same design.

Ashton-Potter (USA) Ltd. printed the stamps by the offset process. They have water-activated gum and conventional perforations. The block of 20 stamps on the pane is

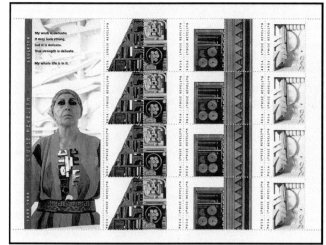

This is an early version of a pane layout, with a different picture of Nevelson in the selvage and two different sculptures shown on the third and fourth stamps in the horizontal row.

enclosed by a single row of perfs. The five horizontal rows of perfs extend to the right side of the pane to facilitate sale of individual stamps by postal clerks.

Unlike the Calder stamps, the Nevelsons weren't made available in uncut press sheets.

Meredith Davis, a member of the Citizens' Stamp Advisory Committee, brought to CSAC's attention the fact that Nevelson's birth centennial was upcoming and that stamp honors would be appropriate. However, the Nevelson stamps, when issued, missed the anniversary by a few months; she was born in Kiev, Ukraine, in the fall of 1899. Her birth name was Leah Berliawsky.

In 1905, her family moved to Maine, where her father worked in the timber trade. She married Charles Nevelson in 1920, the same year in which she began studying painting and drawing at the Art Students League in New York City.

In 1931 she studied with artist Hans Hofmann at his school in Munich, Germany, and she worked with famed Mexican muralist Diego Rivera the following year. Her first solo exhibition didn't take place until 1941, at New York City's Nierendorf Gallery. By then she had begun sculpting with materials such as terra cotta, stone and wood, but the form of her art continued to develop.

It wasn't until the mid-1950s that Nevelson began to enjoy commercial success with geometric arrangements of found wood pieces. Soon after, she began creating wall-size ensembles of adjoining open wood boxes, each containing multiple bits of furniture, decorations or similar objects, all made of wood and

painted a single color. For instance, the components of *Dawn's Wedding Chapel I*, the subject of one of the stamps, included old banister balustrades, bits of molding, finials, newels, slats, knobs, dowels, mitered corners, lintels, studs, porch posts, rough old boards, lion-footed legs, even an old croquet set. Later, Nevelson experimented with plastics, transparent synthetics and metals.

The Whitney Museum of American Art in New York presented the first major retrospective of Nevelson's art in 1967, and today it has the largest collection of her works in the world. Among her most important commissioned sculptures are *Atmosphere and Environment X* for Princeton University, *Bicentennial Dawn* for the James A. Byrne Federal Courthouse in Philadelphia, and *Transparent Horizon* for the Massachusetts Institute of Technology.

During her 50-year career, Nevelson created other artwork, including collages, and sculpture in other forms. She continued to work until her death in 1988.

In *Contemporary Artists*, G.S. Whittet wrote of Nevelson's innovative creations that the "compartmentalization of the relief wall emphasized the contained detail so that on each shelf appeared what seemed the miniature furnishings of a chapel in an overcrowded baroque cathedral." Rosalind E. Krauss noted in *200 Years of American Sculpture* that "Nevelson's modules suggest a dual identity: They are both the model of an interior space in which associations are housed, and the exterior space of real objects from which psychological experience is formed."

The sculptures represented on the stamps are:

SILENT MUSIC I. A triangular sculpture made of small mirrors and wood painted black that Nevelson created in 1964. It is some 7 feet high, 6 feet wide at the base and 10 inches deep. The work is owned by a private collector in Germany. The stamp depicts a portion of the left side of the work, from a photograph provided by the Pace Gallery.

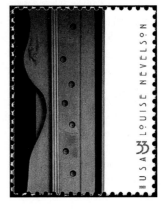

ROYAL TIDE I. Created in 1960, is made of 18 boxes of wooden objects painted gold and is 8 feet high, 3 feet, 4 inches wide and 8 inches deep. It is on long-term loan to the Whitney Museum from the Peter and Beverly Lipman Collection. The stamp depicts two of the boxes in the sculpture. Again, the Pace Gallery was the source of this photo.

BLACK CHORD. A set of boxes full of black-painted wooden objects, *Black Chord* was made in 1964 and stands nearly 10 feet

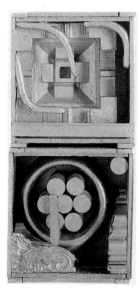

This is the photographic transparency showing two boxes from Royal Tide I *(1961), made of gold-painted wood, from which the stamp image was made. After it was discovered that the boxes in the photo aren't stacked in the way Nevelson intended, the image was changed at the printer to show them stacked correctly.*

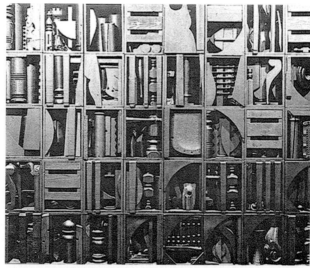

From this black-painted wooden sculpture of 1964, Black Chord, *nearly 10 feet wide by 9 feet high, the second box from the left on the top row was chosen as a stamp illustration.*

wide, 9 feet high and 1 foot deep. It was the gift of Anne and Joel Ehrenkranz to the Whitney Museum, which provided the photo. The stamp depicts the second box from the left on the top row.

NIGHTSPHERE-LIGHT. This black wood wall, stretching 47 feet in length, more than 8 feet high and 1 foot deep, was installed in the lobby of the Julliard Theater at New York City's Lincoln Center for the Performing Arts in 1969. USPS, through PhotoAssist, its research firm, commissioned Jerry L. Thompson to make the photograph. The stamp depicts a detail of the wall.

DAWN'S WEDDING CHAPEL I. Made in the summer of 1959 for a show at the Museum of American Art, this set of boxes full of wooden objects painted white was part of a larger

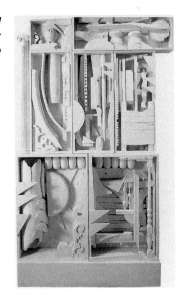

Shown here is Nevelson's white-painted wood sculpture, Dawn's Wedding Chapel I. The box from the lower-left corner is pictured on the stamp. The sculpture was made in 1959.

exhibit called *Dawn's Wedding Feast*. It is 7½ feet high, a little more than 4 feet wide, and 6 inches deep. Its location and ownership were unknown as of August 1999, when PhotoAssist attempted to determine them. The photo of the detail shown on the stamp was provided by the Pace Gallery.

The Designs

Ethel Kessler, a long-time admirer of Nevelson's work, served as art director and designer for the project.

"The problem was, how do you get these room-sized constructions onto a postage stamp?" said Terrence McCaffrey, head of stamp design for USPS. Kessler's solution, which McCaffrey called "brilliant," was to depict a close-up detail of the chosen work at the left or right side of each vertically arranged stamp, with white space and type filling the rest of the design. On each stamp, the depicted sculpture extends to the tips of the perforation teeth on two or three sides.

"One of the things about Nevelson's work is that it consists of units that come together, so there are constructions within squares within boxes," Kessler said. "So I guess it was pretty strong logic to break it down that way. The danger is that you break it down into one single unit and it doesn't really explain what she did, which is, really, to build environments."

By choosing to "stack" stamps of the same design in vertical rows on the pane, rather than arrange the different designs in blocks, Kessler "sort of re-created a Louise Nevelson work as stamps," she said. "Once we structured the pane vertically, which is really the way she structured her sculptures, it fell into place and made sense according to her work."

However, individual stamps must stand alone on envelopes, and the fact is that a person receiving a piece of mail bearing a Nevelson stamp who was unfamiliar with the sculptor would be puzzled as to what he or she was seeing. The only information on the stamps other than the "USA" and denomination is the name "Louise Nevelson." The word "sculptor" and her years of birth and death are in the side selvage; the titles of the featured pieces aren't on the stamps, but are given in the bottom selvage, beneath each vertical row of four stamps that have the same design.

Several factors influenced the choice of the five sculptures to be shown on the stamps. One was the relative importance of the pieces; here, CSAC had the benefit of the expertise of one of its own members, C. Douglas Lewis, curator of sculpture at the National Gallery of Art. Another was the need to present a varied selection. "She did a lot of work that was black on black, but she also did some significant pieces that were white on white and gold on gold," Kessler said. "It seemed appropriate to try to make a pane that had representation of all of that."

USPS ordered a last-minute change in one stamp. After the designs were made public, it was discovered that the photographic transparency used to create the Royal Tide I stamp depicted the two boxes stacked in a way that was the reverse of the way Nevelson had intended. The art was altered at the printer's so that the two boxes were stacked in the correct order.

The unusual, delicate typeface Kessler chose for the stamps and selvage is called ITC Rennie Mackintosh. It was developed by International Typeface Corporation based on the lettering that Charles Rennie Mackintosh, a Scottish architect born in 1868, printed by hand on his drawings. Among the font's striking features are its capital O, which is half the depth of the other letters and has a dot beneath it, and the double horizontal bar on its capital A. Rennie Mackintosh type was used on one previous U.S. stamp, the Wisconsin Sesquicentennial commemorative of 1998.

The selvage photograph is a full-length view of Nevelson, clad in black, with her hand held dramatically over her heart, standing in front of her sculpture *Dawn's Wedding Feast*. The photo was made by Arnold Newman in 1980 during a retrospective of her work at the Whitney Museum, when she was 80 years old.

A striking feature of her face in the photo is the heavy false eyelashes, which she affected in her later years. "In time, the lashes became exaggerated caterpillarlike fur fringes, reminiscent of the stiff doll's eyelashes that had fascinated her so long ago," wrote a biographer, Laurie Lisle. "... Louise sometimes glued several pairs of eyelashes together, because they gave an aging face 'emphasis' and made her feel like 'a playgirl.' "

Superimposed on the selvage picture is the quotation: "My work is delicate. It may look strong, but it is delicate. My whole life is in it. ..." The context of the words is an extended commentary on her sculpture by Nevelson herself.

"I have always felt feminine ... very feminine, so feminine that I wouldn't wear slacks," she wrote. "I didn't like the thought, so I never did wear them. I have retained this stubborn edge. Men don't work this way, they become too affixed, too involved with the craft or technique. They wouldn't putter, so to speak, as I do with these things. The dips and cracks and detail fascinate me. My work is delicate; it may look strong, but it is del-

87

icate. True strength is delicate. My whole life is in it, and my whole life is feminine, and I work from an entirely different point of view. My work is the creation of a feminine mind — there is no doubt. What I wear every day and how I comb my hair all has something to do with it. The way you live a life. And in my particular case, there was never a time that I ever wanted to be anything else. I was interested in being myself. And that is feminine. I am not very modest, I always say I built an empire."

First-day Facts

The stamps were dedicated by Anita J. Bizzotto, USPS vice president for pricing and product, at the spring Postage Stamp Mega-Event show at the New York City Passenger Ship Terminal's Show Pier 92. The show was a presentation of the American Stamp Dealers Association, the American Philatelic Society and the Postal Service.

Speakers were Maria Isak Nevelson, the sculptor's granddaughter; Wayne L. Youngblood of the APS board of directors; and Eugenie Tsai, associate director for curatorial affairs at the Whitney Museum of American Art. Jackson Taylor, president of ASDA, gave the welcome, and New York Postmaster Vinnie Malloy presided.

Honored guests were Ethel Kessler, the stamps' designer; Arnold Newman, whose photograph of Nevelson is shown in the selvage; and Zackary Canter, Morgan Hill, Sarah Lipsey and Ashley Young, the youthful designers of the four Stampin' the Future stamps (see separate chapter).

The earliest-known use of a Nevelson stamp was on a yellow bill-payment envelope hand-canceled Bethesda, Maryland, March 14, 23 days before the official first day of issue. The stamp depicts a detail from Nevelson's *Nightsphere-Light* sculpture.

33¢ EDWIN POWELL HUBBLE (5 DESIGNS)

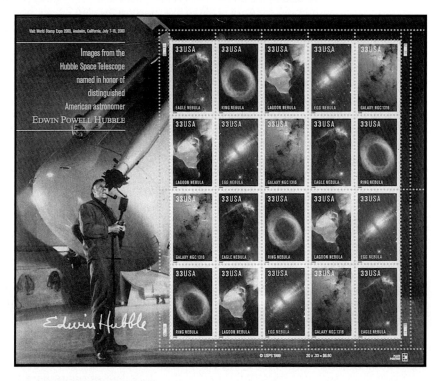

Date of Issue: April 10, 2000

Catalog Numbers: Scott 3384-3388, stamps; 3388a, strip of 5

Colors: magenta, yellow, cyan, black, brown (PMS 468), purple (PMS 209)

First-Day Cancel: Greenbelt, Maryland

First-Day Cancellations: 411,449

Format: Pane of 20, vertical, 5 across, 4 down. Gravure printing plates of 240 subjects (20 across, 12 around) manufactured by Armotek Industries, Palmyra, New Jersey.

Gum Type: water-activated

Overall Stamp Size: 0.99 by 1.56 inches; 25.15 by 39.62mm

Pane Size: 8.76 by 7.23 inches; 222.50 by 183.64mm

Perforations: 11 (APS rotary perforator)

Selvage Inscription: "Visit World Stamp Expo, Anaheim, California, July 7-16, 2000"/"Images from the/Hubble Space Telescope/named in honor of/distinguished/American astronomer/EDWIN POWELL HUBBLE."

Selvage Markings: "©USPS 1999" "20x.33 = $6.60" "PLATE/POSITION" and diagram.

Back Markings: On selvage: "Visit World Stamp Expo 2000, Anaheim, California, July 7-16, 2000"/"EDWIN POWELL HUBBLE/The Hubble Space Telescope, launched in April 1990,/was named by NASA in honor of astronomer/Dr. Edwin Powell Hubble (1889-1953)./Hubble determined that galaxies (very large groups of/stars and associated matter) exist outside of and are/receding from the Milky Way. His work demonstrated/that the universe is expanding. The Hubble Space/Telescope has taken hundreds of thousands of images/of astronomical objects, including the four nebulae/(interstellar clouds of gas and dust) and one galaxy/shown on these stamps./Edwin Powell Hubble at the 48-inch Schmidt Telescope, 1949,/Palomar Observatory, Palomar Mountain, California." Universal Product Code (UPC) "442300."

On individual stamps:

"Galaxy NGC 1316/NASA's Hubble Space/Telescope captured the/aftermath of an ancient/collision between two/galaxies. The remains of/the small galaxy appear/as dark clumps against/the glowing core of the/large galaxy, known/as NGC 1316."

"Egg Nebula/NASA's Hubble Space/Telescope provided this/view of the last gasps of/the sun-like star in the/Egg Nebula. The/intriguing 'searchlight'/beams are emerging/from the dying star, hid-/den behind the dark/central dust band."

"Lagoon Nebula/NASA's Hubble Space/Telescope imaged an eerie/cradle of star formation/called the Lagoon Nebula./The giant clouds of dusty/gas may have been/shaped by high-speed/interstellar winds created/within the clouds by/newly formed stars."

"Ring Nebula/NASA's Hubble Space/Telescope peered at the/Ring Nebula, a barrel of/gas cast off by a dying/star similar to our sun./The barrel, formed over/thousands of years at/the end of the/star's life, appears/as a ring."

"Eagle Nebula/NASA's Hubble Space/Telescope captured the/beauty of a dramatic/region of star formation./This stellar nursery,/known as the Eagle/Nebula, features pillars/of dust and gas that/act as cocoons for/embryonic stars."

Designer, Typographer and Art Director: Phil Jordan of Falls Church, Virginia

Modeler: Donald H. Woo of Sennett Security Products, Chantilly, Virginia

Stamp Manufacturing: Stamps printed for Sennett Security Products by American Packaging Corporation, Columbus, Wisconsin, on Cerutti 950 gravure press. Stamps finished by Unique Binders, Fredericksburg, Virginia.

Quantity Ordered: 105,350,000

Cylinder Number Detail: 1 set of 6 cylinder numbers preceded by the letter S in selvage beside each corner stamp.

Cylinder Number Combination Reported: S111111

Paper Supplier: Westvaco/Ivex Corporation

Tagging: block tagging

The Stamps

On April 10, the Postal Service placed on nationwide sale a pane of 20 stamps — five varieties, four of each — to honor Edwin Powell Hubble, an American astronomer who revolutionized humanity's concept of the universe. The stamps depicted some of the spectacular phenomena of deep space recorded by the orbiting telescope named for Hubble that the National Aeronautics and Space Administration had launched 10 years earlier.

The pane was dedicated at the NASA Goddard Space Flight Center in Greenbelt, Maryland. It consists of four horizontal rows of five stamps with a wide pictorial selvage at the left. The layout is similar to that of the Legends of Hollywood series and recent panes of stamps honoring American artists and sculptors. Unlike those stamps, however, each Hubble stamp bears text on the reverse side explaining the image on the front.

The images — Eagle Nebula, Ring Nebula, Lagoon Nebula, Egg Nebula and Galaxy NGC 1316 — were described by USPS as "visual representations of data taken by the Hubble Space Telescope that have been processed, and in some cases colorized, for scientific purposes."

"We needed the verso text because the images are so abstract," said Terrence McCaffrey, head of stamp design for USPS. "Our policy was not to sell just the whole pane but individual stamps as well, and we felt we had to put some text on them so people wouldn't look at a single stamp and say 'What is this?' "

The reverse side of the selvage also bears a Universal Product Code symbol. It was the second application of a new USPS policy to print bar codes in stamp selvage to help the Postal Service track stamp inventories, beginning with the 33¢ Los Angeles Class Submarine commemorative stamp issued March 27, 2000.

Text is printed on each stamp on the reverse of the pane. The reverse also includes a Universal Product Code symbol to help USPS track stamp inventories.

The stamps were printed by the gravure process by American Packaging Corporation in Columbus, Wisconsin, for Sennett Security Products. They are arranged on the pane so that the horizontal strips of five contain one specimen of each variety, and the horizontal or vertical blocks of six contain two specimens of one variety and one each of the other four varieties.

The portion of the pane containing the stamps is surrounded by a double square of perforations. One square forms the outer edges of the outer stamps, and the second is just outside the first. Perforations also extend through the selvage on the right side, extending from the top, bottom and center of the unit of 20 stamps, to make it easier for postal clerks to remove stamps from the pane.

The perf pattern is the same as that used by Sennett Security Products for the Legends of Hollywood panes. However, the Hubble pane doesn't have the special star-shaped perforations at the corners of each stamp that is a feature of the Hollywood panes. Phil Jordan, art director and designer of the Hubble stamps, had urged that the star-shaped perfs be used for the Hubble pane as well, because of its astronomical subject. "I think stars would have been appropriate, but somebody scotched that at the end," he said, regretfully.

The Postal Service used the Hubble pane to provide advance publicity for World Stamp Expo 2000, which also had a space theme. In the past, USPS has issued pre-event stamps to promote stamp shows in which it participated, such as World Stamp Expo 89 and World Columbian Stamp Expo. This time, however, it settled for a line of type in the selvage of the Hubble pane that read: "Visit World Stamp Expo 2000, Anaheim, California, July 7-16, 2000."

The Eagle Nebula, the image of which is the best known of the five shown on the stamps, is found near the border between the constellations Sagittarius and Serpens, according to the Space Telescope Science Institute at Johns Hopkins University and the Association of Universities for Research in Astronomy. Described as a "bowl-shaped blister on the side of a dense cloud of cold interstellar gas," the nebula is a stellar nursery, containing numerous stars in the process of formation. The color image was created by combining three separate images from 1995.

"Looking down a tunnel of gas at a doomed star" is how Institute scientists describe the image of the Ring Nebula, first cataloged more than 200 years ago by French astronomer Charles Messier. Its central star is shown in a blue haze of hot gas, in the constellation Lyra, 2,000 light years from Earth. The picture reveals that the Ring is actually a cylinder of gas seen almost end-on. Such elongated shapes are common among other planetary nebulae as thick disks of gas and dust form a waist

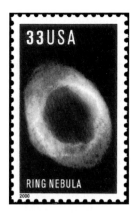

around a dying star.

The Lagoon Nebula is 5,000 light years from Earth in the direction of the constellation Sagittarius. The picture on the stamp shows a pair of interstellar "twisters" one-half light year in length in the heart of the nebula. The hot central star, O Herschel 36, is the primary source of the illuminating light for the brightest region in the nebula, called the Hourglass. The glare from this star is eroding the clouds by heating the hydrogen gas in them.

The Hubble view of the Egg Nebula, located about 3,000 light years from Earth, shows a pair of mysterious "searchlight" beams emerging from a hidden star and crisscrossed by numerous bright arcs. This image is helpful to astronomers in understanding the ejection of stellar matter that accompanies the slow death of sunlike stars. The nebula is really a large cloud of dust and gas ejected by the star, expanding at a speed of 115,000 miles per hour. A dense cocoon of dust — the dark band in the center — enshrouds the star and hides it from view.

The elliptical Galaxy NGC 1316 is 53 million light years from Earth, in the southern constellation Fornax. The beautiful, eerie silhouette of dark dust clouds against the galaxy's glowing nucleus may represent the aftermath of a 100 million-year-old cosmic collision between NGC 1316 and a smaller companion galaxy. A class of small and very faint star clusters has been identified in the galaxy's central region, many of them so small that they are barely held together by the mutual gravity of their constituent stars. Astronomers believe these clusters are among the last visible remains of a galaxy that was "cannibalized" by NGC 1316.

The telescope's namesake, Edwin Powell Hubble, was born November 20, 1889, in Marshfield, Missouri. He attended the University of Chicago and Oxford University, where he studied law as a

Rhodes scholar. He decided to pursue astronomy, and after his military service in World War I he began work at Mount Wilson Observatory near Pasadena, California.

Using the 100-inch telescope at Mount Wilson, Hubble made numerous discoveries, including the finding that galaxies are moving away from each other at a speed relative to the distance between them. Known as the Hubble Constant, the discovery led to the confirmation of the "Big Bang" theory of creation and the insight that the universe is expanding.

He died September 28, 1953, in San Marino, California.

NASA's $2 billion Hubble Space Telescope, launched from the space shuttle *Discovery* April 25, 1990, got off to an inauspicious start. A manufacturing mistake left its 94.5-inch primary mirror flawed, producing fuzzy images. Astronauts returned to the telescope in 1993 to install corrective optics that put everything in focus. Periodic maintenance visits also are required.

The Hubble, by being far above Earth's distorting atmosphere, is able to see distant objects in sharper detail in both visible and infrared light. It also makes ultraviolet observations that are not possible from the Earth. With this capability, astronomers say, the Hubble has increased the volume of space observed by a factor of 1,000.

In its first 10 years — halfway through its currently planned lifetime — the telescope circled Earth more than 58,000 times, made 271,000 observations and investigated 13,670 celestial targets as near as the planets of the Solar System and as remote as galaxies more than 12 billion light years away. Through a survey made possible by the Hubble, astronomers estimated that the observable universe contains at least 120 billion galaxies, each containing upwards of billions of stars.

The Designs

Phil Jordan began the task of choosing the Hubble telescope images for the individual stamps by downloading hundreds of images from the Hubble online archive available through the home page of the Space Telescope Science Institute (www.stsci.edu). As he developed designs involving various combinations of images, "new stuff was coming in every day" on the Web, he said.

"For me, the criteria were, did I think the images would be tremendously interesting to the public, and were they compatible with each other on the pane?" Jordan said.

Once the final combination was selected, PhotoAssist, the firm that handles research for USPS, obtained high-quality color prints from the Space Telescope Science Institute. The following scientists are credited with creating the individual images: Eagle Nebula, Jeff Hester; Ring Nebula, Tom Lutterbie; Lagoon Nebula, Adeline Caulet; Egg Nebula, John Tranger; Galaxy NGC 1316, Carl Grillmair.

The selvage image is based on a black-and-white photo made in 1949 of Hubble beside the 48-inch Schmidt telescope at Palomar Observatory,

This photograph, from the Caltech Astronomy web site, is similar to the selvage photo of Hubble at Palomar Observatory, but shows more detail of Palomar's 48-inch Schmidt telescope.

In this early layout of a Hubble pane by Phil Jordan, the pane consists of 12 semi-jumbo stamps, all different, depicting images downloaded from the Hubble web site. Two of the images, Eagle Nebula and Egg Nebula, were among the five chosen for the finished pane. The others in this layout are identified as Cartwheel Galaxy, Cygnus Loop, Hubble Deep Field, Core of NGC 4261, Orion Nebula, Hourglass Nebula, the planet Mars, Cat's Eye Nebula, Supernova 1987A and the planet Saturn.

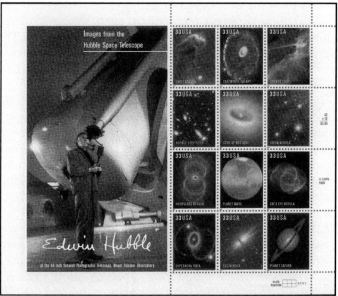

Palomar Mountain, California. The image extends the width of the pane and wraps around the stamps themselves. The photo was made by Edwin L. Wisherd for the National Geographic Society and published in the September 1950 *National Geographic* magazine with this caption:

"Ready for Action, the Big Schmidt Telescope Points at a Target in Outer Space. Dr. Edwin P. Hubble watches the guide star in the eyepiece buttons in the 'guiding head' which he holds."

Hubble has a pipe in his mouth, despite the Postal Service's enduring sensitivity to any suggestion that it might be encouraging smoking. On several previous occasions, artists assigned to create stamp illustrations were ordered not to depict their subjects with cigarettes or pipes, even though the photos on which they based their artwork showed the subjects smoking. Even Santa Claus had his pipe deleted from the old prints adapted for two 1995 Christmas stamps. However, the Postal Service has never altered an actual photograph in this way, and didn't do so in Hubble's case.

"The pipe is shown in the selvage, not on the stamp," Terrence McCaffrey explained. "It was virtually impossible to find a photo of him without a pipe. It was like a pacifier; he had it in his mouth at all times, whether it was lit or unlit. So we left it. We got not a single critical letter."

At the suggestion of CSAC, Jordan placed a facsimile of Hubble's autograph in the selvage near the bottom of the photograph. It was created by combining three versions of the astronomer's signature. The primary version, provided by the Huntington Library, was taken from Hubble's World War I American Expeditionary Forces card.

The exterior of Palomar Observatory, inside which Hubble is shown in the selvage image, was pictured on a 3¢ stamp of 1948 (Scott 966) commemorating the dedication of the facility.

The celestial object pictured on each stamp is identified in dropout-white capitals at the bottom. "33 USA" is at the top. The sans-serif typeface is called Grotesk. Grotesk is also used for the text paragraph in the selvage, while the name "EDWIN POWELL HUBBELL" in the selvage is in Times New Roman.

Because of the dark background of the photograph that covers the selvage, the six-digit plate-number combinations next to the four corner stamps are printed in small rectangular white "windows." Other standard pane information, such as the USPS copyright inscription, the plate-position diagram and the price, is in dropout white characters. The colors used for the Hubble pane were the four standard process colors, for the stamps; a purple shade, for the selvage picture; and tan, for the selvage text.

Varieties

At least two completely imperforate Hubble panes were found. One was purchased by a collector, Tony Sormani of Florida, at the postal store at his local post office August 17, 2000. A short time earlier, a Colorado woman who wished to remain anonymous bought the other pane at a Denver post office. The Scott *Specialized Catalogue of U.S. Stamps & Covers* for 2002 assigns the number 3388b to the pane.

First-day Facts

Postmaster General William J. Henderson dedicated the Hubble stamps at the Goddard Space Flight Center. The ceremony was held in conjunction with NASA's celebration of the 10th anniversary of the launching of the Hubble Space Telescope.

Honored guests included several members of Congress: Senators Paul S. Sarbanes and Barbara A. Mikulski of Maryland, and Representatives Roscoe G. Bartlett, Benjamin L. Cardin, Elijah E. Cummings, Robert L. Ehrlich Jr., Wayne T. Gilchrest, Steny H. Hoyer, Constance A. Morella and Albert R. Wynn. Also listed among the honored guests were three NASA officials, Daniel S. Goldin, administrator, Dr. Edward J. Weiler, associate administrator for space science, and Joseph H. Rothenberg, associate administrator for space flight; George W.S. Abbey, director of the Johnson Space Center; Alphonso V. Diaz, director of the Goddard Space Flight Center; Dr. John H. Campbell, director of flight programs and projects at Goddard; Dr. Steven V.W. Beckwith, director of the Space Telescope Science Institute; and Dr. Maxine F. Singer, president of the Carnegie Institution of Washington, D.C.

USPS held an additional first-day event April 10 at the Carnegie Observatories in Pasadena, California. Participants included Edwin Hubble's only student, astronomer Allan Sandage, and U.S. shuttle astronaut Steven Hawley. Hawley served as primary operator of the robot arm that deployed the Hubble Space Telescope in 1990, and in February 1997 used the robot arm again to retrieve the telescope for maintenance and later to redeploy it. Also taking part were Tirso del Junco, a Postal Service governor, and Augustus Oemler Jr., director of the Carnegie Observatories.

The earliest-known use of a Hubble stamp was on a utility-payment envelope hand-canceled East Andover, New Hampshire, April 5, five days before the official first day of sale. The stamp depicts the Egg Nebula.

33¢ AMERICAN SAMOA

Date of Issue: April 17, 2000

Catalog Number: Scott 3389

Colors: black, cyan, magenta, yellow

First-Day Cancel: Pago Pago, American Samoa

First-Day Cancellations: 107,346

Format: Panes of 20, horizontal, 4 across, 5 down. Offset printing plates of 120 subjects, 8 across, 15 around.

Gum Type: water-activated

Overall Stamp Size: 1.560 by .991 inches; 39.624 by 25.171mm

Pane Size: 7.240 by 5.946 inches

Perforations: 11 (Wista stroke perforator)

Selvage Markings: "©USPS/1999." ".33/x20/$6.60." "PLATE/POSITION" and diagram. Universal Product Code (UPC) "446700."

Designer, Typographer and Art Director: Howard Paine of Delaplane, Virginia

Illustrator: Herb Kawainui Kane of Captain Cook, Hawaii

Modeler: Joseph Sheeran of Ashton-Potter (USA) Ltd., Williamsville, New York

Stamp Manufacturing: Stamps printed by Ashton-Potter on offset portion of Stevens Variable Size Security Documents webfed 6-color offset, 3-color intaglio press. Stamps finished by Ashton-Potter.

Quantity Ordered: 16,000,000

Plate Number Detail: 1 set of 4 plate numbers preceded by the letter P in selvage above or below each corner stamp

Plate Number Combination Reported: P1111

Paper Supplier: Tullis Russell

Tagging: block tagging

The Stamp

In response to strong political pressure, the Postal Service issued a 33¢ stamp April 17 to commemorate the 100th anniversary of the affiliation of the United States and American Samoa. The first-day ceremony was held in the Samoan territorial capital of Pago Pago.

More than a year earlier, in March 1999, Bruce Babbitt, U.S. secretary of the interior, and the governors and representatives to Congress of four U.S. territories and commonwealths signed a petition to Postmaster General William J. Henderson calling for a stamp for American Samoa in 2000. Babbitt's department contains the Office of Insular Affairs, which helps oversee the affiliated overseas areas. The petition also was signed by other executive branch officials, including Mickey Ibarra, assistant to President Clinton and director of the White House office of intergovernmental affairs.

On April 14, 1999, American Samoa's non-voting delegate to Congress, Eni F.H. Faleomavaega, presented USPS with additional petitions that had circulated in the territory and were signed by more than 15,000 persons.

"In spite of the many proud years of our union with the United States, American Samoa remains the only U.S. insular area for which the Postal Service has not issued a commemorative stamp," Faleomavaega told the press. "That's a truly astonishing oversight."

Previous U.S. stamps had honored not only U.S. states, territories and commonwealths, but also independent nations in the Pacific that had formerly been trust territories administered by the United States: the Republic of the Marshall Islands, the Federated States of Micronesia and the Republic of Palau.

In his statement, Faleomavaega invited a comparison of the centennial of American Samoa with several other subjects that "had been deemed worthy of recognition" on U.S. stamps: the Australia bicentennial (1988), hummingbirds (1992), carousel horses (1995), comic strip classics (1995) and automobile tail fins (1996).

"American Samoa's commitment to the United States has been strong throughout the century," he said. "For decades, American Samoa served as a naval coaling station for U.S. ships in the Pacific, and during World War

Herb Kane also painted native sailing vessels in three of his earlier U.S. stamp illustrations: the 20¢ Hawaii Statehood stamp of 1984 and the se-tenant 25¢ stamps issued in 1990 for the Federated States of Micronesia and the Republic of the Marshall Islands.

II American Samoa was the staging point for 30,000 Marines involved in the Pacific theater.

"Our tradition of military service is strong, and our current per capita rate of enlistment in the U.S. military services is as high as any state or territory."

The campaign was successful, and when the Postal Service announced its commemorative stamp program for 2000 on October 14, 1999, the American Samoa stamp was included. The design was formally unveiled late in December 1999, although it had been published earlier in a newspaper in American Samoa that had received it from the local postmaster in violation of release-date instructions.

In acknowledging the success of the stamp campaign, Faleomavaega thanked the postmaster general and took note of the efforts of Tauese P.F. Sunia, governor of American Samoa, former Governor Lutali, "and the many people who worked so hard to achieve this goal."

The stamp, conventionally gummed and perforated, was printed by Ashton-Potter (USA) Ltd. by the offset process and issued in panes of 20. USPS apparently concluded that the stamp would have little sales appeal outside American Samoa (population 64,000), for it ordered a printing of only 16 million stamps, a strikingly low run for a letter-rate U.S. commemorative. No other single-design 33¢ commemorative issued in 2000 had a print order below 55 million (Library of Congress). The largest orders of the year were for the Wile E. Coyote and Road Runner (300 million) and Adoption Awareness (200 million) stamps.

The lowest print run in recent years for a single-design letter-rate commemorative was 10 million each for the 32¢ Glenn "Pop" Warner and 32¢ George Halas stamps of 1997, which were sold in individual panes of 20, with a red bar printed above each stamp's denomination. However, millions more stamps honoring the same two football coaches had been placed on sale only weeks earlier as part of a four-design pane with no red bar in the designs.

American Samoa is an unincorporated and unorganized territory of the United States, administered by the Interior Department. Its constitution provides for an elected governor, lieutenant governor and legislature. Lying in the South Pacific more than 2,000 miles southwest of Hawaii and about 2,700 miles northeast of Australia, the territory consists of five volcanic islands and two coral atolls.

The islands were populated by Polynesian people for centuries before their discovery in 1722 by a Dutch navigator, Jacob Roggeveen. In 1899 the Samoan island group was split into two areas following an agreement between the United States and Germany. In April 1900, local chiefs ceded the eastern islands of Tutuila and Aunuu to the United States. This is the event commemorated by the stamp. The western islands, now known as the independent nation of Western Samoa, came under German domination.

Four years later, the king and the chiefs of the Manua Islands ceded

Tau, Ofu, Olosega and Rose Atoll to the United States. Swains Island, more than 200 miles to the north, became part of American Samoa in 1925. Tutuila, where the capital, Pago Pago (pronounced PAHNG-oh PAHNG-oh), is located, is the largest and most populous island in the group, and has one of the finest natural harbors in the South Pacific.

American Samoa invites tourism with the slogan "Where America's day ends, and paradise begins." Its climate averages between 70 and 90 degrees Fahrenheit the year round. Some 89 percent of its population is Samoan (Polynesian). The Samoan language, which is closely related to Hawaiian and other Polynesian languages, is spoken along with English, with most residents being bilingual.

The Design

For Howard Paine, the USPS art director who was assigned to design the stamp, the choice of illustrator was easy. He called on Herb Kawainui Kane, a Hawaii resident who has made a career of painting Pacific Ocean scenes.

Kane (pronounced Kah-ne) had illustrated several previous U.S. postage items, including the 10¢ Iolani Palace postal card in the Historic Preservation series in 1959 and the 1984 stamp commemorating the 25th anniversary of Hawaii statehood. He also illustrated the aforementioned three stamps of the 1990s commemorating the achievement of self-government by former United Nations trust territories administered by the United States, the Republic of the Marshall Islands, the Federated States of Micronesia and the Republic of Palau, as well as a fourth stamp for the Commonwealth of the Northern Mariana Islands, which chose to retain its U.S. association after its trust-territory status ended.

Those four stamps shared the same design style. Each showed the flag of the country or commonwealth and a representative image, against a solid blue background. For the American Samoa stamp, however, Kane created a conventional illustration, using gouache, or opaque watercolor. His picture shows an 'alia, the traditional native double canoe, its decks crowded with sailors, its triangular sail filled with an easterly wind as it

Herb Kane with one of his large paintings, showing island natives in canoes approaching a visiting sailing ship. This image is taken from his Internet home page, www.hawaiiantrading.com/herb-kane/.

The microprinted word "SAMOA" on the American Samoa stamp (arrow) is extremely small and hard to see, even with a good magnifying glass. (It has been photographically enhanced in this blow-up.) It is located on the canoe, on the yellow edge of the roof section on which four sailors are standing, between the two feet of the sailor on the left and immediately above the head of the first sailor on the deck beneath him.

skims over blue ocean waves. In the background, against a cloud-dappled blue sky, is the dramatic blue-green Sunuitao Peak on the island of Ofu. Two birds, which Kane identified as white-tailed tropic birds, fly just ahead of the vessel.

For the inscription "AMERICAN SAMOA 33 USA" across the top of the stamp, Paine used one of his favorite typefaces, a graceful font called Raleigh.

Three of Kane's previous U.S. stamp designs also featured native sailing ships. The Hawaii statehood anniversary stamp depicted a double-sailed Polynesian voyaging canoe off the coast of the island of Hawaii, while a wa lap canoe was shown on the Marshall Islands stamp and a popo canoe appeared on the Micronesia issue.

The microprinting on the American Samoa stamp — a standard security feature on single-design offset-printed stamps — is extremely small and hard to see, even with a good magnifying glass. It consists of the word "SAMOA," in black, and is located on the canoe, on the yellow edge of the roof section on which four sailors are standing, between the two feet of the sailor on the left and immediately above the head of the leftmost sailor on the deck beneath him.

First-day Facts

The first-day ceremony in Pago Pago was preceded by the "arrival of the 'alias," staged by the American Samoa Voyaging Canoe Society. Edward Broglio, Honolulu's USPS district manager and postmaster, dedicated the stamp. The principal speaker was Tauese P.F. Sunia, governor of American Samoa.

Smitty McMore, postmaster of Pago Pago, presided. Samoan translation was provided by Fagafaga Danny Langkilde.

Collectors who prepared stamped covers for first-day cancellations were instructed to mail them to the postmaster in Honolulu, Hawaii, for processing.

33¢ LIBRARY OF CONGRESS

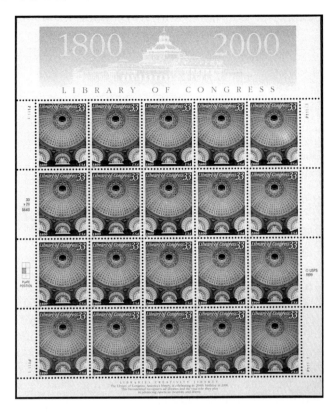

Date of Issue: April 24, 2000

Catalog Number: Scott 3390

Colors: black, cyan, magenta, yellow, red (PMS 188C)

First-Day Cancel: Washington, D.C.

First-Day Cancellations: 115,679

Format: Panes of 20, vertical, 5 across, 4 down. Offset printing plates of 120 subjects, 8 across, 15 around.

Gum Type: water-activated

Overall Stamp Size: 1.22 by 1.56 inches; 31.038 by 39.6240mm

Pane Size: 7.045 by 8.500 inches; 178.79mm by 215.71mm

Perforations: 11 (Ashton-Potter web perforator)

Selvage Inscription: "1800 2000/LIBRARY OF CONGRESS." "LIBRARIES CREATIVITY LIBERTY/The Library of Congress, America's library, is celebrating its 200th birthday in 2000./This bicentennial recognizes all libraries and the vital role they play/in advancing American creativity and liberty."

Selvage Markings: "©USPS/1999." ".33/x20/$6.60." "PLATE/POSITION" and diagram.

Designer, Typographer and Art Director: Ethel Kessler of Bethesda, Maryland

Photographer: Michael Freeman of London, England

Modeler: Joseph Sheeran of Ashton-Potter (USA) Ltd., Williamsville, New York

Stamp Manufacturing: Stamps printed by Ashton-Potter on offset portion of Stevens Variable Size Security Documents webfed 6-color offset, 3-color intaglio press. Stamps finished by Ashton-Potter.

Quantity Ordered: 55,000,000

Plate Number Detail: 1 set of 5 plate numbers preceded by the letter P in selvage next to each corner stamp

Plate Number Combinations Reported: P11111, P22222

Paper Supplier: Tullis Russell

Tagging: block tagging

The Stamp

On May 22, 1996, James H. Billington, librarian of Congress, wrote to the Citizens' Stamp Advisory Committee asking that CSAC approve a stamp to commemorate the Library of Congress' upcoming 200th anniversary. "Ideally," he wrote, "such a stamp would be issued on April 24, 2000, precisely 200 years from the date President John Adams approved the act of Congress creating what is today America's oldest national cultural institution."

CSAC found the proposal worthwhile — in fact, it already had included the library's bicentennial on its list of upcoming significant anniversaries — and, nearly four years later, on the date specified by Billington as most appropriate, the Postal Service issued a 33¢ stamp marking the event.

The stamp is semijumbo in size, vertically arranged, and depicts the interior of the dome of the main reading room of the library's main building, the Thomas Jefferson Building, which is located just east of the Capitol in Washington, D.C. It was printed by the offset process by Ashton-Potter (USA) Ltd. and issued in panes of 20.

The pane has a header, or wide decorative top selvage, featuring an image of the exterior of the Jefferson Building and the inscription "1800 2000/LIBRARY OF CONGRESS." The narrow selvage at the bottom contains the words "LIBRARIES CREATIVITY LIBERTY," followed by the text message: "The Library of Congress, America's library, is celebrating its 200th birthday in 2000. This bicentennial recognizes all libraries and the vital role they play in advancing American creativity and liberty."

The wording on the selvage represented an effort by the Postal Service to meet some of the requests of library officials concerning the stamp project.

"They wanted the 1800 and 2000 on the stamp itself," said Terrence McCaffrey, head of stamp design for USPS. "We don't like to put the current year date in a design. Every stamp carries the current year date in small type down in the corner, so it would be a duplication to put in 2000 twice. In the end, however, we agreed to include the 1800 on the stamp, and put both year dates in the header.

"They also wanted a text message. They proposed that we put it on the back of each stamp. We turned that down; verso printing adds a great deal of cost, and we only use it for selected stamps that need a lot of explanation. So we put the text in the selvage, too."

An early version of the text drafted by library officials was much more wordy than the final version. It read as follows: "The Library of Congress, the nation's oldest federal cultural institution and the world's largest library, is celebrating its 200th birthday. Its Bicentennial theme celebrates libraries everywhere and the creative tie between learning and libraries in a free society." The library revised and shortened it at the Postal Service's request.

The library's bicentennial also was commemorated by the issuance by the U.S. Mint of two commemorative coins, a $10 gold and platinum bimetallic coin and a silver dollar. A congressional bill authorizing the coins was signed into law October 19, 1998, by President Bill Clinton.

The stamp was the second U.S. commemorative to feature the Library of Congress. In 1982 a 20¢ stamp, designed by Bradbury Thompson from a turn-of-the-century photograph and printed in bicolor intaglio (Scott

The U.S. Mint struck two commemorative coins in 2000 to mark the bicentennial of the Library of Congress. A silver dollar depicts on the obverse an open book superimposed over the torch from the library's dome, and on the reverse a depiction of the dome. The gold and platinum ringed bimetallic $10 coin — the first such coin ever struck by the Mint — shows on the obverse the hand of Minerva, the Greek goddess of wisdom, raising the torch of learning above the library's dome, and on the reverse the Library of Congress seal.

105

2004), pictured the exterior of the Jefferson Building.

The bill that President Adams signed April 24, 1800, provided for outfitting the Executive Mansion and Congress in the District of Columbia. It included a section providing "for the purchase of such books as may be necessary for the use of Congress at the said city of Washington, and for fitting up a suitable apartment for containing them, and for placing them therein the sum of five thousand dollars shall be, and hereby is, appropriated."

The first collection, 740 volumes and three maps, was stored in the U.S. Capitol. When British forces burned the building during the War of 1812, the library collection was lost. Congress chose to rebuild the library with the purchase of former President Thomas Jefferson's personal collection of more than 6,000 volumes.

By 1851, the library had grown to 55,000 volumes, but a disastrous fire in the Capitol destroyed more than half of the library holdings. Although the library room was rebuilt, it became apparent that more space would be needed to accommodate the rapidly growing accumulation of material.

Congress required 16 years to select and approve a design for a library building. A commission charged with selecting a plan and a site reviewed submissions by 27 architects and chose an Italian Renaissance Revival design by the Washington firm of Smithmeyer and Pelz. (The firm also designed Healy Hall at Georgetown University in Washington, which is shown on a 15¢ postal card of 1989, Scott UX128.) Dissension and debate followed, but eventually a modified version of this design was settled upon. The main building — later named for Jefferson — opened November 1, 1897, followed by the John Adams Building in 1938 and the James Madison Memorial Building in 1981.

Today, the Library of Congress houses nearly 119 million items, including 18 million books, 2 million recordings, 12 million photographs, 4 million maps, 53 million manuscripts and 100,000 comic books. Among its treasures is a Gutenberg Bible, purchased in 1930, and the Bay Psalm Book, a 1640 volume acknowledged as the first extant book printed in North America.

The Design

Designing the Library of Congress stamp was one of the first projects assigned by Terrence McCaffrey to Ethel Kessler after she joined the

Ethel Kessler developed these two alternative designs in commemorative size, one vertical, one horizontal, from a photograph of the Main Reading room taken from the gallery level.

Postal Service's team of contractual art directors late in 1996. In the interval between the assignment and the stamp's issuance in 2000, several other Kessler-designed stamps were issued, the first of which was the nondenominated Breast Cancer semipostal stamp of 1998.

Because the exterior of the Jefferson Building had been shown on an engraved stamp in 1982, Kessler decided that this one should depict one of the building's many beautiful interior scenes, and that the picture should be a photograph. She reviewed scores of interior shots by well-known photographers, and narrowed the field to those of the Main Reading Room.

Her ultimate choice, endorsed by the other art directors and CSAC, was a color photo of the interior of the dome, along with three of the eight semicircular stained-glass windows that circle the dome's base. The photograph was made by Michael Freeman of London, England, in 1980.

"That view just pulled me in," Kessler said. "My reaction was, 'That's it.' It has such symmetry, and when we actually put 20 stamps together on the pane it created such a beautiful pattern."

At the bottom of Freeman's photograph can be seen two of the eight large statues that stand between the windows and above the giant marble columns that surround the reading room. These two statues represent Reli-

This photograph, showing the entire Main Reading Room dome and the eight surrounding arched windows, was taken from an angle different from that of the photo shown on the stamp.

gion, sculpted by Theodore Baur, and Science, by John Donoghue. Above each statue is a tablet bearing an appropriate inscription. The windows display the seals of the states at the time the building was built, plus the territories, 48 in all; in addition, each window has as its center the Great Seal of the United States.

Above the statues and windows, and dominating the photo and the stamp design, is the great vaulted interior of the dome with its pattern of multiple decorative squares. The predominant color of the dome's interior, and of the stamp, is a warm orange-brown. At the upper center of the stamp, the focal point for the viewer, are Edwin Howland Blashfield's murals, which occupy the central and highest point of the building and form the culmination of the entire interior decorative scheme.

The round mural set inside the dome's lantern depicts Human Understanding. The 12 seated figures in the collar of the dome represent the 12 countries, or epochs, which Blashfield felt contributed most to American civilization. To the right of each figure is a tablet on which is inscribed the name of the country typified and its contribution to human progress. These are: Egypt, written records; Judea, religion; Greece, philosophy; Rome, administration; Islam, physics; The Middle Ages, modern languages; Italy, the fine arts; Germany, the art of painting; Spain, discovery; England, literature; France, emancipation; America, science.

After 1980, when the Freeman photo was made, the interior of the Main Reading Room underwent extensive renovation. Kessler said, "I have a memo from PhotoAssist [the Postal Service's research firm] saying 'The dome is actually brighter now than it is on the stamp. Are we concerned about that? Should we get a new photograph of it?' But there was nothing that had been changed architecturally, so we chose not to change the photo."

Only after settling on a photo of the interior of the dome for the stamp did Kessler and other USPS officials learn that the logo adopted by the Library of Congress for its bicentennial also featured the dome's interior, which was shown inside the first zero of the number "200." "It was a creative coincidence," Kessler said. "The minute we saw what they were doing we knew they would love what we were doing. And that's how it was."

Across the top of the stamp are the words "Library of Congress" and the denomination, "33." In the lower-left corner is "1800," and in the lower right is "USA." The letters and numbers, all in dropout white, are in a typeface called Garamond Condensed Book Italic.

2●0   LIBRARY OF CONGRESS
BICENTENNIAL
1800–2000

Coincidentally, the interior of the dome of the Main Reading Room, featured by USPS on the Library of Congress stamp, also was a graphic element of the logo that the library had chosen for its bicentennial.

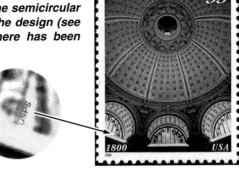

The microprinting on the Library of Congress stamp consists of the letters "USPS," arranged vertically, in the rightmost section of the semicircular window in the lower-left corner of the design (see arrow). The microprinting shown here has been photographically enhanced.

The microprinting on the stamp, which is a standard security feature of offset-printed single-design issues, consists of the letters "USPS" arranged vertically on the rightmost section of the window in the lower-left corner of the design. The letters are quite small and not easy to find, even with a good magnifying glass.

In their early discussions with USPS, library officials had proposed that more than one stamp be issued, with each stamp featuring a different example of the library's collections, such as books, manuscripts, music and film.

"We told them they weren't going to get more than one stamp, but that we would entertain the idea of doing a header that would contain some of that imagery," said Terrence McCaffrey. "Ethel put together a quick dummy mixing some of the elements, the books, the manuscripts, the dome, music and the Gutenberg Bible — things like that. [CSAC] said

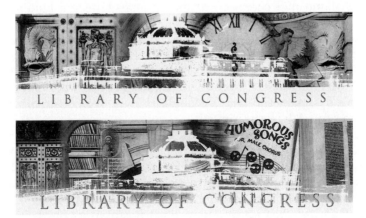

At one point, library officials suggested that several stamps be issued, featuring different parts of the institution's collection. The Postal Service refused to consider more than one stamp, but told designer Ethel Kessler to try to accommodate the library's wishes by creating a montage in the header. CSAC was dissatisfied with these results and opted for simplicity.

This is a preliminary version of the design that ultimately was chosen for the pane header. It features a positive image of the Thomas Jefferson Building rather than the negative that appears on the issued header, and lacks the year dates "1800" and "2000." Ethel Kessler adapted the picture of the building from an early photograph in the book Treasures of the Library of Congress. *She removed the flag and flagpole from the final version.*

'This is just a jumbled mess, and it would need so much explanation as to what these things are. Let's keep the header simple and clean.' "

Kessler's final design for the header fits that description. It features a negative image of the exterior of the Thomas Jefferson Building against a graded golden background, with the large year dates. The words "LIBRARY OF CONGRESS" are printed in a special red (PMS 188C); the rest of the header, and the stamps themselves, are printed in the four standard process colors. Kessler adapted the picture of the building from an early photograph she found in the book *Treasures of the Library of Congress*, which contains contemporary photos by Michael Freeman and Jonathan Wallen.

First-day Facts

Henry Pankey, vice president of the Mid-Atlantic Area for USPS, dedicated the stamp in a ceremony at the Thomas Jefferson building at the library.

Speakers were James H. Billington, librarian of Congress; Donald L. Scott, deputy librarian of Congress; and Sarah Ann Long, president for 1999-2000 of the American Library Association. Delores J. Killette, postmaster of Washington, D.C., presided. Honored guests were Ethel Kessler, the stamp's designer, and Dr. C. Douglas Lewis, vice chairperson of the Citizens' Stamp Advisory Committee.

The Library of Congress encouraged state and local libraries across the country to hold second-day-of-issue ceremonies for the stamp on April 25. Through its Internet web site, the library offered information kits and media guidelines to help the local institutions with these programs. USPS included a Library of Congress media kit in the March 23, 2000, issue of its internal *Postal Bulletin* to advise local postmasters on their involvement in such events.

33¢ WILE E. COYOTE AND ROAD RUNNER
LOONEY TUNES SERIES

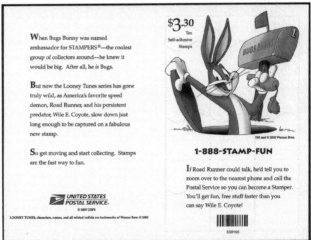

Date of Issue: April 26, 2000

Catalog Number: Scott 3391 (pane of 10); 3391a (single stamp); 3391b (half pane of 9); 3391c (half pane of 1)

Colors: magenta, yellow, cyan, black

First-Day Cancel: Phoenix, Arizona

First-Day Cancellations: 154,903 (includes special printing version)

Format: Pane of 10, vertical, 3 across, 3 down, with 10th stamp set apart in selvage portion, all on backing paper. Offset printing plates of 120 stamps (3 panes across, 4 around). Also sold in uncut half press sheets of 6 panes, 3 panes across, 2 panes down.

Gum Type: self-adhesive

Stamp Size: .99 by 1.56 inches; 25.146 by 39.624mm

Pane Size: 6.830 by 5.125 inches

Uncut Half Press Sheet Size: 21.50 by 11.25 inches

Perforations: 11 (die-cut simulated perforations) (rotary die cutter). Die cutting does not extend through the backing paper. On each pane, backing paper is microperfed vertically so selvage portion with 10th stamp can be separated from remaining 9 stamps.

Back Markings: On portion containing 9 stamps: "$3.30/Ten/Self-adhesive/Stamps/™ and ©2000 Warner Bros./1-888-STAMP FUN/If Road Runner could talk, he'd tell you to/zoom over to the nearest phone and call the/Postal Service so you can become a Stamper./You'll get fun, free stuff faster than you/can say Wile E. Coyote!" Universal Product Code (UPC). On portion containing 1 stamp and selvage: "When Bugs Bunny was named/ambassador for STAMPERS®—the coolest/group of collectors around—he knew it/would be big. After all, he is Bugs./But now the Looney Tunes series has gone/truly wild, as America's favorite speed/demon, Road Runner, and his persistent/predator, Wile E. Coyote, slow down just/long enough to be captured on a fabulous/new stamp./So get moving and start collecting. Stamps/are the fast way to fun./UNITED STATES/POSTAL SERVICE®/©2000 USPS/LOONEY TUNES, characters, names, and all related indicia are trademarks of Warner Bros. ©2000." On back of uncut press sheet, various printers' spray markings are found.

Liner Markings (under stamps): "Beep Beep!" in a repeat pattern

Illustrator and Designer: Ed Wleczyk, Warner Bros., Los Angeles, California

Character Art: Frank Espinosa, Warner Bros.

Concept: Brenda Guttman, Warner Bros.

Art Director: Terrence McCaffrey (USPS)

Stamp Manufacturing: Stamps printed by Banknote Corporation of America, Browns Summit, North Carolina, on Goebel 670 offset press. Stamps finished by BCA.

Quantity Ordered: 300,000,000 stamps, including 200,000 sold in press sheet halves; 10,000 top halves, 10,000 bottom halves.

Plate Number Detail: 4 sets of plate numbers can be found along the lower-right stamp-side selvage on half sheets from lower half of printing sheets, and on the back on half sheets from upper half of printing sheets. Each set consists of 3 digits preceded by the letters LT or LTB.

Plate Number Combinations Reported: LT001-LT001-LT001, front; LTB001-LTB001-LTB001, back.

Paper Supplier: Paper Corporation of the United States/Spinnaker Coatings

Tagging: phosphored paper, with phosphor "blocker" applied over selvage area.

33¢ WILE E. COYOTE AND ROAD RUNNER
SPECIAL PRINTING
LOONEY TUNES SERIES

Date of Issue: April 26, 2000

Catalog Number: Scott 3392 (pane of 10); 3392a (single with die-cut simulated perforations); 3392b (half pane of 9 with die-cut simulated perforations); 3392c half pane containing 1 imperforate stamp and selvage)

Colors: magenta, yellow, cyan, black

First-Day Cancel: Phoenix, Arizona

First-Day Cancellations: 154,903 (includes regular version)

Format: Pane of 10, vertical, 3 across, 3 down, with 10th stamp, imperforate, set apart in selvage portion, all on backing paper. Offset printing plates of

113

120 stamps (3 panes across, 4 around).

Gum Type: self-adhesive

Stamp Size: .99 by 1.56 inches; 25.146 by 39.624mm

Pane Size: 6.830 by 5.125 inches

Perforations: 11 (die-cut simulated perforations) (rotary die cutter) for 9 stamps on left. Die cutting extends through the backing paper. Imperforate 10th stamp on right. On each pane, backing paper is microperfed vertically so selvage portion with 10th stamp can be separated from remaining 9 stamps.

Back Markings: On portion containing 9 stamps: "$3.30/Ten/Self-adhesive/Stamps/™ and ©2000 Warner Bros./1-888-STAMP FUN/If Road Runner could talk, he'd tell you to/zoom over to the nearest phone and call the/Postal Service so you can become a Stamper./You'll get fun, free stuff faster than you/can say Wile E. Coyote!" Universal Product Code (UPC). On portion containing 1 stamp and selvage: "When Bugs Bunny was named/ambassador for STAMPERS ®—the coolest/group of collectors around—he knew it/would be big. After all, he is Bugs./But now the Looney Tunes series has gone/truly wild, as America's favorite speed/demon, Road Runner, and his persistent/predator, Wile E. Coyote, slow down just/long enough to be captured on a fabulous/new stamp./So get moving and start collecting. Stamps/are the fast way to fun./UNITED STATES/POSTAL SERVICE®/©2000 USPS/LOONEY TUNES, characters, names, and all related indicia are trademarks of Warner Bros. ©2000."

Liner Markings (under stamps): "Beep Beep!" in a repeat pattern

Illustrator and Designer: Ed Wleczyk, Warner Bros., Los Angeles, California

Character Art: Frank Espinosa, Warner Bros.

Concept: Brenda Guttman, Warner Bros.

Art Director: Terrence McCaffrey (USPS)

Stamp Manufacturing: Stamps printed by Banknote Corporation of America, Browns Summit, North Carolina, on Goebel 670 offset press. Stamps finished by BCA.

Quantity Ordered: 236,000 panes, each containing 1 imperforate stamp

Plate Number Detail: no plate numbers

Paper Supplier: Paper Corporation of the United States/Spinnaker Coatings

Tagging: phosphored paper, with phosphor "blocker" applied over selvage area.

The Stamps

On April 26, the Postal Service issued the fourth in its series of self-adhesive stamps depicting animated cartoon characters from Warner Bros. Looney Tunes short films. This time the subject was Road Runner and his eternally frustrated pursuer, Wile E. Coyote. The first-day city was Phoenix, Arizona, in the heart of the two characters' desert habitat.

114

The series began in 1997 with a stamp for Bugs Bunny and continued with stamps for Sylvester and Tweety (1998) and Daffy Duck (1999). USPS made a commitment to issue the stamps in return for the studio's permission to use Bugs Bunny free of charge on materials it produced for the Postal Service's Stampers youth program. In 2000, after the Coyote-Road Runner stamp was issued, the Postal Service announced its decision to end the Stampers program, but the Looney Tunes stamp series was scheduled to continue with one more stamp in 2001.

The first three stamps in the series were gravure-printed by Avery Dennison Security Printing Division. The Coyote-Road Runner stamp, however, was produced by the offset process by Banknote Corporation of America. The printing quantity also was sharply reduced. USPS acknowledged that both changes were economy moves dictated by its own financial problems.

Gravure printing is a form of recess printing that uses multiple etched printing cylinders for multicolor projects, one cylinder per ink. It is considerably more expensive than offset lithography, which transfers an inked image from a plate onto a large rubber cylinder and then to stamp paper, one plate per ink. One result of the change was that the colors on the Coyote-Road Runner stamp were less vivid than those of the previous Looney Tunes stamps.

Nevertheless, Coyote-Road Runner is similar to its predecessors in several ways, beginning with its design. Like the others, it is vertically arranged, bears an illustration developed by Warner Bros. cartoonists under USPS supervision, and includes design elements common to the series: an old-fashioned rural wooden mailbox and typography shaped like cloud formations.

Like the others, also, it was sold at post offices in panes of 10. On the left half of the pane is a block of nine stamps, three across by three down, with die-cut simulated perforations. On the right half is an enlarged, less-tightly cropped replica of the stamp design — in effect, a maximum card — with the 10th stamp isolated in an upper corner (the left corner for the first three stamps in the series, the right corner for Coyote-Road Runner). That stamp, too, has die-cut perfs. A vertical line of roulettes, or microperforations, allows the two halves of the pane to be separated.

As USPS had done with the first three stamps in the series, it created a second kind of pane for Coyote-Road Runner. On the special pane, unlike the regular one, the perflike die cuts penetrate the backing paper of the nine stamps on the left side, thus allowing individual stamps to be removed and saved with the liner attached. A more significant difference is that the 10th stamp on the special pane has no die-cut perfs. The entire maximum-card side, including the stamp, is imperforate.

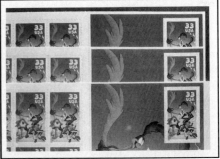

This illustration allows a comparison between the characteristics of the first three Looney Tunes stamps, as represented by the Daffy Duck stamp (left), and the Coyote-Road Runner stamp (right). Shown from top to bottom are the standard post office pane of 10; the special die-cut pane of 10, on which the horizontal and vertical die cuts of the stamps on the left half of the Daffy Duck pane extend to the edges, but on the Coyote-Road Runner pane do not; and the press half sheet, on which the vertical line of roulettes is absent on the Daffy Duck example but present on Coyote-Road Runner.

The special panes were made to fill orders for kits for the Stampers program, although none of the imperforate stamps went to the Stampers. The kits contained Looney Tunes stamps taken from the nine-stamp blocks on the left half of the special panes. The reason the die cuts penetrated the backing paper on those panes was to facilitate the stamps' quick removal. The 10th stamp, in the right half-pane, was left imperforate because it wouldn't have lent itself to speedy removal, even if it had been die cut. In processing the stamps for Stampers, USPS detached and shredded the half-panes containing the imperforate stamps. However, it kept some special panes intact for sale to collectors.

USPS also offered for sale uncut press sheets comprising six Coyote-Road Runner panes, a total of 60 stamps, just as it had done with Bugs, Sylvester-Tweety and Daffy Duck. These uncut sheets actually constituted one-half of the full printing sheets of 12 panes. Collectors could buy either the top or the bottom section for its $19.80 face value through Stamp Fulfillment Services.

Besides being offset-printed, the Coyote-Road Runner issue differed from its predecessors in several other ways, as well (see illustrations):

• Its die cuts are uniform on all stamps. The three previous Looney Tunes stamps were issued with at least two die-cut varieties, which can be termed "perfs up" and "perfs down." On the top edge of the stamp, the die cuts begin at left either with an upward point or peak ("perfs up") or a downward cut often called a valley ("perfs down"). The variations were hard to pin down with the Bugs Bunny stamp, but with Sylvester-Tweety and Daffy Duck they seemed consistent: Perfs up meant the stamp was from the standard post office pane of 10, and perfs down meant it was

116

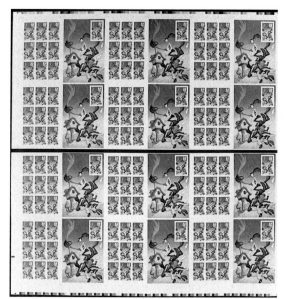

The layout of the Coyote-Road Runner press sheet is three panes across by four down, with the sheets severed into horizontal half sheets of three panes across by two down for sale to collectors. The three previous Looney Tunes stamps were printed in press sheets that were laid out two panes across by six down, severed for marketing purposes into half sheets of two panes across by three down.

from the special pane with the imperforate 10th stamp. That distinction vanished with the Coyote-Road Runner issue, on which all the "perforated" stamps on both types of pane are perfs up.

• Regardless of which kind of pane it is, the horizontal and vertical die cuts on the half that contains the block of nine stamps don't extend to the four edges. That was also true for the standard panes of the previous Looney Tunes stamps. However, on the special panes of those stamps, the die cuts extend to the sides.

• The layouts of the panes on the half sheets differ. Avery Dennison printed Bugs Bunny, Sylvester-Tweety and Daffy Duck in sheets of two panes across by six down, then severed the sheets into top halves and bottom halves of six panes each, configured vertically, two panes across by three down. BCA laid out its Coyote-Road Runner sheets three panes across by four down and separated them into top halves and bottom halves of six panes each, configured horizontally, three panes across by two panes down. The half sheets for the three previous Looney Tunes stamps measure 15.375 inches by 15.0625 inches; the half sheets for the Coyote-Road Runner stamp measure 21.5 inches by 11.25 inches.

• Both the top half sheets and bottom half sheets of Coyote-Road Runner have plate numbers in the selvage, although the numbers on the top half sheets are on the reverse side. On the first three Looney Tunes issues, only the bottom half sheets had plate numbers. With Coyote-Road Runner, the sequence of plate numbers on the bottom half sheets is adjacent to two panes, rather than one as it is on its three predecessors, making it impossible to break out a single pane with all the numbers in its selvage.

• All Coyote-Road Runner panes have vertical rouletting, or microperfs, separating the left and right halves, regardless of whether they are regular panes, special die-cut panes or part of uncut half sheets. With the Bugs Bunny, Sylvester-Tweety and Daffy Duck stamps, panes of 10 stamps cut from half sheets are distinctly different from individually sold panes of those stamps because they lack the vertical line of rouletting.

• The large image on the right half of the Coyote-Road Runner pane has a coating that inhibits or covers the phosphor taggant in the stamp paper. The taggant glows yellow-green when exposed to shortwave ultraviolet light, triggering USPS mail-sorting machinery to position the envelope and apply a postmark. On the previous Looney Tunes issues, the selvage taggant was unblocked, making it theoretically possible to cut a piece of the selvage and apply it to an envelope in a way that would fool the automated postal equipment.

The Postal Service reduced the total number of stamps printed for the Coyote-Road Runner issue to 300 million, down from 427 million for 1999's Daffy Duck stamp. Also cut back were the number of special-die-cut panes ordered (236,000, compared to 1999's 500,000) and the number of press-sheet halves (10,000 each for top and bottom halves, compared to 15,000 in 1999).

The story behind these numbers is one of trial-and-error on the part of the Postal Service. With the first two Looney Tunes issues, for Bugs Bunny and Sylvester and Tweety, USPS seriously underestimated the demand for the special panes and the press-sheet halves, and they were snapped up quickly, in some cases before the general philatelic community was aware they existed. Faced with the prospect of paying dealers many times face value to acquire them, collectors complained loudly. Then, when USPS made belated efforts to correct its mistake by ordering additional quantities of the special Sylvester and Tweety panes printed and offered for sale, it was criticized from the other side for having broken faith with dealers who had bought large numbers of the variety on the assumption that the quantities originally announced would be final.

The result was a surfeit. Sylvester and Tweety special panes remained available from Stamp Fulfillment Services well over two years after their April 27, 1998, issuance, and all Daffy Duck stamp items, including the special panes and press-sheet halves, still were on sale more than a year after their April 16, 1999, issue date. The reduced-quantity Coyote-Road Runner special panes and press-sheet halves still were available as of this writing.

As it had done with the previous Looney Tunes issues, USPS accompanied the Coyote-Road Runner stamp with a picture postal card reproducing the stamp image (see separate chapter).

Collectors of used stamps have encountered difficulties in soaking specimens of many recent U.S. issues from their envelope paper, and this one was no exception. One collector reported to *Linn's Stamp News* that he soaked an imperforate Coyote-Road Runner half pane from its cover and found that not only did it take a great deal of time for the pane to float loose, but portions of the design flaked off in the process.

Wile E. Coyote and the Road Runner have engaged in their unending chase for more than 50 years. According to a Warner Bros. biography of the two animated creatures, writer Michael Maltese and director Chuck Jones set out in the 1940s to find a character combination that they envisioned as a parody of the constant chases that dominated animation.

"They finally settled on an emaciated Coyote chasing a supersonic Road Runner and got it on the screen in *Fast and Furry-ous* in 1949," the studio said. "Audiences laughed, but no one saw it as a parody of anything. So for 15 years, Maltese and Jones had to content themselves with turning out one of the most popular series of cartoons ever made."

The chase sequences all center around Coyote's fantastic but futile schemes to capture the elusive bird. Often, he relies upon the products of the fictitious Acme mail-order company, using rocket packs, earthquake pills and other far-fetched merchandise in his efforts to nab the Road Runner. These inevitably backfire, leaving the coyote, not the bird, as the victim.

Charles Solomon, in his *Enchanted Drawings: The History of Animation*, wrote that Chuck Jones often described Coyote's monomaniacal pursuit of the Road Runner by quoting Santayana's definition of a fanatic: one who redoubles his effort after he loses sight of his goal. "The substance of all the Road Runner-Coyote pictures is not how to catch a road runner; it's how many ways you CAN'T catch a road runner," Jones said. The relationship between the Coyote and the Acme Company was described by Jones as "very much like a squirrel's to a tree. The Coyote supports the Acme Company by buying or at least using the things they manufacture, and the Acme Company survives by supplying them to him."

The only dialog in the cartoons consists of the Road Runner's instantly identifiable "Beep! Beep!" — a sound that designer Paul Julian invented one day while trying to get through a crowded studio hallway — and an occasional hand-lettered sign held up by Coyote to express his dismay as he drops off the edge of a cliff to the desert floor far below.

The Design

When it chose a design for the Bugs Bunny stamp, the Postal Service established the format and concept that would be used on all subsequent Looney Tunes stamps. Before that happened, while the series was in the planning stage, Warner Bros. submitted several proposed illustrations featuring various Looney Tunes characters, in the special stamp size that USPS uses for holiday and Love stamps.

These were tight close-ups, presented in a style that Brenda Guttman, creative director for Warner Bros.' publishing group in Los Angeles, called "in your face." The Coyote-Road Runner illustration showed a sly-looking Wile E. Coyote, obviously in plotting mode, contemplating a nonchalant Road Runner. The studio's cartoonists also worked up the image in commemorative size.

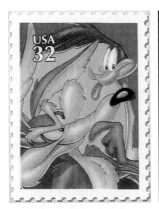

These early design concepts by Warner Bros. Artists were done in what the studio's Brenda Guttman called "in your face" style.

In this concept sketch, the USA and denomination are formed by cactus rather than clouds, as on the previous Looney Tunes stamps.

With this illustration, the studio cartoonists were getting close to the idea they incorporated in the finished design. Wile E. Coyote, a rocket pack strapped to his back, attempts to dive onto the Road Runner from above, but overshoots his mark and is about to plunge into the omnipresent chasm. CSAC wasn't satisfied with this version, however, especially the colors, which included a red-orange sky.

Later, after the Bugs Bunny stamp had set the style for the series, Warner Bros. submitted some additional ideas. In one of them, Coyote is pulling himself out of a hole into which some typical misfortune has plunged him, while stars orbit around his dazed eyes. Instead of clouds forming the USA and the denomination, as in the Bugs Bunny design, the letters and numbers are made of cactus.

But postal officials wanted the rural mailbox to be a unifying element in all the Looney Tunes designs. The cartoonists then created an illustration in which the Road Runner is standing beside the mailbox, mail under his wing, while a rocket-equipped Coyote attempts to dive down on him from above. Naturally, Coyote has overshot his mark and is about to plunge over a cliff. The sky is a deep red-orange, and the clouds and rocket exhaust also are tinged in red.

"The committee felt it wasn't working," said Terrence McCaffrey, head of stamp design for USPS and the art director of the Looney Tunes stamps. "They didn't like the color scheme. Unless the color scheme was the same

as the others in the series, this one would stand out. I called Brenda, and we had a long talk, and a long time passed, and we finally got a revised version with the rocket."

In the new illustration, by Warner Bros.' Ed Wleczyk and Frank Espinosa, Road Runner is perched on top of a rural mailbox beside a stretch of desert road, a mailbag slung around his neck. He is holding out an envelope addressed to Wile E. Coyote, who lies prone on the ground with a sputtering rocket pack on his back and his right paw extended up to accept his mail. Puffs of smoke from the rocket lead to the upper-right corner, where "33 USA" is inscribed in fluffy clouds.

CSAC approved this concept, with some refinements of color and detail. In the process, the committee's often-demonstrated tendency toward political correctness manifested itself when members vetoed the studio's version of the rocket. The shiny golden device "looked too much like a bullet," McCaffrey said. "We said, no, we can't have a bullet." The artists made revisions, and, on the stamp, Coyote's rocket pack is a dilapidated, unbulletlike contraption that looks like something the Acme company might have been trying to unload for years.

An intriguing aspect of the design, as Michael Baadke noted in *Linn's Stamp News*, "is that it features a stamp-on-stamp-on-stamp element that isn't often seen."

"The letter addressed to Wile E. Coyote is franked with the 33¢ Daffy Duck stamp of 1999," Baadke continued. "The actual Daffy Duck stamp included as part of its design two envelopes addressed to Daffy inside a mailbox, one each franked with the 32¢ Bugs Bunny and the 32¢ Sylvester and Tweety stamp.

"In other words, they'll be so tiny that they may not be visible on the actual Road Runner stamp, but the Bugs and Sylvester and Tweety stamps are on the Daffy Duck stamp that is on the Coyote and Road Runner stamp."

In fact, a viewer using a good magnifying glass can see the three earlier stamps — but only on the enlarged reproduction of the Coyote-Road Runner illustration on the right side of the stamp pane.

Because the stamps were offset printed, microprinting was added to the design as a means of security against photocopying. The previous gravure-

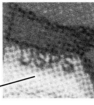

The microprinted letters USPS appear on the front of the mailbox, just under its overhanging roof. As the first Looney Tunes stamp to be offset printed, the Coyote-Road Runner stamp was the first to include microprinting in its design.

Road Runner's familiar "Beep Beep!" is printed in blue on the self-adhesive liner paper.

printed Looney Tunes stamps didn't include that feature. The microtype on the Coyote-Road Runner stamp consists of the letters "USPS" in black on the front of the mailbox, just beneath the roof overhang.

Each of the Looney Tunes panes has had its own message printed in a diagonal repeat pattern in pale blue on the liner paper beneath the stamps. The message becomes visible when a stamp is peeled from the pane. The inscription on this one consists of Road Runner's familiar "Beep Beep!" in uppercase and lowercase letters.

Varieties

A pane of Coyote-Road Runner stamps was found with die cuts completely missing from all 10 stamps. The error is listed by the Scott catalogs as 3391d, a variety of the standard pane.

Dealer Jacques C. Schiff Jr. offered the error pane for sale at his firm's August 25-26, 2000, auction at the American Philatelic Society Stampshow 2000. Schiff told *Linn's* that the stamps came from Oregon, where another dealer had purchased the pane from a customer.

First-day Facts

Johnray Egelhoff, postmaster of Phoenix, Arizona, dedicated the stamp in a ceremony at the city's Pecos Station post office at 10 a.m. April 26. The speaker was Tara Hitchcock of station KTVK-TV, a Warner Bros. affiliate.

A second ceremony was held at 4 p.m. the same day on the Internet's World Wide Web, marking the first time a U.S. stamp was dedicated online. Participating were James Tolbert, executive director of Stamp Services for USPS; Gerald Levin, Time Warner chairman and chief executive officer; and Barry Meyer, Warner Bros. chairman and CEO. The Webcast took place on America Online (keyword: BeepBeep), Warner Bros. Online and on the Postal Service's Web site. The Time Warner Media Center at the Children's Museum of Manhattan was the host site for the online event.

The earliest-known use of a Coyote-Road Runner stamp was on a cover machine-canceled Richmond, Virginia, April 25, one day before the official first day of issue.

33¢ 1990S (15 DESIGNS)
CELEBRATE THE CENTURY SERIES

Date of Issue: May 2, 2000

Catalog Numbers: Scott 3191, pane of 15; 3191a-3191o, stamps

Colors: black, cyan, magenta, yellow (offset); black (offset, back)

First-Day Cancel: Escondido, California. Stamps released nationally the same day.

First-Day Cancellations: 1,172,962

Format: Pane of 15, square, horizontal rows of 3, 3, 5, 4 at 8-degree angle. Printing plates of 4 panes (2 across, 2 around). Also sold in uncut sheets of 4 panes.

Gum Type: water-activated

Overall Stamp Size: 1.225 by 1.225 inches; 31.09 by 31.09mm

Pane Size: 7.5 by 9 inches; 190.36 by 228.43mm

Uncut Press Sheet Size: 16.4 by 19 inches

Perforations: 11½ (Ashton-Potter stroke perforator)

Selvage Inscription: "1990S/CELEBRATE THE CENTURY®." "In Final Decade, Cold War/Ends, Economy Booms." "The Soviet Union collapsed, effectively ending the/Cold War. Troops were deployed by the United States/in the Persian Gulf, in Somalia, and in the Balkans./In 1992—often called the Year of the woman—/a record number of women were elected to political office./American astronauts joined Russian cosmonauts on the Mir/space station, and Mars Pathfinder and Mars Global Surveyor/sent back extraordinary images of the red planet. A grouping of/planets resembling our solar system was found by astronomers./The World Wide Web and e-mail revolutionized communications./Millions of Americans bought cellular phones as service expanded./In Washington, D.C., the Holocaust Museum drew huge crowds,/while in Los Angeles, the Getty Center's architecture got rave/reviews. Moviegoers flocked to see *Titanic* and *Jurassic Park*./Extreme sports, such as snowboarding and BMX biking,/attracted young people, and the U.S. women's softball, soccer,/and basketball teams proved themselves the best in the world./New words: e-commerce, Web site, Y2K." "ART • SPORTS • HISTORICAL EVENTS • TECHNOLOGY • ENTERTAINMENT • SCIENCE • POLITICAL FIGURES • LIFESTYLE."

Back Markings: On selvage: "BACKGROUND PHOTO:/The U.S. economy prospered as the stock market reached/all-time highs. Americans ended the decade with one of the/strongest economies in the world." "CELEBRATE THE CENTURY® 1990S THIS SHEET IS NUMBER 10 IN A SERIES OF TEN SHEETS ©USPS 2000/"Seinfeld © 2000 Castle Rock Entertainment. Major League Baseball trademarks and/copyrights are used with permission of Major League Baseball Properties, Inc. "Jurassic Park"™ & © Universal Studios Inc. and Amblin Entertainment./"Titanic"™ Twentieth Century Fox. ©1998 by Twentieth Century Fox and Paramount Pictures. All rights reserved."

On stamps: "A New York stand-up comic/and his eccentric friends/entertained viewers for nine/seasons on 'Seinfeld,' an/award-winning sitcom/'about nothing' that gave/fans an offbeat and hilarious/look at city life."

"On August 2, 1990, Iraq/invaded and occupied/Kuwait. After negotiations/failed, Operation Desert/Storm was launched on/January 17, 1991./Multinational forces led by/the U.S. liberated Kuwait/within six weeks."

"The pursuit of three/important and long-standing/records thrilled Major/League Baseball® fans./Players set new marks for/career strikeouts, consecutive/games played, and home/runs in a single season."

"Electronic art and computer-/generated animation gained/popularity. Artists, graphic/designers, and moviemakers/used software and powerful,/more affordable computers/to create everything from/abstract paintings to/cinematic special effects."

"Across the U.S., improving/the quality of education/was a priority for educators,/parents, and legislators. Key/approaches included setting/high standards, reducing/class size, supporting/teachers, and creating/access to new technology."

"Extreme sports added an/element of adventure and/increased risk to the sports/world. Daredevil sports such/as aggressive inline skating,/BMX biking, snowboarding,/and street luge achieved/greater popularity."

"Cloned dinosaurs terrorized/visitors at an island theme/park in the 1993 hit 'Jurassic/Park.' Noted for its stunning,/lifelike creatures, the Steven/Spielberg-directed film won/Academy Awards® for Best/Visual Effects, Best Sound, and/Best Sound Effects Editing."

"Employing computers and/interface devices such as/data gloves and head-/mounted displays, virtual/reality created three-/dimensional 'virtual' worlds/used in video games and in/applications ranging from/architecture to surgery."

"In 1998, Special Olympics/marked its 30th anniversary. The/organization provides year-/round sports training and/competition for children and/adults with mental retardation,/giving them opportunities to/develop physical fitness and/demonstrate courage."

"In 1962, aboard the Mercury/*Friendship 7*, John Glenn/became the first American to/orbit Earth. His 1998 return/to space at age 77, on the/shuttle *Discovery,*/heightened interest in the/space program."

"Coordinated efforts led to/the recovery of some/animals that once were/endangered or threatened./In the 1990s, two peregrine/falcon subspecies—arctic/and American—were/removed from the/Endangered Species List."

"The popularity of cellular/phones skyrocketed as the/phones became smaller and/cheaper, sound quality/improved, and service/became more widely/available. In 1999, more than/78 million Americans had/cellular service."

"The World Wide Web/brought the text-based/Internet to life by adding/pictures, sound, and video./Millions of people accessed/the Internet with user-/friendly Web browsers for/business, entertainment, and/educational purposes."

"Originally designed for off-/road driving, sport utility/vehicles became/commonplace on city and/suburban streets. Offering/versatility, comfort, and a/rugged image, SUVs were a/popular choice for American/families and commuters."

"Adding romance and/elaborate special effects to/the tragic story of the ill-fated/luxury liner, James Cameron's/1997 film 'Titanic'™ was a/colossal success at box/offices worldwide and won/11 Academy Awards®, including Best Picture."

Each stamp also bears the inscription "CELEBRATE THE CENTURY—1980S."

Designer and Art Director: Howard Paine of Delaplane, Virginia

Illustrator: Drew Struzan of Pasadena, California

Photographer: Robert McClintock

Typographer: Tom Mann of Vancouver, Washington

Modeler: Joseph Sheeran of Ashton-Potter (USA) Ltd., Williamsville, New York

Stamp Manufacturing: Stamps printed by Ashton-Potter (USA) Ltd. on offset portion of Stevens Variable Size Security Documents webfed 6-color offset, 3-color intaglio press. Stamps processed by Ashton-Potter. Cardboard covers printed in red, yellow and blue (front) and black (back) by

Partners Press, Buffalo, New York.	
Quantity Ordered: 82,500,000	
Plate Number Detail: no plate numbers	
Paper Supplier: International Paper/Ivex	
Tagging: block tagging on stamps	

The Stamps

The final pane of 15 stamps in the Celebrate the Century series featured the events, prominent people and pop culture of the 1990s and was placed on nationwide sale May 2, 2000. The dedication ceremony was held at San Diego Wild Animal Park in Escondido, California, which was chosen as the site because one of the stamp subjects was the recovery of formerly endangered species of wildlife.

The CTC series comprised 150 stamps in 10 panes, each pane marking one of the decades of the 20th century. Four panes were issued in 1998, four in 1999 and the final two in 2000, including the pane for the 1980s, which made its debut January 12, 2000.

Like its predecessors, the 1990s pane was printed by Ashton-Potter (USA) Ltd. on a combination offset-intaglio press. The Postal Service's original plan was to print 14 of the stamps on each pane by multicolor offset and the 15th in single-color intaglio. However, that plan was abandoned for the 1980s and 1990s stamps, all 30 of which were offset-printed.

Beginning with the 1950s pane, the subjects for each decade were chosen by the public from lists nominated by the Citizens' Stamp Advisory Committee, using ballots available at post offices or online. Voting on 1990s subjects took place during May 1999. The ballots offered a total of 30 choices in five categories: People & Events (P&E), Arts & Entertainment (A&E), Sports (S), Science & Technology (S&T) and Lifestyle (L). As was the case with balloting for previous decades, participants could vote for no more than three nominated subjects in each category.

The top two vote-getters in each category, plus the next five highest vote-getters overall, were chosen for the 1990s pane. These were:

P&E: Recovering Species (193,414 votes), Gulf War (160,687), Improving Education (141,124).

A&E: *Titanic* (210,154), *Jurassic Park* (184,370), Computer Art and Graphics (170,449), *Seinfeld* (140,710).

S: Special Olympics (155,802), Baseball Records (151,511), Extreme Sports (151,090).

S&T: World Wide Web (191,292), Virtual Reality (156,944), John Glenn's Return to Space (138,984).

L: Cellular Phones (214,449), Sport Utility Vehicles (164,058).

The also-ran subjects were:

P&E: Cultural Diversity (99,985), Active Older Americans (93,105), Sustained Economic Growth (68,247).

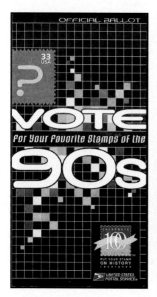
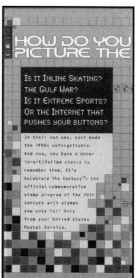

Shown here are the cover and voting portion of the official ballot issued by USPS to enable the public to choose the subjects for the 1990s Celebrate the Century pane.

A&E: Broadway Musicals (97,609), Contemporary Architecture (66,958).

S: Women's Sports (138,752), Inline Skating (129,092), Junior Golf (58,114).

S&T: Dinosaur Fossil Discovery (125,760), Interplanetary Exploration (92,305), Gene Therapy (85,647).

L: Coffeehouse Culture (136,693), Community Service (91,318), Museum Attendance (86,979), Home Offices (76,239).

The overall top vote-getter was Cellular Phones, which finished 4,295

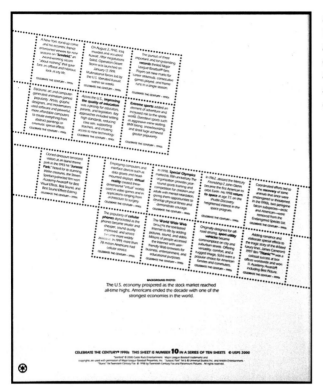

Each stamp bears a few words printed on the reverse, under the gum, describing the design subject. This picture shows the reverse side of a pane of 15 stamps.

votes ahead of *Titanic*. John Glenn's Return to Space was the 15th and last subject chosen, edging out Women's Sports by 232 votes and defeating Coffeehouse Culture by 2,291. Finishing last among the 30 nominated subjects was Junior Golf, 8,844 votes behind the next-to-last-place Contemporary Architecture.

For the first time, the voting categories were equal in size, with six nominated subjects in each one. The 1960s and 1970s ballots had contained categories listing from four to eight subjects; the 1950s and 1980s ballots offered five to seven subjects in each category. Because voters could select only three from each group, these imbalances gave a statistical edge to subjects in the smaller categories.

Michael Baadke, writing in *Linn's Stamp News*, took note of the overall lightness of the list. "With the exception of Glenn's 1998 space shuttle flight and the Gulf War, the subjects by and large don't carry the punch of history-making blockbusters," he wrote. "Popular trends such as in-line skating, sport utility vehicles, home offices and active older Americans make up much of the 1990s ballot. The People & Events category opens the ballot with three social concepts: improving education, cultural diversity and sustained economic growth."

The Postal Service ordered 82.5 million 1980s stamps (5.5 million panes) from Ashton-Potter, the smallest print quantity of the entire Cele-

brate the Century series. For each of the first six decades (1900s to 1950s), 12.5 million panes were printed. Because of diminished demand, the numbers were reduced to 8 million for the 1960s and 6 million each for the 1970s and 1980s.

BASEBALL RECORDS. In the 1990s, two long-standing Major League Baseball records were broken. Cal Ripken Jr. of the Baltimore Orioles set a new mark for consecutive games played of 2,632, replacing Lou Gehrig's 1939 record of 2,130. Roger Maris' 1961 total of 61 home runs — which was commemorated on a Celebrate the Century stamp for the 1960s — was beaten by two players in 1998: Mark McGwire of the St. Louis Cardinals, who hit 70 homers, and Sammy Sosa of the Chicago Cubs, who totaled 66 and won the year's National League Most Valuable Player award. On September 8, when McGwire hit number 62 to top Maris' record, the Cardinals were playing host to the Cubs, and Sosa ran in from right field to embrace the new record-holder.

GULF WAR. On August 2, 1990, Iraq invaded, occupied and annexed Kuwait. After negotiations failed, the United States under President George H.W. Bush led a 30-nation coalition in Operation Desert Storm to drive the Iraqis back across the border. In a six-week war that began January 17, 1991, the allies smashed the Iraqi army and domestic infrastructure in a devastating campaign that resulted in few casualties among the half million American troops, but left an estimated 150,000 Iraqis dead. Although Kuwait was liberated, fulfilling President Bush's announced objective, Saddam Hussein was left in power in Baghdad, and remained a continuing threat to his neighbors.

Participants in operations Desert Shield and Desert Storm were honored with a 1991 commemorative stamp issued in pane and booklet form (Scott 2551-52).

SITCOM SENSATION. *Seinfeld*, a half-hour NBC television situation comedy, ran from May 1990 to May 1998 and was the number one or two program in each of its final five seasons. Calling itself "a show about nothing," it featured four young, single, self-centered Manhattanites and their minor misadventures while dealing with the trivia of life and love. The show starred Jerry Seinfeld, a standup comic who played himself. Included in its ensemble cast were Jerry's ex-girlfriend, Elaine Benes

(Julia Louis-Dreyfus); his closest pal, the worrywart George Costanza (Jason Alexander); and his across-the-hall neighbor, Cosmo Kramer (Michael Richards).

On April 24, shortly before the stamp was issued, Seinfeld told *Linn's Stamp News*: "I'm actually really excited about it. It's very special, a very rare thing for the Postal Service to honor a sitcom like this ... I think it is really one of the most special honors we've ever had."

The *Seinfeld* program was the third TV sitcom to be honored on a CTC stamp. *All in the Family* was a subject on the 1970s pane, and *The Cosby Show* was featured on the pane for the 1980s.

EXTREME SPORTS. Extreme sports, once the province of an elite group of athletes, was transformed in the 1990s into a set of activities in which thousands of youthful participants sought the adrenalin highs that come with inviting risk while pursuing physical achievement. The genre included mountain climbing, rock climbing, skydiving and sky surfing, hang gliding, street luge, snowboarding, mountain biking and parachuting from tall buildings. Television helped promote extreme sports through ESPN's X Games competitions, MTV footage and certain commercials; cult movies like *Point Break*, *Terminal Velocity* and *Cliffhanger* also inspired participation.

Less than a year earlier, four Extreme Sports — snowboarding, skateboarding, in-line skating and BMX bicycling — had been depicted on a block of four commemorative stamps (Scott 3321-24). For the CTC series, the Citizens' Stamp Advisory Committee waived its ban on commemorating any subject more than once in a 10-year period.

IMPROVING EDUCATION. In 1981 a federally commissioned study of U.S. public schools found that American children lagged behind their industrialized-world counterparts in the most basic academic skills. The report, *A Nation at Risk*, cited "a rising tide of mediocrity that threatens our very future as a nation and a people." School reform became a national priority in the 1990s, embraced by liberal and conservative politicians alike, although there was much disagreement over how best to achieve it. Innovative approaches included higher standards for teachers and curricula, increased government funding, statewide testing, extensive preschool education, vouchers, charter schools and school uniforms. At the end of

the decade, some progress had been noted, but the effort — and debate — continued.

COMPUTER ART AND GRAPHICS. Initially a highly specialized tool for scientists and engineers, computer graphics — pictorial images produced on a computer — eventually became part of the artist's kit. By the 1990s every visual medium from video games to ATM machines employed computer graphics. Engineers and architects used computer-aided design to construct space shuttles and skyscrapers. Filmmakers turned to computers to produce dazzling special effects. In 1990 Adobe's Photoshop software enabled designers to manipulate and enhance photographs on screen; using Adobe's Illustrator or CorelDRAW, artists could put down curved and straight lines with a mouse-controlled pen tool.

Starting with the 22¢ Frederic Bartholdi commemorative stamp of 1985 (Scott 2147), the U.S. Postal Service has made extensive use of computer graphics in every phase of stamp design and reproduction.

RECOVERING SPECIES. The plight of the whooping crane, which teetered on the edge of extinction, inspired America's first large-scale effort to protect endangered species and led to passage of the Endangered Species Act in 1973. The law mandated protection for every species of wildlife that was declared endangered. Since ESA, the U.S. Fish and Wildlife Service has helped save such creatures as the brown pelican, the California gray whale, the American alligator and the arctic peregrine falcon. By the end of the 1990s, the gray wolf and the bald eagle were on the road to recovery. And in 1999, two pairs of whooping cranes, part of an experimental flock that was raised in captivity, laid the first eggs in the wild in decades, lifting hopes that the birds could make a comeback.

Endangered animal species were depicted on a pane of 15 stamps issued in 1996 (Scott 3105a-o).

RETURN TO SPACE. On February 20, 1962, John Glenn became the first American to orbit the earth. More than 36 years later, on October 29, 1998, Glenn, now a U.S. senator and 77 years old, returned to space, this time as a payload specialist on the space shuttle *Discovery*, to help investigate similarities between the effects of weightlessness and aging. "John Glenn's return voyage did more than advance our knowledge, it lifted our spirits," said Deborah Willhite, USPS senior vice president for govern-

132

ment relations and public policy, at the stamp's unveiling.

Glenn's original Project Mercury mission in *Friendship 7* was commmemorated by a 4¢ stamp (Scott 1193) that the U.S. Post Office Department designed and printed in secret and issued February 20, 1962, as soon as the astronaut's capsule splashed down safely into the Atlantic Ocean.

SPECIAL OLYMPICS. The nonprofit Special Olympics program, which provides sports training and competition for individuals with mental retardation, was founded by Eunice Kennedy Shriver in the 1960s. Therefore, this subject logically should have been on the 1960s pane. However, it was not one of the subjects nominated on the 1960s ballots distributed to the public. USPS explained, in text on the 1990s ballot and on the back of the stamp itself, that Special Olympics was a 1990s subject because it marked its 30th anniversary in 1998. Today more than one million individuals take part in Special Olympics programs in nearly 150 countries. Every two years, athletes gather for Special Olympics World Games, which alternate between summer and winter.

The Special Olympics previously had been honored on U.S. commemorative stamps in 1979 (Scott 1788) and 1985 (Scott 2142).

VIRTUAL REALITY. VR is a realistic simulation of an environment — including three-dimensional graphics — by a computer system using interactive software and hardware that send and receive information. The user wears these interactive devices as goggles, headsets, gloves or body suits. The illusion of being there (telepresence) is created by motion sensors that pick up the user's movements and adjust the view on the screens accordingly, usually in real time. The basis of VR technology emerged in the 1960s with simulators that taught pilots by using head-mounted displays with tracking systems. In the 1980s, the U.S. military and NASA began creating new systems for interactive computer-generated imagery. VR has potential applications in many different fields.

"JURASSIC PARK". Director Steven Spielberg's 1993 film *Jurassic Park*, based on a 1990 novel by Michael Crichton, told of a modern-day tropic island where dinosaurs cloned from

prehistoric DNA escaped from their pens and terrorized humans. Released by Universal Studios, the film featured extraordinary special effects that combined computer graphics, large models and live action to create the illusion of vicious Velociraptors and a Tyrannosaurus Rex on the rampage, as well as more benign vegetarian species. *Jurassic Park* took in $913 million worldwide to become — for a time — the highest grossing film in history. It won Oscars for best visual effects, best sound and best sound-effects editing.

The stamp was the second in the Celebrate the Century series to honor a film directed by Spielberg. *E.T. The Extra-Terrestrial* was featured on one of the stamps on the 1980s pane.

BLOCKBUSTER FILM ("Titanic"). The sinking of the British luxury liner *Titanic* in 1912 with the loss of some 1,500 lives wasn't a stamp subject on the Celebrate the Century pane for the 1910s. The Citizens' Stamp Advisory Committee wanted to avoid negative events such as ship sinkings and assassinations, a member explained. The same concerns, however, didn't apply to a movie about the sinking. That movie, Twentieth Century Fox's *Titanic*, which opened during the 1997 holiday season, became one of the film industry's all-time smash hits, grossing $1.8 billion in worldwide gate receipts (against a production cost of a record $200 million). The work of writer-director James Cameron, it starred Kate Winslet and Leonardo DiCaprio as doomed shipboard lovers. It won 11 Academy Awards, including best picture.

SPORT UTILITY VEHICLES. A stamp on the 1900s CTC pane honored the Model T Ford, the first mass-produced American car. Nine decades later, among the Model T's distant descendants were Sport Utility Vehicles. SUVs became hugely popular, despite their reputation as gas guzzlers, with sales tripling from 1 million in 1990 to 3.1 million in 1999. The first SUV, a light truck with four-wheel drive, was the Jeep, a civilian adaptation of the workhorse personnel and cargo carrier that helped win World War II. Growing consumer interest in outdoor activities nourished the market for

Ford's Bronco (1966) and Chevrolet's K10 Blazer (1969). By the 1980s, manufacturers were upgrading the vehicles with all the amenities of sedans, and the SUV emerged as an all-purpose family alternative to conventional cars.

WORLD WIDE WEB. Called "the Web" for short, the World Wide Web is the leading information storage and retrieval service of the Internet, the worldwide computer network. The Web gives users access to a wide selection of documents through use of hypertext, a programming language that allows words and phrases to be "clicked on" by a cursor and a mouse and links the user to other related documents, or hypermedia. These contain links to images, sounds, animation and movies. In 1991 Tim Berners-Lee, a British physicist working in Geneva who had been developing the Web since 1980, released it to the general public. Rapid acceptance came with the creation and release in 1993 of a Web browser called Mosaic, which quickly became the most widely used "search engine" on the medium.

CELLULAR PHONES. This communications revolution had its origin in the mid-20th century with the appearance of the Mobile Telephone Service (MTS), a phone service for cars requiring a live operator to place calls. Functioning like a two-way radio, the phone employed a suitcase-sized transceiver that fit in the car's trunk. In 1983 the first commercial cellular service was offered, utilizing cell sites consisting of an antenna tower with a computer at the base. These emit frequencies in concentric circles like a cross-section of a biological cell, hence the name. Usage grew rapidly, and by 2000 more than 100 million subscribers, more than one-third of the nation's population, used the little hand-held phones. Bell Labs predicted that by 2010 there would be more than 1.45 billion cellular subscribers worldwide, about half a billion more than their wireline counterparts.

The Designs

Drew Struzan is an entertainment artist whose work has been featured prominently on numerous film posters. His first assignment for USPS was to paint the portraits of Hollywood composers and Broadway songwriters for the two final sets of Legends of American Music stamps that were released in 1999. That was followed by his painting of Alfred Lunt and

135

Lynn Fontanne that illustrated the 1999 commemorative stamp honoring those two American stage stars. The issuance of the Lunt-Fontanne stamp actually preceded Struzan's Legends of American Music stamps chronologically.

Struzan draws his pictures with a carbon pencil on a gessoed illustration board, then airbrushes the colors in acrylic paint and adds the details with colored pencils. "I love to draw, probably even more than I love to paint, and so the technique has its foundation in the drawing more than anything else," he said. "It's like a tinted drawing, rather than a heavy painting."

For his CTC illustrations, Struzan added what Howard Paine called a "rippling edge" to outline the principal figures and frame the overall picture. "I do that all the time," Struzan said. "I wanted these pieces to be consistent from stamp to stamp, so rather than adapt a style for the subject, I designed a look and then adapted the subject to the style. Some of the edges fall away and bleed out into the white of the stamp — there's kind of an artistic line around [the pictures] instead of a sharp cut.

"I used a style that's of our age, rather than trying to look like the '50s [or some other decade]. I wanted the stamps to look like the '90s as well as represent objects and people from the '90s."

NEW BASEBALL RECORDS. The baseball record breakers of the 1990s, Cal Ripken Jr., Sammy Sosa and Mark McGwire, couldn't be pictured or referred to by name in the stamp design. As an alternative approach, Paine and Struzan worked up symbolic illustrations dominated by a large baseball. In an early sketch, the ball was superimposed against a cloud-filled sky. At Paine's suggestion, Struzan painted the ball ripping through a generic newspaper sports page beneath the banner headline "RECORDS BROKEN." In the artist's first color version, a smaller headline reads "Home Run Derby" and a line above the banner identifies the section as "Games/Events/People." At the request of Terrence McCaffrey, head of stamp design for USPS, this smaller type was made illegible.

GULF WAR. Struzan's dramatic painting shows an American soldier

Shown here are a sketch of the New Baseball Records stamp showing a baseball against a cloudy sky, and a preliminary version of the agreed-on design concept, a baseball tearing through a generic newspaper sports page.

Struzan's original painting for the Gulf War stamp depicted the soldier in short sleeves, behind a sandbag. Although the painting was faithful to the source photograph, the artist was asked to give the soldier long sleeves, and the sandbag in front of the soldier was cropped from the stamp image.

behind what appears to be the barrel of an automatic weapon, facing the viewer and peering through binoculars that conceal his face. Behind him are billowing flames and clouds of orange smoke. In a break in the smoke, two helicopters can be seen. "The binoculars added a 'face' to our stamps, which on the '90s pane lacked portraits because of the 10-year-dead rule," said Howard Paine.

The picture of the soldier was based on a photograph supplied by Folio Inc., and the other elements of the painting came from other photo sources. The soldier's photo was dated December 4, 1990 — before the start of the Gulf War — but no information was available on his identity or where the shot was taken. It showed the soldier in short sleeves and with sandbags piled in front of him, and Struzan painted him that way. Nevertheless, "someone said the poisonous, acidic atmosphere demanded long sleeves, so he had to add them," said Paine. The fact verification process also revealed that the sandbags weren't accurate, McCaffrey added. "A soldier carrying this equipment would be in a vehicle, not behind sandbags," he said. "Therefore, we cropped in on the art."

SITCOM SENSATION ("Seinfeld"). One of Paine's first design ideas was to evoke the coffee shop where the four principal characters of the television show periodically meet. Struzan made two pencil sketches showing tabletop accessories from the restaurant — a ketchup bottle, salt and pepper shakers and a napkin dispenser — with the show's logo worked into the illustration. Another Struzan sketch depicted a director's chair with the *Seinfeld* logo on the back, and two pole-mounted television lights.

However, Castle Rock Entertainment, the holder of the rights to *Seinfeld*, preferred a painting showing the show's main set with the title superimposed — the same solution USPS had used for the two earlier CTC stamps that honored sitcoms, *All in the Family* on the 1970s pane and *The Cosby Show* on the 1980s pane. As was the case with those shows, the *Seinfeld* set featured the interior of the main character's domicile.

Struzan painted the familiar elements of the set, showing the open doorway to the hall in the center, the refrigerator on the right, and in the background at left a washbasin visible through the open doorway to the bathroom. ("A bathroom on a stamp," Paine marveled. "Is this a first?")

Two of Struzan's early pencil sketches for the Sitcom Sensation stamp evoked the coffee shop where Seinfield's four principal characters met; a third sketch depicted a director's chair and TV lights. Each included the TV show's logo.

In order that the scene "wouldn't just look like your room or mine," Paine said, Struzan added elements not seen by the television viewer, namely, the high-wattage TV lights hanging from the ceiling. The artist based his painting on a photograph credited to David Hume Kennerly of Santa Monica, California.

The *Seinfeld* logo consists of uppercase and lowercase letters in a turquoise color, with a purple oval behind. "The colors make it hard to read," Paine complained. "I just wanted the word Seinfeld in white, but [Castle Rock] wanted this purple egg behind it."

Like *The Cosby Show*'s title, the title of *Seinfeld* is the last name of its star. Therefore, the prominent display of that title in the design comes close to violating one of the basic rules for U.S. stamp subjects: "No living person shall be honored by portrayal on U.S. postage."

In his interview with *Linn's Stamp News*, Jerry Seinfeld said he had a hand in shaping the stamp design. "They did allow me to get involved in that," he said, "and we picked this little tableau. We went through a few different iterations of what it would look like.

"The actors always felt like that particular spot on the set was really where the action was. We always enjoyed playing scenes on that part of the floor, right in front of the door, between the couch and the counter. We always felt like that was really the heart and soul of the show, was right in that little area."

EXTREME SPORTS. Struzan painted a male snowboarder in orange coat, black pants, black gloves and goggles, trailing a swirl of snow, against a background that shades from deep blue at the bottom to lighter blue at the top. His original artwork showed the athlete with no helmet and flying hair, but expert opinion held that a helmet should be worn, and Struzan revised the picture accordingly.

"I love what he did with it," Paine said. "It's a romantic, heroic, beautiful design, looking up under the board, and the guy is standing on this frothy spray of ice."

Struzan's first painting of the snowboarder showed him without a helmet. Expert opinion solicited by PhotoAssist held that he should be helmeted, and the artist revised his painting accordingly.

This is Struzan's original finished artwork for the Improving Education stamp. Although CSAC and USPS officials were pleased with it, the art was abandoned after officials discovered that the boy in the source photograph was a French student, not an American.

Artist Drew Struzan and Sean Sturrock, 7, his model for the Improving Education stamp.

IMPROVING EDUCATION. Struzan's first sketch, depicting a boy in a plaid shirt bent over his schoolwork and writing with a pencil, was welcomed by CSAC and USPS officials. "We all agreed it was a very simple, strong design, and we told him to finalize the art," said Terrence McCaffrey. The artist based his drawing and finished painting on a photo supplied by Index Stock Imagery. Only when PhotoAssist set out to obtain the rights to use the image was it learned that the child was French. "We debated whether or not to change the art," McCaffrey said. "After much discussion, we felt we needed to redo it using an American child." USPS declined to identify the French boy.

In January 2000 Struzan found a replacement model. Through a mutual friend he met Walt Sturrock, a computer-training manager for the Walt Disney Studios in Burbank, California, and his son, Sean, 7. "I asked Walt if Sean would like to pose for a stamp, and he said, 'Of course,'" Struzan said. "The whole family came to my studio, my wife baked a cake for the occasion, and I shot a couple of rolls of 35-millimeter film. I changed the lighting and got different angles and had Sean do different things within the framework of the concept. Then I chose the shot that worked best."

In the resulting painting, Sean is wearing a green polo shirt, open at the neck, and, like the boy in the original artwork, is writing with a pencil.

Struzan made no significant changes in his subject's features. "The art is a bit idealized, that's the nature of what I do, but it's Sean; you look at the stamp and you say, 'That's him,' " Struzan said. "He's a redhead, that really is his coloration."

"It's a really pretty shot," Howard Paine said. "There's a good, strong light coming from the upper left, over the child's shoulder, that hits the pencil and causes a nice crescent shadow on his hand."

"We had already sent the [electronic] files to the printer when the decision to change the art was made," said Terrence McCaffrey. "We rushed the new art through, and added it to the pane at the last minute."

Sean, a first-grade student at the Walt Disney Elementary School of Burbank, became a mini-celebrity as a result. His story was featured on NBC television's local affiliate and was written up in the Disney Studios newsletter. Sean told *The Burbank Leader*, a community newspaper: "My friends tell me that it's pretty cool. Very few people get to be on a stamp when they are young — they have to be dead to be on a stamp."

Because only one Sean Sturrock stamp appeared on each pane of stamps, "we had to buy a lot of sheets," his father laughed.

COMPUTER ART AND GRAPHICS. After discussing several concepts, the design team settled on an image of a computer-generated human hand, which, with its lines representing cross-sections of the fingers, palm and wrist, resembles wire mesh. One version prepared by Struzan showed the computerized hand reaching out to touch a flesh-and-blood hand in a juxtaposition reminiscent of Michelangelo's *Creation of Adam* in the Vatican's Sistine Chapel. This "was turned down immediately as having possible 'sacrilegious' overtones," said McCaffrey.

"Then we settled on the abstraction of computers creating nature, namely, the wire-frame hand giving birth to a beautiful butterfly," said Paine. But Struzan's image of the hand "looked like a patterned glove, and his butterfly looked as if it was pinned on a display," Paine continued.

This Struzan concept sketch for the Computer Art and Graphics stamp wasn't accepted by CSAC and USPS officials because its obvious reference to Michelangelo's Creation of Adam *might have been considered sacrilegious by some.*

Struzan's first painting using the image of a computerized blue hand and a yellow and black butterfly was turned down because, as Howard Paine said, the "hand looked like a patterned glove, his butterfly looked pinned on a display."

"With so many other stamps for Drew to finish, I asked Greg Berger to help." Berger is an assistant to another art director, Ethel Kessler, and was the designer of 2000's Adoption commemorative stamp.

"We found a British piece of computer art," Paine said. "We 'flopped' the hand left to right, gave it heavy white lines defining the outline of the hand and fine white lines for the interior, added a glow and a few stars to the greenish-black background, and electronically 'pasted' a new Monarch butterfly [painted by Struzan] into the composition, even letting the wingtips fly into the stamp margin. It was a hard one to crack, but I'm really happy with it. I think it says what we wanted it to say."

RECOVERING SPECIES. "The decision was made collectively to use the peregrine falcon as our illustration, because its recovery was a good success story," said McCaffrey. The painting, the first done by Struzan for the pane, showed the head and upper body of a falcon, in profile, against a dark red background. The artist based the picture on a photograph provided by the Image Bank in New York City. "I picked the one I thought would look good at one inch high," Struzan said.

Struzan later made some minor color changes in the bird's plumage on the advice of ornithologists who examined the illustration for PhotoAssist.

RETURN TO SPACE. USPS could not depict John Glenn, the central figure in the event being commemorated by this stamp, because he was still alive. Nor was the Postal Service willing to use Glenn's name as part of the design, although it had prominently displayed the names of (Jerry) Seinfeld and (Bill) Cosby on the stamps featuring their TV sitcoms on the 1990s and 1980s CTC panes, respectively. Instead, Glenn's name was relegated to the text on the stamp's reverse.

In developing an illustration, Struzan made several pencil and color sketches, including one of a spacewalking astronaut and others of a shuttle in orbit with its cargo doors open. Neither of these scenes represented an actual event during the 1998 *Discovery* mission on which Glenn was a crew member. Also, CSAC felt they didn't say enough about the stamp

Struzan made these pencil sketches for the Return to Space stamp, but the sketches depicted events that didn't take place on the Discovery *mission being commemorated (a space walk, an orbiting shuttle with its cargo bay doors open) and they contained no reference to John Glenn's participation in the mission.*

Shown here are Struzan's first two color sketches illustrating the concept that finally was chosen for the Return to Space stamp: a ghostly Mercury capsule orbiting alongside the Discovery *shuttle. In both, the capsule is too large in relation to* Discovery. *For his finished art, Struzan closed the shuttle's cargo bay doors and showed the two vehicles in the proper scale.*

subject, but "implied only a trip into space," as McCaffrey put it. Finally, at the suggestion of Azeezaly S. Jaffer, head of Stamp Services, it was decided to show *Discovery* with a ghostly *Friendship 7* — the Project Mercury capsule that carried Glenn in orbit in 1962 — alongside. NASA experts who examined Struzan's first drafts of this illustration pointed out that the Mercury capsule was too large in relation to the shuttle. In the finished painting, the two vehicles are in the proper scale.

The Return to Space stamp was the 18th U.S. stamp or stamped envelope to depict a space shuttle. Fred Baumann noted in *Stamp Collector* that, with the exception of the U.S. flag, no subject had been featured more frequently on American postage during the past 20 years. The 1980s CTC pane included a stamp commemorating the start of the shuttle program and depicting the *Columbia* and its booster rocket in the launch position.

The design of the Return to Space stamp, the first of the 1990s group to be made public, was unveiled February 5, 2000, in the rotunda of the Mall of America in Bloomington, Minnesota, America's largest shopping mall. Deborah Willhite, USPS senior vice president for government relations and public policy, was joined at the ceremony by astronaut Timothy J. Creamer and USPS Northland District Manager Wayne Rogers. The unveiling was part of a "Government on Display" exposition at the mall.

SPECIAL OLYMPICS. The stamp's design is a photograph made by Robert McClintock for PhotoAssist of a Special Olympics gold medal. The medal, with attached ribbon, is shown against a blue mesh athletic jersey.

The USPS design team was dissatisfied with this design solution, but accepted it at the insistence of the Special Olympics organization. Paine, in particular, had wanted to show a Special Olympics athlete expressing on his or her face the joy of winning. "The sheet desperately needs a face, some human interest," he wrote in a memorandum during the design process.

Struzan made these sketches of young people in a victory pose with the Special Olympics medal around their necks. In the end, the Special Olympics organization vetoed the depiction of an individual on the stamp.

This is Struzan's painting of the Special Olympics medal, based on a photograph made by Photo-Assist. The Special Olympics organization insisted that USPS use the photograph on the stamp instead.

Struzan made several sketches of the kind Paine had suggested, basing them on photographs he had taken at a school for developmentally disabled children in North Hollywood, California. "I spent the day with them," Struzan said. "It was a delightful experience. I had to photograph every child in the school so that no one's feelings would be hurt — maybe 40 kids in all, all of them wearing the medal around their necks."

But by October 1999 an impasse had developed. Special Olympics officials "were not at all amenable to the idea of using an individual on a stamp," one intermediary wrote in a memo to USPS. "They believe a sole person cannot adequately convey the breadth of the Special Olympics sporting events or diversity of the Olympians who participate in those events." In addition, said the Postal Service's McCaffrey, Special Olympics felt the people in Struzan's sketches were shown as too "handicapped."

With printing deadlines for the 1990s pane drawing near, USPS gave in. Special Olympics exercised one final veto. After Struzan, working from the PhotoAssist photo of the medal, had made a painting of it, the organization rejected the illustration and insisted that USPS use the medal photo itself on the stamp.

The design was unveiled March 25, 2000, at opening ceremonies for the Special Olympics Summer Games in Plant City, Florida. Doing the honors was Michael P. Jordan, USPS Suncoast District manager for customer service and sales. Monty Castevens, president and chief executive officer of Special Olympics, Florida, took part.

VIRTUAL REALITY. Struzan's painting depicted a young man wearing what virtual-reality experts call interface equipment: a head-mounted display device resembling opaque wraparound goggles that cover his eyes, and sensor-tipped data gloves on his hands. His mouth is open in wonder at the three-dimensional simulated world he has entered. The background is pink and orange concentric circles.

The artist based his illustration on photographs he took of a friend, Greg Aronowitz of Studio City, California, a film director and special-effects man. The equipment is Aronowitz's own property. "He looks like he's 16, but he's actually about twice as old as that," Struzan said.

"JURASSIC PARK". Among the subjects on the 1990s ballot was Dinosaur Fossil Discovery, commemorating a major find of Tyrannosaurus Rex bones. To avoid the possibility that T. Rex would be shown on two 1990s stamps, Struzan painted a Velociraptor for the *Jurassic Park* stamp. However, Dinosaur Fossil Discovery wasn't chosen by the public, and Steven Spielberg, director of *Jurassic Park*, asked that T. Rex be depicted on the stamp for his hit film. The artist showed the head of the great carnivore in an appropriately threatening pose.

Struzan created a background that shaded from light green on the left to a darker green on the right. Paine wanted to change the background to

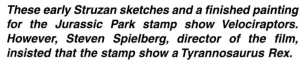

These early Struzan sketches and a finished painting for the Jurassic Park stamp show Velociraptors. However, Steven Spielberg, director of the film, insisted that the stamp show a Tyrannosaurus Rex.

Howard Paine wanted to change the background of the Jurassic Park stamp to white, to make the Tyrannosaurus Rex head "really jump off the page," but Steven Spielberg insisted on a green background.

white — "to push the chin and nose out into the border, and make it really jump off the page" — but Spielberg insisted on the green background. Paine then had the green color lightened on a computer, a decision that disappointed Struzan. The artist said he had chosen "a blackish green background so it had a little more power and oomph. They made it a pastel color, which I thought robbed it of a lot of its power."

BLOCKBUSTER FILM ("Titanic"). CSAC's rules against publicizing commercial products and honoring living people on stamps were breached numerous times in the CTC series. The most flagrant breach, however, came with this stamp and design. It not only advertised a major Hollywood film (as the previous stamp on the same pane had done); it displayed the director's name in the design above the title of the movie. "A James Cameron film" is shown in beige capitals approximately 1mm high, between two red horizontal dashes. By *Linn's Stamp News'* count, 20 living people are in some way depicted or identified in the CTC series, but Cameron is the only one whose first and last name appears on the front of a stamp. Twentieth Century Fox "insisted that the stamp must carry the

In two early pencil sketches by Struzan for the Blockbuster Film stamp, the Titanic *is only partially shown.*

This photograph, made by Digital Domain, was based on the 45-foot-long (¹⁄₂₀ scale) model of the ship made by the special effects company and was published in the book James Cameron's Titanic. *Struzan used it as a model for his stamp painting.*

This is the stamp design before the type referring to the film was added, and with the "33 USA" in a different position.

words 'A James Cameron Film,' " said McCaffrey. "They said that without it, it would be a *Titanic* boat stamp, not the film."

Struzan's painting shows the doomed liner *Titanic* plowing through the water, smoke pouring astern from its four stacks. Two tiny figures are visible at the bow, presumably representing the protagonists of the film, Jack Dawson (Leonardo DiCaprio) and Rose DeWitt Bukater (Kate Winslet), in one of its memorable scenes. The artwork was based on a two-page photograph in the book *James Cameron's Titanic*. The photo, in turn, by Digital Domain, was based on the 45-foot-long ($\frac{1}{20}$ scale) model of the ship made by the special-effects company. Superimposed on the lower part of the ship is the word "TITANIC" as it appears in some of the film's promotional material, in capitals designed to resemble metal plates, complete with rivets.

SPORT UTILITY VEHICLES. "Like most TV commercials showing SUVs scrambling up rocky cliffs and splashing through swamps, Drew's first sketches were pretty macho, with huge tires and a dozen headlights," said Paine. "We didn't want to show SUVs where they're usually found — stuck in commuter traffic or parked out in front of the local Safeway.

"We compromised and quieted the scene, showing an SUV driving along a road with distant mountains at dusk."

Paine's original idea, which "didn't fly," was to show an SUV during the manufacturing process, with the caption "4,000,000 SUVs on the road." He thought this would "avoid having it look macho or commercial, and emphasize the number manufactured and sold," he said. "The naked body wouldn't be identified as a Jeep, Toyota, etc."

Even after the design team settled on the final concept, Struzan made extensive revisions in his artwork. The revisions were based on recommendations by PhotoAssist's consultants, John Martin Smith, president of the National Automotive and Truck Museum of the United States in Auburn, Illinois, and Frank Markus, technical director of *Car and Driver* magazine. These were:

"... Eliminate the upper lights. You seldom see them on SUVs unless they are being used for off-road racing. The lights are not a standard feature, but an after-market accessory, very infrequently used for recreational or commuter use.

"Modify the fog lights so they are rectangular instead of round; nearly

Paine's first idea, illustrated in his sketch shown here, was to show an SUV body being manufactured, "to avoid having it look macho or commercial, and to emphasize the number manufactured and sold."

146

This early Struzan pencil sketch emphasized the muscular appeal of sports utility vehicles.

After receiving detailed recommendations from two experts on SUVs, Struzan eliminated all the lights on this vehicle except the two principal headlights and added a generic grill.

all factory-issued lights and most auxiliary lights in the '90s were that shape.

"Most SUV owners do not add lights to the center grill. Eliminate the middle of the three central lights. It would be preferable to eliminate all three lights, but then the grill would have to be added, which might indicate that the SUV is a particular brand ... The two lights [should] be rectangular. They can sit directly above the lower fog lights.

"One of the main features of SUVs is high ground clearance. Recommendation to raise the clearance about $\frac{1}{16}$ inch. This would also involve slightly raising the fog lights.

"The tires located at the rear driver's and the front passenger's sides should be widened. As painted, the narrow tires makes the SUV look like an Eastern European/Russian SUV ..."

WORLD WIDE WEB. Struzan started with some pencil sketches and a finished painting incorporating large chips and circuitry, including one suggesting an American flag, another a wired North America and a third an electronic polar dawn. In the end, the design team decided that a computer keyboard would be the best way to symbolize the invisible World Wide Web.

Shown here are three allegorical designs, two pencil sketches and a finished painting, developed by Struzan for the World Wide Web stamp before the design team decided to depict a computer keyboard and fragments of URLs.

USPS was unable to use this illustration for the Cellular Phones stamp, showing a woman using a telephone with a cloud-filled sky in the background because the model for the source photograph could not be identified for the purpose of obtaining a release to use her picture.

The artist based his painting for the Cellular Phones stamp on this photograph made by PhotoAssist of one of its employees, Nigel Assam.

The finished illustration shows a keyboard, with bits of Internet URLs floating above it (Universal Resource Locators, which are Internet addresses characterized by the prefix "http:"). These were created by computer-graphics specialist Tom Mann, who was responsible for the typography for the entire CTC series. It was suggested that real URLs for federal agencies be used, including USPS and the White House, but officials decided against doing so.

CELLULAR PHONES. The final stamp on the pane, and in the series, depicts a man speaking on a cellular phone that he holds to his left ear. The image is tightly cropped, so that the phone itself is centered and only half the man's face is seen. Struzan based his painting of the face on a photograph by PhotoAssist of one of the company's employees, Nigel Assam. The artist made no noticeable changes in Assam's features.

Earlier, Struzan had painted a picture of a woman in a yellow blouse using a cell phone, basing his artwork on a stock photograph. But USPS was unable to learn the model's identity in order to obtain legal authorization to use the image.

Because the Celebrate the Century art directors and artists were under extreme time pressure and were unable to delay the design process for each decade's stamps until the ballot results were in, they prepared preliminary designs and, in some cases, final art for most of the nominated subjects, including those that in the end weren't chosen. For the 1990s, the also-ran subjects were:

CULTURAL DIVERSITY. The United States continued in the 1990s to pursue the ideal of being a country that draws strength from its variety of ethnic groups, religions and cultures coexisting in harmony. No artwork was available for this subject.

SUSTAINED ECONOMIC GROWTH. Americans in the 1990s

enjoyed the most sustained period of high economic growth and low inflation in the country's history. For this subject, Struzan painted the face of a bull, representing the great Bull Market, with market letters and numbers superimposed in green. "It's a wonderfully strong, colorful design," Paine said. "I wish this stamp had run!"

ACTIVE OLDER AMERICANS. Improved health and social conditions allowed many Americans over 65 to remain active, working, volunteering in their communities, traveling, continuing their education, and even participating in athletic events. No artwork was available for this subject.

CONTEMPORARY ARCHITECTURE. Many contemporary architects combined unexpected forms and angles in surprising patterns and colors to create free-flowing, asymmetrical designs. For this stamp that never was, Struzan made a pencil sketch of the Getty Museum of Art in Los Angeles, California.

BROADWAY MUSICALS. In the 1990s, Broadway was host to fewer new musicals than ever before, but those that opened and prospered tended to be heavy on spectacle. Struzan prepared two pencil sketches featuring the half-mask worn by the title character in Andrew Lloyd Webber's *Phantom of the Opera*, which was one of the hit musicals of the 1990s.

WOMEN'S SPORTS. The success of American women's teams in international competition during the 1990s sparked a growing interest in women's professional sports that saw, among other things, the creation of two new pro bas-

ketball leagues. For this subject, Struzan prepared two pencil sketches, one showing women volleyball players in action, the other depicting the bodies of two women runners, numbers pinned to their singlets.

INLINE SKATING. For several years during the 1990s, inline skating was the fastest-growing sport in the country. Young skaters led the way, from 8 million in 1993 to more than 14 million in 1995. Struzan made a pencil sketch of a youthful male skater in racing position.

JUNIOR GOLF. The popularity of golf continued to grow in the 1990s, particularly among the young, who were the beneficiaries of junior golf programs throughout the country. No artwork was available for this subject.

DINOSAUR FOSSIL DISCOVERY. In 1990, one of the world's largest and most complete Tyrannosaurus Rex skeletons was discovered in South Dakota. Buried for 65 million years, the fossil, nicknamed Sue, was nearly 90 percent complete. Struzan sketched his impression of Sue, its formidable jaws agape. (The sketch mistakenly was given the caption "Jurassic Park," which was one of the subjects that actually made it to the 1990s pane. "Obviously, two dinosaurs on one sheet wouldn't have worked," Paine said.)

GENE THERAPY. Since 1990, more than 200 human clinical trials in gene therapy have been approved. This and future research may well lead to the successful treatment of many diseases. For this subject, Paine made a mockup of a stamp from a magnified photograph in colorful blue and orange.

INTERPLANETARY EXPLORATION. The ambitious 10-year NASA program to study Mars with robotic spacecraft began in November 1996 with the launch of Mars Global Surveyor, which began mapping the planet from orbit in March 1998. For this illustration, Struzan painted a probe vehicle in orbit around a cratered red planet. The vehicle is loaded with accessories for gathering and transmitting information and generating power. A brilliant sun or star radiates light across the picture. The result was "a confusing abstraction," Paine admitted.

MUSEUM ATTENDANCE. American museums drew younger and bigger crowds with major exhibitions, state-of-the-art interactive displays, and after-hours cultural attractions. By the late 1990s, museum attendance nationwide exceeded 850 million visits per year. No artwork was available for this subject.

HOME OFFICES. Technological advances made it easier for more Americans to work at home. In 1996, 30 million households had home offices; the number of telecommuters rose from 4 million in 1990 to 15 million in 1998. "We didn't want to show another person at a computer," Paine said. "Drew posed 'Miss Kitty' near a laptop computer and a cell phone. The picture clearly said 'home.' Nice!"

COMMUNITY SERVICE. The 1990s saw a resurgence in people's commitment to volunteerism. Citizens, private corporations and government agencies agreed to work together to help fight crime and improve the lives of at-risk youth. For this stamp, Struzan sketched a scene at a soup kitchen. Hands belonging to a client of the kitchen hold a paper plate while a ladle held by an unseen volunteer places food on it.

COFFEE. Gourmet coffee beverages, such as latte, espresso and iced cappuccino revived the coffeehouse culture in America. Struzan made two pencil sketches featuring a paper cup of steaming coffee.

Struzan also prepared some additional preliminary designs for two subjects that didn't get as far as the official ballot:

CHICAGO BULLS. This National Basketball Association team, starring Michael Jordan, won six NBA titles in the 1990s under Coach Phil Jackson. Rather than depict players, Struzan produced a pencil sketch depicting what Paine called "a choreography of hands," against the team's home-floor display of the Bulls logo. "It probably wouldn't have 'read' very well at stamp size," Paine said.

AMERICA'S CUP. For this subject, Struzan sketched an overhead view of two racing yachts side by side.

For the selvage image, Paine created a pane with a photograph of a blue sky with sunlight breaking through the clouds, "to suggest the dawn of a new century," he said. But CSAC turned thumbs down. "Everyone felt the picture was inappropriate," said Terrence McCaffrey. "The background selvage should reflect the 1990s, not the future."

The committee suggested that the selvage theme be the decade's stock market boom and prosperous economy — a subject that failed to make it onto a stamp in the public balloting (see above). A photograph was obtained of a brokerage office, full of workers at computer monitors. Paine conceived the idea of superimposing a jagged white graph line representing the Dow-Jones average, to show the upward trend of stock prices, with black vertical dashes at equal intervals indicating each of the 10 years. Because the decade hadn't yet ended, "We had to guess at where the end of the line would go," Paine said. "We hoped for no decade-ending crash!"

However, "the committee felt that the image didn't convey the idea of the stock market," McCaffrey said. "It looked too much like a typical office environment."

In the end, it was decided to use a photo, in green tones, depicting U.S. currency, bills and coins, with the Dow-Jones graph line. PhotoAssist created the graph; the money photograph came from Corbis Inc.

Two early illustrations for the 1990s pane selvage were a blue sky with sunlight breaking through the clouds, suggesting the dawn of a new century and millennium, and a brokerage office with a graph showing the upward trend of stock prices during the decade. The first image was turned down because the subject of the pane was the 1990s, not the future. The second looked too much like a typical office environment, with nothing in it to connote the stock market.

152

First-day Facts

Diane M. Regan, associate vice president for sales for the Postal Service's Pacific Area, dedicated the 1990s stamps at a ceremony in the Village Amphitheater of San Diego Wild Animal Park. To attend, collectors had to pay the park's admission fee. A USPS retail booth offering stamps for sale, first-day cancellations and a limited number of free ceremony programs was set up outside the park entrance.

Speakers were Mike Mace, the park's curator of birds, and Robert Mesta, lead biologist for the U.S. Fish and Wildlife Service's Peregrine Falcon Recovery Effort. Joan Embery, the San Diego Zoo's conservation ambassador, was mistress of ceremonies. Doug Myers, executive director of the Zoological Society of San Diego, opened the ceremony, and John E. Platt, manager for the USPS San Diego District, introduced the honored guests.

The earliest-known use of a 1990s stamp was on a cover hand-canceled East Northport, New York, April 10, 22 days before the official first day of issue. The stamp commemorates John Glenn's Return to Space.

33¢ DISTINGUISHED SOLDIERS (4 DESIGNS)

Date of Issue: May 3, 2000

Catalog Number: Scott 3393-3396, stamps; 3396a, block or strip of 4

Colors: black, cyan, magenta, yellow

First-Day Cancel: Washington, D.C.

First-Day Cancellations: 322,278

Format: Panes of 20, horizontal, 4 across, 5 down. Offset printing plates of 120 subjects, 15 across, 8 around.

Gum Type: water-activated

Overall Stamp Size: 1.560 by 1.225 inches; 39.624 by 31.115mm

Pane Size: 7.421 by 7.539 inches; 188.493 by 191.491mm

Perforations: 11 (Wista perforator)

Selvage Inscription: "DISTINGUISHED SOLDIERS/John L. Hines, 1918/4th Division Insignia, Meuse-Argonne, 1918." "Omar N. Bradley, 1942/First Army Insignia, Normandy, 1944." "Alvin C. York, 1919/82nd Division Insignia, Meuse-Argonne, 1918." "Audie L. Murphy, 1945/3rd Infantry Division Insignia, Colmar Pocket, 1945."

Selvage Markings: "©USPS/1999." ".33/x20/$6.60." "PLATE/POSITION" and diagram. Universal Product Code (UPC) "441000."

Designer, Typographer and Art Director: Phil Jordan of Falls Church, Virginia

Modeler: Joseph Sheeran of Ashton-Potter (USA) Ltd., Williamsville, New York

Stamp Manufacturing: Stamps printed for Ashton-Potter by Sterling Sommer, Tonawanda, New York, on Akiyama 628 offset press. Stamps finished by Ashton-Potter.

Quantity Ordered: 55,000,000

Plate Number Detail: 1 set of 4 plate numbers preceded by the letter P in selvage next to each corner stamp

Plate Number Combinations Reported: P1111, P2222

Paper Supplier: Tullis Russell

Tagging: block tagging

The Stamps

For many years, admirers of Audie Murphy, the most decorated U.S. soldier in World War II, had lobbied for a stamp depicting him. Their efforts were rewarded May 3 when the Postal Service issued a block of four commemoratives honoring Distinguished Soldiers that included Murphy in the quartet.

Others featured on the stamps were another World War II veteran, General Omar N. Bradley, and General John L. Hines and Sergeant Alvin C. York, who served in World War I.

The stamps, semijumbo in size, are conventionally gummed and perforated. They were printed by the offset process by Sterling Sommer of Tonawanda, New York, for Ashton Potter (USA) Ltd., and issued in panes of 20, four across by five down, with a decorative top selvage, or header.

Among the leaders of the campaign for a Murphy stamp was Stan H. Smith of Potomac, Maryland, a member of the Congressional Medal of Honor Society and founder of the Audie Murphy National Fan Club. Organizations backing the effort included the American Veterans of World War II, Korea and Vietnam (AMVETS), the Disabled American Veterans and the Vietnam Veterans of America. *The New York Daily News* editorial page lent its support. Philatelic writer Robert Rabinowitz weighed in frequently in favor of a Murphy stamp, citing long lists of what he called "lesser individuals" who had been honored on U.S. stamps while Murphy went stampless.

In recent years, the effort was joined by Einar V. Dyhrkopp of the USPS Board of Governors, himself a veteran of World War II, who often spoke publicly in favor of postal honors for Murphy. On September 16, 1999, Louis Caldera, secretary of the Army under President Bill Clinton, wrote

to Postmaster General William Henderson asking for a Murphy stamp.

By this time, however, the stamps for Murphy and the others already were in preparation for 2000 release. Azeezaly S. Jaffer, head of stamp services for USPS, was passing the word as early as June 1999 that Murphy would get his stamp the following year.

Alvin York, like Murphy, had been on the Citizens' Stamp Advisory Committee's list of proposed subjects for some time. Among York's advocates was a fellow Tennesseean, Marvin Runyon, Henderson's predecessor as postmaster general. Once CSAC warmed to the idea, its plan was to issue a pane containing two stamp varieties, honoring York, as a soldier of World War I, and Murphy, of World War II. Phil Jordan, one of the Postal Service's contract art directors and a Navy Seabee's son who "grew up around military posts," volunteered to oversee the design process.

"Then Karl Malden raised another issue in a CSAC meeting," Jordan recalled. "Malden [a distinguished film actor] had played Omar Bradley in the movie *Patton* and had become a close friend of Bradley and his wife. He said, 'This is a genuinely warm human being who deserves all the accolades he has received.' "

CSAC agreed to add Bradley to the group. "We realized we had an asymmetrical pane," Jordan said. "We needed a World War I figure to pair with York and a general to complement Bradley. So the committee said, 'We'll put John Pershing [commander of the American Expeditionary Force] in there.' Now I had a block of four to work with.

"Several months after all this started, I approached CSAC and Terry McCaffrey [head of stamp design], and pointed out that we had already done Pershing [Scott 1042A, an 8¢ definitive issued in 1961]. Surely, in all that World War I effort, there were other generals worthy of a stamp.

"PhotoAssist [the Postal Service's research firm] began compiling lists of World War I generals, and I started doing research, too."

Jordan read portions of Pershing's biography and memoirs, S.L.A. Marshall's *World War I*, Coffman's *War to End All Wars*, Laurence Stallings' *The Doughboys*, and some 16 other volumes with relevant information about units and personalities. After discussing the possibilities with David

156

Eynon, the military history expert on CSAC's subject subcommittee and a World War II veteran, Jordan narrowed his own preferred list to two. One was John Hines. The other was James Harbord, a major general who served as Pershing's AEF chief of staff and later commanded the 4th Marine Brigade of the Army's 2nd Infantry Division, which distinguished itself at the Battle of Bellau Wood, and then the 2nd Division itself.

"I concluded that Hines was the more attractive one for a stamp because of his combat career and his later administrative successes with the Army," Jordan said. Eynon concurred, and recommended to CSAC that it approve Hines as the fourth member of the quartet.

Hines (1868-1968), the son of Irish immigrants, was from White Sulphur Springs, West Virginia. He graduated from the U.S. Military Academy in 1891, served in the Spanish-American War and was cited for gallantry in the Battle of San Juan Hill. He was an adjutant to General Pershing during the expedition against Pancho Villa in Mexico. Later, with Pershing's AEF, Hines became the first U.S. soldier since Thomas "Stonewall" Jackson to command in combat successively a regiment, brigade, division and corps. He was awarded the Distinguished Service Cross and Distinguished Service Medal for bravery and leadership under fire.

"In spite of his legend as a man of few words, he seemed to have a zest for life and lived every moment at full gallop, whether in combat or in retirement," Jordan said. "He also was a legendary dancer who once literally danced himself to exhaustion, as well as an amateur botanist."

Hines served a single term as Army chief of staff in 1924-26. Events of his tenure included the court-martial of Brigadier General William "Billy" Mitchell, who was depicted on a U.S. stamp in 1999 (Scott 3330). He retired in 1932. In 1941, as World War II was spreading, Hines, now 73, requested an Army command but was turned down. Until his death in 1968 at 100, he was the oldest living graduate of West Point.

Alvin Cullum York (1887-1964), considered the greatest U.S. hero of World War I, was born into a fundamentalist Christian family in Pall Mall, Tennessee. Ironically, in light of future events, he was taught to oppose war and killing. As a noncommissioned officer with the 82nd Division in World War I, however, he distinguished himself October 8, 1918, when he

led a small detachment of men against 35 German machine guns. Using skills he learned as a Tennessee hunter, York killed 25 enemy soldiers with his rifle and pistol and captured 132. Allied Commander Marshal Ferdinand Foch called York's feat "the greatest thing accomplished by any private soldier of all the armies of Europe."

York received the Congressional Medal of Honor. In 1919, he returned home to a hero's welcome and a ticker-tape parade in New York City. The 1941 movie *Sergeant York* was based on his life and war record, with Gary Cooper winning the Academy Award for his performance in the title role.

Omar Nelson Bradley (1893-1981) was born in Missouri, the son of a schoolteacher. He graduated from West Point in 1915. In 1943, during World War II, he succeeded General George S. Patton as commander of the II Corps and led it in the Tunisia and Sicily campaigns. He commanded the First Army in the June 6, 1944, D-Day landings in Normandy on the French coast, the largest field command in history.

An unpretentious officer, Bradley was known as the "GI general" for his concern for the welfare of ordinary soldiers. After the war, he served as Army chief of staff (1948-49) and as the first chairman of the Joint Chiefs of Staff (1949-53). In 1950, he was promoted to general of the Army and received his fifth general's star.

Bradley is one of seven U.S. Army and Navy officers over the years who have held five-star rank. Six of them now have been depicted on U.S. stamps: Bradley, George Marshall, Douglas MacArthur, Henry "Hap" Arnold and Dwight Eisenhower, all generals of the Army, and Fleet Admiral Chester Nimitz. The seventh, still awaiting postal recognition, is Fleet Admiral Ernest King, chief of naval operations during World War II. (Pershing, although he wore only four stars, was given the unique rank "General of the Armies of the United States" by act of Congress.)

Audie Leon Murphy (1924-1971), the son of poor Texas sharecroppers, learned to shoot by hunting rabbits to feed his family. A small, slight, boyish-looking Army enlistee, he was called "Baby" by his fellow recruits. But, first in Sicily, then in Italy and France, he proved to be the fiercest of warriors.

As an infantry noncommissioned officer and later a lieutenant commissioned in the field, Murphy fought in nine major campaigns and was wounded three times. Among the 23 U.S. and foreign medals he received were the

Bronze Star, Silver Star and Distinguished Service Cross. He won the Congressional Medal of Honor January 26, 1945, near Holtzwihr, France, when he single-handedly stopped six German tanks and 250 troops, then led a successful counterattack. His citation says in part: "Murphy's indomitable courage and his refusal to give an inch of ground saved his company from possible encirclement and destruction, and enabled it to hold the woods which had been the enemy's objective."

After the war, Murphy was invited to Hollywood by actor James Cagney. He went on to star in 26 Universal-International films over the next 15 years, including *The Red Badge of Courage* and *To Hell and Back*, the latter based on his autobiography. His acting career spanned nearly a quarter century. He also wrote songs that were recorded by such well-known performers as Dean Martin, Charley Pride and Roy Clark.

Murphy died in a plane crash in 1971. Before receiving postal honors from his native country, he was depicted on stamps of Sierra Leone in 1991, Guyana in 1993 and Nevis in 1995.

Three of the soldiers honored — Murphy, Bradley and Hines — are buried in Arlington National Cemetery.

The Designs

Each stamp features a photograph of the soldier it honors, printed in a rich sepia tone suggestive of Army olive drab. The photos are shown off center, which Jordan believes "increases the drama of the photograph and gives it a little more power." A touch of color is added by the separate depiction of each individual's unit shoulder-sleeve insignia, with a partial white outline and a dropped shadow to make the patch stand out. The name of the soldier, in a dropped-out type called Officina Serif, is at the bottom of the stamp; "USA 33," in the same typeface in tan or black, is in an upper corner.

The header has a tan background and the words "DISTINGUISHED SOLDIERS" in black in a font called Stencil Antique, which recalls the stenciled lettering on boxes of military supplies. The tan color ends with a torn edge, created with computer software called Page Edges, which "seemed to suggest the nature of their business," Jordan said.

The header includes two lines of small type over each of the four top-row stamps. These lines, in a font with the odd name of Akzidenz Grotesk, identify the soldier in the adjacent stamp, with a year date indicating when the photo was made, an identification of the insignia, and the battle or theater in which the soldier distinguished himself, along with its year date.

"From the initial concept, I wanted to use 'in the field' photos rather than studio 'bemedaled, spit-and-polish' photos," Jordan said. "The fundamental quality that made each soldier a good subject for honor was their combat skills. They were all infantrymen. I chose the photos with that in mind.

"All the backgrounds of the photos have been subdued in order to make the heads predominant. I picked photos that I felt best captured the char-

In this version of the Omar Bradley stamp, the helmeted general is shown with four stars. The photograph was replaced with an earlier photo showing Bradley as a two-star major general.

acter of each individual, such as the steely resolve and deep faith of Alvin York and the baby-faced, freckled nature of Audie Murphy, the big helmet emphasizing his small physical stature and youth. To me, the Omar Bradley photo implies his great professional expertise and warm personality, and the John Hines photo clearly captures the character of this rock-hard professional soldier who loved to dance and of whom one Marine said, 'This general ran one hell of a tight ship!' "

The Hines photo, credited to the U.S. Signal Corps, was made in 1918 in Metz, France, then part of the German province of Lorraine, while the general was commanding the 4th Division. The source of the York image was a family photo of the soldier and his mother taken in 1919 in front of their home in Tennessee by Marvin W. Wiles of Wiles Studio, Nashville. Bradley's photograph, also made by the Signal Corps, was taken at Camp Gordon in Johnston, Florida, February 15, 1943. Murphy, shown as a lieutenant, was photographed June 7, 1945, a month after the end of the war in Europe, at a parade in Salzburg, Austria; the picture is credited to Keystone Photos.

Jordan experimented with depicting a ribbon on each stamp indicating a medal won by the soldier depicted — the Congressional Medal of Honor for York and Murphy, the Silver Star for Hines, the Distinguished Service Cross for Bradley — but decided that he wanted to show instead the patch

Designer Phil Jordan experimented with displaying ribbons representing medals won by the depicted soldiers rather than unit insignia, but dropped the idea. Hines is shown with the Silver Star, Bradley the Distinguished Service Cross, and York and Murphy the Congressional Medal of Honor.

160

of the Army unit most closely identified with each soldier's great accomplishments.

"With York and Murphy, that was easy, since each served in combat with only one division," Jordan said. "York's was the 82nd, which became an airborne division during World War II. Murphy's was the 3rd Infantry Division. With Bradley and Hines, it was more complex, since each had a long, distinguished career and served in combat with multiple units.

"For Hines, I chose the 4th Infantry Division, which he commanded during the battles of St. Mihiel and the Meuse-Argonne. For Bradley, the natural choice was the First Army, which he commanded at Normandy on D-Day.

"I felt it was important to select photos that showed the subjects in the field during the period of their most important accomplishments. For many reasons, we simply couldn't find suitable photos from the exact dates of the patches shown. This caused negative comments from some critics.

"For example, the photo of Omar Bradley was taken when he was a major general and commanding the 28th Infantry Division, a year before he became a lieutenant general and before he commanded the First Army. However, the Bradley family agreed that the photo captured the essence of the 'Soldier's General' and approved it.

"In the final analysis, the patches recognize the units each served with during their recognized accomplishments, while the photos capture the character of the individual. The header text clarifies this."

Adding the patches accomplished another purpose, as well, Jordan believes. "For all those people who served with those units over the years, it gives them some participation, too," he said. "It gives them a nice identifier, making them feel a part of it. To me, that was important."

PhotoAssist went to great lengths to verify the appearance of one of the patches, that of Alvin York's 82nd Division. Patches weren't universally worn during World War I, and the AEF-approved patch for the 82nd at the time of York's heroism, October 8, 1918, was a simple blue circle on a red square. Jordan incorporated this patch in early versions of the York stamp.

However, York's family wanted the patch shown on his stamp to include the embroidered letters "AA." PhotoAssist found copies of Army internal correspondence to show that in April 1918 division headquarters had adopted the name "All American Division" and authorized the addition of

PhotoAssist made this photograph of a homemade 82nd Division patch for use on the Alvin York stamp. The "AA," for "All American" Division, was added by the soldiers themselves before being retroactively approved by the American Expeditionary Force headquarters.

the "AA" to the blue circle without AEF sanction. Some division members were able to find French seamstresses to make the alteration for them. AEF headquarters didn't retroactively approve the "AA" until February 1919, after the war was over.

The research satisfied the design team that it would not be incorrect to depict the patch with the "AA" added. PhotoAssist obtained a photo of a "homemade" example from the Military History Institute at Carlisle Barracks, Pennsylvania.

The First Army patch originally chosen for the Bradley stamp included a square of red beneath the "A." Research showed that this color combination was adopted after World War II and that the patch as it existed on June 6, 1944, when the First Army landed in Normandy, was black and olive drab, which is how it is shown on the stamp as issued.

Hines' 4th Division patch, and Murphy's 3rd Division insignia, underwent no changes during their period of use. But, in the case of Murphy's patch, care had to be taken to orient the cloth correctly on the stamp. "It's amazing that you can take something that has four blue stripes and three white ones and turn that thing in the wrong direction three different ways if you're not careful," Jordan said.

First-day Facts

Einar V. Dyhrkopp, chairman of the Board of Governors of the Postal Service, and Louis Caldera, secretary of the Army, dedicated the stamps in a ceremony at the Pentagon in Arlington, Virginia. Honored guests included family members of the four honored soldiers; John F. Walsh, another member of the USPS Board of Governors; Delores J. Killette, postmaster of Washington, D.C.; and Phil Jordan, the stamps' designer.

33¢ SUMMER SPORTS

Date of Issue: May 5, 2000

Catalog Number: Scott 3397

Colors: black, cyan, magenta, yellow

First-Day Cancel: Spokane, Washington

First-Day Cancellations: 110,768

Format: Panes of 20, horizontal, 4 across, 5 down. Offset printing plates of 120 subjects, 8 across, 15 around.

Gum Type: water-activated

Overall Stamp Size: 1.560 by .991 inches; 39.624 by 25.171mm

Pane Size: 7.045 by 5.946 inches; 183.896 by 151.028mm

Perforations: 11 (Ashton-Potter stroke perforator)

Selvage Markings: "© USPS/1999." ".33/x20/$6.60." "PLATE/POSITION" and diagram. Universal Product Code (UPC) "440600."

Designer, Typographer and Art Director: Richard Sheaff of Scottsdale, Arizona

Photographer: David Madison of Portola Valley, California

Modeler: Joseph Sheeran of Ashton-Potter (USA) Ltd., Williamsville, New York

Stamp Manufacturing: Stamps printed by Ashton-Potter on offset portion of Stevens Variable Size Security Documents webfed 6-color offset, 3-color intaglio press. Stamps finished by Ashton-Potter.

Quantity Ordered: 90,600,000

Plate Number Detail: 1 set of 4 plate numbers preceded by the letter P in selvage above or below each corner stamp

Plate Number Combinations Reported: P1111, P2222

Paper Supplier: Tullis Russell

Tagging: block tagging

The Stamp

"The thrill of watching and participating in athletics will be celebrated May 5 with the issuance of a new United States postage stamp honoring Summer Sports," said the Postal Service announcement. No mention was made of the Summer Olympic Games that would open the following September 15 in Sydney, Australia. Nor did the stamp, when issued, bear any reference to the Olympics. Nevertheless, the two events were linked.

From 1972 through 1996, the Postal Service explicitly commemorated each quadrennial Olympic Games, winter and summer, with a stamp or set of stamps bearing the five interlocked Olympic rings. In 1996, however, friction developed between USPS and the International and U.S. Olympic committees over several details related to that year's Summer Games in Atlanta, Georgia.

The following year, the IOC asserted tight control over the designs, number and denominations of any postage stamps issued by any nation to commemorate the Olympic Games. The Postal Service decided it had had enough, and that it would go its own way in the future.

"Before they [the Olympic committees] began making it very difficult for us, we were committed to issuing stamps to commemorate Olympic Games," Azeezaly S. Jaffer, then the director of stamp services for USPS, told *Scott Stamp Monthly* editor Peter Martin. "But after what we went through in Atlanta, as long as I sit in this job you will never see rings on stamps again. It's not worth it."

In January 1998, shortly before the 18th Winter Games opened in Nagano, Japan, USPS issued what might be called an "un-Olympic" stamp: a Winter Sports commemorative that showed an athlete participating in one of the Winter Olympics' premier events — downhill skiing — but without the rings and without the O-word.

In 2000, with the Summer Olympics pending, USPS took the same route. The stamp it issued May 5 bore a design evocative of an Olympic-style footrace, but its only commemorative reference was the inscription: "Summer Sports." "Track and field events are representative of the summer season's invigorating athletic activities and competitions," was how the Postal Service news release explained the design subject.

"Some feel we're thumbing our nose at the Olympics," said Terrence McCaffrey, head of stamp design. "It's not an official thumbing, but it's our way of saying 'We'll do sports stamps, but we don't have to do Olympics stamps.' And sports stamps sell well."

The Summer Sports stamp has water-activated gum and conventional perforations. It was printed by the offset process by Ashton-Potter (USA) Ltd. and issued in panes of 20.

Numerous U.S. stamps in the past, both Olympic and non-Olympic, have depicted runners, including well-known achievers like track star Jesse Owens. A 1996 commemorative marked the 100th anniversary of the Boston Marathon. Jogging was among the subjects nominated for inclusion in the Celebrate the Century pane for the 1960s, and a design was prepared for it, but the subject wasn't among the 15 chosen for the pane by the public in balloting sponsored by the Postal Service.

The Design

Richard Sheaff, one of the Postal Service's art directors, was assigned to design the Summer Sports stamp, using a photograph. He was instructed by Terrence McCaffrey to avoid showing any recognizable individuals.

"I didn't want anyone saying 'Oh, we're honoring that specific person,' or 'That person was in the Olympics, and the Olympics people are coming after us,' " McCaffrey explained.

There were no people at all in the first group of photos adapted by Sheaff as stamp designs. These featured lines and stenciled lettering on the surface of an all-weather running track. Sheaff had taken the pictures at the Dartmouth College track in Hanover, New Hampshire.

"They were a little too abstract and esoteric," McCaffrey said. "The [Citizens' Stamp Advisory] Committee loved them, but they said the public is not going to understand or appreciate them; they are too subtle. We need people in the image."

Sheaff's next group of designs, using stock photography, included overhead shots of sprinters in action and a series in which only the elongated shadows of a group of distance runners are visible. "The shadow pictures were very interesting. The committee was intrigued," McCaffrey said. "But, again, we weren't sure how the public was going to react. The shadows are upside down, and people weren't going to know which side was up on the stamps. We said, 'Let's not confuse the issue.' "

The design ultimately selected by CSAC "is strong, it's colorful, it says Summer Sports, it's track and field, it's biracial," McCaffrey said. The stamp depicts the hips and legs of three runners, two white and one black, moving from left to right on a reddish-brown track against a green infield.

 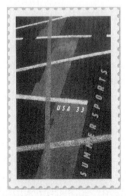 

Art director Richard Sheaff used photographs he had taken at the Dartmouth College track to develop these proposed images for the Summer Sports stamp. CSAC found them "a little too abstract and esoteric" and chose a design showing actual runners.

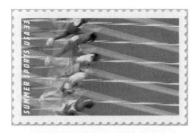

This group of proposed designs incorporated overhead photos of sprinters breaking from the starting line and crossing the finish line.

CSAC was intrigued by these designs, featuring the elongated shadows of distance runners competing in a crowded stadium. However, officials decided the designs would be confusing to postal customers, who wouldn't know "which side was up."

Their hips are in relatively sharp focus — the number 4 can be read on the lane number pinned to the middle runner's shorts — but their legs are blurred.

The photo was made by David Madison (www.davidmadison.com), a sports photographer from Portola Valley, California, at the 1994 Commonwealth Games in Victoria, British Columbia, Canada. The race was 1,500 meters, Madison believes. He purposely framed his picture to show only the lower half of the competitors.

"A lot of my work is more illustrative than journalistic," he explained. "My style is not so much to get the news picture of who won as it is to get a picture that somehow is symbolic of the sport or the athlete — or the body parts. This photo is sort of typical of the kind of things I'll shoot."

To capture the effect of strenuous action provided by the blurred legs, Madison set his Canon camera with a 200mm or 300mm telephoto lens at a slow shutter speed — between $^1/_{15}$ and $^1/_{125}$ of a second — and swung the camera to follow the runners as they passed. Under such conditions,

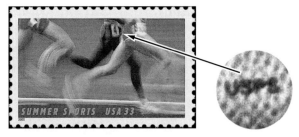

The microprinted letters "USPS" can be found on the white sheet of paper bearing the lane number "4" that the middle runner is wearing on his shorts.

"where you have motion going in a lot of different directions, frequently you'll get little bits of the image that are relatively sharp because the motion you've introduced with the camera coincides with the motion in the subject," he said. "In this case, I was pretty well synchronized on the hips, and the hips aren't bouncing up and down very much, whereas when you get out to the end of some of those guys' feet, especially on their back legs, where they're flipping them up, you get a lot more blur because the motion is going crosswise to the motion of the camera, as opposed to par-allelling with it.

"That's one of the intriguing things about slow-motion techniques; the effects vary with the kind of subject motion, the shutter speed and the other factors."

For the inscription "SUMMER SPORTS" and the "USA 33," Sheaff chose a typeface called Block Berthold extra-condensed italic. The micro-printed letters "USPS" can be found on the white card bearing the lane number "4" that the middle runner is wearing on his shorts.

The previous running stamp that most closely resembles this one is the 20¢ Physical Fitness commemorative of 1983 (Scott 2043). It also shows three runners moving from left to right, although its illustration by Don-ald Moss depicts them in full and adds an electrocardiograph tracing to suggest the benefits of exercise to the cardiovascular system.

First-day Facts

The first-day ceremony for the Summer Sports stamp was held outside the Spokane, Washington, Convention Center, on a floating stage at the Riverfront Park, in conjunction with Spokane's annual 12-kilometer Lilac Bloomsday Run. With nearly 60,000 registrants, the event is one of the largest individually timed races in the nation.

Richard "Digger" Phelps, a member of CSAC and a commentator on the cable sports channel ESPN, dedicated the stamp. Don Kardong, a U.S. Olympian and founder of the Bloomsday Run, was the speaker. Clair A. Brazington, Spokane District manager for customer service and sales for USPS, gave the welcome, and Spokane Postmaster Kenneth Symbol presided. Honored guests were U.S. Representative George R. Nethercutt Jr. and Karen Heaps, Lilac Bloomsday Association race coordinator.

33¢ ADOPTION AWARENESS

Date of Issue: May 10, 2000

Catalog Number: Scott 3398

Colors: black, cyan, cyan (selvage), magenta, yellow

First-Day Cancel: Los Angeles, California

First-Day Cancellations: 137,903 (includes Adoption stamped card)

Format: Panes of 20, vertical, 5 across, 4 down. Offset printing plates of 120 subjects (8 across, 15 around).

Gum Type: self-adhesive

Overall Stamp Size: 1.23 by 1.56 inches; 31.24 by 39.62mm

Pane Size: 7.63 by 7.74 inches

Perforations: 11½ (die-cut simulated perforations) (in-line rotary perforator)

Selvage Inscription: "Adopting a CHILD/Shaping a LIFE/Creating a WORLD/Building a HOME."

Selvage Markings: "©USPS/1999" ".33/x20/$6.60" "PLATE/POSITION" and diagram. Universal Product Code (UPC) "447100."

Illustrator, Designer and Typographer: Greg Berger of Bethesda, Maryland

Art Director: Ethel Kessler of Bethesda, Maryland

Stamp Manufacturing: Stamps printed by Banknote Corporation of America, Browns Summit, North Carolina, on Goebel webfed 670 offset press.

Quantity Ordered: 200,000,000

Plate Number Detail: 1 set of 5 plate numbers preceded by the letter B in selvage above or below each corner stamp

Plate Number Combinations Reported: B11111, B22222

Paper Supplier: Paper Corporation of the United States/Spinnaker Coatings

Tagging: block tagging

The Stamp

When a proposal for a stamp to publicize the need for adoptive homes for children was put before the Citizens' Stamp Advisory Committee, the members reacted warily. They considered it a risky subject because of the controversy surrounding international and interracial adoptions.

But influential citizens wanted the stamp. Prominent among them was Dave Thomas, founder of Wendy's Restaurants and the Dave Thomas Foundation for Adoption.

Thomas, who was adopted at the age of six weeks and never knew his natural parents, previously had served as national spokesperson for President George H.W. Bush's "Adoption Works ... For Everyone" campaign. He had persuaded corporations to provide adoption benefits to its employees, similar to maternity benefits, and had lobbied Congress and state legislatures for tax credits for adoptive families. Beginning in 1998, he enlisted members of Congress in a stamp campaign, and they in turn persuaded Postmaster General William J. Henderson.

"[Management] sent the word back down that 'You need to reconsider this,' " recalled Terrence McCaffrey, head of stamp design for USPS. "What they were suggesting didn't necessarily involve the controversial side of adoption. The committee took it to its next meeting and agreed that it was a good cause, but that we had to design the stamp and be very careful in promoting it so it didn't lend an endorsement to international adoptions."

The result was the 33¢ Adoption Awareness stamp that was issued May 10 in Beverly Hills, California. Its design also was used on the imprinted stamp and the picture side of a 20¢ picture stamped card (see separate chapter). The design was unveiled in October 1999 by Thomas, Postmaster General Henderson and television star Rosie O'Donnell, an adoptive mother.

Adoption Awareness was another of the "message" stamps that USPS has issued over the years to publicize social causes. Recent stamps in this category have promoted the awareness of AIDS, breast cancer and

prostate cancer; the donation of organs and tissue; charitable giving; and hospice care. A self-adhesive, the Adoption Awareness stamp was printed by the offset process by Banknote Corporation of America and distributed in panes of 20.

After its issuance, Thomas and celebrities from sports and show business embarked on an 100-event tour to promote the stamp. The group included retired athletes Gale Sayers and Muhammad Ali, comedian Paula Poundstone and actress Rhea Perlman. Thomas challenged Wendy's employees, franchisees and suppliers to promise to buy 1 million Adoption Awareness stamps. The group surpassed that goal, pledging to buy 2.5 million.

The stamp posed a problem for collectors, who discovered that it was extremely difficult to soak canceled specimens from envelopes. Charles Snee of *Linn's Stamp News*, after receiving complaints from several readers, tried soaking some used Adoption Awareness stamps and found the results "not encouraging."

Experimental soaks ranging from one hour to 16 hours resulted in stamps to which adhesive residue and portions of the envelope continued to cling, and, even worse, stamps with large thin spots, Snee reported. In a handful of other cases, however, the stamps, with careful handling, came away cleanly and were gum-free after drying.

"Overall, the results ... are inconclusive," Snee wrote. "The length of a water soak appears to have no bearing on whether or not a given Adoption stamp can be successfully removed from its envelope clipping."

The Design

Two of the Postal Service's contractual art directors volunteered to develop design proposals for the stamp. One, Derry Noyes, had a direct link to the subject of adoption; the other, Ethel Kessler, had an indirect link. Their design efforts followed different routes.

Noyes — whose oldest son, William Craig, is adopted — asked two artists to take a literal route and create illustrations of mothers with small children. Vivienne Flesher of Sausalito, California, made three pictures in pastels, and Augusta Talbot of San Francisco used the scratchboard technique for her sketch. Although CSAC members were pleased with the results, they felt that by focusing on mothers and infants the designs excluded other adoption situations, such as the adoption of older children.

Kessler, head of Kessler Design Group of Bethesda, Maryland, produced the symbolic illustration that eventually was chosen for the stamp. It was the work of another independent designer, Greg Berger, with whom she shares office space, who was himself adopted as a small child. In ask-

Using pastels, Vivienne Flesher created these images of a mother with a young adoptive child, which Derry Noyes incorporated in stamp designs.

Shown here is another proposed design, depicting a mother and adopted child, this one based on a scratchboard drawing by Augusta Talbot.

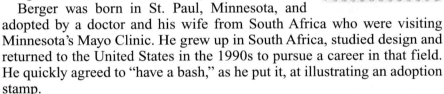

ing Berger to help find a design solution, Kessler knew from her own experience the satisfaction of creating a stamp that is, in her words, "very close to the soul." A breast cancer survivor, she had designed the Breast Cancer semipostal of 1998.

Berger was born in St. Paul, Minnesota, and adopted by a doctor and his wife from South Africa who were visiting Minnesota's Mayo Clinic. He grew up in South Africa, studied design and returned to the United States in the 1990s to pursue a career in that field. He quickly agreed to "have a bash," as he put it, at illustrating an adoption stamp.

"There are so many angles to adoption," Berger said. "Everyone has a different experience, being an adopted kid. How was I going to find an image that would relate to such a diverse topic? That was the challenge."

Berger decided to "go back to the beginning" and suggest how a child in his first art class, "untouched, innocent," would depict the idea of adoption. Without his usual preliminary sketching, "I went straight to the computer. I wanted it to be spontaneous, the way kids would do it. I didn't want it to be planned. When kids are in kindergarten, they have big crayons and off they go without even thinking. I was trying to capture that kind of feeling."

Using Freehand and Photoshop software, he drew stick-figure children, a boy and girl, against a backdrop of bright colors. The children's circular faces intersect so they share a single smile. They hold hands with one

171

An early version of Greg Berger's adoption stamp design lacked wording and included an additional pair of stick-figure children in the lower-left corner. To simplify the illustration, Berger eliminated the smaller child figures and made the dog larger.

another and with other stick figures, representing the adoptive father and mother, who are out of sight beyond the edges of the stamp. A dog stands at their feet. Behind them a path divides, with one path leading toward a night scene, with a crescent moon, stars and planets overhead, and the other to a sunlit cottage.

An early version of the drawing included a second, smaller pair of children in the lower corner, but Berger eliminated them to simplify the artwork and prevent it from being confusing.

Kessler found the illustration exciting. "What blew me away," she said, "was that there's nothing I've ever seen on a stamp that looks like this." She felt, however, that words were needed to supplement the visual message: "I had a feeling somebody [at the Postal Service] was going to say, 'Why don't we just put Adoption Awareness on this thing?' because that would be the automatic word solution."

She and Berger talked about his personal feelings about adoption, and out of their conversation came a set of three-word phrases that seemed just right: "Adopting a CHILD/Shaping a LIFE/Building a HOME/Creating a WORLD." They used these phrases, set in a typeface called Avant-Garde, to frame the illustration.

The design process didn't stop with the stamp itself. A continuing theme among USPS art directors, Kessler said, is "What have we not done? What would be different and interesting? How can we push the envelope of design? One thing we had not done was design a pane of 20 stamps with additional designs all the way around on the selvage."

Borrowing graphic elements from the stamp, along with its four defining phrases, Berger created a pictorial border for the pane. The result, Kessler said, was something "very playful" and helps confirm the impression that "it's a happy stamp." And, as Terrence McCaffrey pointed out, it had the advantage to USPS of making the full pane "more collectible."

Because the stamp is offset-printed, the printer included microprinting in its design as a security measure. The letters "USPS," arranged diagonally, can be found in the grass at the corner of the house.

172

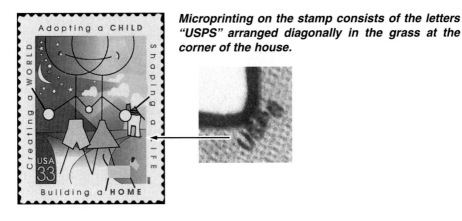

Microprinting on the stamp consists of the letters "USPS" arranged diagonally in the grass at the corner of the house.

While Greg Berger was working on the stamp illustration, another drama was being played out in his life.

Some time earlier, he had decided to try to find and meet his birth mother. His adoptive parents in South Africa, Dr. and Mrs. Mike Berger, were very supportive of the idea. "It's just a little thing you need to do," Berger explained. "You need to find out what happened in your first chapter, to work out where you came from."

Through the adoption agency that had placed him some 30 years before, he learned that his mother not only was willing to meet him; she herself had contacted the agency in hopes of initiating a reunion. The agency served as an intermediary through which the mother and son wrote to each other over a period of several months, and finally arranged a telephone conversation between them.

On a winter day in 2000, Berger was at Dulles International Airport near Washington, ready to fly to Minnesota to meet his mother in person. As chance would have it, during a takeoff delay he telephoned Kessler, who gave him the good news that CSAC had just approved his design for the Adoption stamp. The reunion, Berger said, was a happy one.

First-day Facts

S. David Fineman and Tirso del Junco of the USPS Board of Directors dedicated the stamp in a ceremony at the former Beverly Hills Post Office building in Beverly Hills.

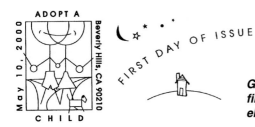

Greg Berger designed this pictorial first-day cancellation, using design elements from his stamp illustration.

Dave Thomas (left), chief advocate of the Adoption Awareness stamp, and actor Henry Winkler spoke at the first-day ceremony.

Speakers were Dave Thomas, the stamp's principal advocate; actor Henry Winkler of Children's Action Network; the Douglas family; and Postmaster General William J. Henderson. Deborah K. Willhite, senior vice president of USPS for public policy and government relations, presided.

Honored guests included Larry King, CNN talk show host; Paula Poundstone; Rhea Perlman; Azeezaly S. Jaffer, vice president for public affairs and communications of USPS; Karl Malden and Michael Brock of CSAC; and stamp illustrator Greg Berger.

After the ceremony, Thomas, Winkler, Perlman and Poundstone sold stamps and picture postal cards to persons attending the ceremony. The celebrities, each accompanied by a postal clerk, signed autographs and talked with their fans.

33¢ YOUTH TEAM SPORTS (4 DESIGNS)

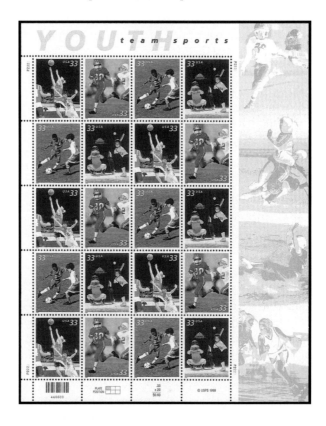

Date of Issue: May 27, 2000

Catalog Numbers: Scott 3399-3402, single stamps; 3402a, block or strip of 4

Colors: black, cyan, magenta, yellow

First-Day Cancel: Lake Buena Vista, Florida

First-Day Cancellations: 309,349

Format: Panes of 20, vertical, 4 across, 5 down. Offset printing plates of 120 subjects (12 across, 10 around).

Gum Type: water-activated

Overall Stamp Size: 1.225 by 1.560 inches; 31.115 by 39.624mm

Pane Size: 7.116 by 9.104 inches; 180.746 by 231.242mm

Perforations: 11 (Wista perforator)

Selvage Inscription: "YOUTH team sports"

Selvage Markings: "©USPS 1999." ".33/x20/$6.60." "PLATE/POSITION" and diagram. Universal Product Code (UPC) "446600."

Photographers: William Sallaz, Mike Powell, Zoran Milich, Bob Wickley, David Madison, Lan Li-Hua

Designer and Art Director: Derry Noyes of Washington, D.C.

Typographer: John Boyd of New York, New York

Modeler: Joseph Sheeran of Ashton-Potter (USA) Ltd., Williamsville, New York

Stamp Manufacturing: Stamps printed for Ashton-Potter by Sterling Sommer, Tonawanda, New York, on Akiyama 628 offset press. Stamps finished by Ashton-Potter.

Quantity Ordered: 88,000,000

Plate Number Detail: 1 set of 4 plate numbers preceded by the letter P in selvage next to each corner stamp

Plate Number Combinations Reported: P1111, P2222, P3333

Paper Supplier: Tullis Russell

Tagging: block tagging

The Stamps

On May 27, as part of a continuing effort to issue stamps that will appeal to young people, the Postal Service issued a set of four stamps displaying photographs of youthful competitors playing basketball (girls) and football, soccer and baseball (boys). The stamps are contained in a pane of 20 — five of each variety — with a wide decorative selvage on the right and a narrower selvage at the top bearing the words "YOUTH team sports."

"Youth team sports encourage a healthy lifestyle, promote socialization and provide opportunities for children to learn cooperation and teamwork," USPS said in a news release.

Although the stamp photos depicted recognizable individuals, USPS made no effort to electronically "morph," or alter, any of the faces. With previous stamps that displayed photographs — the American Ballet commemorative of 1998 and the Xtreme Sports block of four of 1999 — the designers altered the features, because of the rule of the Postal Service and the Citizens' Stamp Advisory Committee that "no living person shall be honored by portrayal on U.S. postage." But the USPS art directors and some members of CSAC considered the morphing process unsatisfactory and, in fact, unnecessary.

"It's difficult to alter faces on the computer, and many times it makes them look strange," said Terrence McCaffrey, head of stamp design for USPS. "We thought the way the Xtreme

176

Sports stamps came out was detrimental to the design of the stamps and the people on them. When we blew up the designs for unveiling purposes, the faces looked terrible.

"We need to have it understood that when we use a photograph of a living person on a stamp we are not honoring these models as individuals; they're just symbolic. We decided that where the model could be identified, we would get a signed release, and then not change them."

In an early version of the pane, art director and designer Derry Noyes proposed five designs: the four that eventually were used, plus a second soccer stamp depicting the girls' game. The decision was made to keep the number of varieties at four and eliminate girls' soccer.

The stamps, semijumbo in size, vertically oriented and conventionally gummed and perfed, were printed by the offset process by Sterling Sommer for Ashton-Potter (USA) Ltd. The stamps are arranged so that either blocks or horizontal strips of four can be taken from the pane.

Amateur sports has been a frequent topic of U.S. commemorative stamps. Among the more recent examples have been the aforementioned Xtreme Sports block of four (Scott 3321-3324) and the five Recreational Sports stamps of 1995 (Scott 2961-2965).

The Designs

"With youth team sports, we're all used to seeing photographs," said Derry Noyes. "We thought that by handling the design job photographically, we would make the stamps more contemporary looking than if we had an illustrator paint them. I think illustration would have felt a little old-fashioned, a little dated, for this particular subject."

Her goal in choosing photographs for the stamps as well as the selvage was "to give [the pane] the overall feeling of movement and action," Noyes said.

"It turns out, interestingly, that there really aren't that many good photographs of youth sports made by professionals and available in stock," she said. "There are tons of photos for adult sports.

"There are plenty of amateur photographers out there — parents are always shooting photos — and I tried some of those, but the colors were murky and the grass was muddy, with no contrast. The assignment really called for professional photographs."

BASEBALL. The photo, which Derry Noyes calls her favorite, is a pitcher's-eye view of a batter, catcher and home plate umpire against a solid black background. The batter's bat is cocked and his eye is on the ball, which is on its way to the plate. His face is clearly visible beneath his batting helmet; the catcher's and umpire's faces are masked.

The batter is Aaron Wickley of San Antonio, Texas, who was an 11-year-old Little League outfielder in 1992, when the photo was made. In 2000, Aaron was 19 and on a church mission in Chile during a two-year sabbatical from his pre-med studies at Brigham Young University's Hawaii campus. Thus he was a long way from home when he learned that his unaltered image, as a child, was on a newly issued U.S. postage stamp.

The picture was taken by Aaron's father, Bob Wickley, a professional photographer (www.wickley.com), and was obtained by USPS from SuperStock, a stock company that owns rights to a number of Wickley's sports photos. "I always took a camera to my kids' Little League games," Wickley said.

He made the picture at Northeast Little League Field in San Antonio. Aaron was playing for a team called the Pirates (the letters TES are visible on his yellow shirt in the picture). His father shot the scene with a Nikon camera and 300mm lens from behind the center-field fence.

BASKETBALL. In this dramatic action picture, a girl player in red jersey and blue-and-white shorts, her blond hair flying, launches a two-handed shot, while a defending player in a white uniform, her arms also raised, falls backward toward the camera. A teammate of the shooter is partly visible on the left. In the background are an official at the scorer's table and a crowd of spectators.

The shooter, the only player whose face can be seen, was Jenny Roulier of Cherry Creek High School in Colorado. (The word "Creek" is visible on the front of her tank-top jersey.) The defending player is Ann Mattock of Horizon High School. William Sallaz, a veteran sports photographer from Fort Collins, Colorado (www.sallaz.com), took the photo for stock purposes at the 1997 Colorado state girls' high-school basketball tournament at the Denver Coliseum, using a Nikon camera.

The Postal Service obtained rights to the photo from Sports Illustrated Pictures. By the time the stamp was issued, Jenny Roulier had graduated from high school and was playing varsity basketball for the University of Colorado.

SOCCER. The image is of two boys, one in a blue uniform preparing to kick the ball with his right foot, the other, in white shirt and blue shorts, attempting to reach the ball first.

The photograph, from a slight elevation, was made by Zoran Milich of Toronto, Ontario, Canada, for Allsport Photography Inc. June 7, 1997.

FOOTBALL. A football player is shown running, the ball in his right hand, while a second player gives chase in an effort to bring him down. Their features can be only partly seen because of their face masks. The background is out of focus.

The photo was made by Mike Powell for Allsport Photography Inc. Because the boys couldn't be identified for the purpose of obtaining model releases, the colors of their uniforms — red and white for the ball carrier, white and green for the defender — were electronically changed, first to turquoise and white for the ball carrier ("the turquoise was really hideous," said McCaffrey) and white and brown for the defender, and finally to burgundy and white for the ball carrier and white and teal for the defender. The uniform numbers also were changed, from 20 to 80 and from 7 to 2.

For the pane selvage, Noyes "tried to get the feeling of movement," she said, "and something different from what we normally do with just a title at the top."

Her first selvage design was a header that incorporated a full-color photo of a baseball player sliding into a base where the infielder waits, the ball already in his glove, to try to tag him out.

Noyes' second proposal was for a wide selvage down the right side of the pane displaying four sports photos in a subdued gray tone that contrasted with the bright colors of the stamps. But the use of additional pho-

Derry Noyes' proposed 15-stamp layout shown here incorporated a fifth stamp design, depicting girls' soccer, and a full-color header image showing a sliding baserunner and a waiting infielder.

This proposed side-selvage design incorporates four photographs in muted gray tones. On the pane as issued, the selvage images are negatives, not positives as they appear here, and three of them are different: soccer, football and baseball. The picture of the girls' basketball player at the bottom of this layout is the same one that appears on the issued pane as a negative. The player is Jenny Roulier of Cherry Creek High School in Colorado, who also appears in the photograph seen on the basketball stamp.

tos would have made it necessary to identify still more recognizable youngsters and obtain releases for the use of their pictures.

Then Noyes suggested that the photos be shown as negatives rather than positives, making the individuals more difficult to recognize. "Our legal team said that would be fine, and I said, 'Let's go with it,' " said Terrence McCaffrey.

The selvage football picture shows a runner carrying the ball while a defensive player lunges at him, a scene similar to the one on the football stamp. The photograph, like the football stamp photo, was made by Mike Powell.

The soccer picture is a negative black-and-white version of the color image Noyes originally had proposed for a fifth stamp featuring girls' soccer. It was made by Li-Hua Lan of Woodstock, New York in 1996 for The Image Works.

The basketball photo in the selvage, like the stamp photo, was made by William Sallaz and depicts Jenny Roulier, who is featured on the stamp as well. This time, instead of shooting, she is dribbling left-handed and attempting to drive by a defensive player.

The selvage photo of a baseball player sliding home was made in 1992 by sports photographer David Madison of Portola Valley, California. It was a staged shot that Madison made to illustrate an article in *Little League* magazine. He took the color picture from atop a stepladder at a diamond in Pittsburg, California, where he had assembled some Little League players for the photo project. The boy's raised arm obscures his features.

Earlier in 2000, USPS issued a Summer Sports commemorative, which also incorporated a photograph by David Madison (see separate chapter).

For her stamp and selvage type, Noyes chose a simple font called Universe Italic. "I wanted to keep the type as low-key as possible, so it wouldn't take over and be too prominent," she said.

180

First-day Facts

David S. Fineman, a member of the USPS Board of Governors, dedicated the stamps in a ceremony at the Promenade section of Disney's Wide World of Sports Complex in Lake Buena Vista, Florida. The event was held in conjunction with the Amateur Athletic Union National Tournaments, in which more than 3,000 players and coaches participated at the complex during the weekend.

Bobby Dodd, executive director and president of the AAU, was the speaker. Viki M. Brennan, USPS manager for the Central Florida District, presided, and Reggie Williams, vice president and executive director of Disney Sports and Recreation, gave the welcome.

The admission fee to events at the Disney's Wide World of Sports Complex was waived for persons attending the first-day ceremony only. First-day cancellations and stamps also could be obtained at the main post office in Orlando, Florida.

The earliest-known use of a Youth Team Sports stamp was on a cover machine-canceled Fresno, California, May 19, eight days before the official first-day sale. The stamp was a Soccer stamp. The collector who submitted it to *Linn's Stamp News* told the newspaper that he had bought a pane of the stamps from a postal store May 17 and immediately used one on a cover that he mailed to himself, but when he received it the next day he found that the May 17 cancel date wasn't clearly marked, so he tried again May 19.

33¢ THE STARS AND STRIPES (20 DESIGNS)
CLASSIC COLLECTION SERIES

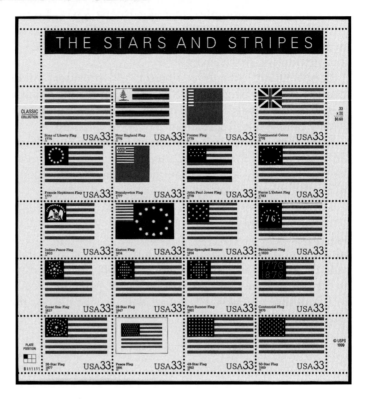

Date of Issue: June 14, 2000

Catalog Number: Scott 3403, pane of 20; 3403a-3403t, stamps

Colors: black, green (PMS 356), brown (PMS 126), red (PMS 200, 2 plates), blue (PMS 280)

First-Day Cancel: Baltimore, Maryland

First-Day Cancellations: 1,121,071

Format: Panes of 20, horizontal, 4 across, 5 down. Offset printing plates of 120 subjects (10 across, 12 around). Also sold in uncut press sheets of 6 panes.

Gum Type: water-activated

Overall Stamp Size: 1.56 by 1.23 inches; 39.62 by 31.24mm

Pane Size: 7.24 by 7.75 inches

Uncut Sheet Size: 22.75 by 15.50 inches

Perforations: 10½ by 11 (rotary perforator)

Selvage Inscription: "THE STARS AND STRIPES."

Selvage Markings: "CLASSIC/COLLECTION" "©USPS/1999" ".33/x20/ $6.60" "PLATE/POSITION" and diagram.

Back Markings: On header: "THE STARS AND STRIPES/One of the world's most powerful and widely recognized symbols, the United States flag has evolved over the past 200-plus years from a/variety of local, regional, and national designs, including unofficial and semiofficial ones. Many designs incorporated horizontal stripes;/many—but not all—had stars. These 20 examples, which are based on the most recent research available, offer a visual sampling of/variations on a theme. For artistic consistency, flag widths have been made uniform, and the same shades of red and blue have been used/throughout. The date on each stamp may reflect the most significant year in a flag's history, not necessarily the year the flag was created." On selvage: Universal Product Code (UPC) "55330."

On individual stamps:

"Continental Colors 1776/The British Union Jack on our/first national flag, in use during/the early years of the Revo-/lution, sent a clear message./Until the colonies proclaimed/independence in July 1776,/they were fighting for their/rights as subjects of the King."

"Forster Flag 1775/According to Forster family/tradition, this flag was cap-/tured/from the British by Minutemen/on April 19, 1775, the first day of/the Revolution. White stripes/then replaced its original canton;/with the red background, they/represented the 13 Colonies."

"New England Flag 1775/George Washington's military/secretary, Col. Joseph Reed, pro-/posed that all American ships fly/the Massachusetts Navy flag./This 'Americanized' version of/the flag links a regional sym-/bol,/a New England pine, with the/now familiar national colors."

"Sons of Liberty Flag 1775/The Sons of Liberty, activists in/defense of Amer-/ican rights,/used this flag of 13 horizontal/stripes to represent the unity of/the Colonies. This flag probably/inspired the stripes in Old Glory./Its red and white colors derived/from the English flag."

"Pierre L'Enfant Flag 1783/Pierre L'Enfant—the architect/who would create the original/plans for the nation's capital—/sketched this flag on a pro-/posed/membership diploma for the/Society of the Cincinnati, a/veterans' organization for offi-/cers of the Revolutionary War."

"John Paul Jones Flag 1779/After John Paul Jones and the/crew of *Bonhomme Richard* cap-/tured HMS *Serapis* on Septem-/ber 23, 1779, a Dutch artist/painted a watercolor of this flag,/which Jones had hoisted in/victory. Blue was considered/America's prime national color."

"Brandywine Flag 1777/In the Revolution, military units/often had different flags (or no/flags). Reputedly carried at the/Battle of Brandywine on Sep-/tember 11, 1777, this flag was/one of the first with stars and/stripes. New research indicates/it may have been a militia color."

"Francis Hopkinson Flag 1777/Continental Congress member/Francis Hopkinson designed the/first Stars and Stripes. His stars/may have formed rows or a ring;/the exact design is not known./In a resolution of June 14, 1777,/they were said to represent/'a new constellation.'"

"Bennington Flag c.1820/Long believed to date from the/Revolution, the Bennington Flag/was possibly made between/1810 and 1830. It could have/been created during the War of/1812, or in 1826 to celebrate

183

the/50th anniversary of the/Declaration of Independence."

"Star-Spangled Banner 1814/At Baltimore's Fort McHenry in/1814, the Star-Spangled Banner/came under British fire in the/War of 1812. Its 'broad stripes/and bright stars' inspired/Francis Scott Key to write words/that, set to music, later became/our national anthem."

"Easton Flag 1814/During the War of 1812, patriotic/citizens of Easton, Penn-sylvania,/presented this flag to their First/Company, First Regiment of/Vol-unteers. The striped canton/and starry field of this design/reversed the official placement/of the stars and stripes."

"Indian Peace Flag 1803/The American government often/presented the Stars and Stripes/to friendly Indian nations. These/'Indian Peace Flags' displayed/the U.S. coat of arms and/usually accompanied other gifts,/including medals with the/words 'peace and friendship.' "

"Centennial Flag 1876/Americans celebrated the Cen-/tennial with renewed faith in a/nation stretching from Atlantic/to Pacific and encouraging/inven-tion and industry. This un-/official flag, reflecting patriotic/spirit, shows that Old Glory has/always belonged to the people."

"Fort Sumter Flag 1861/This flag was flying over/Charleston's Fort Sumter on/April 12, 1861, when the Civil/War began. More than half a/million brave men from North/and South died before the very/same flag was hoisted there/again in 1865."

"29-Star Flag 1847/In 1845, the diamond pattern/became standard on garri-son/flags, enormous versions of the/Stars and Stripes flown at large/Army posts. Such flags could be/easily updated after new states/were admitted; in 1847, the 29th/star (for Iowa) was added."

"Great Star Flag 1837/An 1818 act established that the/flag include a star for each state/and 13 stripes. Capt. Samuel C./Reid, a naval hero of the War of/1812, recommended arranging/the stars into one large star/pattern, a common design in the/19th century."

"50-Star Flag 1960/When the 50th star (for Hawaii)/was added on July 4, 1960, our/current Stars and Stripes was/born. The U.S. flag stands for/our Constitution and the/American way of life, as well as/our past achieve-ments and/dreams for the future."

"48-Star Flag 1912/This version of Old Glory was/official from 1912 to 1959 —the/longest period any fixed star/pattern has been used. Ameri-/cans saluted this flag during two/World Wars, the growth decades/of the 1920s and 1950s, and the/Great Depression."

"Peace Flag 1891/Using their First Amendment/rights, Americans have enthusi-/astically pursued religious,/social, and political goals and/modi-fied the flag to show com-/mitment to country and cause./Dedication to world peace was/once symbolized by this flag."

"38-Star Flag 1877/The unusual pattern of this/1877 design includes a star for/Colorado, admitted as the 38th/state on August 1, 1876./Until 1912, when rows of stars/became standard, flagmakers/could use imaginative designs/to accommodate new stars."

Designer, Typographer and Art Director: Richard Sheaff of Scottsdale, Arizona

Stamp Manufacturing: Stamps printed by Banknote Corporation of America, Browns Summit, North Carolina, on Goebel webfed 670 offset press.

Stamps perforated by Sennett Security Products, Fredericksburg, Virginia and finished by BCA.

Quantity Ordered: 80,000,000

Plate Number Detail: 1 set of 6 plate numbers preceded by the letter B in selvage next to lower-left corner stamp

Plate Number Combination Reported: B111111

Paper Supplier: Paper Corporation of the United States/Ivex

Tagging: block tagging

The Stamps

On June 14, Flag Day, the Postal Service issued a pane of 20 stamps depicting 20 historic American flags that USPS described as "linked to the evolution of the Stars and Stripes since 1775."

The first-day sale was held at Fort McHenry National Monument and Historic Shrine in Baltimore, Maryland. It was at Fort McHenry during the War of 1812 that Francis Scott Key saw "by dawn's early light" that the flag and fort had survived a British bombardment, inspiring him to write the words to what would become the U.S. national anthem, *The Star Spangled Banner*.

The pane was the eighth in what USPS calls its Classic Collection series. Conventionally gummed and perforated, it was printed by offset lithography by Banknote Corporation of America. It resembles its predecessors in the series in several respects. It has a header, or decorative top selvage. Each stamp bears a few lines of descriptive text on the back. In addition to being sold in individual panes, it was offered to collectors in uncut press sheets of six panes for their face value, $39.60. And, like some of the previous Classic Collections, the Stars and Stripes stamps were supplemented by a set of 20 picture postal cards reproducing the stamp designs on the picture sides and in the imprinted postage (see separate chapter).

In an unusual contractual arrangement, the stamps were perforated by another independent stamp printer, Sennett Security Products, then were returned to BCA for final processing and shipping. The Postal Service's major stamp suppliers rarely work together on a single issue. Cathy Yarosky, a USPS spokesperson, explained that the Sennett firm has special perforating equipment made to process panes of 20 stamps with a header.

BCA used selective block tagging on the untagged paper used to print the stamps. The tagging mat used to apply the phosphorescent material was cut in different ways, so that on some stamps the stripes glow under shortwave ultraviolet light, while on others the glowing portion is the flag's canton, or rectangular area in the corner. By tagging the stamps in this manner, wrote Wayne Youngblood in *Stamp Collector*, USPS was able to protect perforating equipment, enhance security against counterfeiting,

Each stamp bears a few words printed on the reverse, under the gum, describing the design subject.

THE STARS AND STRIPES

One of the world's most powerful and widely recognized symbols, the United States flag has evolved over the past 200-plus years from a variety of local, regional and national designs, including unofficial and semiofficial ones. Many designs incorporated horizontal stripes; many — but not all — had stars. These 20 examples, which are based on the most recent research available, offer a visual sampling of variations on a theme. For artistic consistency, flag widths have been made uniform, and the same shades of red and blue have been used throughout. The date on each stamp may reflect the most significant year in a flag's history, not necessarily the year the flag was created.

Continental Colors 1776 The British Union Jack on our first national flag, in use during the early years of the Revolution, sent a clear message. Until the colonists proclaimed independence in July 1776, they were fighting for their rights as subjects of the King	**Forster Flag 1775** According to Forster family tradition, this flag was captured from the British by Minutemen on April 19, 1775, the first day of the Revolution. White stripes then replaced its original canton; with the red background, they represented the 13 Colonies.	**New England Flag 1775** George Washington's military secretary, Col. Joseph Reed, proposed that all American ships fly the Massachusetts Navy flag. This "Americanized" version of the flag links a regional symbol, a New England pine, with the now familiar national colors.	**Sons of Liberty Flag 1775** The Sons of Liberty, activists in defense of American rights, used this flag of 13 horizontal stripes to represent the unity of the Colonies. This flag probably inspired the stripes in Old Glory. Its red and white colors derived from the English flag.
Pierre L'Enfant Flag 1783 Pierre L'Enfant — the architect who would create the original plans for the nation's capital — sketched this flag on a proposed membership diploma for the Society of the Cincinnati, a veterans' organization for officers of the Revolutionary War.	**John Paul Jones Flag 1779** After John Paul Jones and the crew of *Bonhomme Richard* captured HMS *Serapis* on September 23, 1779, a Dutch artist painted a watercolor of this flag, which Jones had hoisted in victory. Blue was considered America's prime national color.	**Brandywine Flag 1777** In the Revolution, military units often had different flags (or no flags). Reputedly carried at the Battle of Brandywine on September 11, 1777, this flag was one of the first with stars and stripes. New research indicates it may have been a militia color.	**Francis Hopkinson Flag 1777** Continental Congress member Francis Hopkinson designed the first Stars and Stripes. His stars may have formed rows or a ring; the exact design is not known. In a resolution of June 14, 1777, they were said to represent "a new constellation."
Bennington Flag c.1820 Long believed to date from the Revolution, the Bennington Flag was possibly made between 1810 and 1830. It could have been created during the War of 1812, or in 1826 to celebrate the 50th anniversary of the Declaration of Independence.	**Star-Spangled Banner 1814** At Baltimore's Fort McHenry in 1814, the Star-Spangled Banner came under British fire in the War of 1812. Its "broad stripes and bright stars" inspired Francis Scott Key to write words that, set to music, later became our national anthem.	**Easton Flag 1814** During the War of 1812, patriotic citizens of Easton, Pennsylvania, presented this flag to their First Company, First Regiment of Volunteers. The striped canton and starry field of this design reversed the official placement of the stars and stripes.	**Indian Peace Flag 1803** The American government often presented the Stars and Stripes to friendly Indian nations. Those "Indian Peace Flags" displayed the U.S. coat of arms and usually accompanied other gifts, including medals with the words "peace and friendship."
Centennial Flag 1876 Americans celebrated the Centennial with renewed faith in a nation stretching from Atlantic to Pacific and encouraging invention and industry. This unofficial flag, reflecting patriotic spirit, shows that Old Glory has always belonged to the people.	**Fort Sumter Flag 1861** This flag was flying over Charleston's Fort Sumter on April 12, 1861, when the Civil War began. More than half a million brave men from North and South died before the very same flag was hoisted there again in 1865.	**29-Star Flag 1847** In 1845, the diamond pattern became standard on garrison flags, enormous versions of the Stars and Stripes flown at large Army posts. Such flags could be easily updated after new states were admitted; in 1847, the 29th star (for Iowa) was added.	**Great Star Flag 1837** An 1818 act established that the flag include a star for each state and 13 stripes. Capt. Samuel C. Reid, a naval hero of the War of 1812, recommended arranging the stars into one large star pattern, a common design in the 19th century.
50-Star Flag 1960 When the 50th star (for Hawaii) was added on July 4, 1960, our current Stars and Stripes was born. The U.S. flag stands for our Constitution and the American way of life, as well as our past achievements and dreams for the future.	**48-Star Flag 1912** This version of Old Glory was official from 1912 to 1959 — the longest period any fixed star pattern has been used. Americans saluted this flag during two World Wars, the growth decades of the 1920s and 1950s, and the Great Depression.	**Peace Flag 1891** Using their First Amendment rights, Americans have enthusiastically pursued religious, social, and political goals and modified the flag to show commitment to country and cause. Dedication to world peace was once symbolized by this flag.	**38-Star Flag 1877** The unusual pattern of this 1877 design includes a star for Colorado, admitted as the 38th state on August 1, 1876. Until 1912, when rows of stars became standard, flagmakers could use imaginative designs to accommodate new stars.

allow for cancellation ink absorption and make the stamps more attractive.

"The signal given off by each stamp is more than strong enough to trigger the [post office facer-canceler] equipment," Youngblood explained. "Also, the selective nature of the tagging keeps the abrasive substance away from the processing equipment, and such an unusual feature would be extremely difficult to counterfeit.

"In addition, with only certain areas of each stamp ... tagged, cancellation ink will be absorbed by the stamp paper, making it very difficult for crooks to chemically remove the cancellation from the stamps for illegal reuse. Finally, few would [deny] that this unexpected feature makes the stamps more attractive to any interested observer."

Collectors who bought uncut press sheets found that the sheets include a number of different printer's color boxes in the vertical gutters between the panes (see illustrations). Such boxes are used to check color printing and alignment before and during the printing process. On most of the previous press-sheet issues, most or all printer's marks have been trimmed away from the sheet paper that surrounds the unsevered panes.

The set was conceived by Richard Sheaff, one of the Postal Service's contract art directors and designers. To assemble a variety of early American flags on a pane to illustrate the evolution of the present Stars and Stripes, Sheaff thought, would be "pretty powerful, graphically." Based on his own research, he chose 20 visually interesting and historically signif-

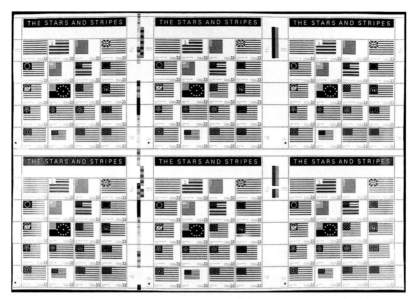

Color bars appear in the left and right vertical gutters of the Stars and Stripes press sheet.

Shown here are the various position pieces, listed as collectible configurations in the Scott Specialized Catalogue of United States Stamps & Covers, *that can be extracted from an uncut press sheet of six* The Stars and Stripes *panes (120 stamps). These position pieces show portions of the gutters, or uncut margin paper between adjoining panes, that prove that they come from a press sheet. At top, what Scott describes as the horizontal block of eight with vertical gutter. At lower left, the vertical block of 10 with horizontal gutter. At lower right, the cross-gutter block of 20 stamps that are portions of four panes.*

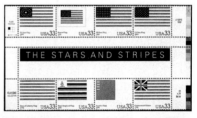

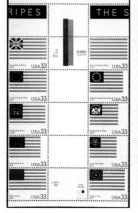

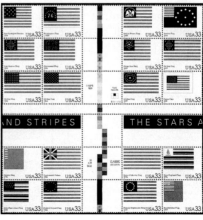

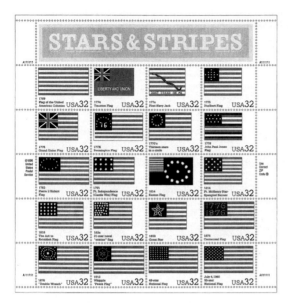

Richard Sheaff made this sample pane of 20 historic flags of his own selection, with a header bearing the inscription "Stars & Stripes," to show the Citizens' Stamp Advisory Committee what such a pane might look like. Most of the original 20 flags were retained for the finished pane, although with some variations. Those that didn't make the final 20 included the Liberty and Union flag and the well-known "Don't Tread on Me" rattlesnake flag, both in the top row.

icant flags and made a sample of a Classic Collection pane to show to the Citizens' Stamp Advisory Committee.

"At first the committee's reaction was, 'Ho hum,' " recalled Terrence McCaffrey, head of stamp design. But when Sheaff produced his sample pane, McCaffrey said, "the members were intrigued. They thought it had a nice design pattern to it, that it was visually very exciting, and that it would be a good history lesson. PhotoAssist [the Postal Service's research firm] was brought in to find a vexillologist, or flag expert, to review Dick's flags and make recommendations."

The specialist chosen by PhotoAssist was Whitney Smith, author and executive director of the Flag Research Center in Winchester, Massachusetts. His assignment was not only to advise on the final selection of 20 flags for the pane but to make certain, as well, that their designs were based on the most recent scholarship and that the year date that would appear on each stamp represented either the year of the flag's creation or a significant year in its history. Smith also wrote the text for the back of the stamps.

Continental Colors 1776 · USA33

Francis Hopkinson Flag 1777 · USA33

Brandywine Flag 1777 · USA33

"Dr. Smith was great on the proportions of each flag, the size and style and number of stars, and what constitutes an official flag," Sheaff said. "In the early days there were regimental flags and homemade flags and state-generated flags. Whatever anyone decided was official was official.

"Along the way there were a million other picky details about one thing or another, which we dealt with, and PhotoAssist then ran the results past other experts, and they of course disagreed with Dr. Smith. I tried to stay out of the way as much as possible. I said, 'Just tell me the bottom line, and I'll adjust.' "

Smith suggested only a few substitutions for the flags on Sheaff's original pane of 20, and these were made. Among his additions were two all-red flags, the Forster and Brandywine, while the Sheaff flags that fell by the wayside included the famous First Navy Jack, with a rattlesnake stretched across the stripes and the slogan "Don't Tread on Me." Smith also recommended the use of a different version of the Great Star flag, on which the stars in the star-shaped constellation are of varying sizes.

On the finished pane, the four flags in the top row, dated 1775 and 1776, show horizontal stripes but not stars. The first of these, consisting simply of seven red and six white stripes, is the flag of the Sons of Liberty, an activist group defending colonists' rights. The Sons used 13 stripes to symbolize the unity of the colonies. The fourth flag in the row, the Continental Colors, displayed the 13 stripes, but with the British Union Jack in the canton. In use during the early days of the Revolution, this flag sent the message that the colonists at that point weren't fighting for independence, but rather for their rights as subjects of the British king.

Stars didn't appear until 1777, after the Declaration of Independence, when Francis Hopkinson, a member of the Continental Congress, designed a flag with a field of 13 stars. In a resolution of the Continental Congress June 14, 1777 — the date that gave us today's Flag Day — Hopkinson's stars were said to represent "a new constellation." This flag is depicted on the first stamp in the second row; all the following flags on the pane contain stars as well as stripes.

When the U.S. government was created, the plan was to add a star AND a stripe for each new state entering the Union. The Star Spangled Banner that flew over Fort McHenry in

John Paul Jones Flag 1779 · USA33

1814, shown on the 11th stamp of the pane, displayed 15 stars and 15 stripes. However, it quickly became obvious that adding stripes wasn't a practical idea, and the number of stripes reverted to 13, representing the 13 original U.S. colonies.

Pierre L'Enfant Flag 1783 — USA 33

The original design of the 29-Star Flag (14th on the pane), as released by USPS, bore the year date 1845. This was changed to 1847 on the finished pane as the result of an inquiry by *Linn's Stamp News* on behalf of one of its readers, John Schatzlein.

Schatzlein saw the preliminary stamp designs in October 1999 and pointed out to *Linn's* that the 1845 date on the 19-Star Flag stamp didn't match the date when the 29th state was admitted to the Union. Texas was admitted as the 28th state in December 1845, and, under the terms of the Flag Act of 1818, the 28th star was added to the flag the following July 4. The 29th state was Iowa, which didn't join the Union until 1846.

USPS replied to the *Linn's* inquiry in November 1999, saying:

"We reviewed the 29-star flag and found that an inadvertent error had been made in indicating 1845 as the date.

"Our primary emphasis on that particular flag was in terms of its use by the U.S. Army as a garrison flag. While the standard pattern garrison flag was introduced in 1845, the 29-star flag itself was not introduced until 1847 ... [T]he star representing the December 1846 admission of Iowa as the 29th state was added to the U.S. flag in 1847.

"The fact that the number of stars did not correlate with a date of 1845 was unfortunately overlooked in the effort to emphasize the significance of the garrison flag and the date that design was introduced. This error will be corrected before the stamp pane is released to the printer."

Other year dates that were changed between the time the designs first were made public and the actual printing of the stamps were: John Paul Jones flag, from 1778 to 1779; the Indian Peace flag, from 1795 to 1803; and the Bennington flag, from 1826 to circa 1820. The text printed on the reverse of the Bennington flag stamp is testimony to the uncertainty, and changeableness, of flag scholarship:

"Long believed to date from the Revolution, the Bennington Flag was possibly made between 1810 and 1830. It could have been created during

Indian Peace Flag 1803 — USA 33

Easton Flag 1814 — USA 33

Star-Spangled Banner 1814 — USA 33

Bennington Flag
c.1820
USA33

the War of 1812, or in 1826 to celebrate the 50th anniversary of the Declaration of Independence."

USPS also furnished information at *Linn's* request on other flags on the pane. One was the unfamiliar New England Flag, with alternating red, white and blue stripes and a green pine tree in the canton. Helen Skillman, a Postal Service representative, told *Linn's* the design came from a partially furled flag depicted on a John Paul Jones coat of arms designed just after the Revolutionary War began.

"The evidence for this particular coat of arms is a line drawing, painted in watercolors, from the collection of the Masonic Library in Boston," Skillman said.

"The coat of arms is illustrated on page 201 in Edward Richardson's book *Standards and Colors of the American Revolution* (University of Pennsylvania Press, 1982), and in Samuel Eliot Morison's article, 'The Arms and Seals of John Paul Jones,' published in the October 1958 issue of *The American Neptune*. On page 205 of his book, Richardson also included an illustration of how that particular flag would have appeared unfurled.

"A number of New England flags were created between 1634 and approximately 1836; most, but not all, included a pine tree. Further, Col. Joseph Reed, George Washington's secretary, recommended, probably at Washington's behest, that the flag of the Massachusetts navy be used for all American ships.

"The New England flag shown on the stamp is an Americanized version of the Massachusetts flag, since the stripes of red, white and blue were beginning to be recognized as a national symbol. This may have been a flag flown by people who didn't like the Union Jack in the Continental colors; it is not known, however, whether this flag was ever widely used. It was included on the stamp pane to illustrate the link between the pine tree as a regional symbol and the stripes as a national symbol."

Another flag about which *Linn's* inquired was the Francis Hopkinson flag, with its circle of 13 white stars on the blue canton. *Linn's* cited authorities that said the 13 stars actually had been arranged in alternating rows of three, two, three, two and three, a pattern technically known as

Great Star Flag
1837
USA33

29-Star Flag
1847
USA33

Fort Sumter Flag
1861
USA33

Centennial Flag 1876 — USA33

38-Star Flag 1877 — USA33

Peace Flag 1891 — USA33

quincuncial because it is based on the repetition of a motif of five units.

The Postal Service's Skillman reported that while some authorities attribute the quincuncial star pattern design to Hopkinson, "his exact design is not known and current thinking favors the ring of stars as the Hopkinson design," which is believed to have been in use from 1777 to 1795.

She noted additionally that the ring-of-stars pattern was part of a proposed design by William Barton for a coat of arms of the United States, as described in a 1976 U.S. Department of State publication, *The Eagle and the Shield*, by Richard S. Patterson and Richardson Dougal.

"Although the 13 stars in circle is a popular design in the minds of most Americans, there is no proof that this was the design Francis Hopkinson proposed to the Congress," Skillman said. "The exact arrangement of the stars on the Hopkinson flag is not known."

A much earlier U.S. commemorative stamp had attributed the Hopkinson flag to Betsy Ross. The 3¢ stamp, issued in 1952 to mark the 300th anniversary of the seamstress' birth (Scott 1004), reproduces a painting by Charles H. Weisgerber showing Ross sewing a flag with the circle-of-stars pattern while George Washington, Robert Morris and George Ross look on.

U.S. vexillologists put little credence in the story that Betsy Ross created the first flag. William R. Furlong and Byron McCandless wrote in *So Proudly We Hail* (Smithsonian Institution Press, 1981) that although the Ross story "has an enormous popularity ... the known facts do not substantiate it."

Some of the flags on the Stars and Stripes pane previously had appeared on U.S. postage. A 1968 set of 10 Historic Flags (Scott 1345-1354) included four of them: the Continental Colors (Grand Union flag), the Francis Hopkinson flag, the Star Spangled Banner and the Bennington flag, the

48-Star Flag 1912 — USA33

50-Star Flag 1960 — USA33

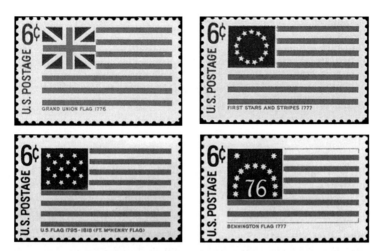

Four of the flags on the Stars and Stripes pane were also depicted on 6¢ stamps of the 1968 Historic Flag set, in some cases with different names and dates: the Continental Colors (here described as the Grand Union flag), the Francis Hopkinson flag (First Stars and Stripes), the Star Spangled Banner (Ft. McHenry flag), and the Bennington flag.

last-named flag accompanied on its stamp by the year date 1777. The Star Spangled Banner had waved on two other U.S. stamps, as well: a 1948 3¢ commemorative honoring Francis Scott Key (Scott 962) and a 1978 15¢ definitive in the Americana series (Scott 1597-98). The Francis Hopkinson flag was shown over Independence Hall on a 1975 13¢ definitive (Scott 1622).

The 48-star flag that was in use during both World Wars, featured on the 19th stamp on the Stars and Stripes pane, had been depicted on a handful of previous U.S. stamps, although only once in full color (Scott 1094). The pane's 20th and final flag, however, is the current 50-star U.S. flag, and it has been shown repeatedly on U.S. definitive and commemorative stamps and postal stationery, always in full red, white and blue.

The Designs

Richard Sheaff drew the flags for the stamp designs on his computer, using Photoshop software, and placed each flag against a white background. He based the drawings on visual reference materials provided by Whitney Smith, including diagrams and paintings.

For example, Sheaff copied the John Paul Jones flag, with its eight-point stars and its irregular sequence of colors among the stripes (five red, four white and four blue), from a watercolor painting by a Dutch artist of the flag Jones had raised over the British frigate *Serapis*. Jones captured *Serapis* September 23, 1779, off the English coast, in a battle in which he lost his own flagship, *Bonhomme Richard*. When the American fleet,

193

This watercolor painting by a Dutch artist was used as the model for the John Paul Jones flag, with eight-point stars and blue stripes in the first, sixth, tenth and twelfth positions, which Jones raised on the captured British frigate Serapis. *The Dutch script beneath the painting indicates that it was made October 5, 1779.*

including *Serapis*, sailed into Texel, The Netherlands, for repairs, the British minister demanded that the neutral Dutch arrest Jones as a pirate. To refute the charge, the Dutch sought to establish that Jones was sailing under a recognized flag by sending an artist to make paintings of the American ships' flags. The Dutch script beneath the paintings indicates that the *Serapis* flag was painted October 5, 1779.

For the sake of visual uniformity, Sheaff made all 20 flags on the pane the same depth. That meant that their widths on the stamps would vary, depending on the ratio of each flag's actual width to depth. "Otherwise, the pane would have been a visual hodgepodge," he explained. "There had to be some standardization to it."

"Originally, I considered stylizing the flags even more, and, for at least some of them, making them fill the whole width of the stamp, even if that didn't match their real dimensions. But the scholars didn't appreciate that, so we agreed to be accurate."

The Peace flag, in the bottom row, had a white border around the Stars and Stripes. Sheaff indicated this by outlining the flag in black. Because the Bennington flag, unlike any of the others, had white stripes at the top and bottom rather than red ones, the designer defined those white stripes with horizontal black lines.

BCA used six plates to print the pane. One plate each was used for black, dark blue, green and brown, the latter two colors appearing only on the pine tree emblem on the New England flag. The remaining two plates applied the red color.

Cathy Yarosky of USPS told *Linn's* that one red plate was used to print two of the stamps, the Forster flag and the Brandywine flag, because both have unusually intense red saturation. The second red plate printed the less intense red areas of the other 18 flags. Had a single red plate been used for the pane, Yarosky said, the printing of the 18 stamps might have been smeared or blurry because of the large amount of ink the plate would have required.

BCA didn't screen the colors, as stamp printers usually do, but printed them as solid colors.

The typography chosen by Sheaff for the stamps is a font called Serifa Roman, uppercase and lowercase, and is printed in black. The sans-serif letters dropped out of a blue bar on the header are in a Universe typeface.

First-day Facts

W.C. Miner, district manager for the Baltimore Performance Cluster of USPS, dedicated the stamps in a ceremony at Fort McHenry. He substituted in that role for Einar V. Dyhrkopp, chairman of the Postal Service's Board of Governors, whose flight was delayed. The event was part of a two-hour Flag Day Celebration at the national monument.

Honored guests included U.S. Representative Benjamin L. Cardin; Thomas V. (Mike) Miller Jr., president of the Maryland State Senate; Howard (Pete) Rawlings, chairman of the House Appropriations Committee, Maryland General Assembly; Martin O'Malley, mayor of Baltimore; Henry A. Rosenberg Jr., chairman of the National Flag Day Foundation Inc.; Laura Joss, general superintendent of the Fort McHenry National Monument and Historic Shrine; and Ronald E. Becker, associate director for capital programs, National Museum of American History, Smithsonian Institution.

The earliest-known use of a Stars and Stripes stamp was on covers machine-canceled Columbia, South Carolina, June 10, four days before the official release date. One cover bore a 38-Star Flag stamp; the other, a 50-Star Flag stamp.

33¢ LEGENDS OF BASEBALL (20 DESIGNS)
CLASSIC COLLECTION SERIES

Date of Issue: July 6, 2000

Catalog Numbers: Scott 3408, pane of 20; 3408a-3408t, stamps

Colors: black, cyan, magenta, yellow; black (back of liner paper)

First-Day Cancel: Atlanta, Georgia

First-Day Cancellations: 1,214,413

Format: Panes of 20, vertical, 5 across, 4 down. Offset printing plates of 120 subjects (8 across, 15 around). Also sold in uncut press sheets of 6 panes, 3 across, 2 down.

Gum Type: self-adhesive

Overall Stamp Size: 1.225 by 1.560 inches; 31.115 by 39.620mm

Pane Size: 7.125 by 7.750 inches

Uncut Sheet Size: 21.5 by 16.5 inches

Perforations: 11¼ (die-cut simulated perfs) (Arpeco die cutter)

Selvage Inscription: "Legends of Baseball" with All-Century Team logo.

Selvage Markings: "CLASSIC/COLLECTION." ".33/x20/$6.60." "©USPS/2000." "PLATE/POSITION" and diagram.

Liner Back Markings: On header: "Legends of Baseball/In this Classic Collection, the U.S. Postal Service honors 20 nominees for the Major League Baseball® All-Century Team./These players embody the glory and tradition of our national pastime./Tales of their extraordinary abilities and larger-than-life personalities have made them much more than just ballplayers:/THEY ARE LEGENDS." All-Century Team logo. In selvage: "Major League Baseball trademarks and/copyrights are used with permission/of Major League Baseball Properties, Inc." Universal Product Code (UPC).

On individual stamps:

"GEORGE SISLER/The St. Louis Browns'/George Sisler won two/batting titles, set the record/for hits in a season, and/produced a 41-game hitting/streak—all while/maintaining a reputation as/one of the true gentlemen in/Major League Baseball."

"TY COBB/Known for his aggressive/style at the plate and on the/base paths, Ty Cobb may have/been the greatest all-around/player in Major League/Baseball. In his 24-year/career, 22 with the Detroit/Tigers, the 'Georgia Peach'/won 9 straight American/League batting titles."

"CHRISTY MATHEWSON/In 1901, 21-year-old/Christy Mathewson won 20/games for the New York/Giants. With his 'fadeaway'/pitch, he posted three/consecutive 30-victory/seasons and in the 1905/World Series threw three/shutouts in only six days."

"EDDIE COLLINS/Eddie 'Cocky' Collins/played the game of baseball/for 25 seasons, a 20th-/century record for/nonpitchers. His brilliant/baserunning and batting/helped four teams/win World Championships."

"JACKIE ROBINSON/Jackie Robinson broke the/Major League Baseball color/barrier when he came to the/Brooklyn Dodgers in 1947./Two years later, he hit a/league-leading .342, drove/in 124 runs, and was voted/the Most Valuable Player/in the National League."

"ROBERTO CLEMENTE/The first Hispanic elected to/the Hall of Fame, Roberto/Clemente was admired for/his superb hitting, rifle-like/arm, and philanthropic/spirit. He helped the/Pittsburgh Pirates win two/World Championships."

"WALTER JOHNSON/Walter 'Big Train' Johnson/used a sweeping sidearm/ motion to fire fastballs over/home plate. In his 21-year/career with the Washington/Senators, he fanned 3,509/batters, won 417 games,/and pitched a record/110 shutouts."

"BABE RUTH/Babe Ruth was the most/celebrated athlete of his/time. Before beginning play/with the New York Yankees/in 1920, the 'Sultan of/Swat' was a successful/pitcher for the Boston/Red Sox. In 1927,/he hit a record-setting/60 homers."

"MICKEY COCHRANE/Mickey Cochrane sparked/the Philadelphia Athletics'/championship teams/of 1929-1931 with his/potent bat, skill behind/the plate, and fierce,/competitive spirit."

"ROGERS HORNSBY/Rogers Hornsby was the/most impressive right-/handed hitter in the history/of the game. He won seven/batting championships/(six in a row) and managed/the 1926 St. Louis/Cardinals to their/first World Championship."

"PIE TRAYNOR/Rated as one of the finest/third basemen of all time,/the Pittsburgh Pirates'/Pie Traynor had a defensive/prowess that often/overshadowed his strong/hitting. His nickname/reportedly came from a/childhood fondness/for pastry."

"JIMMIE FOXX/One of the top Major League/Baseball sluggers of all/time, Jimmie Foxx hit 30 or/more home runs for 12/seasons in a row. Foxx won/the Triple Crown for the/Philadelphia Athletics in/1933, leading the American/League in home runs,/batting, and RBIs."

"CY YOUNG/Denton True Young,/nicknamed Cy (short for/'Cyclone'), won 511/games in his 22-year/Major League Baseball/career—almost 100 more/than any other pitcher./A durable athlete, Young/pitched an astonishing/749 complete games."

"TRIS SPEAKER/Tris Speaker revolutionized/outfield play by positioning/himself in shallow center/field. As a result, this/Cleveland Indian recorded/more assists than any/other outfielder in the long/history of Major League/Baseball."

"LEFTY GROVE/One of the finest left-handed/pitchers in the history of/Major League Baseball,/Lefty Grove went 31-4 for/the 1931 Philadelphia/Athletics. In the process,/he put together a 16-game/winning streak."

"LOU GEHRIG/First baseman for the New/York Yankees, Lou Gehrig/played in 2,130 consecutive/games. In 1934 the 'Iron/Horse' led the American /League in batting average/(.363), home runs (49),/and RBIs (165)."

"DIZZY DEAN/Dizzy Dean, fastball-/throwing member of the St./Louis Cardinals' 'Gas House/Gang,' was a legend in his/own time, once holding the/modern single-game record/of 17 strikeouts. In 1934 he/and brother Paul led the/Cardinals to the/World Championship."

"JOSH GIBSON/Among the biggest draws/in the Negro Leagues,/popular Josh Gibson/is generally considered/one of the most/prodigious power hitters/in the history of/professional baseball."

"HONUS WAGNER/The Pittsburgh Pirates' star/shortstop, Honus Wagner/also was a league-leading/batter and base stealer./The 'Flying Dutchman'/enjoyed 15 consecutive/.300 seasons, 8 as/the National League/batting champ."

"SATCHEL PAIGE/A legend after two decades/in the Negro Leagues,/pitcher Satchel Paige signed/with the Cleveland Indians/in 1948. At age 42, this/'veteran-rookie' helped his/team win the American/League pennant."

Illustrator: Joe Saffold of Savannah, Georgia

Designer, Typographer and Art Director: Phil Jordan of Falls Church, Virginia

Modeler: Joseph Sheeran of Ashton-Potter (USA) Ltd., Williamsville, New York

Stamp Manufacturing: Stamps printed by Ashton-Potter (USA) Ltd. on offset portion of Stevens Variable Size Security Documents webfed 6-color offset, 3-color intaglio press. Stamps finished by Ashton-Potter.

Quantity Ordered: 225,000,000

Plate Number Detail: 1 set of 4 plate numbers preceded by the letter P in selvage next to lower-left corner stamp

Plate Number Combinations Reported: P1111, P2222, P3333, P4444

Paper Supplier: International Papers/Flexcon

Tagging: block tagging

The Stamps

On July 6, in Atlanta, Georgia, the Postal Service issued a pane of 20 stamps in its Classic Collection series honoring "Legends of Baseball." Each of the stamps depicted a member of the National Baseball Hall of Fame, which comprises players of the past who starred in the major leagues or the old Negro leagues.

The 20 featured players were Jackie Robinson, Eddie Collins, Christy Mathewson, Ty Cobb, George Sisler, Rogers Hornsby, Mickey Cochrane, Babe Ruth, Walter Johnson, Roberto Clemente, Lefty Grove, Tris Speaker, Cy Young, Jimmie Foxx, Pie Traynor, Satchel Paige, Honus Wagner, Josh Gibson, Dizzy Dean and Lou Gehrig.

The set, the ninth Classic Collection, was the first in the series to be self-adhesive. In other respects, however, it resembles its series predecessors, from Legends of the West in 1994 through the Stars and Stripes set that was issued just three weeks earlier, on June 14, 2000.

Like those, the Legends of Baseball pane has a header, or decorative top selvage; each stamp bears a few lines of descriptive text on the back (although in this case the text is on the liner rather than on the stamp itself); and the stamps were offered for sale in two formats: individual panes, and, through Stamp Fulfillment Services, uncut press sheets of six

Legends of Baseball

In this Classic Collection, the U.S. Postal Service honors 20 nominees for the Major League Baseball® All-Century Team. These players embody the glory and tradition of our national pastime. Tales of their extraordinary abilities and larger-than-life personalities have made them much more than just ballplayers: —THEY ARE LEGENDS

GEORGE SISLER — The St. Louis Browns' George Sisler won two batting titles, set the record for hits in a season, and produced a 41-game hitting streak—all while maintaining a reputation as one of the true gentlemen in Major League Baseball.

TY COBB — Known for his aggressive style at the plate and on the base paths, Ty Cobb may have been the greatest all-around player in Major League Baseball. In his 24-year career, 22 with the Detroit Tigers, the "Georgia Peach" won 9 straight American League batting titles.

CHRISTY MATHEWSON — In 1901, 21-year-old Christy Mathewson won 20 games for the New York Giants. With his "fadeaway" pitch, he posted three consecutive 30-victory seasons and in the 1905 World Series threw three shutouts in only six days.

EDDIE COLLINS — Eddie "Cocky" Collins played the game of baseball for 25 seasons, a 20th-century record for nonpitchers. His brilliant baserunning and batting helped four teams win World Championships.

JACKIE ROBINSON — Jackie Robinson broke the color barrier when he came to the Brooklyn Dodgers in 1947. Two years later, he hit a league-leading .342, drove in 124 runs, and was voted the Most Valuable Player in the National League.

ROBERTO CLEMENTE — The first Hispanic elected to the Hall of Fame, Roberto Clemente was admired for his superb hitting, rifle-like arm, and philanthropic spirit. He helped the Pittsburgh Pirates win two World Championships.

WALTER JOHNSON — Walter "Big Train" Johnson used a sweeping sidearm motion to fire fastballs over home plate. In his 21-year career with the Washington Senators, he fanned 3,509 batters, won 417 games, and pitched a record 110 shutouts.

BABE RUTH — Babe Ruth was the most celebrated athlete of his time. Before beginning play with the New York Yankees in 1920, the "Sultan of Swat" was a successful pitcher for the Boston Red Sox. In 1927, he hit a record-setting 60 homers.

MICKEY COCHRANE — Mickey Cochrane sparked the Philadelphia Athletics' championship teams of 1929–1931 with his potent bat, skill behind the plate, and fierce, competitive spirit.

ROGERS HORNSBY — Rogers Hornsby was the most impressive right-handed hitter in the history of the game. He won seven batting championships (six in a row) and managed the 1926 St. Louis Cardinals to their first World Championship.

PIE TRAYNOR — Rated as one of the finest third basemen of all time, the Pittsburgh Pirates' Pie Traynor had a defensive prowess that often overshadowed his strong hitting. His nickname reportedly came from a childhood fondness for pastry.

JIMMIE FOXX — One of the top Major League Baseball sluggers of all time, Jimmie Foxx hit 30 or more home runs for 12 seasons in a row. Foxx won the Triple Crown for the Philadelphia Athletics in 1933, leading the American League in home runs, batting, and RBIs.

CY YOUNG — Denton True Young, nicknamed Cy (short for "Cyclone"), won 511 games in his 22-year Major League Baseball career—almost 100 more than any other pitcher. A durable athlete, Young pitched an astonishing 749 complete games.

TRIS SPEAKER — Tris Speaker revolutionized outfield play by positioning himself in shallow center field. As a result, this Cleveland Indian recorded more assists than any other outfielder in the long history of Major League Baseball.

LEFTY GROVE — One of the finest left-handed pitchers in the history of Major League Baseball, Lefty Grove went 31–4 for the 1931 Philadelphia Athletics. In the process, he put together a 16-game winning streak.

LOU GEHRIG — First baseman for the New York Yankees, Lou Gehrig played in 2,130 consecutive games. In 1934 the "Iron Horse" led the American League in batting average (.363), home runs (49), and RBIs (165).

DIZZY DEAN — Dizzy Dean, fastball-throwing member of the St. Louis Cardinals' "Gas House Gang," was a legend in his own time, once holding the modern single-game record of 17 strikeouts. In 1934 he and brother Paul led the Cardinals to the World Championship.

JOSH GIBSON — Among the biggest draws in the Negro Leagues, popular Josh Gibson is generally considered one of the most prodigious power hitters in the history of professional baseball.

HONUS WAGNER — The Pittsburgh Pirates' star shortstop, Honus Wagner also was a league-leading batter and base stealer. The "Flying Dutchman" enjoyed 15 consecutive .300 seasons, 8 as the National League batting champ.

SATCHEL PAIGE — A legend after two decades in the Negro Leagues, pitcher Satchel Paige signed with the Cleveland Indians in 1948. At age 42, this "veteran-rookie" helped his team win the American League pennant.

Major League Baseball trademarks and copyrights are used with permission of Major League Baseball Properties, Inc.

560700

Each stamp bears a few words printed on the reverse, under the gum, describing the design subject.

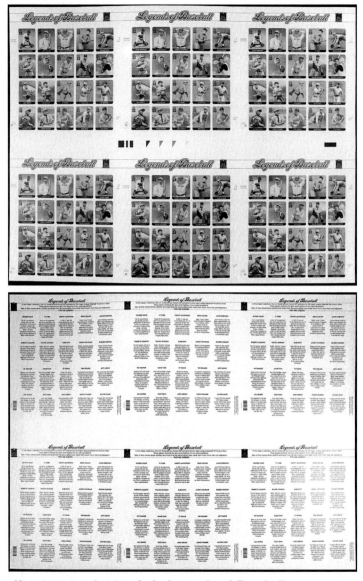

Uncut press sheets of six Legends of Baseball panes were available to collectors.

panes, 120 stamps in all. Postal clerks were instructed to sell nothing less than a full pane of 20 — no separate stamps.

Legends of Baseball was offset-printed by Ashton-Potter USA, the same company that produced the two previous Classic Collections. Like several of its predecessors in the series, it was accompanied by 20 picture postal cards imprinted with the same stamped images as the stamps (see separate chapter).

The set was eight years in the making. When it was conceived in 1992, it was intended to be the first of the Classic Collections, and some of the features that would become standard for the series were developed for this set. But legal difficulties forced USPS to shelve the project. When the stamps finally were issued, it was on short notice; the Postal Service didn't announce they were coming until April 19, 2000.

The proposal for a set of stamps honoring past baseball stars came from Carl Burcham, then the general manager of the Postal Service's stamp marketing division. In a memorandum, Burcham suggested that the subject would have special appeal for stamp collectors because of "the American public's fascination with 'all things baseball,' " and because of the great popularity of a similar hobby, baseball-card collecting. The stamps could be issued in 1994 to coincide with producer-director Ken Burns' forthcoming Public Broadcasting System television series on the national pastime, Burcham wrote. "Baseball stamps offer unlimited marketing opportunities," he enthused.

As Burcham envisioned it, the set would comprise 20 stamps or more in a pane as well as in four to five booklets, each featuring five different "Baseball Greats" in a particular category. For the booklets, he suggested what he called "fun" names: "The Hurlers," "The Clutch Players," "Sultans of Swing," "The Brains" and "The Underrated." The individuals honored would be members of the National Baseball Hall of Fame and would include not only players, but also famous managers and owners.

"By issuing four to five different booklets featuring different players and managers, the Postal Service can promote the collectibility and 'trading' aspects of the Baseball Greats stamps to both stamp collectors and card collectors," Burcham concluded.

Phil Jordan, who recently had been named one of the Postal Service's contract art directors for stamp development, was asked to oversee the design work. In late April 1992, Jordan and Burcham went to Cooperstown, New York, home of the National Baseball Hall of Fame and Museum, to describe the project to William J. Guilfoyle, the Hall's associate director, and to solicit its support.

Guilfoyle was enthusiastic and offered to enlist the members of the Hall's Veterans Committee to recommend the names of baseball personalities to be included on the pane. The committee consisted of 17 experts on the game, including ex-players Roy Campanella, Monte Irvin, Buck O'Neil, Ted Williams and Stan Musial, baseball executives Gabe Paul and "Buzzie" Bavasi, and sportswriter Shirley Povich. Guilfoyle wrote to each member, asking him to nominate 35 Hall of Fame honorees who met the Postal Service's 10-years-dead requirement for stamp eligibility.

Fourteen members of the committee responded, and in June 1992 Guilfoyle forwarded to Jordan the 30 names that appeared most frequently on their ballots. They were: Gehrig, Robinson, Wagner, Speaker, Ruth, Johnson, Mathewson and John McGraw (manager), 14 votes each; Hornsby, Cobb, Clemente, Grove, Gibson, Young and Connie Mack (manager), 13 each; Paige, Collins and Paul Waner, 12 each; Kenesaw Mountain Landis (commissioner), Sisler, Grover Cleveland Alexander and Bill Klem (umpire), 11 each; Casey Stengel (manager), Branch Rickey (executive), Napoleon Lajoie and Cochrane, nine each; and Foxx, Traynor, Dean and Alexander Cartwright (credited with inventing baseball), eight each.

The Citizens' Stamp Advisory Committee decided that Burcham's idea for stamps in booklets was excessive, but gave the go-ahead to develop a pane of 20, and Jordan began the design process. In consultation with Burcham and Joe Brockert, another USPS stamp development official, he assigned spots on the pane to the top 18 individuals on the Hall of Fame

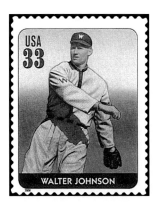
WALTER JOHNSON

ROBERTO CLEMENTE

LEFTY GROVE

list — everyone who had received 12 votes or more — and, to round out the 20, picked Sisler and Klem over Landis and Alexander "to get balance in our selection and to include an umpire." Then, working with outside designers and illustrators, Jordan developed a set of stamp designs and a header that bore the title "Hall of Fame Heroes/Cooperstown Collection" and the Hall of Fame logo.

At this point, the project came to a halt.

Postal Service attorneys had been contacting the estates of the selected players, one at a time, seeking the rights to use their names and images on the planned stamps. USPS policy is not to pay for such rights, although it will pay estates a percentage of the royalties it receives for the use of stamp designs on commercial products. The attorneys also opened negotiations with Major League Baseball Properties, which licenses the use of team names and uniforms.

Kelly Spinks, a Postal Service lawyer who took over the baseball project file the following year, in 1994, recalled the problems her predecessors had encountered. "Some of the estates wanted royalties for the stamps themselves," she said "and at least four of the estates wanted money up front against future royalties on products, which would have amounted to an advance licensing fee."

TRIS SPEAKER

A bigger problem was the attitude of Major League Baseball Properties, the game's licensing agency. Its officials offered to license the use on stamps of team names and uniforms for a flat fee — but the fee was estimated by USPS staffers at a prohibitive $300,000 to $1 million.

"We could have painted the players in generic uniforms, without identification," said Terrence McCaffrey, head of stamp design for USPS. "But it would have created a false impression. You expect to see players in their actual uniforms. We have always tried to be authentic in our depictions."

Informed of the impasse, then-Postmaster General Marvin Runyon "tossed it back to us," McCaffrey said. "He said, 'I don't even want to look at this until you've cleared all the hurdles.'"

In 1996, USPS tried to revive the baseball pane for inclusion in the following year's stamp program. "We went out to the families and their agents again," Spinks said. "Again, there was a problem. We were having trouble locating families, and the agents wanted to control the licensing of the stamp images, which wasn't acceptable to us. [The project] went away again."

Meanwhile, however, USPS had begun developing its Celebrate the Century (CTC) series of 150 stamps. Among the intended subjects were several baseball events and players. "Whether it was that CTC wasn't solely a baseball project, or just that the tides were turning, we had no trouble with the estates or Major League Baseball and no questions about royalties," Spinks said. "Getting all those baseball-related subjects in CTC put us in a better position to say, 'Maybe we can get Major League Baseball to sit down and talk about doing a whole baseball sheet.'"

In 1999, USPS again broached the subject — and this time the timing was right.

Major League Baseball had created a promotion called the "All Century Team," consisting of 30 great players of the past and present. Twenty-five of the 30 were chosen by fans from a list of 100 nominees, and the remaining five were added by a special panel. In the process, baseball officials obtained licensing rights to most of the 100 players' names and pictures, usable through 2001. The officials willingly gave USPS permission to use those rights to issue a pane of stamps, on the sole condition that the stamps would be linked to the All Century Team. No licensing fees or royalties would be demanded.

"We didn't have to go to each individual estate for the players, because

the estates already had made arrangements with Major League Baseball," Spinks said. "We probably couldn't have done it if that hadn't already been set up.

"But we were up against the clock, because it meant we had to do the stamps in 2000."

Fortunately, the 100 nominees to the All Century Team included all 17 of the players who had been selected by the Hall of Fame Veterans Committee for the "Hall of Fame Heroes" pane that had been planned back in 1993. This enabled USPS to use Joseph Saffold's 1993 paintings of those players, with some modifica-

tions, on the new pane.

Because three non-players were included in the 1993 group, however — umpire Klem and managers McGraw and Mack — it was necessary to replace them with All Century Team nominees, and new illustrations had to be made for them. At the same time, a player — Paul Waner — also was dropped from the original pane. The four players who were added to fill the now-empty spots were Mickey Cochrane, Jimmie Foxx, Pie Traynor and Dizzy Dean.

Roberto Clemente, who had been among the original 20, also was dropped, because Major League Baseball hadn't obtained the necessary clearance from his family. USPS replaced Clemente on the new pane with Al Simmons, an outfielder who played from 1924 to 1944, mostly for the Philadelphia Athletics, and recorded a .334 lifetime batting average.

However, Phil Jordan, the Citizens' Stamp Advisory Committee and USPS officials wanted to find a way to keep Clemente in the group, both because of his stature as a player and because they felt it essential to include on the pane an individual from Latin America, a region that today is heavily represented in professional baseball. With Major League Baseball's help, Kelly Spinks won permission from Clemente's family for the

Postal Service to depict him on one of the stamps of the set, and Simmons was sent back to the philatelic "bench."

Clarence E. Lewis Jr., chief operating officer for USPS, unveiled the designs of the 20 stamps during a pre-game ceremony on the field at Busch Stadium in St. Louis, Missouri, home of the St. Louis Cardinals, May 4, 2000.

Outfielder Al Simmons briefly owned a spot on the Legends of Baseball pane until he was replaced by Roberto Clemente.

Taking part were former Cardinals stars Lou Brock and Ozzie Smith; Jack Buck, the long-time "Voice of the Redbirds," who served as master of ceremonies; Tim Brosnan, executive vice president of Major League Baseball; and Richard "Digger" Phelps, a sports broadcaster and member of the Citizens' Stamp Advisory Committee.

Stamp collectors encountered a practical problem with the Legends of Baseball stamps: It was difficult to remove the backing paper from a single that had been separated from its 20-stamp pane. The panes have die cuts that extend through the stamps and the liner release paper, thus making it possible to separate and save mint singles. However, the liner paper behind each stamp lacks a slit that would make it easy to peel away from a single. *Linn's Stamp News* reported success in removing the backing paper from a single stamp by carefully bending back the stamp's corner to release it, which allowed the stamp to be peeled. "It was not particularly easy, and patience was needed to avoid permanently creasing the corner of the stamp," *Linn's* reported.

In addition, collectors of used stamps found that the Legends of Baseball stamps, like certain other modern U.S. issues, tended to curl tightly after being soaked from their envelope paper and needed careful flattening during the drying process.

Four of the players on the Legends pane were making their second or third appearance as stamp subjects. Jackie Robinson was honored on a 20¢ Black Heritage stamp in 1982 (Scott 2016). A second Robinson stamp was included among the 15 33¢ stamps on the Celebrate the Century pane for the 1940s, issued in 1999 (Scott 3186c). Babe Ruth also appeared on two previous stamps, a 20¢ American Sports Series commemorative of 1983 (Scott 2046) and a 32¢ stamp on the Celebrate the Century pane for the 1920s in 1999 (Scott 3184a). Roberto Clemente was depicted on a 20¢ commemorative in 1984 (Scott 2097), and Lou Gehrig on a 25¢ American Sports Series stamp in 1989 (Scott 2417). Baseball has been a topic of numerous other U.S. stamps, beginning in 1939, when the centennial of the game's alleged invention in Cooperstown by Abner Doubleday was marked by a 3¢ commemorative (Scott 855).

The Designs

In 1993, when the design process began, Phil Jordan called on three professionals for help: Bart Forbes, an illustrator who had created the images for previous U.S. sports stamps, including the Lou Gehrig commemorative of 1989; Mark Hess, who would go on to paint the portraits for two later Classic Collection sets, Legends of the West and Civil War; and Don Trousdell, a designer from Atlanta, Georgia, with a long-time interest in baseball. Trousdell, in turn, asked Joseph Saffold, a fellow Georgian, to provide illustrations for his design concepts.

From the outset, Jordan and Carl Burcham agreed that the stamps should resemble baseball trading cards, in which players are shown in characteristic poses on the diamond. They instructed the artists to include in each design, in addition to the player's portrait and name, his team affiliation, the words "Hall of Fame" and the year of his induction, and some kind of symbol, such as a baseball, bats or a glove.

When the first sketches came back, however, the officials saw that using all these elements would clutter a stamp-sized design. "It became very difficult to pick out the denomination," Jordan said. "CSAC told me, 'It has to be simpler than this. We're having trouble sorting all this stuff out.' So we began to distill it down."

Eventually, working with Trousdell's designs and Saffold's illustrations, Jordan and CSAC agreed on what would become basically the finished "look" of the stamps. The player's portrait dominated each stamp. His name, in orange or yellow capitals, was dropped out of a black band across the bottom. The year of his Hall of Fame induction was in the upper right. "USA" and the denomination occupied the upper left. The entire design was surrounded by a hairline border with rounded corners.

Saffold worked from old photographs, most of them supplied by the Hall of Fame. These included some portraits that previously had appeared on baseball cards. His painting of Ty Cobb, for example, is based on the

same photo that is reproduced on a 1912 card issued by the Honest Long Cut and Miners Extra tobacco brands. Saffold's artwork itself is almost photographic, featuring crisply outlined images of the players, blurry, out-of-focus backgrounds and pastel colors. He achieves his effect with Prismacolor pencils and acrylic and oil paints applied with an airbrush.

The design of the Ty Cobb stamp is based on the same photograph used for a 1912 baseball card issued by the Honest Long Cut and Miners Extra tobacco brands.

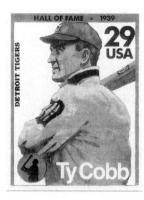
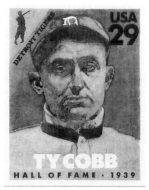

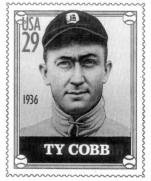

These are concept sketches, each featuring Ty Cobb, prepared in 1992 by three professionals at Phil Jordan's request. Each incorporated the typographical elements Jordan had asked for: player's name and team affiliation, the words "Hall of Fame" and the year of the player's induction into the Hall, and a symbol or symbols of the game of baseball. The designs are by Bart Forbes (top), Mark Hess (first two, second row) and Don Trousdell and Joseph Saffold (remaining sketches). After examining them, Jordan and CSAC concluded that they had asked for too many elements and that the designs were cluttered as a result.

Shown here and on the next page are the photographs on which Joseph Saffold based his paintings for the Legends of Baseball stamps.

Rogers Hornsby

Josh Gibson

Satchel Paige

Lefty Grove

Christy Mathewson

Mickey Cochrane

Eddie Collins

Pie Traynor

Jackie Robinson

Honus Wagner

Lou Gehrig

Dizzy Dean

Ty Cobb

Babe Ruth

George Sisler

Tris Speaker

Jordan laid out the pane of 20 stamps in a way that became the Classic Collection prototype, with stamps at the four corners "that would sort of turn the action in" on the pane, he said. The corner stamps depicted two non-players, Mack and McGraw, along with players Josh Gibson and Cy Young. Young was shown in a still pose, because, said Jordan, "unfortunately, most action photos of Cy were taken when he was in the twilight of his career and a tad portly." Don Trousdell prepared several proposed designs for the pane header, featuring the set's working title, "Hall of Fame Heroes."

At this point, the Postal Service's efforts to obtain the necessary rights to depict the players failed, and the project was put aside.

Six years went by. "In 1999 I got a message from Kelly [Spinks], telling me there was a possibility we could revive the thing, but to be prepared to move very fast," Jordan recalled. Among other things, new artwork would be needed for the players who would replace some of the people on the original pane.

PhotoAssist, the Postal Service's research firm, located artist Joseph Saffold, who had retired to Savannah, Georgia. Saffold agreed to supply portraits of Cochran, Foxx, Traynor and Dean, in addition to Al Simmons, who would enjoy a brief inclusion in the lineup before being replaced by Roberto Clemente.

Saffold also made new paintings of Cy Young and Lou Gehrig. Jordan and CSAC had been dissatisfied with the earlier, static image of Young, and Saffold created a composite action picture. He based the head on a photograph of Young pitching for the Boston Pilgrims around 1904-05 and the body on a photo of another pitcher of the early 20th century, Rube

Because the available action photographs of Cy Young showed the pitcher, in Phil Jordan's words, "in the twilight of his career and a tad portly," Saffold based the final version of his painting of Young on these two photos. The head is from a photo of Young pitching for the Boston Pilgrims circa 1904-05; the body is from a picture of another early 20th century pitcher, Rube Benton of the Cincinnati Reds and New York Giants. To make the southpaw Benton into a right-hander, like Young, Saffold "flopped," or reversed, the image.

Benton. Benton, unlike Young, was left-handed, so Saffold reversed the image. His original painting of Gehrig in the batter's box awaiting a pitch was replaced with a picture of the great Yankee first baseman smiling and resting three bats on his shoulder.

In addition, Saffold had to revise numerous details in his earlier paintings, most of them related to the players' uniforms and equipment. The artwork had been done before the Bill Pickett affair, in which the Postal Service misidentified one of the subjects of the first Classic Collection set actually to be issued, Legends of the West in 1994. That embarrassment led USPS, now obsessed with accuracy, to hire PhotoAssist to do its research and fact checking. PhotoAssist showed the Saffold illustrations to baseball experts, and the artist made the alterations they recommended.

In painting Josh Gibson, for example, Saffold had worked from a black-and-white photograph and had guessed at the color of the Negro Leagues catcher's long-defunct Pittsburgh Crawfords uniform. The cap, stripes and

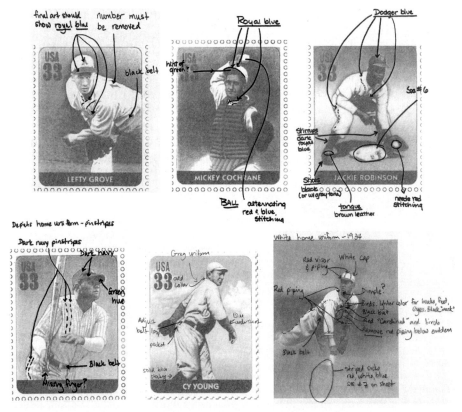

These annotations by PhotoAssist's baseball-uniform experts, made on tissue overlaid on Saffold's illustrations, indicate the lengths to which USPS went in striving for accuracy. The consultant assigned to Babe Ruth even noted that only four of the Babe's fingers are visible at the end of the bat. (Saffold added a little finger on his final version.)

212

lettering should be maroon instead of blue, the consultants said, and the artist revised them accordingly. Christy Mathewson's uniform and cap colors, also blue in the original version, were changed to brown. To Honus Wagner's collar, Saffold added a small red embroidered "P" for "Pittsburgh"; the detail can be seen on the stamp, but only with a magnifying glass. Because the consultant questioned the accuracy of Satchel Paige's belt loops, Jordan simply re-cropped the illustration above Paige's waist. (The art director commented that Paige, Honus Wagner and Tris Speaker were his favorite illustrations of the group.)

Meanwhile, Jordan was making typographical changes, as well. Because the stamps now were linked to the All Century Team rather than the Hall of Fame, the years of the players' induction into the Hall were eliminated. The typeface for the players' names is Kabel, as before, but Jordan changed the "USA" to a font called Berthold Akzidenz Grotesk, and the "33" is in ITC Century Bold Condensed. The "USA" and "33" are purple in color.

Shown here is one of Phil Jordan's 1993 trial layouts for the "Hall of Fame Heroes" pane, as it then was called, using artwork by Joseph Saffold. Individuals depicted on this pane that were dropped when the "Legends of Baseball" set finally was issued in 2000 were managers John McGraw (upper right) and Connie Mack (lower left), and umpire Bill Klem and player Paul Waner (bottom row). Also, the portraits of Cy Young (upper left) and Lou Gehrig (second row, right) were changed before the set was issued. Note the misspellings in this version of "Heroes" and Christy Mathewson's and Rogers Hornsby's last names.

The old header, with the title "Hall of Fame Heroes/Cooperstown Collection" and the Hall of Fame logo, was replaced by a new one bearing the title "Legends of Baseball." The title is in the same typeface, Sports Script, that Don Trousdell had chosen for his "Hall of Fame Heroes" header. Jordan enhanced the font by adding yellow and red bands around the letters, using PhotoShop software. As per the Postal Service's agreement with Major League Baseball Properties, the new header also displays the All Century Team logo.

First-day Facts

S. David Fineman, a member of the USPS Board of Governors, dedicated the stamps in a ceremony at International Plaza in Atlanta, Georgia. The event was held in conjunction with what USPS described as the "Club MLB Road Show Presented by Jif Smooth Sensations" and with Major League Baseball's 2000 All-Star Week, which concluded July 11 with the 71st All-Star Game at Atlanta's Turner Field.

Also participating in the dedication ceremony were Henry (Hank) Aaron, an Atlanta Braves executive, member of both the National Baseball Hall of Fame and the Major League Baseball All Century Team and holder of the major league career home-run record of 755; Kathy Francis, vice president for marketing of Major League Baseball; and Marjorie M. Brown, Atlanta's postmaster.

Honored guests were: for the Babe Ruth Estate, Julia Ruth Stevens, Tom Stevens, Ron Tellefsen and Brent Stevens; for the Josh Gibson family, Josh Gibson Jr. and Shawn Gibson; for the George Sisler family, Dorothy Sisler and Rick Sisler; for the Lou Gehrig family, George Pollack and Dorothy Pollack; for the Rogers Hornsby family, Rogers Hornsby 3d, Rogers Hornsby 4th and Ronna Hornsby; for the Jackie Robinson family, Rachel Robinson and Sonya Pankey; for the Roberto Clemente family, Roberto Clemente Jr. and Luis Clemente; for the Pie Traynor family, Michael Dale Helmer and Robert Helmer; for the Honus Wagner family, Leslie A. Blair; for the Dizzy Dean estate, Father William Cantrell; for the Walter Johnson family, Carolyn Johnson Thomas and Henry (Hank) Thomas; for the Christy Mathewson family, Laura Peck; for the Ty Cobb family, Shirley E. Cobb; for the Satchel Paige family, Warren Paige and Pam O'Neal; for the Lefty Grove family, Wayne Craig.

Also, Mrs. Billye Aaron, wife of Hank Aaron; Jim Hummerstone, director of licensing for Major League Baseball; James "Red" Moore, former Negro Leagues player; Joseph Saffold, the stamps' illustrator; John Kelly, president of Expedited and Package Services for USPS; Anderson Hodges Jr., Atlanta District manager for USPS; and James C. Tolbert Jr., USPS executive director, stamp services.

The earliest-known use of a Legends of Baseball stamp was on a cover machine-canceled Los Angeles, California, June 19, 17 days before the official first day of issue. The stamp depicts Honus Wagner.

$11.75 SPACE ACHIEVEMENT AND EXPLORATION SOUVENIR PANE

Date of Issue: July 7, 2000

Catalog Number: Scott 3412

Colors: magenta, yellow, cyan, black, plus hologram

First-Day Cancel: Anaheim, California

First-Day Cancellations: 12,070

Format: Pane of 1, circular, with circular selvage. Hologram affixed. Printed with 4 other souvenir panes, all different, from same gravure printing cylinder manufactured by Southern Gravure. Also sold in uncut sheets containing all 5 panes.

Gum Type: water-activated

Overall Stamp Diameter: 1.778 inches; 45.16mm

Pane Diameter: 3.65 inches; 92.075mm

Uncut Sheet Size: 16 by 20 inches; 406.4 by 508mm

Perforations: 10¾ (APS rotary perforator)

Selvage Inscription: "SPACE ACHIEVEMENT AND EXPLORATION/ WORLD STAMP EXPO 2000."

Designer, Typographer and Art Director: Richard Sheaff of Scottsdale, Arizona

Hologram Designer: Fernando Catta-Preta of Charlottesville, Virginia

Stamp Manufacturing: Selvage printed for Sennett Security Products by American Packaging Corporation, Columbus, Wisconsin, on Rotomec gravure press. Hologram embossed by Wavefront Technologies, Paramount, California. Stamps finished by Unique Binders, Fredericksburg, Virginia.

Quantity Ordered: 1,695,000, including 305,000 in uncut sheets

Cylinder Number Detail: no cylinder numbers

Paper Supplier: Glatfelter/Ivex Corporation

Tagging: block tagged

$11.75 LANDING ON THE MOON SOUVENIR PANE

Date of Issue: July 8, 2000

Catalog Number: Scott 3413

Colors: magenta, yellow, cyan, black, plus hologram

First-Day Cancel: Anaheim, California

First-Day Cancellations: 11,639

Format: Pane of 1, horizontal. Hologram affixed. Printed with 4 other souvenir panes, all different, from same gravure printing cylinder manufactured by Southern Gravure. Also sold in uncut sheets containing all 5 panes.

Gum Type: water-activated

Overall Stamp Size: 1.96 by 1.41 inches; 49.78 by 35.81mm

Pane Size: 7.25 by 5 inches; 184.15 by 127mm

Uncut Sheet Size: 16 by 20 inches; 406.4 by 508mm

Perforations: 10½ (APS rotary perforator)

Selvage Inscription: "LANDING ON THE MOON"

Designer, Typographer and Art Director: Richard Sheaff of Scottsdale, Arizona

Stamp Manufacturing: Stamps printed for Sennett Security Products by American Packaging Corporation, Columbus, Wisconsin, on Rotomec gravure press. Hologram embossed by Wavefront Technologies, Paramount, California. Stamps finished by Unique Binders, Fredericksburg, Virginia.

Quantity Ordered: 1,695,000, including 305,000 in uncut sheets

Cylinder Number Detail: no cylinder numbers

Paper Supplier: Glatfelter/Ivex Corporation

Tagging: block tagged

$3.20 ESCAPING THE GRAVITY OF EARTH (2 DESIGNS) SOUVENIR PANE

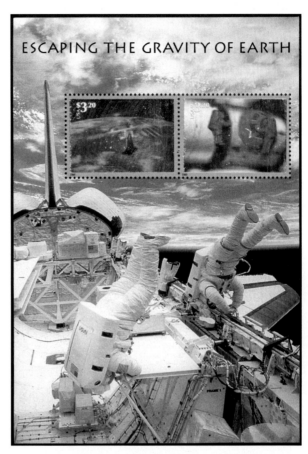

Date of Issue: July 9, 2000

Catalog Numbers: Scott 3411, full pane; Scott 3411a-3411b, stamps

Colors: magenta, yellow, cyan, black, plus holograms

First-Day Cancel: Anaheim, California

First-Day Cancellations: 22,321

Format: Pane of 2, horizontal. Holograms affixed. Printed with 4 other souvenir panes, all different, from same gravure printing cylinder manufactured by Southern Gravure. Also sold in uncut sheets containing all 5 panes.

Gum Type: water-activated

Overall Stamp Size: 1.96 by 1.41 inches; 49.78 by 35.81mm

Pane Size: 5 by 7.25 inches; 127 by 184.15mm

Uncut Sheet Size: 16 by 20 inches; 406.4 by 508mm

Perforations: 10½ (APS rotary perforator)

Selvage Inscription: "ESCAPING THE GRAVITY OF EARTH"

Designer, Typographer and Art Director: Richard Sheaff of Scottsdale, Arizona

Stamp Manufacturing: Stamps printed for Sennett Security Products by American Packaging Corporation, Columbus, Wisconsin, on Rotomec gravure press. Holograms embossed by Wavefront Technologies, Paramount, California. Stamps finished by Unique Binders, Fredericksburg, Virginia.

Quantity Ordered: 1,695,000, including 305,000 in uncut sheets

Cylinder Number Detail: no cylinder numbers

Paper Supplier: Glatfelter/Ivex Corporation

Tagging: block tagged

60¢ PROBING THE VASTNESS OF SPACE (6 DESIGNS) SOUVENIR PANE

Date of Issue: July 10, 2000

Catalog Numbers: Scott 3409, pane of 6; 3409a-f, stamps

Colors: magenta, yellow, cyan, black

First-Day Cancel: Anaheim, California

First-Day Cancellations: 296,252

Format: Pane of 6, horizontal. Printed with 4 other souvenir panes, all different, from same gravure printing cylinder manufactured by Southern Gravure. Also sold in uncut sheets containing all 5 panes.

Gum Type: water-activated

Overall Stamp Size: 1.56 by 0.99 inches; 39.62 by 25.14mm

Pane Size: 7.25 by 5 inches; 184.15 by 127mm

Uncut Sheet Size: 16 by 20 inches; 406.4 by 508mm

Perforations: 10½ by 11 (APS rotary perforator)

Selvage Inscription: "PROBING THE VASTNESS OF SPACE"

Designer, Typographer and Art Director: Richard Sheaff of Scottsdale, Arizona

Photographers: David Nunuk, Photo Researchers; Roger H. Ressmeyer,

Corbis; David Parker, Photo Researchers; John Bedke, Huntington Library

Artist: Vincent Di Fate, National Geographic Society

Stamp Manufacturing: Stamps printed for Sennett Security Products by American Packaging Corporation, Columbus, Wisconsin, on Rotomec gravure press. Stamps finished by Unique Binders, Fredericksburg, Virginia.

Quantity Ordered: 1,695,000, including 305,000 in uncut sheets

Cylinder Number Detail: no cylinder numbers

Paper Supplier: Glatfelter/Ivex Corporation

Tagging: block tagged

$1 EXPLORING THE SOLAR SYSTEM (5 DESIGNS) SOUVENIR PANE

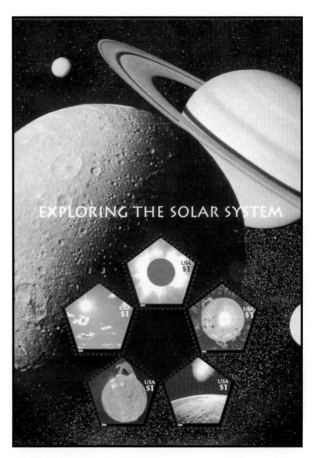

Date of Issue: July 11, 2000

Catalog Numbers: Scott 3410, full pane; 3410a-3410e, stamps

Colors: magenta, yellow, cyan, black

First-Day Cancel: Anaheim, California

First-Day Cancellations: 49,500

Format: Pane of 5, pentagonal, arranged around pentagonal label. Printed with 4 other souvenir panes, all different, from same gravure printing cylinder manufactured by Southern Gravure. Also sold in uncut sheets containing all 5 panes.

Gum Type: water-activated

Overall Stamp Size, Each Side: 0.8125 inch; 20.630mm

Pane Size: 5.00 by 7.25 inches; 127.00 by 184.15mm

Uncut Sheet Size: 16 by 20 inches; 406.4 by 508.0mm

Perforations: 10¾ (APS rotary perforator)

Selvage Inscription: "EXPLORING THE SOLAR SYSTEM"

Designer, Typographer and Art Director: Richard Sheaff of Scottsdale, Arizona

Photographers: Dan McCoy, Rainbow; Craig Aurness, Corbis

Artist: Jim Lamb

Stamp Manufacturing: Stamps printed for Sennett Security Products by American Packaging Corporation, Columbus, Wisconsin, on Rotomec gravure press. Stamps finished by Unique Binders, Fredericksburg, Virginia.

Quantity Ordered: 1,695,000, including 305,000 in uncut sheets

Cylinder Number Detail: no cylinder numbers

Paper Supplier: Glatfelter/Ivex Corporation

Tagging: block tagged

The Souvenir Panes

World Stamp Expo 2000, the second international stamp show to be sponsored by the U.S. Postal Service, ran from July 7 through 16, 2000, at the Anaheim, California, Convention Center. As USPS had done with its first show, World Stamp Expo 89 in Washington, D.C., it celebrated the event by issuing some innovative philatelic material.

This time, the main course for collectors was a set of five souvenir panes comprising 15 stamps, all with space themes. Grouped under the title Space Achievement and Exploration, they incorporated several U.S. postal firsts:

• The first U.S. stamps bearing holograms — two-dimensional pictures that, when viewed at the proper angle and in the proper light, appear to have three dimensions and display iridescent colors.

• The first circular U.S. stamp.

• The first pentagonal U.S. stamps.

• The first printing of five different issues from one plate.

Collectors could buy the five panes individually, but they also could purchase uncut press sheets made from the single printing plate, with each posterlike sheet containing one specimen of each pane.

All the stamps carried denominations higher than the 33¢ first-class rate then in effect, and the total face value of the five souvenir panes (or of a single uncut sheet) was $38.50. The panes and their subjects were as follows:

• Space Achievement and Exploration. A circular pane containing a single circular stamp with a hologram. The face value, $11.75, met the then-

The five Space Achievement and Exploration panes also were available to collectors in uncut press sheets. Each sheet contained one specimen of each pane.

prevailing Express Mail rate. This is the "title pane," bearing the inscriptions explaining the subject and purpose of the press sheet.

• Landing on the Moon. A rectangular pane containing a single rectangular hologram stamp. The stamp is of the standard jumbo Express Mail-Priority Mail size and also has a face value of $11.75.

• Escaping the Gravity of Earth. A rectangular pane containing two jumbo-size rectangular stamps with holograms. The face value of each stamp is $3.20, to cover the Priority Mail rate then in effect.

• Exploring the Solar System. A rectangular pane containing five small pentagonal stamps arranged in a pentagonal pattern. Each stamp has a face value of $1, a widely used denomination.

• Probing the Vastness of Space. A rectangular pane containing six commemorative-size stamps, each with a face value of 60¢, which covered the international first-class letter rate.

The panes are arranged on the press sheets with the circular Space Achievement and Exploration pane at the center and the rectangular panes in each of the four corners. There are no plate numbers or other marginal markings on the press sheets.

Sennett Security Products printed the sheets and the 11 non-hologram

225

stamps by the gravure process on paper pregummed with conventional water-activated adhesive. The four hologram stamps, which consist of thin pieces of polyester film, were embossed by Wavefront Technologies of Paramount, California. After perforating the printed sheets, Sennett affixed the hologram stamps within the appropriate spaces, which are round in the case of the Space Achievement and Exploration stamp, rectangular for the others.

The ambitious issue was conceived in 1997 by Richard Arvonio, then the Postal Service's manager of international and direct marketing, who wanted a philatelic blockbuster with a space theme to accompany World Stamp Expo 2000.

To implement Arvonio's plan, Richard Sheaff, art director and designer of the issue, worked closely with Terrence McCaffrey, head of stamp design for USPS, and Catherine Caggiano, USPS manager of stamp acquisition and distribution.

"Rick [Arvonio] said he wanted to take this to the next level and do something that had never been done before," said McCaffrey. "He wanted to have different elements that could all be put together in one big sheet.

"Not being a designer, he had trouble interpreting what he wanted, so Dick and I sat down and talked for a long time and tried to get an idea of what he was after. He wanted a marketing tool, with stamps that could be used but still promote the stamp show, and he wanted to make it something entirely different — to explore cutting-edge technology things. He wanted to do a hologram, and add other bells and whistles.

"We had reached that point in our technology where we could do a hologram stamp. Up until then we hadn't been able to, because we didn't meet environmental standards. Hologram materials weren't biodegradable. But with the new technology we found a way of doing them."

Other countries had been issuing hologram stamps since Austria pioneered the format in 1989. In fact, USPS also had produced holographic postage — but in the form of stamped envelopes, with the hologram showing through a die-cut window in the envelope corner. The first of these, a 25¢ envelope issued at World Stamp Expo 89 in 1989, depicted an imaginary space station.

Out of the planning talks among Arvonio, McCaffrey and Sheaff came the idea of a sheet with four quadrants that could be cut into individual souvenir panes but also could be kept together as a unit. "That basic concept became the basis for this whole development," McCaffrey said.

Sheaff recalled that he began "doodling around with some different things," trying to settle on what the four corners of the sheet should represent. Ultimately, it was his idea to have the individual panes feature different stages in space exploration.

As Sheaff developed the idea, the Earth itself, the home of humans and the starting point for all their ventures into space, is at the center. The lower-right pane represents learning to escape Earth's gravitational pull and send missions into orbit. (At the suggestion of the National Aeronau-

Before the decision was made to divide the press sheet into individual-pane quadrants, Richard Sheaff assembled what he called "a very quick, very rough" poster onto which individual stamps, once they were selected and designed, would be superimposed.

tics and Space Administration, the subject of this pane, which originally was intended to be one of NASA's fleet of space shuttles, was changed to the international space station then under construction.)

The upper-left pane celebrates the Apollo missions that took men to the moon. The lower-left pane carries the theme farther out into space by recognizing the exploration of the solar system — the sun and the planets that orbit it — while the upper-right pane features the probing of deep space with various kinds of telescopes.

As early as the spring of 1997, USPS officials let it be known they were planning a hologram stamp. In its original announcement of the Space Achievement panes in 1999, USPS said it would include only one hologram, on the circular Express Mail stamp. In April 2000, however, the agency disclosed that there would be three additional hologram stamps, as well. Stamp acquisition manager Caggiano said the decision to increase the number of holograms was made in response to collector requests.

"We had been asked over and over by our customers when we would issue a hologram stamp," she told *Stamp Collector.* "Of course, in addition to the technological challenges, there is a cost factor. ... We felt that the special [World Stamp Expo] 2000 issue lent itself well to the need for a high-value stamp. We followed suit with several world postal administrations by issuing our first holographic stamps as high values.

"Once the prepress work was completed — which presents its own set

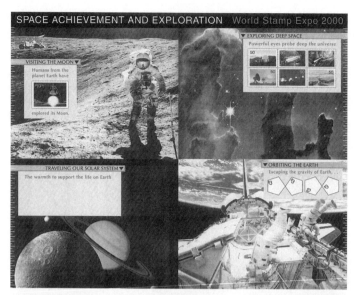

Shown here are two preliminary layouts for the press sheet. Both layouts incorporate a box within each souvenir pane to enclose the stamps, and differ in numerous other ways from the issued sheet. On the first layout (top), which consists of four panes, the sheet includes a header with a title and a plug for World Stamp Expo 2000. Each pane contains a line or lines of expository information, and the pentagonal stamps are allocated to the Escaping the Gravity of Earth pane. On the second layout, a circular fifth souvenir pane, with the word SPACE superimposed upon it, has been added at the center of the sheet. At the urging of the Citizens' Stamp Advisory Committee's design subcommittee, and one member, Meredith Davis, in particular, Sheaff simplified the design by abandoning the interior boxes surrounding the stamp.

of challenges for each new stamp — we broached the issue of adding the holograms. We worked closely with Dick Sheaff to determine which elements of the designs would best adapt themselves to three-dimensional holography."

Sheaff added: "I originally suggested that all the stamps be issued at the first-class rate. But for such an expensive product — one that was to include the use of holograms — that just wasn't feasible."

Among other "bells and whistles" proposed for the sheet was the use of foil paper on a portion of it. The shiny paper could show through in appropriate places, officials thought, and give an impression of twinkling stars. The plan was "foiled," McCaffrey said, because after much experimentation the printers were unable to get good ink coverage. "We had to go back to using regular paper," he said. "We walked away from it with much frustration."

In addition to the Space Achievement sheet, Arvonio wanted a commemorative stamp that would be issued several months ahead of World Stamp Expo 2000 for advance publicity, similar to stamps that had provided early promotion for World Stamp Expo 89, World Columbian Stamp Expo 92 and other philatelic shows. However, he was persuaded to settle for a line of type in the selvage of the Edwin Hubble space pane of five varieties issued April 10, 2000, that read: "Visit World Stamp Expo 2000, Anaheim, California, July 7-16, 2000."

Azeezaly S. Jaffer, vice president of public affairs and communications for USPS and former manager of Stamp Services, called the space souvenir panes "the most prestigious product that we will put out" in 2000.

"When I came to the stamps job," he told *Stamp Collector*'s Fred Baumann, "part of what I challenged my people to do was to ask the question 'How can we make the stamp program better? How can we produce stamps that have both uniqueness and collectibility?' " Part of the answer to those questions, he suggested, were the Space panes.

However, the high face value of the panes drew criticism from collectors. In a letter to Jaffer dated December 10, 1999, Peter P. McCann, president of the American Philatelic Society, wrote:

"We recogize that new formats and new technology require higher face values to both cover costs and assure a reasonable profit. But issues such as these have a tremendous potential to hook the interest of new adherents to the hobby, and the high face values will discourage that. We hope that in the future such items will be more affordable so that a broader range of our members and other collectors new to the hobby can save and enjoy them."

McCann also urged Jaffer to make the space panes widely available — "at a minimum through all of the postal store outlets" — and to keep them on sale "for a significant period of time beyond World Stamp Expo 2000." The Postal Service complied with those requests and, after a few months, went beyond them.

Originally, the panes were sold only at postal stores and post office philatelic centers and by mail from Stamp Fulfillment Services in Kansas City, Missouri, while the uncut press sheets were available only from Kansas City and postal stores. In its October 19, 2000, *Postal Bulletin*, however, USPS announced that as of October 5 the souvenir panes could be purchased at post offices, and that uncut press sheets were available at philatelic centers.

The change of plans came about because of disappointing sales. Although USPS initially had ordered 2,000,000 of each pane — 1,695,000 to be sold individually and 305,000 in the form of uncut press sheets — as of October, 2000, fewer than 125,000 of each pane and only 45,915 press sheets had been sold. The items were still on sale in 2002.

Because the stamps had unique features, collectors reported some unique problems in dealing with them. Removing the circular Space Achievement and Exploration stamp from its souvenir pane without damaging the perforations was extremely difficult, inasmuch as the stamp could not be folded and refolded along the perfs beforehand, which is what collectors customarily do before separating stamps with normal straight sides. The fact that the stamp had a face value of $11.75 raised the stakes considerably. Some collectors also reported problems in removing the pentagon-shaped $1 Exploring the Solar System stamps from their pane, although this could be done by patiently folding them along the five sides of each stamp.

Collectors of used stamps discovered that they had to use extreme caution in removing hologram stamps from covers. Soaking the stamps in water long enough to cause them to float from the envelope tended to cause the holographic overlays to separate from the perforated stamp paper to which they were attached.

Sandra Lane, president of Sennett Security Products, explained that the holograms were affixed to the stamps with the same kind of water-soluble barrier between the overlay and the stamp paper that is used on U.S. self-adhesive stamps to enable collectors to soak them from envelopes. The reason, Lane said, was to ensure that the stamps were environmentally friendly. If standard pressure-sensitive adhesive without a barrier had been used to affix the holograms to the stamps, any piece of paper bearing the stamps would have been unrecyclable.

However, collectors were able to deal with the problem. *Linn's Stamp News* associate editor Charles Snee, after receiving a tip from a reader, successfully removed a $3.20 Escaping the Gravity of Earth stamp from a Priority Mail envelope by cutting off the corner of the envelope in a way that allowed him to stand the paper upright in a cup. He added enough water to the cup to bring the level in contact with the envelope paper but not the stamp itself. Capillary action then drew the water into and through the envelope paper. After about 90 minutes, Snee reported, he lifted the still-intact stamp easily and cleanly from the clipping. A trace of the water-activated gum remaining on the back of the stamp itself was removed by gentle wiping with a damp sponge.

RETURNED FOR POSTAGE

Some USPS personnel didn't recognize the Space Achievement and Exploration panes as valid postage, as shown by this close-up of a cover bearing an $11.75 Express Mail stamp that didn't make it to its destination.

Another problem, *Linn's* reported, was that some Postal Service personnel didn't recognize the unorthodox-looking labels as valid stamps. One reader told of getting back his cover franked with the circular Space Achievement and Exploration stamp with the imprint: "RETURNED FOR POSTAGE."

The Designs

In determining what images would be used on the stamps and the selvage, Sheaff examined hundreds of photographs. "PhotoAssist [the Postal Service's research firm] sent me things, I went on the Internet and got things, NASA sent me things — it was a variety of sources," he said. "It was hard to find good ones. We kept looking, and eventually we found a set that covered the bases in terms of technology and that I thought worked."

To develop the first U.S. holographic stamps, USPS and Sennett Security Products called on Fernando Catta-Preta, a holographer and computer animator who is president of Trace Holographic Art & Design of Charlottesville, Virginia. Catta-Preta began working in holography in 1980 and, as a resident of Sao Paulo, Brazil, in 1989, developed the world's second holographic stamp, an emblem on a souvenir sheet issued by Brazil to commemorate Sao Paulo's 20th International Art Biennial (Scott 2210).

"They needed somebody who understood holography to act as a designer and a liaison between the designers at the Postal Service and getting the thing into holographic form," Catta-Preta said.

"There are certain things a hologram can do that regular printing can't. I worked with Dick Sheaff, taking his designs and adapting them, as it were, to optimize them for holography. Dick would give me a concept, and over several months I would suggest things to him, having in mind not only his design but also the several different effects only holography can offer and that could be used selectively to enhance his ideas.

"Sandra Lane [of Sennett Security Products] was basically the person I worked with on the production side. She suggested that we use these stamps as a showcase for everything holography can do. So instead of making four stamps using the same technique, Sandy was trying to stimulate us to use as many different techniques as possible, and take this opportunity — the first holographic stamps in the United States — to showcase the state of the holographic art.

"So, not only did we vary techniques, but we also incorporated something else holography can do very well — security. ... We embedded microtext into the stamps, in order to show holography's potential not only aesthetically but also as a security device."

Catta-Preta did his preliminary designing, including computer work, at his offices in Charlottesville. The holographic images were created at two companies specializing in this field. The hologram that depicts the space-walking astronauts was shot at Blue Ridge Holographics, also in Charlottesville, and the other three were made at Chromagem, in Youngstown, Ohio. Finally, the holograms themselves were embossed by Foilmark.

Holograms are possible because of a property of laser light known as coherence, which is best understood as light that is only one wavelength of the visible spectrum and possesses a high degree of organization.

When a hologram is made, the laser shoots a beam of light that is split in two. The two beams each pass through a series of lenses, prisms and mirrors. One beam, the object beam, illuminates the object or scene being imaged. The other beam, the reference beam, illuminates the film plate on which the hologram will be recorded. Some of the light shining on the object will be reflected toward the film, where it will interfere with light shining directly on the film. This interference pattern is recorded in the light-sensitive emulsion of the film.

A hologram can be made to appear as a three-dimensional image floating in space by illuminating the developed film with a laser from the same angle as the original reference beam. The interference pattern recorded on the film bends some of the light, striking it into a re-creation of the pattern of light that originally came from the object beam, because of a property of light known as diffraction. The reconstructed object beam contains

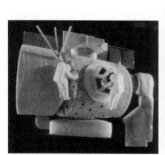 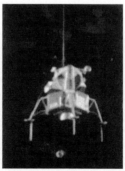 

These are enlarged photos of the models that were made for three of the hologram stamps. The models are the same size as the stamp images for which they were created. In the end, the model of the full space station proved too difficult to work with, and a computer-generated image was used to make the hologram. (Photos courtesy of Sennett Security Products).

all the original information it once carried, so the viewer sees the object in full three-dimensionality, just as if it were actually there.

To create a "white-light viewable rainbow hologram," or "H2," on foil, viewable in ordinary, or white, light, the manufacturer makes a second hologram from the first. The emulsion is developed, rendering the interference pattern as a series of ultra-fine ridges. "We take that plate and electroplate it," Catta-Preta said. "We spray it with silver and put it in a nickel bath. From that plate, we then remove a nickel shim, which is basically a shiny nickel stamp that has all the 3-D information on it. That shim is what we will use to print the hologram.

"There are different techniques for embossing, but the simplest is this: The shim goes on a cylinder, and with heat and pressure the image is embossed into silver Mylar, which is silvered polyester. We call it printing without ink, because once the hologram comes out you'll get the colors of the rainbow, but there's no ink involved. The color is coming from the light that illuminates the hologram, which is acting like a prism."

All four stamps were embossed at the same time by Foilmark and the rolls were shipped to Sennett's processing plant in Fredericksburg, Virginia. Here, the individual stamps were coated with adhesive, die-cut from the rolls and applied to the printed and perforated web in the designated locations at high speed. The web then was sheeted out into press sheets and cut into panes.

LANDING ON THE MOON. This pane's single stamp was the first of the four holograms on the sheet to be created. It depicts a lunar lander hovering on a plume of flame a few feet over the moon's surface, against the symbolic backdrop of an immense moon rising over the horizon. The lander is three-dimensional; the viewer can see "around" it by tilting the stamp from side to side. When the stamp is tilted up and down, the flame seems to burst out of the lander's rocket nozzle and change color, from a bright red-orange to a deep blue-violet, while reflecting vividly off the underside of the lander. The moonscape and the typography, "$11.75 USA," also change colors as the stamp is moved.

"Traditionally, when you make a hologram, you use one of two techniques," Catta-Preta said. "One way is to work with flat graphics on several planes, and that's done by shooting flat art with a few millimeters' difference in depth. Most of the holograms you see, such as the one on your MasterCard credit card, are done in this fashion. The three-dimensionality comes from the difference in the depth.

"The other technique is to use a model, and make what we call a truly 3-D hologram. The dove on the Visa credit card, for example, was actually shot from a tiny model of a dove. The model has to be exact size. You can't enlarge or reduce in holography; you can't make a large dove and shoot it small, because of the optical aberrations that occur, the distortions.

"[For Landing on the Moon,] we decided to do a combination of 3-D sculpture and 2-D artwork — with a little bit of animation to boot. I work with different sculptors around the world, but one of the best is Allen Suffield of Aztec Model Makers in England. He made the plastic sculpture of the lunar lander that you see on the stamp. It's actually that size.

"The deeper the hologram is, the better the light source has to be for it to be sharp. Since this was a stamp, we figured most people weren't going to have it under a perfect light at all times. So we used a technique called foreshortening or forced perspective to make sure our models suggested more depth than they actually had. That way, the hologram remains sharp under diversified lighting conditions. It becomes 'illumination friendly,' we say. The lunar lander model actually was only a few millimeters deep."

The image of the moon rising over the horizon came from a black-and-white NASA photograph. "The picture actually is a whole moon that we put behind the photograph of the mountain range," Catta-Preta said. "The mountain range and the moon have depth in relation to each other, but they're actually flat pieces of art." The plume of flame was created by using what Catta-Preta described as a traditional technique in two-dimensional animation called color chasing or color cycling.

The microprinting on the hologram, visible through a good magnifying glass, consists of the letters "USPS," arranged vertically, on the door near the center of the lunar lander. Microprinting was added "not so much to deter counterfeiting, but to show the security possibilities," Catta-Preta said. "The hologram itself is a security device."

The selvage of the Landing on the Moon pane, printed by Sennett in conventional four-color gravure, bears a NASA photo from the Apollo 16 mission in April 1972. Lunar module pilot Charles M. Duke Jr. is standing on the moon, collecting soil samples at the rim of Plum crater near the Descartes landing site. A lunar roving vehicle is visible in the distance, in the upper-left corner of the picture. The photo was taken by the mission commander, John W. Young. The inscription "LANDING ON THE MOON," in white Lithos capitals, is dropped out of the photograph above the stamp.

SPACE ACHIEVEMENT AND EXPLORATION. The second holographic image to be created was the circular one for the Space Achievement and Exploration stamp, featuring Earth as it might be seen from outer space, with North America and most of South America facing the viewer.

The only usable photographs available from NASA showed the Eastern Hemisphere, with Africa and the Indian Ocean visible through a swirl of clouds. These were used to create the stamp design that USPS first released to the public. But Sheaff and other officials wanted the United States portion of the globe to be prominent on the stamp.

"We didn't have any photographic reference, so we had to use another

234

technique," said Catta-Preta. "We couldn't work with an actual model.

"I generated a 3-D model of the Earth on the computer, as seen from the angle we wanted. I did it in layers. We have a layer of wispy transparent clouds that you can see through, and then we have the blue water and the green and brown land masses. If you were to see Earth from space, the colors wouldn't be that lively, but Dick wanted me to force the colors, as an artistic decision, to convey the beauty that there must be in seeing such a thing from space.

"I rendered the computer model by using what in 3-D terms we call 'bump maps' and 'texture maps' ... I used bump maps to make the mountain ranges look higher than the rest of the land, and texture maps to make the Earth seem covered with forests and the ocean rippling with waves. ...

"Plus, this whole thing had to rotate."

Using a proprietary holographic technique, Catta-Preta and technicians at Chromagem combined stereography with holography and state-of-the-art computer animation ("imagine a virtual camera floating out in space looking at the Earth and shooting 100 frames as the Earth rotates on its axis from point one to point 100"). The ultimate result was a convex-looking globe that appears to rotate slightly if the stamp is tilted from side to side, with the west coast of Africa and Europe emerging and retreating in the process.

This hologram also contains the microprinted letters "USPS," but the microprinting is of a more secure kind that is extremely difficult to see even with a strong magnifying glass. According to Catta-Preta, the microprinting was incorporated on only two or three of the photographic frames and thus can be seen only under very specific conditions, with a point-source light coming from about a 45-degree angle and the hologram tilted horizontally so that the blue color is predominant. The letters are "east of the top of Brazil over the ocean, just above one of the cloud formations," Catta-Preta said.

On the pane selvage, the inscription "SPACE ACHIEVEMENT AND EXPLORATION," in Lithos capitals, curves along the top part of the green outer ring, while "WORLD STAMP EXPO 2000" balances it at the bottom. Next comes a star-flecked black ring extending to the edge of the hologram and containing the stamp's perforations. In an earlier version of the design, the word "Space" was laid horizontally across the selvage above the stamp, in bold yellow letters. However, CSAC and the design team found this placement of the word unattractive.

ESCAPING THE GRAVITY OF EARTH. The two hologram stamps depict the International Space Station that was then in the early construction stages. The first shows a space shuttle docking with the completed station as seen from some distance away in space. The second is a close-

 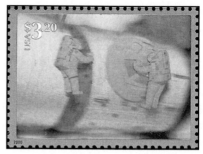

up of the station's cabin module, with two astronauts "standing" in space outside.

The design team worked closely with NASA to make sure the stamps depicted the latest configuration of the space station, because the details of its design were continually changing, right down to the shape of the exterior handles provided for space-walking astronauts.

"It was highly political," Catta-Preta said. "There were so many countries cooperating in designing the space station that if we left out one country's module or another, even though it would be just a tiny thing on the hologram, it would be a big problem.

"I even worked with the designer of the space suits to make sure all the patches on the astronauts were in the right place. We wanted this to be as authentic as possible."

On the first of the two holograms, the space station is shown in orbit, its eight sets of solar panels extended. Far below is the Earth, with Mexico's Yucatan peninsula in the foreground, while beyond it lie the Gulf of Mexico and, partly concealed by the station, the peninsula of Florida.

Catta-Preta originally intended to use another of Aztec Model Makers' models in creating his hologram, but, in his words, "the gods of holography reared their ugly heads."

The first problem was that the model arrived from England in pieces, and Catta-Preta had to glue it back together. Things got worse when the model was placed on the laser table at Blue Ridge Holographics and the object beam was directed at it.

Holography requires that the object be totally motionless. "There can be no vibrations from the ground, sound, heat from your body — anything," Catta-Preta said. "Although the model was wonderfully sculpted — again, with the forced perspective that would give it more apparent depth than it had — its solar panels, on a microscopic level, were acting like tiny tuning forks. They were vibrating. They were paper-thin and were reacting to differences in temperature. We couldn't for the life of us register them for the hologram.

"We tried letting the model spend the night on the table to see if the temperature would equal out and things would stabilize, but they didn't. I made an 'exoskeleton' out of a paperclip and tried gluing it behind the

236

solar panels so it wouldn't be visible, but that didn't solve the problem. The clock was ticking, and we were already nine or ten days over schedule with this last one."

After consulting Sandra Lane, Catta-Preta decided to abandon the model and create a computer-generated image with animation, as he had done with the Earth for the Space Achievement and Exploration stamp. Using a computer-generated model of the space station and the shuttle created by Marco Zambetti of NASA's Johnson Space Center, "I composited it into a scene featuring the station against a background of the Earth," Catta-Preta said. "Dick Sheaff had asked that it be a readily recognizable part of the United States, so Florida was chosen because of its characteristic shape." As a result, both the space station in the foreground and the clouds and surface features in the background seem to move in a subtle way when the stamp is moved.

"It turned out to be the best solution," Catta-Preta said. "Although the original physical model was fantastic, it was nowhere near as detailed as the computer-generated space station was."

Like the Space Achievement and Exploration hologram, which also was created using computer animation, this hologram has microprinting on two or three of the multiple photographic frames used to make it. According to Catta-Preta, if a point-source light is directed on the hologram at about a 45-degree angle and coming in from the left side (as opposed to directly above and at 45 degrees) and the stamp is tilted horizontally so the

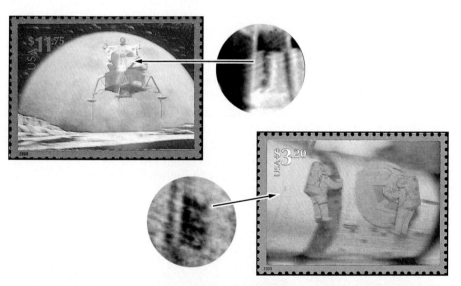

Microprinting on the Landing on the Moon hologram stamp consists of the letters "USPS," arranged vertically, on the door near the center of the lunar lander. The microprinting on only one of the Escaping the Gravity of Earth stamps is photographable: It is on the exterior of the space station module on the left, and also consists of the vertically arranged letters "USPS."

red color is dominant, the letters "USPS" can be seen through magnification "on the top right-hand corner of the Earth, close to the tip of the rightmost solar panel of the space station."

By contrast, the second hologram on the pane, depicting the two astronauts, was the easiest and quickest of all the holograms to make. It, too, was based on a shallow model by Aztec Model Makers, and in this case the model was usable. Aztec created the model by referring to computer drawings made by Catta-Preta, who in turn had based his drawings on plans furnished by NASA.

The image is in black and white, an "achromat," except for the glow in the cabin windows, "which was a little twist I added to give it color," Catta-Preta said. As on the other hologram stamps, the denomination and "USA" also are in colors that change with the viewing angle. The stamp's microprinting consists of the initials "USPS," arranged vertically, on the exterior of the cabin module on the left side.

The pane's vertically oriented selvage bears a photograph of astronauts David C. Leestma and Kathryn Sullivan at work in the open cargo bay of the *Challenger* space shuttle during an October 1984 mission, with a cloud-dappled blue Earth hanging above them. Although there is no "down" or "up" in space, the two astronauts are upside down relative to the viewer. The words "ESCAPING THE GRAVITY OF EARTH," in black Lithos capitals, are at the top of the pane.

PROBING THE VASTNESS OF SPACE. The six gravure-printed stamps on this pane depict various telescopes and other devices used by U.S. astronomers to observe the solar system and deep space. They are:

• An illustration of the Hubble Space Telescope by Vincent Di Fate for the National Geographic Society.

• A photograph by David Nunuk of some of the 27 dish antennae that make up the National Science Foundation's Very Large Array radio telescope on the Plains of San Agustin, west of Socorro, New Mexico. Each antenna is 25 meters across and weighs 235 tons. The dishes can be moved to various positions along the arms of a Y-shaped railway network. The data from all the dishes can be combined using interferometry techniques to produce a single detailed radio image.

• A photo, also by David Nunuk, of twin domes housing the optical and infrared telescopes at the Keck Observatory in Mauna Kea, Hawaii, seen

against a deep red sunset sky, with the constellation Orion dimly visible overhead. Each telescope has a 10-meter mirror made up of 36 hexagonal units mounted on a computer-controlled motor that makes tiny adjustments to keep astronomical objects in precise focus. The two telescopes can be used to observe the same object, with their signals combined by interferometry to obtain a more accurate image.

• A photo by Roger Resmeyer of optical telescopes at NSF's Cerro Tololo Inter-American Observatory east of La Serena, Chile. The domes are bathed in a pink light that also illuminates the horizon.

• A photo by John Bedke of the 100-inch Hooker optical telescope inside Mount Wilson Observatory, near Pasadena, California.

• An aerial photo by David Parker, using a fish-eye-lens camera, of the radio telescope at NSF's Arecibo Observatory in Puerto Rico. This radio telescope, with a 305-meter fixed dish that is the largest in the world, is located in a natural crater. The subreflector system with two mirrors, newly installed in 1997, is housed in a 90-ton movable dome receiver shown suspended 130 meters above the dish. It can send and receive signals to examine planets and asteroids and to analyze Earth's upper atmosphere. The upgrading of the observatory included installation of a 16-meter-high buffer screen around the dish and a new transmitter that increased its power by 20 times.

The selvage bears a digitally enhanced image from the Hubble Space Telescope showing the stellar nursery known as the Eagle Nebula. A more tightly cropped version of the same picture was shown on one of the five 33¢ stamps in the set honoring Edwin Powell Hubble that was issued the previous April 10. The words "PROBING THE VASTNESS OF SPACE," in white Lithos capitals, are dropped out of the photograph.

The stamps have dark blue borders running to the perforations. "In the beginning, there were no borders, and the selvage picture would have gone right up to the telescope picture," Sheaff said. "That was just too confusing visually. I didn't want that, but I didn't want to do white borders on the stamps because they would have been too bright and contrasty. So we picked a color that was dark but still gave us separation of the images."

Across the bottom of each stamp, in extremely small black type that is difficult to read against the dark blue borders, is a description of the depicted subject and the year date "2000." The type was added after the images were made public. The design team had decided that simply using the pictures without identification was insufficient.

"We needed [the type] there, but we could live without it on the other stamps, where there was a chance the holograms, if they were slightly out of place, would cover up the information," Sheaff said.

EXPLORING THE SOLAR SYSTEM. The five pentagon-shaped $1 stamps depict various aspects of the sun. Four were existing images: a photograph of a solar eclipse with corona, taken from a satellite and credited to Dan McCoy; a digitally restored NASA image of a sunrise as seen from space; an image of a solar eruption taken by Skylab December 19, 1973, and a photo from Earth of the sun in a partly cloudy sky, by photographer Craig Aurness. The fifth, a cutaway view of the sun, exposing its core, was commissioned by Sheaff from artist Jim Lamb, who had created similar artwork for a book on the sun published by the Smithsonian Institution.

Why pentagons? "I thought, why not, given that we were breaking other new ground with the circular stamp and the holograms," Sheaff said. "I had wanted to do a pentagonal stamp for a while. There was no reason not to — it didn't matter what size and shape the individual stamps were — so that's what we did."

The design concept originated with an idea Sheaff had illustrated early in the planning stage, before the total number of stamps and their denominations had been established. It consisted of a pane of 20 first-class-rate stamps, showing the sun as seen by different interpreters ranging from ancient cultures to modern science. Four of these image concepts ultimately were included on the finished pane.

The selvage depicts a NASA montage consisting of the ringed planet

Saturn and a few of its moons, with the heavily cratered Dione in the foreground, from images made by *Voyager 1* in November 1980. Sheaff originally had hoped to show the planets of the solar system in the selvage, but "there were a lot of problems with that, mainly because of the distances the planets are from each other and the difference in their sizes," he said. The inscription "EXPLORING THE SOLAR SYSTEM," in white Lithos capitals, is dropped out of the selvage image.

The four rectangular panes were trimmed on all four sides when they were extracted from the press sheet, with large areas of pictorial selvage cut away.

For the Landing on the Moon pane, the trimmed area consisted of an

The forerunner of the Exploring the Solar System pane was this concept illustrated by Richard Sheaff early in the planning stage, before the total number of stamps and their denominations had been determined. It consisted of a block of 20 first-class-rate stamps, showing the sun as seen by different interpreters ranging from ancient cultures to modern science. Four of the ways of showing the sun were retained on the finished pane.

241

additional three inches of selvage, displaying all of the astronaut's shadow on the lunar soil.

The Probing the Vastness of Space pane on the press sheet includes an additional 2⅛ inches of selvage above the stamps and another 2½ inches to the left. The additional selvage on the left includes a towering pillar of hydrogen dust and gas, as was shown on the Eagle Nebula stamp of the Edwin Powell Hubble set issued earlier in 2000. On the separated souvenir pane, only the extreme edge of this pillar is visible.

In the case of Exploring the Solar System, the approximately 3½ inches of selvage that was trimmed from the right side of the individual pane — but which remains on the press sheet — contains part of Saturn's rings, plus an additional moon.

The Escaping the Gravity of Earth pane lost 4½ inches of selvage on the left side, including a large part of the shuttle and the cloud-flecked Earth hanging overhead.

Errors and Freaks

An imperforate Exploring the Solar system pane, with no perfs around the sheet's five pentagonal $1 stamps, was purchased in August 2000 at the Radio City, New York City, postal store of USPS. The buyer was Vincent Cosenza, who found the pane in its shrink-wrapped packaging on display at the store along with several normal panes of the same issue and reported his find to *Linn's Stamp News*.

Numerous freak production varieties of the souvenir panes also were reported by collectors.

For example, two different collectors reported buying Space Achievement and Exploration panes that have normally placed circular hologram overlays in the center of the panes and partial holograms just to the right of, and slightly above, the normal holograms. These are eye-catching freaks, resembling an imminent total solar eclipse, with the moon about to pass in front of the sun.

Three other collectors reported purchasing uncut press sheets that are missing the circular hologram from the Space Achievement and Exploration portion. On each one, the area where the hologram should have appeared is perforated normally.

On another uncut press sheet, the Landing on the Moon hologram is missing from the normally perforated area of that portion of the sheet. On still another uncut sheet, two Landing on the Moon holograms are present, one in the correct position within the perforated boundaries, the other just to the right of the first.

Several freak examples of the Exploring the Solar System pane were reported. On one, a sliver of what looks like the hologram of the circular $11.75 Earth stamp shows on the top edge of the pane at the right side. Two others bear a partial hologram overlay from one of the two $3.20 Escaping the Gravity of Earth stamps, one on the upper-right side, the other on the upper left.

242

Shown here are two freak production varieties of the space souvenir sheet. A Space Achievement and Exploration sheet bears a partial circular hologram overlay just to the right of the hologram overlay that is positioned normally in the center of the sheet. And a Landing on the Moon sheet, pictured inside its shrink-wrap packaging, has a complete additional hologram overlay just to the right of the normal stamp.

First-day Facts

All five first-day ceremonies were held at World Stamp Expo in the Anaheim Convention Center.

The dedicating officials were: Space Achievement and Exploration, July 7, Postmaster General William J. Henderson; Landing on the Moon, July 8, Tirso del Junco of the USPS Board of Governors; Escaping the Gravity of Earth, July 9, John Wargo, USPS vice president for strategic marketing; Probing the Vastness of Space, July 10, Benjamin Paul Ocasio, USPS vice president for diversity development; Exploring the Solar System, July 11, Deborah K. Willhite, USPS senior vice president for government relations and public policy. July 11 also was the issue date for the uncut press sheet.

Principal speakers at the ceremonies were: Space Achievement and Exploration, astronauts Sally Ride and Marsha Ivins and USPS Governor Tirso del Junco; Landing on the Moon, Walter M. "Wally" Schirra, one of the original Mercury astronauts, and Marsha Ivins; Escaping the Gravity of Earth, David C. Leestma, deputy director of engineering for the Lyndon B. Johnson Space Center in Houston, Texas, who is one of the two astronauts depicted in the selvage of that sheet; Probing the Vastness of

Space, Paula Cleggett, NASA deputy associate administrator for public affairs, and Dr. Augustus Oemler Jr., director, Carnegie Observatories; Exploring the Solar System, William F. Readdy, deputy associate administrator for the space shuttle in NASA's Office of Space Flight, and Larry Dumas, deputy director of the Jet Propulsion Laboratory in Pasadena, California.

Honored guests at one or more of the ceremonies were Azeezaly S. Jaffer, USPS vice president for public affairs and communications; James C. Tolbert Jr., USPS executive director, stamp services; Dickey B. Rustin of USPS, director, World Stamp Expo 2000; Richard Sheaff, designer of the souvenir sheets; John Hotchner, a member of CSAC; David P. Shapiro, Santa Ana District manager for USPS; Robert C. Gillis, USPS senior plant manager at Santa Ana; and Larry A. Webster, postmaster of Anaheim. Robert E. Lamb, executive director of the American Philatelic Society, gave the welcome at the July 10 ceremony, and Jackson Taylor, president of the American Stamp Dealers Association, welcomed the audience July 11.

33¢ STAMPIN' THE FUTURE (4 DESIGNS)

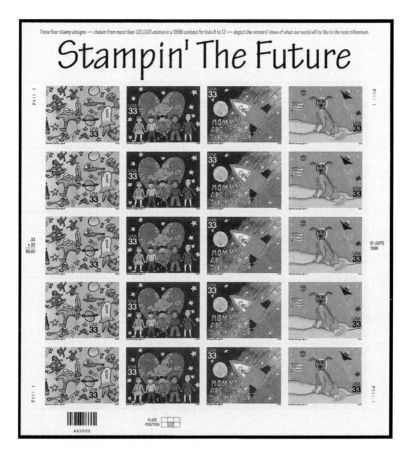

Date of Issue: July 13, 2000

Catalog Numbers: Scott 3414-3417, stamps; 3417a, horizontal strip of 4

Colors: black, cyan, magenta, yellow, red (PMS 187)

First-Day Cancel: Anaheim, California

First-Day Cancellations: 294,434

Format: Pane of 20, horizontal, 4 across, 5 down. Offset printing plates of 120 (10 across, 12 around).

Gum Type: self-adhesive

Overall Stamp Size: 1.560 by 1.225 inches; 39.624 by 31.115mm

Pane Size: 7.734 by 7.115 inches; 196.443 by 180.721mm

Perforations: 11¼ (die-cut simulated perforations)

Selvage Inscription: "These four stamp designs — chosen from more than 120,000 entries in a 1998 contest for kids 8 to 12 — depict the winners'

views of what our world will be like in the next millennium./Stampin' The
Future."

Selvage Markings: "©USPS/1999" ".33/x20/$6.60" "PLATE POSITION" and
diagram. Universal Product Code (UPC) "449900."

Illustrators: Zachary Canter, Morgan Hill, Sarah Lipsey, Ashley Young

Designer, Typographer and Art Director: Richard Sheaff of Scottsdale, Arizona

Modeler: Joseph Sheeran of Ashton-Potter (USA) Ltd., Williamsville, New
York

Stamp Manufacturing: Stamps printed by Ashton-Potter (USA) Ltd. on offset
portion of Stevens Variable Size Security Documents webfed 6-color offset, 3-color intaglio press. Stamps finished by Ashton-Potter.

Quantity Ordered: 100,000,000

Plate Number Detail: 5 plate numbers preceded by the letter P in selvage
next to each corner stamp

Plate Number Combinations Reported: P11111, P22222, P33333

Paper Supplier: Westvaco/Fasson

Tagging: block tagged

The Stamps

On July 13, at World Stamp Expo 2000 in Anaheim, California, the
Postal Service issued a block of four stamps with illustrations by four
American schoolchildren. Each stamp bore the name and age of its illustrator in small type at the bottom, a perquisite that USPS does not allow
to its adult artists.

The set of stamps, which USPS called "Stampin' the Future," depicts
whimsical visions of a space-centered future life for American families.
The pictures were chosen in a competition that attracted 120,000 participants, aged 8 to 12, who were asked to create stamp designs expressing
their dreams, hopes and visions of the coming millennium.

From these submissions, 110 children were named as finalists: two
from each state, the District of Columbia, Puerto Rico, the Virgin Islands,
Guam and overseas military addresses. The four winners were recom-

mended by members of the Citizens'
Stamp Advisory Committee's design subcommittee, and these recommendations
were accepted by Postmaster General
William J. Henderson.

The competition was reminiscent of a
similar one held a few years earlier. In
1995, USPS issued four environmentally
themed 32¢ stamps under the title "Kids
Care!" (Scott 1951-54) with designs cre-

246

The Postal Service sent special promotional packets to educators across the country, inviting children aged 8 through 12 to design a stamp for the Stampin' the Future block of four.

ated by youngsters who had won a contest sponsored by the Postal Service and McDonald's Corporation. Those four stamps were the first U.S. issue to include the name of the designers; Stampin' the Future was the second.

The Stampin' the Future stamps are semijumbo in size, with pressure-sensitive gum and die-cut simulated perforations. They were printed by the offset process by Ashton-Potter (USA) Ltd. and issued in panes of 20 with a header, or extra-wide decorative top selvage. Each of the four vertical rows contains five stamps with the same design.

Azeezaly S. Jaffer was manager of stamp services for USPS when the idea for the stamps "was born on a cocktail napkin on a flight between Los Angeles and Washington," he told *Stamp Collector's* Fred Baumann. "What better way to let the 21st century's dawning be depicted than by stamps showing what kids think about it?" he added.

Jaffer said he then sat down with Dickey Rustin, World Stamp Expo 2000 director, and fleshed out the idea of a global kids' convention in which all Universal Postal Union nations would be invited to take part. Twenty-seven agreed to do so, and 17 of them were represented at the World Kids' Congress at World Stamp Expo 2000. Among the countries that held Stampin' the Future contests, and issued blocks of four stamps bearing the winning designs, were Aruba, Argentina, Brazil, Canada, China, the Faroes, France, Gibraltar, Hong

Kong, Iceland, Ireland, Israel, San Marino, Singapore, Switzerland, Suriname and Uruguay.

Jaffer's plan first was disclosed to the public in the November 3, 1997, issue of *Newsweek* and confirmed shortly afterward by USPS. The U.S. competition took place between August 24 and October 17, 1998, and USPS unveiled the winning designs August 22, 1999, in Beijing, China, one day before that city played host to the Universal Postal Union's 22nd Universal Postal Congress.

Their young artists were Zachary Canter, of Kailua, Hawaii, who was 9 when he entered the contest; Morgan Hill, of Montclair, New Jersey, who also was 9; Sara Lipsey, 11, of Memphis, Tennessee; and Ashley Young, 11, of Sandy, Utah. Besides the celebrity, each received a Pentium-class computer system, complete with a CD-ROM and a printer. Each also received a trip for four to the Spring Postage Stamp Mega-Event show in New York City in April 2000 and to World Stamp Expo 2000 for the stamps' dedication.

Terrence McCaffrey, head of stamp design for USPS, was a member of a panel that had screened the submissions and narrowed the number down to 110. When he met with the CSAC design subcommittee before it took on the job of choosing the final four, he told the members he had been "a bit disappointed at the quality of the entries and the lack of originality."

"The rest of the [screening] panel was disappointed, too," McCaffrey recalled. "We analyzed it, and realized what had happened.

"When the criteria were given out, and entry blanks sent out, suggestions were made to the contestants: 'Give us examples of what life will be like in the future, for space travel, for kids, for home life, that sort of thing.' The kids read those instructions literally as 'OK, I have to do space travel, I have to do what my home is going to look like in the future.'

"Fifty to sixty percent of all the entries were space travel, showing rocket ships. Then it got into homes of the future — futuristic glass homes.

"The panel also noted something that I had seen right away but was attuned to, having worked with kids in art classes. The older kids get, the more inhibited they are, because they listen to the teacher more. The younger kids are less inhibited; they just draw what they want to draw. You could see that the younger contestants, 8, 9 and 10, were more creative and free; the older ones were more inhibited and structured."

The 110 finalists, by state or territory, were:

Alabama, Jeremy Covington and Jared Mathis; Alaska, Jessica Davis and Peter Lizardi; Arizona, Sherry Cross and Michele Venidis; Arkansas, Sara Campbell and Tasha Thompson; California, Kseniya Juchinskaya and Aaron Yamagata; Colorado, Jordan Kropp and Eric Sugano; Connecticut, Max Drzewinski and Hilary Scalcon; Delaware, Justin Dorman and Julie Ramone; District of Columbia, Benjamin J. Cecil and Edgar Chavez; Florida, Kyle Deluca and Casey Moro.

Georgia, Ken Avila and Hannah Dibble; Guam, Erika David and Michael Miracle; Hawaii, Lhery Claire Abella and Zachary Canter; Idaho, Kelsey Jardine and Nikki Knox; Illinois, Matthew J. Kou and Paul Valentine; Indiana, Chantel R. McAhren and Stephanie Seger; Iowa, Erin Brocka and Jenna L. Skophammer; Kansas, Ali Ehlers and Kayla Kuhl; Kentucky, Crystal Hackel and Jingyi Zhang; Louisiana, Troy Herbert and Dexter L. Monroe Jr.

Maine, Whitney Leblanc and Jessica Osborne; Maryland, Angela Riley and Allison Smith; Massachusetts, Peter Gillooly and John Her; Michigan, Forrest Cohn and Jessica Tater; Minnesota, Jennifer Lee and Dan Levar; Mississippi, Sarah Baker and Emily Rodriguez; Missouri, Tasha Daily and Larry McQueen; Montana, Nick Econom and Casey Krenzer.

Nebraska, Nathan Dubs and Alexander Lin; Nevada, Tasha Deleon and Rosa Lopez; New Hampshire, Victor Leclair and Heather Ortakales; New Jersey, Morgan Hill and Jessica Sainato; New Mexico, Michael Eaglestar and Evan Richardson; New York, Michael Jordan and Benjamin Morejon; North Carolina, Daniel Lloyd and Lakiesha N. White; North Dakota, Lindsey Heupel and Bonnie Patton.

Ohio, Abby Larosa and John Szezucinski; Oklahoma, Stevi McQueen and Josh Speer; Oregon, Marin Ewing and Zoe Shipley; Pennsylvania, Cheryl Dingman and Leah Hershey; Puerto Rico, Pedro de Jesus and Madai Mateo; Rhode Island, Tim Fiore and Casuarina Hart; South Carolina, Joshua Anderson and Elizabeth Hope; South Dakota, William Schultz and Anna L. Wonnenberg; Tennessee, Ernie Havener and Sarah E. Lipsey.

Texas, Breeanne Batts and Jimmy Watson; Utah, Garrett Debruyn and Ashley Young; Vermont, Brendan Dempsey and Erin McCreary; Virginia, Leigh Grossman and Tommy Yi; Virgin Islands, Terrance Bartley and Andrea Russell; Washington, Christa Curry and Kit Radosevich; West Virginia, Matthew Bowles and Nadia Rahi; Wisconsin, Jamie Becker and Jesse Kamsler; Wyoming, Justin Rose and Ji Su Yi; overseas military, Gilmer McMillan and Chelsi Melvin.

Before the Kids Care! block of stamps of 1995, several other U.S. stamp issues had been designed by children.

The first (Scott 1085) was a 3¢ 1956 commemorative promoting children's friendship. Its artist, Ronald Dias, was a high-school student in Hawaii who submitted his design in response to a nationwide competition sponsored by the old U.S. Post Office Department.

Two 1984 stamp designs were chosen from entries in a contest sponsored by the Postal Service. The 20¢ Family Unity stamp (Scott 2104) was illustrated by Molly LaRue, a Shaker Heights, Ohio, high-school student. Her stick-figure designs were intended to emulate the artwork of younger children. Third-grade student Danny LaBoccetta depicted Santa Claus on the 20¢ contemporary Christmas design (Scott 2108).

The winners of the 1995 Kids Care! competition were Brian Hailes, 13; Melody Kiper, 9; Jennifer Michalove, 10; and Christy Millard, 12.

The Designs

Zachary Canter's design shows a sky filled with astronauts, spaceships, stars and planets. Some of the spacewalkers are upside down, and one space-suited girl appears to be riding a rocket-powered skateboard. Zachary is from an artistic family; his mother is an artist, and his grandfather, Saul Mandel, designed the 22¢ "puppy love" Love stamp of 1986 (Scott 2202).

"This is the illustration that stood out for me," said Terrence McCaffrey. "It had more good illustration potential for a future artist than any of the others I saw.

"I told the CSAC [design] subcommittee, 'There's one in here that, if it's not in the final four, I'll never speak to you again. But I'm not going to tell you which one it is. You'll have to find it.' " To a person, the subcommittee picked it. "I told them, 'You're redeemed,' " McCaffrey said.

Morgan Hill's entry pictured a woman and two children taking an interplanetary vacation, with the words "Mommy, are we there yet?" in large letters near the lower-left corner. *Linn's Stamp News* reported that she hand-drew the individual elements, then scanned each piece and used her computer to arrange the elements to her liking. She thought of and drew her winning picture in less than an hour, she told *The Star-Ledger* of Newark.

Morgan said she arrived at her inspiration by taking a common question she and her 6-year-old sister, Shannon, pose to their mother and combining it with the idea of outer space — a possible career choice.

"Sometimes I want to travel in space, but there's a lot of other jobs I might want to do," she told *The Star-Ledger*.

Morgan, like Zachary Canter, benefits from artistic genes. Her mother designs children's clothing, and her father is a free-lance set designer.

Sarah Lipsey used felt-tip color markers to draw a multi-ethnic group of five youngsters holding hands in front of a heart-shaped Earth surrounded by yellow stars. Sarah, a seventh grader, told *The Commercial Appeal* of Memphis, Tennessee, that she created the picture late at night over a two-day period. "I want world peace, and that's what I drew," she said. "I think a lot of people [contestants] want that, but I guess I want it more."

Like her fellow winners, Sarah comes from an artistic family. Her mother is a free-lance artist, and her sister, Bohne, was the Tennessee state winner — and one of the 50 finalists — in the competition that produced the four Kids Care! stamps of 1995. "Our house is filled with lots of art

The Stampin' the Future stamp artists, with their stamp designs, top left: Zachary Canter with Astronauts, *top right: Sarah Lipsey with* Children, *bottom left: Morgan Hill with* Rocket, *and bottom right: Ashley Young with* Dog.

things, and my sister inspires me too, because she is a real good artist," Sarah told *The Commercial Appeal*.

Ashley Young's illustration depicts a dog wearing a transparent round astronaut's helmet on some alien world, with an American flag planted in the soil at the left and a saucerlike spacecraft zooming off into the sky at the right. A ringed green planet hangs in the upper right.

"We were studying space in school," Ashley explained, according to a Postal Service news release. "I thought about showing myself in space, but then I love animals so I decided on a dog." The dog is named Fetch and is a golden retriever, she said.

In making its selections, the CSAC design subcommittee found that "the hardest thing was to get four that would work together in a block, color-wise and subject-wise," said Terrence McCaffrey. "The [Sarah Lipsey] picture of the kids holding hands was different enough, the committee felt, and the colors worked well, so it was chosen for variety.

"Everybody loved the space dog, and they loved the 'Mommy, are we there yet?' Even though it had wording drawn on the design, which normally we don't like, we thought it was so original and so typical of what kids would say that we just had to have it."

This four-stamp layout shows the young winners' original artwork, without stamp typography added. Art director Richard Sheaff later touched up the illustrations on his computer, lightening some of the colors and removing the brushmarks from the solid-color areas and making those areas uniform. He also "cleaned up" the planetary surface around Ashley Young's space-traveling dog.

In 1995, Richard Sheaff, a Postal Service art director, had adapted the Kids Care! winning illustrations as stamp designs and added typography. Now he did the same thing for the Stampin' the Future illustrations. Using his computer, he lightened some of the colors, strengthened crayoned areas and made the solid-color areas uniform. The only change he made in any of the artwork was to remove some little mounds of dark color surrounding Ashley Young's space dog.

"They looked like dog litter," McCaffrey explained. "It looked as if the dog had been left on the moon too long without being walked. We said, 'This won't work, let's clean it up.' We never told Ashley, and if she noticed she didn't say anything."

Sheaff inserted "USA 33" into each design, in dropout or black type. The font is Helvetica and Helvetica Bold. His header design consists of the words "Stampin' the Future" in large black Tekton letters, and, across the top in smaller Tekton characters, the explanatory inscription, "These four stamp designs — chosen from more than 120,000 entries in a 1998 contest for kids 8 to 13 — depict the winners' views of what our world will be like in the next millennium." The latter inscription is printed in a special red (PMS 187). The rest of the pane, including the stamps, is printed in the four standard process colors, black, cyan, magenta and yellow.

First-day Facts

Patricia M. Gilbert, USPS vice president for retail, consumers and small business, dedicated the stamps in a ceremony at the Anaheim Convention Center.

252

Joyce Carrier, USPS manager of public affairs, gave the welcome. Honored guests included the four young stamp designers; Azeezaly S. Jaffer, vice president for public affairs and communications of USPS; James C. Tolbert Jr., executive director, stamp services; Dickey B. Rustin of USPS, director of World Stamp Expo 2000; and Anaheim Postmaster Larry A. Webster. "Mickey Mouse" made a special appearance.

The earliest-known prerelease use of a Stampin' the Future stamp was on a cover machine-postmarked from the Irving Park Road packaging and delivery center in Chicago, Illinois, July 12, one day before the official first day of issue. The stamp bore Ashley Young's space dog design.

33¢ CALIFORNIA STATEHOOD

Date of Issue: September 8, 2000

Catalog Number: Scott 3438

Colors: yellow, magenta, cyan, black, metallic gold

First-Day Cancel: Sacramento, California

First-Day Cancellations: 119,729

Format: Panes of 20, vertical, 5 across, 4 down. Gravure printing cylinders of 200 subjects, 2 panes across, 5 panes around.

Gum Type: self-adhesive

Overall Stamp Size: .990 by 1.560 inches; 25.146 by 39.624mm

Pane Size: 5.875 by 6.500 inches; 149.23 by 165.10mm

Perforations: 11 (die-cut simulated perforations) (Comco Commander rotary die cutter)

Selvage Markings: "©USPS/1999." ".33 x 20/=$6.60." "PLATE/POSITION" and diagram. Universal Product Code (UPC) "447200."

Photographer: Art Wolfe of Seattle, Washington

Designer and Art Director: Carl Herrman of Carlsbad, California

Typographer: John Boyd of New York, New York

Stamp Manufacturing: Stamps printed by Avery Dennison Security Printing Division, Clinton, South Carolina, on 8-color Dia Nippon Kiko webfed gravure press. Stamps processed by Avery Dennison.

Quantity Ordered: 53,000,000

Plate Number Detail: 1 set of 5 plate numbers preceded by the letter V in selvage next to each corner stamp

Plate Number Combination Reported: V11111

Paper Supplier: Fasson Division of Avery Dennison

Tagging: phosphored paper

The Stamp

On September 8, the Postal Service issued a 33¢ commemorative stamp to mark the 150th anniversary of California's admission to the Union as the 31st state.

The stamp, a self-adhesive, was printed by the gravure process by Avery Dennison Security Printing Division and issued in panes of 20. Only 53 million stamps were ordered, a relatively low print run for a U.S. commemorative. In keeping with USPS policy for statehood stamps, this one was sold only at California post offices, at philatelic centers and postal stores nationwide, and by mail from Stamp Fulfillment Services in Kansas City, Missouri.

The limited distribution of selected modern U.S. stamps and postal stationery began in 1998 with the announcement that the forthcoming 32¢ Wisconsin statehood stamp would be sold only in Wisconsin post offices, plus postal stores in other states and by mail from Stamp Fulfillment Services. The news came as a shock to politicians and others who had worked for issuance of the Wisconsin stamp, and they were shocked further to learn that only 16 million Wisconsins would be printed.

Although USPS initially defended the limited production and release of the Wisconsin stamp, it eventually issued another 16 million stamps after Rep. F. James Sensenbrenner of Wisconsin, along with Wisconsin Sesquicentennial officials and others, expressed strong opposition.

Stamp collectors also complained, and the American Philatelic Society voted to protest the USPS regional-issue policy. The reaction had a positive effect. On April 1, 1999, postal officials announced an end to the practice of restricting the distribution of stamps. The change didn't apply to commemorative stamped cards, however, which have continued to be released regionally and in low quantities, beginning with the 20¢ University of Wisconsin stamped card of 1999.

Nor did it apply to all stamps, as it turned out. In an April 15, 1999, press release for the forthcoming 33¢ Ayn Rand commemorative stamp (which originally was slated for post office distribution only in New York and California), USPS stated that the Rand stamp would be "the first stamp to be issued following the Postal Service's recent decision to continue nationwide distribution of all commemorative stamps other than 'statehood' stamps."

John Hotchner, APS president at the time and now a member of the Citizens' Stamp Advisory Committee, said he was disappointed at the Postal Service's flip-flop on statehood commemoratives. He told *Linn's Stamp News* that he remained "convinced that any regionalization of stamp issuance is not in the interests of either the collector or the Postal Service."

California statehood became possible on February 2, 1848, when Mexico and the United States signed a treaty ending the Mexican War. Mexico agreed to cede a large portion of the Southwest, including present-day California, to the United States. Just a few days before, on January 24, gold had been discovered at Sutter's Mill on the American River near Sacramento. The ensuing rush of gold seekers hastened the territory's admittance to the Union, which took place September 9, 1850.

In 1950, the U.S. Post Office Department issued a gold-colored 3¢ stamp to commemorate the 100th anniversary of the state of California (Scott 997). As Fred Baumann pointed out in *Stamp Collector*, more than 121 million of those stamps were printed, at a time when California had only 10.6 million residents. In 2000, however, when the state's population had grown to 33.2 million, only 53 million statehood sesquicentennial stamps were issued, fewer than 44 percent of the number released in 1950.

California was the subject of one of the 50 State Flags stamps (Scott 1663) and the 50 State Birds and Flowers stamps (Scott 1957). Stamps also commemorated the 200th anniversaries of California's settlement (Scott 1373) and of the first civil settlement in Alta California (Scott 1725), as well as the 450th anniversary of explorer Jean Rodriguez Cabrillo's discovery of San Diego Bay (Scott 2704). A 44¢ airmail stamp honored Father Junipero Serra, "the patron saint of California" (Scott C116). The centennial of the discovery of gold at Sutter's Mill was the subject of a 3¢ commemorative in 1948 (Scott 954). Fifty-one years later, a 33¢ stamp marked the 150th anniversary of the gold rush that brought the "Forty-niners" to California (Scott 3316).

Many California scenes and attractions have been featured on U.S. stamps and postal cards, including the Golden Gate and Golden Gate Bridge, Yosemite National Park, San Francisco's cable cars, Stanford University, Hearst Castle at San Simeon, the Dominguez Adobe at Rancho San Pedro, the Sonoran Desert, California redwood trees, and the *Super Chief* and *Daylight* passenger trains.

California events that inspired commemorative stamps include the Panama-Pacific Exposition of 1915 and the Golden Gate International Exposition of 1939, both in San Francisco; the California-Pacific Exposition of 1935, in San Diego; the Summer Olympic Games of 1932 and 1984, in Los Angeles; the Winter Olympic Games of 1960, in Squaw Valley; and the Pacific 97 and World Stamp Expo 2000 stamp shows, in San Francisco and Anaheim, respectively.

Native Californians who have been honored on U.S. stamps include Richard M. Nixon, Adlai Stevenson, Earl Warren, Robert Frost, Jack London, John Steinbeck, William Saroyan, George S. Patton, Hazel Wightman, Amadeo Giannini, Lawrence Tibbett and Marilyn Monroe. Monroe is only one of dozens of subjects related to the Hollywood film industry that have been featured on stamps over the years.

The Design

Carl Herrman, a USPS art director, has overseen the design process of stamps honoring two states in which he was living at the time. As a resident of Ponte Vedra, Florida, he served as art director for the 1995 Florida statehood sesquicentennial stamp. Later, after moving to California, he asked for and got the same assignment for the 2000 California commemorative.

For the Florida stamp, Herrman used a stylized illustration of an alligator. "I really wanted to pursue some illustration ideas for California, too, but the [Citizens' Stamp Advisory] Committee suggested I try to find some good photographs," he said.

While examining photos, Herrman also developed two proposed stamp designs using details from paintings by Albert Bierstadt (1830-1902), a painter of romanticized Western scenes whose *The Last of the Buffalo* was shown on one of the Four Centuries of American Art stamps of 1998. One of the two paintings, *The Yosemite Valley*, an oil on canvas painted in 1868, is in the Oakland, California, Museum. The other, *Giant Redwood Trees of California*, an undated oil on canvas, is owned by the Berkshire Museum in Pittsfield, Massachusetts.

The problem was that neither painting said "California" unmistakably, Herrman said. The Yosemite scene could have been a generic Western landscape; the redwood forest would have looked like an ordinary stand of trees once the picture had been reduced to stamp size, which would have caused the human beings whom Bierstadt had included in the painting to virtually disappear.

To make the design more specifically Californian, the art director and the committee decided to depict a Pacific coast scene. Herrman's favorite was one of his own photographs, showing the coast at Laguna Beach from Vista Point. "It had aloe blooming in the foreground, with big red blossoms," he said. "It had the surf hitting both the rocks and the beautiful white sandy beach, and in the distance the coastline is curving around, with nice clouds and beautiful blue water."

But CSAC opted for Big Sur, the spectacular stretch of coast south of Monterey, along which California Route 1 wends its breathtaking way. The committee turned down two horizontal treatments of photographs showing the Bixby Bridge, and chose instead a vertical layout showing a close-up of an extremely rugged section of the coast. The photo, by Art Wolfe, a prominent nature photographer from Seattle, Washington, was taken in May 1996 at the extreme southern end of Big Sur, just south of Ragged Point. It shows sun-dappled cliffs plunging down to the ocean; surf breaks on rocks at their base. The clifftops are covered by the pink blossoms and green leaves of the iceplant, or sea fig, with several blossoms prominent in the foreground.

The inclusion of the iceplant proved controversial. In a letter to USPS, Tony Morosco, a University of California botanist who is plant manager of the CalFlora Database, said that to postally promote the plant in this fashion would mislead the public into believing it was native and harmless. Instead, Morosco said, the iceplant is "an invasive weed responsible for enormous destruction of California coastal habitats." He contended

Carl Herrman developed these two proposed California stamp designs using details from oil on canvas paintings by Albert Bierstadt: Yosemite Valley *and* Giant Redwood Trees of California.

This proposed design, showing Laguna Beach from Vista Point with red-blossomed aloe in the foreground, features one of Herrman's own photographs.

These two concepts used photographs of the Big Sur coastline and the Bixby bridge at two different times of day and from different distances.

that the species, scientifically known as Carpobrotus edulis, is "actively smothering native California wildflowers while converting pristine coastal dune, cliff and prairie habitats into desolate biological wastelands that our native flora and fauna cannot survive in."

"If the goal of the stamp is to show California as it may have looked in 1850, historical accuracy is done disservice by showing a landscape that probably did not exist at the time of first contact," Morosco said. "The best scientific evidence to date analyzing pollen samples taken from soil

258

cores in the Monterey area shows Carpobrotus as an introduction from Africa well after first European contact. The inclusion of a noxious weed on a postal stamp (C. edulis is classified by the California Exotic Pest Plant Council as a threat of rank 1-A: 'Most Invasive Wildland Pest Plants: Widespread') does not celebrate the rich history of the state of California but features one of its worst problems."

The botanist conceded that the iceplant "is now so widespread and difficult to eradicate that it is understandable how it would show up in the final round of images selected for this stamp." Nevertheless, he called on the Postal Service to change the stamp's design — or, at least, to "modify the accompanying marketing and distribution information to include education materials on the dangers of this invasive plant."

USPS did neither. Officials had been alerted by PhotoAssist during the design selection process that the iceplant wasn't indigenous to California, and Carl Herrman said he pointed out the flowers in the photograph when he showed the proposed design to an assistant to Governor Gray Davis in Sacramento. According to Herrman, the aide said "no problem" and approved the design on the governor's behalf. The Postal Service's news release announcing the stamp quoted Davis as calling the stamp "a wonderful keepsake" and "a magnificent addition to our Celebrating California lineup and a fitting tribute to the spectacular beauty our state offers."

"We're not honoring that particular plant," Don Smeraldi, a USPS spokesman, told *Linn's Stamp News.* "It just happens to be part of the design."

After experimenting with several fonts and sizes of type, Herrman settled on a font called Huxley Vertical. The word "CALIFORNIA" is stripped across the bottom of the design. It is printed in metallic gold ink, as is appropriate for a state nicknamed "the Golden State." "Because we used gold, I needed a typeface with some heft to it," Herrman said. "The Huxley was able to hold the color with more strength than the others I tried, which were too delicate." Above the gold letters, on the right, the year date "1850" is in white dropout type, and "USA/33" is dropped out of the upper-right corner of the photograph.

Herrman tried several sizes and fonts of type with the Art Wolfe photograph that was chosen for the stamp design. The design team turned down this concept because the type, in a font called Compacta, seemed to overwhelm the photo.

259

First-day Facts

Deborah K. Willhite, USPS senior vice president for government relations, dedicated the stamp in a ceremony on the west steps of the California state capitol in Sacramento. She was introduced by mistress of ceremonies Bette Vasquez, host of *Central Valley Chronicles* on KVIE-TV (PBS). The principal speaker was Governor Gray Davis.

The ceremony helped launch Sacramento's three-day Admission Day 2000 celebration.

33¢ DEEP SEA CREATURES (5 DESIGNS)

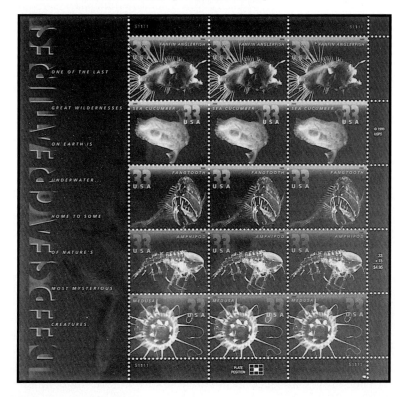

Date of Issue: October 2, 2000

Catalog Numbers: Scott 3439-3443, stamps; 3443a, vertical strip of 5

Colors: magenta, yellow, cyan, black

First-Day Cancel: Monterey, California

First-Day Cancellations: 385,406

Format: Panes of 15, horizontal, 3 across, 5 down. Gravure printing cylinders of 135 subjects, 9 across, 15 around, manufactured by Armotek Industries, Palmyra, New Jersey.

Gum Type: water-activated

Overall Stamp Size: 1.56 by 1.23 inches; 39.59 by 31.21mm

Pane Size: 7.25 by 7.00 inches; 183.99 by 177.65mm

Uncut Sheet Size: 22.25 by 21.25 inches

Perforations: 10 by 10¼ (APS rotary perforator)

Selvage Inscription: "DEEP SEA CREATURES/ONE OF THE LAST/GREAT WILDERNESSES/ON EARTH IS/UNDERWATER.../HOME TO SOME/OF NATURE'S/MOST MYSTERIOUS/CREATURES."

Selvage Markings: "©1999/USPS." ".33/x15/$4.95." "PLATE/POSITION" and diagram.

Photographers: Bruce H. Robison of Monterey, California, fanfin anglerfish and fangtooth; Laurence P. Madin of Falmouth, Massachusetts, deep sea medusa, sea cucumber and amphipod.

Art Director: Ethel Kessler of Bethesda, Maryland

Designer and Typographer: Greg Berger of Bethesda, Maryland

Stamp Manufacturing: Stamps printed for Sennett Security Products, Chantilly, Virginia, by American Packaging Corporation, Columbus, Wisconsin, on Rotomec 5 gravure press. Stamps processed by Unique Binders, Fredericksburg, Virginia.

Quantity Ordered: 85,000,000

Plate Number Detail: 1 set of 4 plate numbers preceded by the letter S in selvage above or below each corner stamp

Plate Number Combination Reported: S1111

Paper Supplier: Ivex/Paper Corporation of the United States

Tagging: block tagging that covers all 15 stamps on the pane

The Stamps

On October 2, the Postal Service issued a pane of 15 stamps comprising five varieties, each bearing a photograph of an exotic creature from the ocean depths. The release of the stamps marked the beginning of the 20th annual Stamp Collecting Month, which is observed each October.

The set was the second in two years to feature underwater wildlife. In 1999, USPS had issued a pane of 20 stamps containing four varieties that depicted fish and other flora and fauna commonly kept in freshwater and marine aquariums.

The Deep Sea Creatures stamps were gravure-printed by American Packaging Corporation for Sennett Security Products and have water-activated gum and conventional perforations. Semijumbo in size and horizontally oriented, they are arranged on the pane three across by five down. Each horizontal strip comprises stamps of the same design; each vertical strip contains one of each variety. A wide decorative selvage on the left bears the words "DEEP SEA CREATURES" and a brief explanatory text. The tagging is a single large block of phosphor that fully covers the 15 stamps on the pane.

Although USPS sometimes prohibits window clerks from breaking apart commemorative panes with decorative selvage, the *Postal Bulletin* informed clerks that the Deep Sea Creatures pane "can be split and the stamps can be sold individually."

The Postal Service also offered collectors the option of buying the stamps in uncut press sheets of nine panes for $44.55, the face value of the 135 stamps on the sheet, through Stamp Fulfillment Services.

An uncut press sheet of the Deep Sea Creatures stamps.

The creatures shown on the stamps, from top to bottom of the pane, are the fanfin anglerfish, the sea cucumber, the fangtooth, the amphipod and the medusa.

The Citizens' Stamp Advisory Committee chose the subject of deep sea creatures after market research conducted by the old Stampers program showed it would appeal to youthful stamp buyers. USPS says the 8- to 12-year-old age group "has become the largest participating group in National Stamp Collecting Month and one of the fastest growing segments of stamp collectors in the U.S." The 2000 event, with the theme "Stamp COOL-lecting: Your Window to the World," was the 20th annual observance since Stamp Collecting Month began in 1981.

The five creatures seen on the stamps are rarely viewed by humans. They dwell in the midwater range of the ocean. The midwater range includes the mesopelagic zone, which begins at a depth of approximately 330 feet and extends down to about 3,300 feet, where sunlight no longer penetrates, and the bathypelagic zone, 3,300 feet and below, which is eternally dark, except for light produced by its bioluminescent inhabitants.

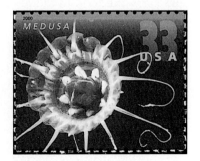

The deep sea is the most expansive animal habitat on Earth, where the dominant physical factors are darkness, cold and brutal pressure. Inhabitants of this environment possess significant modifications, including bizarre body forms and

unusual lifestyles.

One example is the fanfin anglerfish. The female, as shown on the stamp, has a fleshy glowing extension that resembles a fishing pole protruding from her head. The anglerfish uses the lurelike extension as bait for meals, as well as an attraction for potential mates.

The sea cucumber has a cylindrical body and lives on the ocean floor, catching its food using tentacles that surround its mouth. There are some 500 species of sea cucumber, making it one of the most common of the deep sea creatures. The *Concise Columbia Electronic Encyclopedia* says that many sea cucumbers eject most of their internal organs when sufficiently irritated and later regenerate a new set.

The ferocious appearance of the fangtooth helps it survive at depths up to 6,000 feet, where food is a precious commodity. Though small in size, the fangtooth has long, sharp teeth and a gaping jaw to help it capture and consume fish, squid and other prey.

There are almost 200 families and tens of thousands of species of amphipod, according to Australia's Museum Victoria in Melbourne. Most amphipods range in size from 1 millimeter to 10 millimeters. Classified as crustaceans, amphipods have seven pairs of walking legs. They may burrow in the sand or live among sea plants. Although they can swim, a quick flip of the tail is often used to propel them away from danger.

The deep sea medusa of the class Hydrozoa is a relative of the jellyfish that is found in shallower waters. The medusa has no skeletal structure, and it drives its dome-shaped jellylike membrane through the water with undulating movements. Long tentacles bearing stinging cells capture prey and carry the food to the mouth on the underside of the dome.

The Designs

The stamps have solid black backgrounds. The black printing actually includes the other three process colors, magenta, cyan and yellow, which adds richness to the tone. There are no borders on the stamps; the black bleeds across the perforations into adjacent stamps and covers the pane selvage.

"Our hope was that looking at the whole pane, with all the black, would really give you a sense of being in the dark ocean depths," said Ethel Kessler, the project's art director.

The subject matter also helped determine the way the five varieties are laid out on the pane. Rather than being arranged in a block pattern, or with stamps of the same design stacked vertically, they are placed in horizontal rows of identical stamps.

"These fish live at the same level of the deep sea," Kessler said. "We also took into consideration the concept of schools of fish. If you're bouncing these five different fish images around the pane, you're not suggesting schools of fish any longer. So this horizontal placement gave us a nice structure that made sense with the subject."

Stamps that make extensive use of black, such as Deep Sea Creatures and the American Ballet commemorative of 1998, must be designed in such a way that the phosphor in the paper or the applied coating will activate post office facer-canceler machines. This requires the inclusion of a certain amount of white or light-colored design elements.

With Deep Sea Creatures, art director Ethel Kessler and designer Greg Berger met the requirement by placing across the top of each stamp a strip of color that grades into the black background. The color is different on each stamp, and the sequence of colors from top to bottom of a vertical strip corresponds to that of the spectrum: red, orange, green, blue and violet. The two lower-stamp colors are relatively dark, but the creatures shown on those stamps — amphipod and medusa

Early in the design process, Ethel Kessler and Greg Berger created these four designs with white borders. Only one of the creatures shown here, the fangtooth, was among the five on the issued stamps. The anglerfish in this group is of a different kind from the fanfin variety in the final group of five.

265

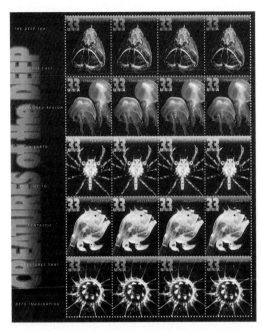

This alternative pane layout comprises 20 vertically arranged stamps rather than the 15 horizontal stamps that ultimately were issued. It also includes images and species that are different from those on the issued pane. The title of the set used here, "Creatures of the Deep," was rejected in favor of "Deep Sea Creatures," and the descriptive text on the selvage was changed for the finished product.

— have enough white in their bodies to compensate.

Because the stamps have no borders, and because the color strip on each stamp extends to the very top and portions of the tightly cropped photographs extend to the bottom edge, the perforating of the pane had to be very precise to prevent parts of a design from appearing on the stamp above or below it. With such designs, stamp printers "get wildly concerned that they're not going to be able to hold the line," Kessler said. But on this issue, Stamp Venturers was generally successful in putting the perfs exactly where they should be.

On each stamp, the denomination, "33," is printed in the same graded color as the color strip, and appears just below it on either the left or right side. The typeface, called Futura Extra Bold, was modified by Berger on the computer. "USA," in the same color as the strip but not graded, is superimposed on the denomination. The depicted creature's name, in a font called Frutiger, also appears below the strip of color.

The extensive use of black on the pane required other deviations from standard practice, as well. On most U.S. stamps, the year date is printed in small black type on the white border at the lower left. On Deep Sea Creatures, it appears on the color strip at the top of each stamp, on either the left or right side. On the Medusa stamp, the dark violet of the color strip makes the black "2000" printed on it very difficult to see.

The standard selvage markings, including the cylinder-number sequences, are dropped out of the black background. The number representing the black plate is lightly screened, making it look gray against the solid black of the selvage.

Shown here are two alternative selvage designs, one with text, one without.

In choosing the five creatures to depict on the stamps, the design team consulted experts, principally Bruce Robison, senior scientist at the Monterey Bay Aquarium Research Institute in Monterey, California. Kessler and Berger considered several ocean dwellers that didn't make the final cut, including scalloped ribbonfish, stinging jellyfish, siphonophore, viperfish and plankton.

The selection process involved several considerations. "The mix had to include species that lived at the same depth, that were diverse, that were differently shaped, and that would 'read' [be legible] against the black at stamp size," Kessler said.

The availability of good images was a key factor. For example, the work of one well-known photographer of undersea life was "extensive and spectacular," Kessler said, but he demanded too high a price for use of his photos. The design team also rejected the idea of using photographs of dead specimens, which typically are injected with dye to bring out the details of skeletal structure and other internal parts.

All five creatures on the pane were photographed alive in tanks. Bruce Robison, the consultant from Monterey, made the pictures of the fanfin anglerfish and the fangtooth, while Laurence Madin of the Woods Hole Oceanographic Institute in Woods Hole, Massachusetts, photographed the sea cucumber, the amphipod, and the medusa.

First-day Facts

Daryl A. Ishizaki, postmaster of San Jose, California, dedicated the stamps in a ceremony in the auditorium of the Monterey Bay Aquarium Research Institute. He was assisted by Bruce Robison, senior scientist at the institute and the photographer of two of the creatures on the stamps. Robert D. Spadoni, postmaster of Monterey, presided.

The speakers were Marcia McNutt, president and chief executive officer of the institute, and Jennifer Lazaroff of North Canton, Ohio, listed in the program as a "stamp collector and future marine biologist." Julie Packard, executive director, Monterey Bay Aquarium, gave the welcome.

Guests at the ceremony watched as a first-day cancellation was unveiled by a robot arm on the remotely operated vehicle *Ventana*, an underwater robot tethered to the research vessel *Point Lobos* and operating at a depth of 1,476 feet below the ocean's surface.

The aquarium is located at 886 Cannery Row in Monterey, a street made famous by a John Steinbeck novel named for it. At the time of the first-day event, the aquarium hosted a living exhibit titled Mysteries of the Deep, with more than 40 species of deep sea creatures on display.

33¢ THOMAS WOLFE
LITERARY ARTS SERIES

Date of Issue: October 3, 2000

Catalog Number: Scott 3444

Colors: black, cyan, magenta, yellow, yellow (PMS 129)

First-Day Cancel: Asheville, North Carolina

First-Day Cancellations: 112,293

Format: Panes of 20, horizontal, 4 across, 5 down. Offset printing plates of 120 subjects, 8 across, 15 around.

Gum Type: water-activated

Overall Stamp Size: 1.560 by .991 inches; 39.624 by 25.171mm

Pane Size: 7.420 by 5.946 inches; 183.896 by 151.028mm

Perforations: 11 (Wista stroke perforator)

Selvage Markings: "©USPS/1999" ".33/x20/$6.60" "PLATE/POSITION" and diagram. Universal Product Code (UPC) "442700."

Illustrator: Michael Deas of New Orleans, Louisiana

Designer, Typographer and Art Director: Phil Jordan of Falls Church, Virginia

Modeler: Joseph Sheeran of Ashton-Potter (USA) Ltd., Williamsville, New York

Stamp Manufacturing: Stamps printed by Ashton-Potter on offset portion of Stevens Variable Size Security Documents webfed 6-color offset, 3-color intaglio press. Stamps finished by Ashton-Potter.

Quantity Ordered: 53,000,000

Plate Number Detail: 1 set of 5 plate numbers preceded by the letter P in selvage above or below corner stamp

Plate Number Combinations Reported: P11111, P22222

Paper Supplier: Tullis Russell

Tagging: phosphored paper

The Stamp

The 17th stamp in the Postal Service's Literary Arts series marked the centennial of the birth of novelist Thomas Wolfe and was issued October 3 in Wolfe's hometown of Asheville, North Carolina.

Ashton-Potter (USA) Ltd. printed the stamp by offset lithography. It has water-activated gum and conventional perforations and was issued in panes of 20.

The Literary Arts series was launched with a John Steinbeck stamp in 1979 and in recent years has honored Tennessee Williams, F. Scott Fitzgerald, Thornton Wilder, Stephen Vincent Benet and, most recently, Ayn Rand.

Thomas Clayton Wolfe was born October 3, 1900, in Asheville, the youngest of the eight children of William Oliver Wolfe, a tombstone cutter, and Julia Wolfe, a former teacher who operated a boarding house. He was an outstanding student in public and private schools, and at age 15 entered the University of North Carolina at Chapel Hill, where he wrote plays and edited *The Tar Heel*, the student newspaper. He graduated in 1920 and earned a master's degree at Harvard two years later.

He taught English at the Washington Square College of New York University while unsuccessfully seeking backing to produce his dramatic works. In 1925, he met and fell in love with Aline Bernstein, a married New York theatrical designer many years his senior. With aid from Bernstein, Wolfe was able to quit teaching and focus on writing.

The massive raw material for his first novel caught the attention of Scribner editor Maxwell E. Perkins in 1928. *Look Homeward, Angel* was published the following year, after Perkins and Wolfe worked together to bring form to the huge work.

Look Homeward, Angel is an autobiographical novel that transforms Asheville into the town of Altamont. It tells the story of Wolfe's early years in the boarding house through the eyes of fictional protagonist Eugene Gant. Although it was ill-received in Asheville, where many citizens resented its candor, the novel won great acclaim around the world. Its sequel, *Of Time and the River*, was published in 1935.

The tempestuous Wolfe ended his relationship with Bernstein early in the 1930s and changed editors in 1937, following a series of disagreements with Perkins. He continued writing at a feverish pace, but contracted pneumonia during a West Coast trip, and died of tubercular meningitis September 1, 1938, at age 37.

Two novels with another semi-autobiographical protagonist, George Webber, were shaped from the mass of manuscripts left after Wolfe's death. *The Web and the Rock* was published in 1939, and *You Can't Go Home Again* appeared in 1940.

During his lifetime, Wolfe also published dozens of short stories, several short novels, and *The Story of a Novel*, a book that describes the effort to create *Of Time and the River*.

The Design

Four of the past five stamps in the Literary Arts series were illustrated by Michael Deas of Brooklyn Heights, New York, and had a uniform "series look" to them. Each of the horizontal designs featured a head-and-shoulders portrait of the writer in the foreground, with an image behind him evocative of one of his major works.

For the 1999 stamp, honoring Ayn Rand, however, the Citizens' Stamp Advisory Committee switched illustrators — and styles. It chose Nicholas Gaetano, who had done the illustrations for editions of several of Rand's books, to create the stamp design. Gaetano produced a vertically oriented, art deco-flavored picture that featured a graphic portrait of Rand partly obscured by a group of skyscrapers.

When the Thomas Wolfe illustration assignment came up, Phil Jordan, art director for both the Rand and Wolfe stamps, called on Gaetano again. Deas had a number of other professional commitments at the time, Jordan explained. Besides, Rand and Wolfe came out of the same period of American literature, and Gaetano, as a resident of Fletcher, North Carolina, had ready access to research material on Wolfe.

Although CSAC "went along initially" on the choice of Gaetano to do Wolfe, Jordan said, the committee members had second thoughts when Jordan showed them his layout using Gaetano's artwork. They thought the stylized image, made up of sharply outlined planes with starkly contrasting lighting, "lacked the introspective depth that characterized Wolfe's novels," Jordan said, and in addition was "way out of step with the series." This was of particular concern to Howard Paine, another art director, who often had expressed his belief that a set of stamps should have visual continuity. The Rand stamp had been an aberration, the committee acknowledged, but that could be justified because she was such an idiosyncratic writer, whereas Wolfe was "not that far out of the mainstream," Jordan said. In the end, CSAC asked that sketches be commissioned from Michael Deas, and Deas, despite his workload, agreed to take the assignment.

Deas examined several possible source photographs for the Wolfe portrait, finally choosing a profile photo of the author in his late 20s, made by Doris Ulmann to help publicize *Look Homeward, Angel*. The photo is in the Wolfe Collection at the University of North Carolina. "For stamps,

Nicholas Gaetano, who had illustrated the previous stamp in the Literary Arts series, honoring Ayn Rand, developed this design for the Thomas Wolfe stamp. Members of CSAC felt it was too different in appearance from earlier stamps in the series illustrated by Michael Deas, and that it would be better to return to the "series look" that Deas had established.

I try to get a fresh image that shows the person in their prime, at the peak of their powers, but that also isn't too well known," Deas said. Coincidentally, the source photo was the same one Gaetano had used.

For the background picture, Deas first sketched a street scene near his home in Brooklyn Heights that included the brownstone where Wolfe once lived. "I wanted to give it an Edward Hopper kind of feel," Deas said, referring to the American realist artist whose starkly lit scenes were said to be suggestive of modern alienation. "I think Hopper is the visual equivalent of Wolfe's writings. To show a lonely city street behind his portrait, particularly one with his residence in it, seemed to be a good idea. But it turned out to be too heavy-handed and didn't really work."

A Wolfe expert consulted by PhotoAssist, the Postal Service's research firm, recommended that the stamp depict a carved stone angel to represent the sculpture that played a part in the plot of *Look Homeward, Angel*. In the book, the fictional Oliver Gant, father of the protagonist and a stonecutter like Wolfe's own father, was inspired to take up his trade by the sight of a stone angel, and although he never learned to carve an angel he later purchased one for resale to adorn a grave. "For six years it had stood on the porch, weathering, in all the wind and the rain," Wolfe wrote. "It was now brown and fly-specked. But it had come from Carrara in Italy, and it held a stone lily delicately in one hand. The other hand was lifted in benediction, it was poised clumsily upon the ball of one phthisic foot, and its stupid white face wore a smile of soft stone idiocy." Deas found an angel of the same period in a New Orleans cemetery, photographed it and used it as a model for his background art. The

This is the photograph on which Michael Deas based his painting of a stone angel for the Thomas Wolfe stamp. Deas found the sculpture in a New Orleans cemetery.
(Photo by Michael Deas)

Deas adapted the lettering of the book titles on the Wolfe stamp from the letters on this inscription on the base of the statue of Admiral David Farragut in New York City's Madison Square Park.

Shown here is Michael Deas' original pencil sketch of Thomas Wolfe with the stone angel in the background. Note that the name of a third Wolfe book, You Can't Go Home Again, *is lettered on the author's shoulder. Deas removed it for the finished art.*

The word "AUTHOR," in black microtype, can be found in the curls on the side of the stone angel's head.

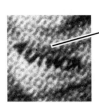

angel, clutching flowers in both hands, fills the space behind Wolfe on the left side of the finished oil painting.

On the right side, Deas lettered the titles of the two Wolfe novels that were published during his lifetime, *Look Homeward, Angel* and *Of Time and the River*. Originally he included the title of one of the posthumous novels, *You Can't Go Home Again*, superimposed on the right shoulder of the portrait, but he thought it might conflict with the type containing Wolfe's name, so he omitted it. "I wish, in retrospect, I had put it in," he said. "I think it would have given more balance to the image." Seeking a style of lettering for the titles that would have been in vogue in the early part of the 20th century, Deas found it in New York City's Madison Square Park, on the base of a pedestal designed by Stanford White for a statue of Admiral Farragut by Augustus Saint-Gaudens.

"With this stamp, and all the others in the Literary Arts series, I've deliberately tried to find a visual analogy to each author's writings, trying to capture in a picture what Wolfe and the others caught with words," Deas said. "Wolfe's work is fairly dark, often dealing with themes of memory and a sense of loss. Hence, the Wolfe stamp is a bit dark — deliberately so — but with flashes of light, too."

Unlike previous stamps in the Literary Arts series, this one has a soft edge to its design. "It was a deliberate choice on my part," Deas said. "The rounded corners and darkened edges are meant to conjure the feeling of an old snapshot (perhaps one taken with a pinhole camera), hopefully reinforcing that feeling of 'looking back' that is so prevalent in Wolfe's works."

The name "THOMAS WOLFE," in gold-colored Times New Roman type, stretches across the top of the design.

The printer inserted the word "AUTHOR," in black microtype, in the curls on the side of the stone angel's head. (See illustration.)

First-day Facts

Henry A. Pankey, vice president for area operations of the Postal Service's Mid-Atlantic Area, dedicated the stamp in a ceremony at the author's boyhood home, now the Thomas Wolfe Memorial, a national historic landmark in Asheville. The large wood-frame house was undergoing renovation after suffering substantial damage from a July 1998 arson fire, but a visitor's center and exhibition hall were open to visitors.

Speakers were Steven Hill, manager of the historic site; Dr. Jeffrey J. Crow, director of archives and history for the North Carolina Department of Cultural Resources; Betty Ray McCain, secretary of the cultural resources department; and author Wilma Dykeman. Four fourth-grade students read essays they had written for the occasion. Gordon Jacobs, USPS district manager for the mid-Carolinas, presided.

Honored guests were Dr. R. Deitz Wolfe Sr., Dr. Thomas Clayton Wolfe, Mr. and Mrs. Greg Gambrell, Mr. and Mrs. Edward Gambrell, Mr. and Mrs. R. Dietz Wolfe Jr., Mr. and Mrs. Richard Gambrell, Tina D. Gambrell, Jack and Ann Westall, Juliana Gambrell, Steven Gambrell, Mildred Gambrell, Jan Gambrell, Lisa Gambrell and Asheville Postmaster James Antill.

33¢ THE WHITE HOUSE

Date of Issue: October 18, 2000

Catalog Number: Scott 3445

Colors: black, cyan, magenta, yellow

First-Day Cancel: Washington, D.C.

First-Day Cancellations: 135,844

Format: Pane of 20, horizontal, 4 across, 5 down. Offset printing plates of 180 subjects, 15 across, 12 around.

Gum: self-adhesive

Overall Stamp Size: 1.19 by 0.91 inches; 30.226 by 23.114mm

Pane Size: 5.95 by 5.46 inches; 151.130 by 138.684mm

Perforations: 11¼ (die-cut simulated perforations) (Arpeco die cutter)

Selvage Markings: "©USPS/1999." ".33/x20/$6.60." "PLATE POSITION" and diagram. Universal Product Code (UPC) "446900."

Photographer: Patricia Fisher of Washington, D.C.

Designer, Art Director and Typographer: Derry Noyes of Washington, D.C.

Modeler: Joseph Sheeran of Ashton-Potter (USA) Ltd., Williamsville, New York

Stamp Manufacturing: Stamps printed by Ashton-Potter on offset portion of Stevens Variable Size Security Documents webfed 6-color offset, 3-color intaglio press. Stamps processed by Ashton-Potter.

Quantity Ordered: 125,000,000

Plate Number Detail: 1 set of 4 plate numbers preceded by the letter P in selvage above or below each corner stamp

Plate Number Combinations Reported: P1111, P2222, P3333

Paper Supplier: Fasson/Glatfelter

Tagging: phosphored paper

The Stamp

On November 1, 1800, President John Adams moved into the still-unfinished U.S. Executive Mansion on Pennsylvania Avenue in Washington, D.C. Thereafter, all U.S. presidents and their families would reside in the building that has become universally known as the White House.

On October 18, 2000, a few days short of the mansion's bicentennial, the Postal Service commemorated the anniversary by issuing a 33¢ commemorative stamp depicting a winter view of the White House at twilight, its front lawn blanketed in snow.

"Ron Robinson [a member of the Citizens' Stamp Advisory Committee] said, 'We really should do the White House on a stamp,' " recalled Terrence McCaffrey, head of stamp design for USPS. "I said, 'We've done the flag over the White House and many others.' He said, 'Well, the anniversary is coming up.' I said, 'I know, but they haven't really contacted us.'

"Right after that, Hugh Sidey, president of the White House Historical Association, called me and asked me how they would go about getting a stamp for the 200th anniversary. I told him we were working up something."

Postal officials initially planned to issue the White House stamp in panes to be dispensed in automated teller machines. Because participating banks like to have new ATM stamps available during the winter holiday season with appropriate designs, the officials thought it would be appropriate to show the building in winter.

Later, however, they realized that a stamp marking an anniversary of such national significance should be more widely available than through ATMs alone, and decided to issue the stamp in panes for over-the-counter sale at post offices.

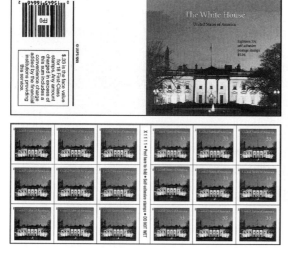

Postal officials considered issuing the White House stamp in the form of a dollar-bill-sized pane of 18 for sale through automated teller machines. Derry Noyes created this layout, using a different photograph of the building for the stamp and cover design. Note that in this photo, the Washington Monument is visible behind the left side of the executive mansion.

"It proved to be one of the more popular stamps of the year," McCaffrey said. "Because we didn't sell a new Christmas stamp in 2000, people used it a great deal on Christmas card mailings." Thus, the stamp saw rather extensive use, even though the first-class rate it met — 33¢ — was scheduled to be increased by a penny less than three months after its date of issue.

The self-adhesive stamp is the special size used for holiday and Love stamps, arranged horizontally. It was printed by the offset process by Ashton-Potter (USA) Ltd. and issued in panes of 20.

The Postal Service and the Treasury Department's Bureau of Engraving and Printing collaborated to produce a pricey collectible called "The White House 200th Anniversary Commemorative Stamp and Note Portfolio." Costing $198, it consisted of a pane of White House stamps, together with a $20 currency note bearing an engraving of the White House. The note bore a special serial number range not available in general circulation.

These items were packaged in a portfolio that also contained the engraved portraits of John Adams and William J. Clinton, the first and last presidents to reside in the White House during its first 200 years. A total of 30,000 portfolios were produced.

The White House was designed by Irish-born James Hoban, who won a competition to design the new nation's presidential residence, and was built under Hoban's supervision on a spot amid apple orchards that was selected by President George Washington. It was the largest house in America at the time.

When Adams moved in, half the rooms were unplastered, only a twisting back stair had been built between floors, and scaffolding stood against the basement walls. Adams spent the day greeting visitors. After supper, he climbed the one usable staircase, candle in hand, to go to bed. The next day, on a plain sheet of paper, which he headed "President's House, Washington City, Nov. 2, 1800," he wrote a letter to his wife Abigail containing this benediction:

"I pray heaven to bestow the best of blessings on this house and all that shall hereafter inhabit it. May none but honest and wise men ever rule under this roof."

Since those times, the White House has seen many changes and improvements. Running water and an indoor bathroom were installed in 1833 and electric lights in 1891. During the presidency of Theodore Roosevelt, the West Wing offices were built.

The building also has undergone two comprehensive renovations. The first, overseen by its architect, James Hoban, came after British troops burned it during the War of 1812 and was completed in 1817; it was then that the building's sandstone walls were painted white, to conceal burn marks. The second was in 1948, during the Truman administration, after an examination of the building showed it to be structurally unsafe. It was gutted, reinforced with steel and concrete, and rebuilt within its original walls. Truman also had a balcony installed inside the south portico, an addition that was criticized at the time but has become an accepted part of the mansion.

The first U.S. stamp to show the White House was the 4½¢ value of the 1938 Presidential definitive series. Since then, 12 other face-different stamps, including the bicentennial commemorative, and one picture postal card have depicted the building. These include a Christmas stamp (5¢, 1963) with the National Christmas Tree in the foreground; 18¢ and 20¢ commemoratives issued in 1981 to honor James Hoban, part of a joint issue with Ireland; a World War II commemorative of 1995 showing President Truman meeting the press in the Oval Office; and three different "Flag Over White House" definitives. The most recent of these, a 29¢ coil stamp issued in 1992, bore the dates "1792-1992," to note the fact that the cornerstone for the White House had been laid 200 years earlier.

The Design

Derry Noyes, a Postal Service contract art director, was asked to design the stamp, using an appropriate photograph of the White House in winter. After examining some 300 photos, she narrowed the field to three and used them to make layouts for an ATM pane of 18 and, subsequently, for a post office pane of 20.

The photo she and CSAC liked best was by Patricia Fisher, a veteran commercial photographer in Washington, and was part of Fisher's large archive in the stock agency Folio Inc. It depicts the mansion's north facade at nightfall, with light illuminating the building and the fountain in front. The lawn is covered with a blanket of fresh snow, which, like the sky, is deep blue in color. Bare tree branches flank the building on both sides.

Fisher found the setting "one of those lovely scenes with fresh snow that photographers can't resist," but doesn't remember when the photo was made. "Early 1990s would be my best guess, but it might have been even earlier," she said. "The White House is so classic, it virtually hasn't changed appearance in the two decades I've been photographing it.

"The photo probably was taken during January, as that is when D.C. is most likely to get major snow. The time is around 5 p.m., as that is when 'blue time' or twilight occurs during December and January. This is a very short window, when exterior light drops to the same level as interior, and the exterior light on a cloudy day is soft blue."

Fisher set up her Canon 35mm camera on a tripod on the sidewalk outside the iron perimeter fence on Pennsylvania Avenue so the lens protruded through the bars of the fence, and shot the building from a point slightly to the left of dead center. She set her lens for maximum sharpness — around f.8 — and, after making reflected meter readings off the sky, the snow and the lit exterior of the White House itself, bracketed exposures around a basic exposure time of 3 to 4 seconds.

Frank Van Riper, a photography expert writing in *The Washington Post*, called what resulted "the image of a lifetime."

Microprinting on the stamp consists of the year date "2000" on the right side of the White House, near the bottom of the illuminated portion, between the second and third windows.

"Pat noted that her final picture worked so well because of a number of factors, all revolving around the theme of less being more," Van Riper wrote. "First, the uniformity of the snow and sky focuses the eye directly on the beautiful contours of the Executive Mansion. Second, there are no clouds in the sky to distract the viewer." Third, he added, because the holidays were past, there were no decorations, "thereby making the image a more universal — not seasonal, or holiday-related — depiction of the White House."

Noyes offered to CSAC a design incorporating the photograph in a larger format. "We kept getting reduced down, smaller and smaller," she said. The committee's conclusion was that printing the stamp in the special size "was the way it would probably get the most use, but it did kind of take away from the photograph, having it so tiny. It would have been a really spectacular-looking semijumbo stamp."

The designer used dropout white Garamond letters to spell "The White House" across the top of the image. "USA 33" is in the lower-right corner. The microprinting, which is a standard feature of single-design offset-printed issues, consists of the year date "2000" on the right side of the building, near the bottom of the illuminated portion, between the second and third windows.

First-day Facts

Jerry Lane, Capital District manager for the Postal Service, dedicated the stamp in a ceremony at the White House Visitors' Center, located in the Department of Commerce, a block from the executive mansion.

Speakers were Hugh S. Sidey, president, White House Historical Association; Gary J. Walters, chief usher at the White House; and Jim McDaniel, director for White House liaison for the National Park Service. Delores J. Killette, postmaster of Washington, presided.

"John Adams" made a special appearance, portrayed by Steven J. Perlman, park ranger and historian for the Independence National Historical Park in Philadelphia, and helped Lane unveil the stamp. Honored guests were Azeezaly S. Jaffer, USPS vice president for public affairs and communications; Ron Robinson, a Citizens' Stamp Advisory Committee member; and Derry Noyes and Patricia Fisher, the stamp's designer and photographer, respectively.

At the ceremony, Fisher asked Gary Walters if he could obtain President Clinton's signature on a first-day cover for her. Walters took the envelope and agreed to try. A short time later, the chief usher returned the photographer's cover, complete with the presidential autograph.

The earliest-known prerelease use of a White House stamp was on a cover machine-canceled in Worcester, Massachusetts, October 13, five days before the official first day of sale.

33¢ EDWARD G. ROBINSON
LEGENDS OF HOLLYWOOD SERIES

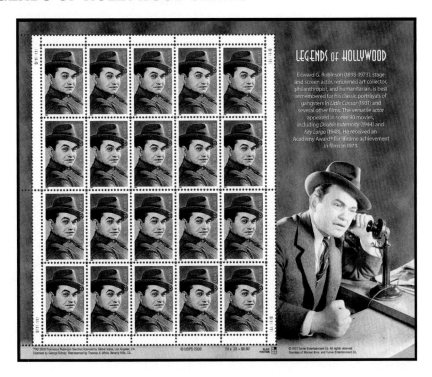

Date of Issue: October 24, 2000

Catalog Number: Scott 3446

Colors: stamps, magenta, cyan, yellow, black, gold (PMS 872); selvage, brown, black

First-Day Cancel: Burbank, California

First-Day Cancellations: 120,125

Format: Panes of 20, vertical, 5 across, 4 down. Gravure printing cylinders of 120 subjects (10 stamps across, 12 around) manufactured by Southern Graphics. Also sold in uncut sheets of 6 panes, 2 panes across, 3 panes down.

Gum Type: water-activated

Overall Stamp Size: 0.99 by 1.56 inches; 25.15 by 39.63mm

Pane Size: 8.75 by 7.25 inches; 222.25 by 184.15mm

Uncut Press Sheet Size: 17.75 by 22 inches

Perforations: 11 (APS rotary perforator) (star-shaped perforations at corners of each stamp)

Selvage Inscription: "LEGENDS OF HOLLYWOOD/Edward G. Robinson (1893-1973), stage/and screen actor, renowned art collector,/philanthropist, and humanitarian, is best/remembered for his classic portrayals of/gangsters in Little Caesar (1931) and/several other films. The versatile actor/appeared in some 90 movies,/including Double Indemnity (1944) and/Key Largo (1948). He received an/Academy Award® for lifetime achievement/in films in 1973." "™/©Francesca Robinson Sanchez licensed by Global Icons, Los Angeles, CA./Licensed by George Sidney. Represented by Thomas A. White, Beverly Hills, CA." With selvage illustration: "©1931 Turner Entertainment Co. All rights reserved./Courtesy of Warner Bros. and Turner Entertainment Co."

Selvage Markings: "©USPS 2000." "20 x .33 = $6.60." "PLATE/POSITION" and diagram.

Illustrator: Drew Struzan of Pasadena, California

Designer, Typographer and Art Director: Howard Paine of Delaplane, Virginia

Modeler: Donald H. Woo of Sennett Security Products, Chantilly, Virginia

Stamp Manufacturing: Stamps printed for Sennett Security Products by American Packaging Corporation, Columbus, Wisconsin, on Rotomec Roto 5 gravure press. Stamps finished by Unique Binders of Fredericksburg, Virginia.

Quantity Ordered: 52,000,000

Cylinder Number Detail: 1 set of 7 cylinder numbers preceded by the letter S in selvage beside each corner stamp

Cylinder Number Combination Reported: S1111111

Paper Supplier: Paper Corporation/Spinnaker Coatings

Tagging: full block tagging extends to the perforations on the block of 20 stamps

The Stamp

The sixth stamp in the Postal Service's Legends of Hollywood series honored actor Edward G. Robinson, who played tough-guy characters in many of his 100-plus films and numerous stage and television productions. It was issued in Los Angeles, California, October 24.

The stamp originally was scheduled to be dedicated September 14. But because of a USPS decision to change the location of the ceremony to Los Angeles from the Warner Bros. Studios in Burbank, the issue date was postponed. This abrupt change of plans, together with an internal communications lapse, caused many U.S. post offices to sell the Robinson stamp beginning in mid-September, unaware that they were violating USPS rules.

The Postal Service had intended for Robinson to be the Legends of Hollywood series subject for 1999. In mid-1998, however, the company that licenses James Cagney's name and image asked USPS for a Cagney stamp the following year, which would be the 100th anniversary year of Cagney's birth. Postal officials agreed, and postponed Robinson's stamp appearance to 2000.

The Robinson stamp has several things in common with its predecessors in the series, which honored Marilyn Monroe, James Dean, Humphrey Bogart, Alfred Hitchcock and Cagney. It has water-activated gum, is vertically arranged, was gravure-printed by Sennett Security Products (formerly Stamp Venturers) and was issued in panes of 20 with a wide selvage containing a picture and text on the right side. In addition to the normal round perforations, there are star-shaped perfs at the four corners of each stamp. A second row of perfs around the outer edges of the block of 20 stamps creates a narrow inner selvage, which is blank except for a set of plate numbers in each corner.

The tagging also is the same as that on previous Legends of Hollywood stamps. It consists of a large block of taggant applied over the 20 stamps so that it covers only the design areas, leaving the outer margins of the 14 outside stamps untagged.

USPS offered uncut sheets of six panes for sale to collectors at face value ($39.60), as it had done with the five previous Legends stamps. Like those sheets, the Robinson sheets have a vertical row of perforations down the middle, the stated purpose of which is to stabilize the sheets during the perforation process by allowing the mechanism perforating the sheet to hold it more securely as it goes through. When the sheets are cut into panes for sale at post offices, the internal row of perforations is on a one-eighth-inch strip of paper that is cut off.

Edward G. Robinson was born Emanuel Goldenberg December 12, 1893, in Bucharest, Romania, the fifth of six sons of Morris and Sarah Goldenberg. The family moved in 1902 to the United States, where Robinson grew up on New York City's Lower East Side.

He studied at City College of New York and the American Academy of Dramatic Arts and began acting on the stage in his early 20s. He also appeared in the 1916 film *Arms and the Woman*. His big break in motion pictures came in 1930, when he was cast as mobster Rico Bandello in Mervyn Le Roy's *Little Caesar*.

Because of his scowling face and often-imitated voice, Robinson frequently was cast as a criminal or gangster, although he was admired for his ability to portray other types, including the role of a German physician in *The Story of Dr. Erlich's Magic Bullet* (1940).

He starred in dozens of features from the 1930s through the 1960s, including *The Sea Wolf* (1941), in which he played the cruel captain, Wolf Larsen; *Double Indemnity* (1944); *Key Largo* (1948) and *The Ten Commandments* (1956). As the years went by, he undertook a diminished workload in order to enjoy his other interests, including his collection of art, his own paintings and his family. He devoted much of his time and money to charitable causes.

Although Robinson was awarded the Cannes Film Festival best-actor award for *House of Strangers* (1949), the Academy Award eluded him until 1973, when he received an Oscar for lifetime achievement. He died at age 79 shortly after receiving his award in the hospital.

The Design

Producing the final design of the Edward G. Robinson stamp and selvage proved to be a complicated task. Before it was over, three different artists had been involved, and three persons who had been close to Robinson had influenced the process.

At the outset, Terrence McCaffrey, head of stamp design for USPS, and art director Howard Paine gave the job of painting the star's portrait to veteran illustrator Ren Wicks. Wicks, then in his 80s, hadn't illustrated a U.S. stamp since the William Saroyan commemorative of 1992, and he had pleaded for another stamp assignment.

Working from photographs, Wicks produced several concept sketches in color. One, showing the actor in a gangster role puffing on a cigar, violated CSAC's no-smoking-on-stamps policy. The committee liked another Wicks sketch, but one of the members, movie actor Karl Malden, a longtime friend of Robinson, "didn't like it at all," recalled McCaffrey. "He said, this is just not Edward G."

Additional reference photographs were found and sent to Wicks. Meantime, however, the artist had been badly hurt in a fall and was unable to continue working. He eventually died of his injuries. McCaffrey and Paine had to find another illustrator.

These designs were based on paintings by Ren Wicks, the original artist on the Robinson stamp project. CSAC quickly rejected the image of Robinson with a cigar in his mouth. Committee member Karl Malden, a friend of Robinson, was dissatisfied with the other portrait. Wicks suffered a fatal fall before he could complete the stamp assignment.

Artist Thomas Blackshear's painting of Robinson had its admirers on CSAC but was vetoed by one of the members, fellow screen actor Karl Malden, and by George Sidney, another Robinson associate.

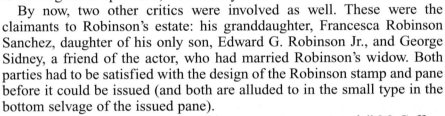

Their choice was Thomas Blackshear, a well-known painter of posters and other artwork for Hollywood films. Among several stamps that Blackshear had illustrated for USPS were the Classic Films block of four stamps of 1990 and the Joe Louis commemorative of 1993.

Blackshear produced a painting of Robinson that pleased McCaffrey and others on the committee — but not Malden. "Karl said Robinson looked 'too soft,' and needed to be toughened up a little," McCaffrey said.

By now, two other critics were involved as well. These were the claimants to Robinson's estate: his granddaughter, Francesca Robinson Sanchez, daughter of his only son, Edward G. Robinson Jr., and George Sidney, a friend of the actor, who had married Robinson's widow. Both parties had to be satisfied with the design of the Robinson stamp and pane before it could be issued (and both are alluded to in the small type in the bottom selvage of the issued pane).

"Getting them to agree on anything was not an easy task," McCaffrey sighed. "The granddaughter loved Thomas Blackshear's painting, but Sidney said it was the most hideous portrait he had ever seen and refused to accept it.

"We got to the point where, before we even started on artwork, we were sending black-and-white photos to the two estate holders AND to Karl Malden. 'If you can all agree, this is what we will paint from,' we told them, 'but we're not going to paint until you all agree on the pose.' Finally, one photograph got their approval.

"We went back to Thomas Blackshear and told him we would give him a new contract to paint a new portrait. A few weeks later he telephoned us and said he was having his studio remodeled and his house was torn up, and he couldn't do any work. So now we had gone through two artists and still had nothing. We were starting to wonder if this stamp was really meant to be."

McCaffrey and Paine now turned to Drew Struzan, another noted artist in the entertainment field, whose stamp credits included, in 1999, the portraits of Alfred Lunt and Lynn Fontanne, six Hollywood composers and six Broadway songwriters, and, in 2000, the Celebrate the Century stamps for the decade of the 1990s.

The publicity still photo on which Struzan based his portrait of Robinson was made by Warner Bros. staff photographer Elmer Fryer and shows the actor, in suit and fedora, facing right, his head turned to look at the viewer. Struzan's acrylic painting, with details in colored pencil, gives the proper prominence to the distinctive Robinson facial features, the heavy arched eyebrows and full lips. Its predominant colors are browns and greens.

The typography consists of the words "EDWARD G. ROBINSON USA 33" in a line of simple sans-serif capitals running up the right side of the stamp, in a style first used in the series on the James Cagney stamp of 1999. The type is in gold ink, superimposed on the illustration. Viewed at a certain angle, the letters virtually disappear from view.

Deciding on the proper selvage image also was a challenge. An assortment of photographs was tried and rejected as being too static. "We wanted some action, to differentiate the selvage picture from the stamp portrait," McCaffrey said. But one proposed picture, a drawing by Thomas Blackshear, had the wrong kind of action; it showed Robinson, as Rico Bandello in *Little Caesar*, clutching his arm after being shot. "We didn't want to show violence, even in the selvage," McCaffrey explained.

Finally, the committee settled on a publicity photo from the 1931 Warner Bros. film *Five Star Final* that shows Robinson as Randall, a tough newspaper editor, pounding his desk as he talks on the telephone. ("I loved Randall because he wasn't a gangster," Robinson wrote in his posthumously published autobiography *All My Yesterdays*. "*Five Star Final* is one of my favorite films.") The picture was printed in the selvage in a sepia tone, using brown and black plates. Francesca Sanchez didn't like the image, McCaffrey recalled, and promised to provide some alternative photographs, but didn't do so.

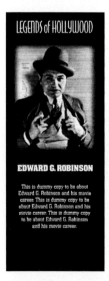 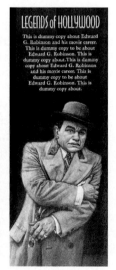  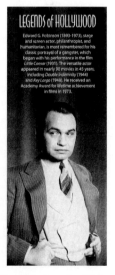

The design team tried out a number of alternative images for the selvage, including stills from Robinson's movies and a drawing by Thomas Blackshear of the star "taking a bullet" in the film Little Caesar, *before settling on a publicity photo for 1931's* Five Star Final.

First-day Facts

Karl Malden of CSAC and Tirso del Junco, a member of the USPS Board of Governors, dedicated the Robinson stamp at the historic Egyptian Theatre on Hollywood Boulevard. The event was held in conjunction with the American Film Institute's AFI Fest 2000, an international film festival that ran from Oct. 19 to 26.

The Postal Service's original plan to hold the dedication at the Warner Bros. Studios in Burbank was abandoned after Warner Bros. and USPS officials were unable to agree on the details of the event and how the cost would be apportioned. On short notice, Frank Thomas, the Postal Service's manager of special events, worked out an agreement with AFI to tie the stamp dedication to the festival.

Among those taking part in the dedication ceremony was comedian and television personality Steve Allen, who performed a piano interlude of music by George Gershwin. Allen, 78, died of a heart attack October 30, less than a week later. Comedian-impressionist Rich Little also entertained the crowd, noting how Robinson's distinctive voice offered rich material for impersonators.

Remembrances of Robinson were offered by Nanette Fabray; Florence Henderson, who appeared with Robinson in the 1970 film *Song of Norway*; Charlton Heston, who starred with Robinson in the 1956 epic *The Ten Commandments* and in Robinson's last film, *Soylent Green* of 1973; and Norman Lloyd.

Jean Picker Firstenberg, director and chief executive officer of the American Film Institute, gave the welcome. Robert Osborne, prime-time host and anchor for cable television's *Turner Classic Movies*, was the master of ceremonies.

Honored guests included Robinson's granddaughter, Francesca Robinson Sanchez; Adam Edward Sanchez, Robinson's great grandson; Drew Struzan, the stamp's illustrator; Azeezaly S. Jaffer, USPS vice president for public affairs and communications; and Michael Brock, a member of CSAC.

A screening of the 1965 Norman Jewison film *The Cincinnati Kid*, in which Robinson appeared with Steve McQueen, Ann-Margret and Malden, followed the first-day ceremony.

Postal clerks often use the USPS publication *Postal Bulletin* as a guide to when stamps are to be placed on sale. The original September 14 release date for the Robinson commemorative was published in the August 10 issue, and the announcement of the postponement didn't appear until September 21, a week after the stamp was supposed to have been released. As a result, according to *Linn's Stamp News* readers in several states, the Robinson stamp was available for purchase at post office counters well before the official release date.

The earliest-known use of the stamp was on a cover hand-canceled in Bradenton, Florida, September 9, 45 days early.

60¢ GRAND CANYON
SCENIC AMERICAN LANDMARKS SERIES

Date of Issue: January 20, 2000

Catalog Number: Scott C135

Colors: black, cyan, magenta, yellow

First-Day Cancel: Grand Canyon, Arizona

First-Day Cancellations: 64,282

Format: Pane of 20, horizontal, 4 across, 5 down. Offset printing plates of 180 subjects, 15 across, 12 around.

Gum Type: Self-adhesive

Overall Stamp Size: 1.56 by 0.99 inches; 39.62 by 25.15mm

Pane Size: 7.25 by 6.00 inches

Perforations: 11¼ by 11½ (die-cut simulated perforations)

Selvage Markings: "©USPS1999." ".60/x20/$12.00" "PANE POSITION" and diagram.

Designer, Typographer and Art Director: Ethel Kessler of Bethesda, Maryland

Photographer: Tom Till of Moab, Utah

Stamp Manufacturing: Stamps printed by Banknote Corporation of America (BCA), Browns Summit, North Carolina, on a Goebel 670 offset press. Stamps processed by BCA.

Quantity Ordered: 100,800,000

Cylinder Number Detail: 1 set of 4 cylinder numbers preceded by the letter B in selvage above or below each corner stamp

Cylinder Number Combinations Reported: B1111

Paper Supplier: Paper Corporation of the United States/Spinnaker Coatings

Tagging: block tagged

The Stamp

On January 20, the Postal Service issued a corrected version of a stamp it had planned to issue in 1999 but postponed because of an inscription error.

The item was a 60¢ international-rate airmail stamp in the Scenic American Landmarks series that depicted Arizona's Grand Canyon, the famous gorge through which the Colorado River flows. The entire initial printing of 100,750,000 specimens was ordered destroyed, at an estimated cost of $500,000, because the tiny printing beneath the image read "Grand Canyon, Colorado" instead of the correct "Grand Canyon, Arizona."

The day after the revised stamp, with the right identification line, was placed on sale, it became apparent how truly jinxed this issue was. Alerted by a staff member of the U.S. Park Service at Grand Canyon, Arizona, postal officials were chagrined to find that the photographic transparency used to create the image of the canyon in the design had been "flopped," or reversed, during the preparation of the design, so that the stamp shows a mirror image of the way the scene actually looks.

By now, however, the stamps had been distributed and were on general sale. USPS gave no thought to a second round of stamp destruction and revision.

Azeezaly S. Jaffer, director of stamp services for USPS, in a telephone conference with several journalists June 4, 1999, offered an explanation of how the first mistake — the wrong-state inscription — occurred.

"First, it was a human error, it was an honest human error," Jaffer said. "The design for the Grand Canyon was part of what we call a rate-change package that the [Citizens' Stamp Advisory] committee and the design committee can all work on and we keep in our bank so that if we're moving for an international-rate change we have the designs available and we're not starting from scratch."

The designs for the first three stamps in the Scenic American Landmarks series, depicting the Grand Canyon, Niagara Falls and the Rio Grande, were approved by then-Postmaster General Marvin Runyon, Jaffer said.

"It was about a month and a half or maybe two months [after] there was a design coordinators' meeting going on at which some members were present and the international rates were looking like they were going to change so we were doing all the prepress work, getting stuff to the printers, etc., and there was a discussion among the design coordinators and the committee members as follows:

" 'This is the Grand Canyon and if it's international it really ought to say something on there so that people overseas know what they're looking at, this American landscape, this American monument.'

"Then the discussion pursued about, 'Is it the Colorado River that runs through it, what river runs through it, what side of the canyon are we looking at?'

"... Ethel [Kessler] was the design coordinator on this one and she called the typographer at the printer and said, 'Grand Canyon, Colorado, needs to be microtyped into this thing.'

"And you know since the Bill Pickett [stamp] we have been super-careful on everything that we do. And it was an honest mistake that she made."

In 1994 a 29¢ stamp that was meant to honor rodeo star Bill Pickett was inadvertently illustrated with the likeness of another man, believed to be the cowboy's brother, Ben Pickett. Some specimens of the stamp were sold to the public before the Postal Service could withdraw the issue and reprint it using a portrait of the correct man. USPS subsequently contracted with a private firm, PhotoAssist, to do its subject and design research and fact verification.

"What we've done now," Jaffer said, "is that any changes that are even made at the printer come back in-house for three independent reviews."

Terrence McCaffrey, head of stamp design for USPS, provided some additional information in an interview with the *Yearbook*. As Jaffer had indicated, he said, there originally was no wording on the Grand Canyon, Niagara Falls and Rio Grande stamps.

"It wasn't until the last minute, when we were ready to go to printing, that the committee said, 'You know, these are going overseas, and we Americans know what these scenes are but foreigners don't, so we need to put place names on them,' " McCaffrey said.

"Contrary to what Mr. Jaffer said to the media, the inscription wasn't added at the printer [Banknote Corporation of America] at the request of Ethel Kessler. It was done at Ethel's studio."

The identifying information accompanying the transparency that was the source of the stamp image included the words "Colorado River," McCaffrey said.

"Ethel looked down and saw 'Colorado,' didn't connect 'River,' and just put in 'Grand Canyon, Colorado,' " he said. "She did it on her layout and then it was sent off to the printer.

"We weren't looking at enlarged-size images, because it was so late in the process. Normally we'd all see it at stamp size and four times up [four times stamp size]. PhotoAssist didn't see it; because it was added at the last minute, it didn't go through the normal process of approvals and reviews. If we had done it through that system, it would have been caught, but it wasn't, unfortunately."

How many people actually saw the wording before it went to press?

"Ethel, myself, probably a couple of people at Dodge Color who do the final preparation of files," said McCaffrey. "But everybody was looking at it at stamp size, and it was so minuscule it was hard to see, and nobody really paid attention, and it was one of those rush things. We were doing all the rate-change designs at the same time. So in the heat of things, it just got bypassed."

The error was called to McCaffrey's attention by a former USPS headquarters employee, Robin Wright, now deceased, who had been transferred to the Pacific Coast. "He was a very loud and boisterous guy," McCaffrey said. "We had just released the stamp images to the media, and he called me at home one night and yelled: "Terry!" and I knew who it was. "He said to me, 'Where in the blankety-blank is the Grand Canyon?' I said, 'What are you talking about?' He kept saying, 'Where is it?' I said,

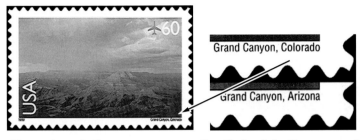

Shown here is the erroneous wording that originally appeared on the Grand Canyon stamp and the correct version that was on the stamp as issued.

'What are you getting at, Robin?'

"He said, 'We got all the press information and all the transparencies and at the bottom of the stamp it says, 'Grand Canyon, Colorado.' I said, 'Are you sure it doesn't say Colorado River?' He said, 'It doesn't.' "

"The next morning I checked and sure enough, there it was, 'Grand Canyon, Colorado,' as big as life. I called Cathy [Caggiano, head of stamp acquisition and distribution] and she said the stamp was still at the printer, we hadn't released any, and asked why I was inquiring. I told her, and the air was blue for a little bit."

Officials discussed the consequences of doing nothing about the mistake and releasing the stamps as they were, McCaffrey said. "It was actually not that long a conversation," he said. "Fortunately, it was not a major press run with hundreds of millions of stamps involved. We just felt that it would be worth it to go back and correct it. It was a matter of getting it right for posterity rather than having that error out there for everybody to look at for years to come."

McCaffrey, Caggiano and James Tolbert, manager of stamp development, made the joint recommendation that the error stamps be destroyed, and Jaffer concurred.

The job was done at the printer, using quarter-inch shredders. (McCaffrey has a shred the width of the press sheet that Caggiano gave him, angled so that the words "Grand Canyon, Colorado" can be seen.) Despite predictions by some philatelic journalists that whole stamps with this inscription would reach collectors' hands, no such instances have been reported as of this writing.

Inevitably, the jokes followed. *USA Today* reported the story on page one with the advice, "Get those people an atlas." The Associated Press said, "The Grand Canyon is an awfully big piece of real estate to misplace." And *The Record* of Bergen County, New Jersey, in an editorial approving the decision to reprint the stamps, concluded: "After all, if the Postal Service doesn't know where the Grand Canyon is, why should anyone expect it to deliver a letter to the right address?"

The Postal Service disclosed the second mistake — the reversing of the

After the fact, the Postal Service made this layout to show how the Grand Canyon should have looked, with Tom Till's photograph correctly displayed.

photograph — in a February 1, 2000, telephone press conference held by James Tolbert, in his first month as Jaffer's successor as manager of stamp services, and USPS spokespersons Don Smeraldi and David Failor. According to these officials, on January 21, the day after the first-day ceremony, the Denver office of USPS got a voice mail message from a U.S. Park Service staff member at Grand Canyon, saying he thought there was "something wrong" with the image.

Officials checked with Tom Till, the photographer who took the picture, and Ethel Kessler, and confirmed that the photo had been flopped. Tolbert said he took full responsibility for the error, which he characterized as an "oversight," but noted that the stamp's design had been on public view for several months. At no time, however, had Till been asked to verify the accuracy of the picture. Till told the *Yearbook* he hadn't known what the stamp looked like until USPS sent him a reproduction after the damage had been done.

"In their defense," Till said, "I get so many of my photographs published flopped. It happens all the time. I've gotten books where half the pictures are flopped.

"I've had stuff published in a lot of National Geographic Society publications and they've never gotten it wrong, but they've never called me in advance to say 'Hey, is this right?', either. So it wasn't a standard in the industry to worry about [picture reversal] so much until this."

With modern films, it's difficult to tell from looking at a transparency which side is the front and which is the back, Till said. "There's no substitute for checking with the photographer," he added.

The errors resulted in two separate investigations by the Postal Service's inspector general, Karla W. Corcoran. Her 1999 report concluded that the wrong-state inscription occurred because the Stamp Services Division didn't follow its established control processes. The 2000 review found that the reversing of the photograph wasn't detected because of insufficient internal controls.

Such controls now are in place, said McCaffrey, and they include Till's recommended remedy: consulting the photographer in advance to make sure the picture hasn't been reversed.

The Grand Canyon stamp wasn't the first to depict an image that was inadvertently flopped, although it got much more publicity. The 25¢

Americas commemorative of 1989 depicted a carved and painted wooden figure from the Mimbres culture of the American Southwest of several centuries earlier. Because artist Lon Busch, in painting the picture, worked from a museum-supplied photographic color transparency with the wrong side up, his artwork shows a mirror image of the actual figure.

The Grand Canyon stamp was the first in the American Scenic Landmarks series to be printed by offset lithography. Its predecessors, the 48¢ Niagara Falls and the 40¢ Rio Grande, were gravure-printed by Avery-Dennison Security Printing Division. The 60¢ denomination covered the then-prevailing rate for a half-ounce airmail letter to countries other than Canada and Mexico.

Carved by the rushing waters of the Colorado River over the course of some six million years, the Grand Canyon is one of the most spectacular natural landmarks in the United States. Through the exposure of multiple layers of earth, the canyon provides one of the world's best records of geologic history. Located in northwest Arizona, it is 217 miles long and averages a mile deep. Congress officially created Grand Canyon National Park in 1919, and today more than five million people visit the park each year.

A view of the Grand Canyon from the park lodge was shown on the 2¢ stamp of the 1934 National Parks series (Scott 741). A 6¢ commemorative of 1969 marked the 100th anniversary of the trip of John Wesley Powell, who led the first party to go through the gorge end to end (Scott 1374). In 1990 a 25¢ Americas series stamp (Scott 2512) showed the canyon from the south rim. A 32¢ stamp on the Celebrate the Century pane for the 1910s (Scott 3183h), issued in 1998, reproduced a representative view of the canyon by artist Dennis Lyall. The canyon also was pictured on a 9¢ Tourism Year of the Americas airmail postal card in 1972 (Scott UXC12) and on the back of a 6¢ card in the same series (Scott UX63).

The Design

In choosing images for the Scenic American Landmarks series, designer-art director Ethel Kessler examined a wide selection of stock photos assembled by PhotoAssist. The one she chose for the Grand Canyon was made by Tom Till, of Moab, Utah (web site www.tomtill.com), who has had more than 13,000 photos appear in print since 1977 and who has shot landscapes, nature and history in all 50 states and nearly 40 countries.

"As soon as I picked it up, I knew this was the one," Kessler said. "The lighting is gorgeous."

Till's picture, made in the summer of 1997, shows a sunrise over Lipan Point, in the Desert View portion of the park, some 25 miles to the east of Grand Canyon Village. The scene is a study in oranges, purples and blues. It was made with a 4 by 5 Toyo 45 A 11 Field Camera.

"It had rained all night, and I was camped out," Till recalled. "I got up before dawn and was hoping for something good, but when you're dealing with unpredictable weather you're just as likely to get nothing.

"Off to the east there's a lot of desert and often there are no clouds over

The letters "USPS," in black microtype, can be found on a ridge at the center of the stamp design, near the bottom.

that area when there are clouds over the Grand Canyon. So the sun came up, and really lit the clouds up beautifully above the canyon. I've spent at least six months of my life photographing the 'Can,' maybe more, and that was the most beautiful sunrise I've ever seen!"

When the picture was reversed on the stamp, east became west and the sunrise became a sunset.

In designing the stamps in the Scenic American Landmarks series, Ethel Kessler's aim has been to get the type "out of the way of the image and let the image have as much space on that stamp as possible," she said. On Grand Canyon, the "USA" and "60" are in a simple thin sans-serif typeface and are dropped out of the lower-left and upper-right corners of the design, respectively.

A little jet-plane silhouette, printed next to the denomination, is a hallmark of the series, indicating that the primary purpose of the stamps is to pay postage on international airmail. The intention of the Postal Service was that the plane be printed in silver ink, as it was on the Niagara Falls and Rio Grande stamps. However, on the Grand Canyon stamp the plane is in gray — actually, a screened black. McCaffrey attributed the change to an "oversight" that occurred during the hectic events involving the stamp's printing, destruction and reprinting.

Because the stamp is an offset-lithography product, the Postal Service required the use of microtype in the design as a security feature. The letters "USPS" are printed on the top of a ridge at the center of the design near the bottom edge. The letters are black and the background dark brown, making them difficult to find, even with a good magnifying glass (see illustration).

Varieties

At least six vertical pairs of the Grand Canyon stamp exist with no die-cut simulated perforations. The pairs come from a pane of 20 that originally was purchased from the USPS substation at the 2000 American Philatelic Society Stampshow in Providence, Rhode Island.

"The original owner bought three Grand Canyon panes at the APS show," Jacques C. Schiff Jr., a dealer who specializes in stamp errors, told *Linn's Stamp News*. "Two of the panes had partial die-cut impressions that did not completely penetrate the stamp paper. The third pane was similar to the first two, except that a portion of it had no die-cut impressions whatsoever. Six die-cut-missing pairs were taken from this third pane."

The vertical error pairs are listed in the 2002 Scott *Catalogue of U.S. Stamps & Covers* with the number C135a.

First-day Facts

Ruth E. Brooks, manager of marketing for the Postal Service's Western Area, dedicated the stamp in a ceremony in the Shrine of the Ages at Grand Canyon Village, Arizona. Charles M. Davis, USPS Arizona District manager for customer service and sales, gave the welcome. American Indian dancers and children from the Grand Canyon School shared stories about their lives in and around the canyon.

Instead of the usual folded event program issued at most U.S. first-day ceremonies, USPS representatives distributed a 6-inch by 9-inch never-folded program card. Roberta Wojtkowski developed the new format, which was done to reduce printing costs, and designed the card. It features an enlarged image of Tom Till's canyon photograph that was used on the stamp. Like the picture on the stamp, the program photo is reversed.

The earliest-known use of a Grand Canyon stamp was on a cover machine-canceled Charlotte, North Carolina, December 13, 1999, 38 days before the first day of issue. The cover was mailed to himself by a collector whose daughter had bought a pane of 20 stamps December 11 at the Carmel branch of the Charlotte post office.

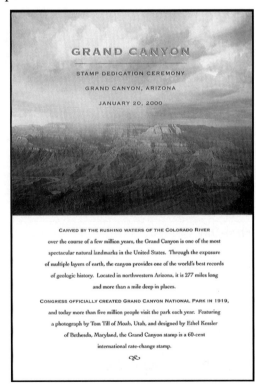

The unfolded card that served as a first-day ceremony program featured the same reversed image of the Grand Canyon that appears on the stamp.

33¢ FRUIT BERRIES (4 DESIGNS)
DOUBLE-SIDED CONVERTIBLE BOOKLET of 20

Date of Issue: March 15, 2000

Catalog Number:3294a, 3295a, 3296a, 3297a, single stamps; 3297d, double-sided pane of 20; 3297e, block of 4

Colors: magenta, yellow, cyan, black

First-Day Cancel: Ponchatoula, Louisiana

First-Day Cancellations: 40,911

Format: Convertible booklet of 20, vertical, with stamps on both sides, 2 across by 4 down plus booklet cover on one side, 2 across by 6 down on other side, with 2 horizontal peel-off strips on each side. Liner paper and peel-off strips on booklet-cover side are scored to facilitate folding. Gravure printing cylinders of 320 subjects (16 across, 20 around), cover side; 480 subjects (20 across, 24 around), other side.

Gum Type: self-adhesive

Overall Stamp Size: .870 by .982 inches; 22.10 by 24.94mm

Pane Size: 1.740 by 6.192 inches; 44.19 by 157.27mm

Perforations: 8½ (die-cut simulated perforations) (George Schmitt & Co. rotary die cutter)

Selvage Markings: On peel-off strips: "©USPS 1998 • Peel here to fold • 2-sided self-adhesive stamps." Plate numbers and "• Peel here to fold • DO NOT WET." "Peel here to fold • 2-sided self-adhesive stamps" • "DO NOT WET." "© USPS 1998 • Peel here to fold."

Back Markings: "FRUIT/BERRIES." "Twenty 33¢ stamps." "SELF-ADHE-SIVE/Four different designs." "$6.60." Universal Product Code "0 660500 1."

Illustrator: Ned Seidler of Hampton Bay, New York

Designer and Art Director: Howard Paine of Delaplane, Virginia

Typographer: Tom Mann of Vancouver, Washington

Stamp Manufacturing: Stamps printed by Guilford Gravure, Guilford, Connecticut, for Banknote Corporation of America, Browns Summit, North Carolina, on Cerutti R118 gravure press. Stamps processed by Guilford Gravure.

Quantity Ordered: 3,600,000,000

Plate Number Detail: 1 set of 4 plate numbers preceded by letter B on one peel-off strip on cover side.

Plate Number Combination: B1111

Paper Supplier: Paper Corporation of the United States/Spinnaker Coatings

Tagging: phosphored paper. Phosphate blocker applied to the cover portion of the pane.

The Stamps

On March 15, the Postal Service issued four different self-adhesive Fruit Berries definitives in a convertible booklet pane of 20 with stamps on both sides of the liner release paper.

The designs are the same as those used by USPS in 1999 for stamps in three self-adhesive formats: convertible booklet pane of 20 (with stamps on only one side), vending booklet of 15 and coil roll of 100. They feature bunches of blueberries, strawberries, raspberries and blackberries. However, the new stamps readily can be distinguished from the earlier ones by the black "2000" year date in the lower-left corner. The stamps issued in 1999 bear that year's date.

Like the 1999 Fruit Berries stamps, the new ones were printed by the gravure process by Guilford Gravure for Banknote Corporation of America.

The paper-saving double-sided format was introduced in 1999 with four Tropical Flowers commemorative stamps and was used again with that year's Christmas Madonna and Child stamp.

As was the case with those issues, the Fruit Berries stamps are arranged on the pane in blocks of four, with blueberries and raspberries above, strawberries and blackberries below. One side of the pane consists of eight stamps in two blocks, plus a panel bearing descriptive text and an enlargement of the strawberries design. The other side contains 12 stamps in three blocks of four.

The blocks on each side are separated by horizontal peel-off strips. When these are removed, the pane can be folded into a compact booklet, with the imprinted panel serving as the cover. To facilitate folding, the backing paper is scored with dashlike cuts that penetrate the peel-off strips on the front of the pane. Each stamp has one or two straight edges, depending on its location.

The stamps were printed on phosphored paper. The imprinted panel was coated with a transparent phosphor blocking compound so that if any portion of it was placed on an envelope in lieu of a stamp it would be rejected by the Postal Services' phosphor-sensitive facer-canceler machines.

The Designs

The designs of the stamps, by Howard Paine based on illustrations by Ned Seidler, are the same as those used on the 1999 Fruit Berries stamps.

Seidler's painted berries are in bunches, each bunch sitting on a mottled pinkish surface and casting shadows. "We wanted to show the berries as a product," Paine said. "The little shadows are suggestive of the fact that these have been bought and brought home and are on a plate or something; they're not a botanical thing, hanging on a vine."

The "33 USA" in the each stamp's upper-left corner is in black Galliard type.

First-day Facts

The stamps first went on sale in Ponchatoula, Louisiana, where the 1999 Fruit Berries stamps had made their debut. This time there was no first-day ceremony. The city is the home of the annual Ponchatoula Strawberry Festival, which USPS described as "the largest free two-day festival in Louisiana."

33¢ CORAL PINK ROSE
DOUBLE-SIDED CONVERTIBLE BOOKLET OF 20

Date of Issue: April 7, 2000

Catalog Number: Scott 3052E, single stamp; 3052Ef, booklet of 20

Colors: green (PMS 364), pink (PMS 219), black

First-Day Cancel: New York, New York

First-Day Cancellations: 18,199

Format: Convertible booklet pane of 20, horizontal. Stamps on both sides, 8 (2 across by 4 down) plus booklet cover on one side, 12 (2 across by 6 down) on other side, with 2 horizontal peel-off strips on each side. Gravure printing cylinders of 288 (18 across, 16 around), cover side; 432 (18 across, 24 around), all-stamp side.

Gum Type: self-adhesive

Overall Stamp Size: 0.98 by 0.87 inches

Pane Size: 5.53 by 1.96 inches; 140.46 by 49.78mm

Perforations: 10¾ by 10½ (die-cut simulated perforations) (Comco custom die-cutter)

Selvage Markings: "• Peel here to fold • DO NOT WET" plus cylinder numbers on first peel-off strip on all-stamp side; "©USPS 1998 • Peel here to fold • Double-Sided Booklet" on second peel-off strip on all-stamp side.

Back Markings: "Coral Pink/Rose/Twenty/33c/Self-adhesive/stamps/$6.60" plus Universal Product Code (UPC) on booklet cover.

Illustrator: Ned Seidler of Hampton Bay, New York

Designer and Art Director: Derry Noyes of Washington, D.C.

Typographer: John Boyd of New York, New York

Modeler: Donald Woo of Sennett Security Products of Chantilly, Virginia

Stamp Manufacturing: Stamps printed for Sennett Security Products by American Packaging Corp. of Columbus, Wisconsin, on Rotopak 3000-ES gravure press. Stamps finished by Unique Binders of Fredericksburg, Virginia.

Quantity Ordered: 350,000,000 stamps

Cylinder Number Detail: 1 set of 3 cylinder numbers preceded by the letter S on 1 peel-off strip.

Cylinder Number Combinations Reported: S111, S222, S333

Paper Supplier: Nichimen of America

Tagging: phosphored paper. Phosphate blocker applied to the cover portion of the pane.

The Stamp

On April 7, the Postal Service issued a new variety of the 33¢ Coral Pink Rose self-adhesive definitive that had made its debut the previous August 13. The new stamp bore a "2000" year date in the lower-left corner and was sold in two-sided convertible booklets of 20. The first version carried a "1999" date and was issued in two formats: convertible booklets of 20 with stamps on only one side, and prefolded vending-machine booklets of 15.

Like its predecessor, the 2000 Coral Pink Rose was printed by the gravure process by American Packaging Corporation of Madison, Wisconsin, for Sennett Security Products. The stamps were processed by Sennett's Unique Binders of Fredericksburg, Virginia.

The 2000 Coral Pink Rose was the second stamp issue of 1999 to be brought back the following year in the paper-saving two-sided booklet form and with the year dates changed. The first was the Fruit Berries set of four designs, which made its 2000 return as a two-sided booklet March 15 (see separate chapter).

Like the Fruit Berries, the Coral Pink Rose stamps are arranged on the pane in blocks of four. One side of the pane consists of eight stamps in two blocks, plus a panel bearing descriptive text and an enlargement of the rose design. The other side contains 12 stamps in three blocks of four. All 20 stamps have at least one straight edge.

The blocks on each side are separated by horizontal peel-off strips.

When these are removed, the pane can be folded into a compact booklet, with the imprinted panel serving as the cover. To facilitate folding, the backing paper is scored with dashlike cuts that penetrate the peel-off strips.

The stamps were printed on phosphored paper. The imprinted panel was coated with a transparent phosphor blocking compound so that if any portion of it was placed on an envelope in lieu of a stamp it would be rejected by the Postal Services's phosphor-sensitive facer-canceler machines.

Collectors of used stamps who attempted to soak specimens of the 2000 Coral Pink Rose from envelopes encountered a problem they hadn't seen since self-adhesive stamps were introduced on a permanent basis in 1989. Normally, a water-soluble buffer between the stamp and the pressure-sensitive adhesive dissolves after a few minutes of soaking in room-temperature water and the stamp floats free of the envelope or can be peeled off easily. However, the 2000 Coral Pink Rose — unlike its 1999 predecessor — couldn't be removed without damaging the stamp even after several days of soaking.

Charles Snee, in *Linn's Stamp News*, described an experiment in which he conducted separate water soaks of three used 2000 Coral Pink Rose stamps, increasing both the time and water temperature on each occasion. The third soak lasted 100 minutes and was done in water "hot enough to brew a cup of tea," which Snee replaced halfway through the test to keep the temperature up. Each attempt resulted in stamps that were torn or severely thinned.

Pressed for an explanation, the Postal Service's stamp acquisition office at first reported that there was nothing different about the paper used for the 2000 Coral Pink Rose. Several months later, however, the office acknowledged that there was a problem, and issued this statement:

"International Paper used to produce their stamp paper with starch sizing on the wire side of the paper. Since the process is done with wet paper, some of the fiber is exposed when the paper is dried. When the pressure-sensitive adhesive was laminated to the face paper, the adhesive had direct contact with the paper fibers and, therefore, affected the water removability of the stamp.

"International Paper agreed to change the wire side coating by using a primer coat developed specifically to improve the fiber sealing and, therefore, improve the water removability requirements of their stamp paper."

The Design

The design of the 2000 Coral Pink Rose stamp is identical to that of the 1999 version except for the year date. It features an enlarged, tightly cropped image of a pink rose blossom framed by green leaves. The original artwork was by Ned Seidler of Hampton Bay, New York. Seidler also had painted the four varieties of fruit berry used on definitive stamps of 1999 and 2000, as well as the illustrations for many other U.S. stamps depicting flowers or fruit.

Shown here is the 12-stamp side of a convertible booklet that is completely missing the black ink. The missing black is most obvious in the absence of the "33 USA" inscription that appears in the top left corner of each normal stamp. The two horizontal selvage strips on the error side of the pane also are missing the black. Only the top selvage strip bears any printing: two "1" digits from the plate number, representing the pink and green of the flowers. The bottom selvage strip is blank.

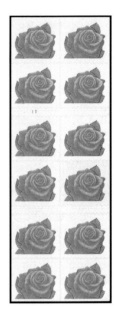

Varieties

In 2001, a convertible booklet was found on which the 12-stamp side was completely missing the black ink on the stamps and horizontal selvage strips. The eight-stamp side of the pane was normal. A single stamp from the error pane was scheduled to be sold during the November 8-9, 2001, unreserved public auction of Jacques C. Schiff Jr. Schiff told *Linn's Stamp News* that he probably would sell other singles from the pane in the near future.

Two examples of production varieties caused by misregistration between the printed web and the cutters were reported to *Linn's Stamp News*.

On one, the vertical cut that normally would separate two panes on the web was made between two vertical rows of stamps on a pane. The resulting freak pane shows no evidence of vertical cutting between pairs of stamps.

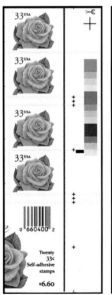
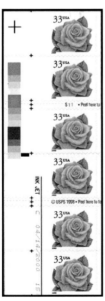

Shown here at the left and center are the two sides of the freak Coral Rose pane described in the text. The cover side of a normal pane is illustrated at right.

302

The other, more dramatic in appearance, is a pane that contains only 10 stamps instead of 20 and shows marginal markings from the original printed roll of stamp paper (see illustration). A black vertical line runs the length of the miscut pane. Several markings, including a plus sign, registration crosses and color test bars, appear to the right of the line. Similar markings appear on the reverse side of the pane, including a sprayed-on "04/14/2000" that may indicate when the stamps were printed.

In each case, at some point during the finishing process (slicing the die-cut, printed web of stamp paper into individual panes), a misregistration occurred, either with the paper roll or the cutters, resulting in the shift.

First-day Facts

Because the stamp has the same design as the one issued in 1999, the Postal Service at first said there would be no first-day ceremony. But later it was announced that the 2000 Coral Rose would be issued in New York City on the second day of the April 6-9 Postage Stamp Mega-Event.

For a limited time, Stamp Fulfillment Services offered uncacheted first-day covers for 54¢.

33¢ FRUIT BERRIES (4 DESIGNS), LINERLESS COIL

Date of Issue: June 16, 2000

Catalog Numbers: Scott 3404-3407, single stamps; 3407a, strip of 4

Colors: magenta, yellow, cyan, black

First-Day Cancel: Buffalo, New York

First-Day Cancellations: 35,671

Format: Coils of 100, horizontal. Gravure printing cylinders of 384 subjects, 16 across, 24 around.

Gum Type: self-adhesive, with no liner paper

Overall Stamp Size: .982 by .870 inches; 24.94 by 22.10mm

Perforations: 8½ (die-cut simulated perforations) (George Schmitt & Co. rotary die cutter)

Illustrator: Ned Seidler of Hampton Bay, New York

Designer and Art Director: Howard Paine of Delaplane, Virginia

Typographer: Tom Mann of Vancouver, Washington

Stamp Manufacturing: Stamps printed by Guilford Gravure of Guilford, Connecticut, on Cerutti 8/C gravure press. General Electric-made front-side release coating added and stamps processed by Guilford Gravure.

Quantity Ordered: 330,000,000

Cylinder Number Detail: 1 set of 4 cylinder numbers preceded by the letter G on every 12th stamp

Cylinder Number Combination Reported: G1111

Paper Supplier: Westvaco

Tagging: phosphored paper

The Stamps

On June 16, the Postal Service issued a linerless roll of 100 self-adhesive coil stamps bearing four now-familiar Fruit Berries designs. The designs, featuring bunches of blueberries, strawberries, raspberries and blackberries, had been used in 1999 on stamps in three different self-adhesive formats — coil with liner and two kinds of booklet — and were used again for a double-sided convertible booklet of 20 stamps issued March 15, 2000 (see separate chapter).

All previous Fruit Berries stamps had been laid out vertically. For the linerless coil stamps, however, the designs were revised to fit a horizontal layout, with die-cut simulated perforations at top and bottom rather than on the sides. They were the first regularly issued horizontal U.S. coil stamps since the 3¢ Francis Parkman Prominent Americans stamp of 1975 (Scott A1297). The experimental variable-rate coil stamp of 1992 also was horizontal.

The layout requires a top-to-bottom arrangement of the stamps on the coil roll, creating what collectors call a vertical coil. In a press release, the Postal Service explained that this arrangement was intended to "facilitate use by left-handed as well as right-handed customers."

(Of this explanation, dealer Robert Rabinowitz wrote in a column in *Linn's Stamp News*: "This writer happens to be a pure left-hander. I have had absolutely no trouble handling traditional horizontal coil stamps. I hold the roll in my right hand and readily pull off what I need with my left hand.

("As a matter of fact, I think the traditional arrangement favors left-handed people. So what is the Postal Service talking about? What's the real reason for the new format?")

The stamps are linked to each other by their interlocking die-cut simulated perforations and are coiled upon themselves like a roll of transparent adhesive tape, allowing them to be dispensed one at a time as necessary for postage.

USPS pointed out in its press release that the linerless Fruit Berries stamps were "environmentally friendly and less costly to produce when compared to previously issued coils with liner paper." The elimination of

A roll of 100 Fruit Berries linerless coil stamps.

the backing paper and a plastic dispenser that had been offered as an option with previous linerless coils "saves material resources and could potentially reduce production and storage costs," the release said.

The earlier Fruit Berries stamps were gravure-printed by Guilford Gravure of Guilford, Connecticut, as a subcontractor for Banknote Corporation of America. For the linerless coils, however, Guilford was both the printer and prime contractor. For this reason, the four-digit cylinder number that appears on every 12th stamp is preceded by the letter G, rather than B, as on the previous versions.

After applying the four process colors that create the stamp design, Guilford covered the front of the stamps with a silicone release coating to prevent the stamps from sticking to each other. The product is called G.E. Release, after its manufacturer, General Electric. A small tab of liner paper is attached to the first stamp in each roll to facilitate the stamp's separation from the roll, and a strip of liner paper is attached to the last eight stamps on the roll for what USPS called "adhesive protection."

The linerless rolls were individually shrink-wrapped and packaged in vertical groups (or "sticks," in Postal Service terminology) of five rolls for distribution to post offices.

Linerless U.S. self-adhesive stamps made their debut in 1997 with the release of the two experimental issues with limited distribution: the 32¢ Flag Over Porch linerless coil (Scott 3133), with die-cut simulated perfs, and the nondenominated (25¢) service-inscribed Juke Box linerless coil (Scott 3132), which was imperforate.

Flag linerless coils were sold only in rolls of 100. For an extra 25¢, buyers could get the aforementioned plastic dispenser, similar to those made for rolls of transparent tape. Included with the rolls were storage strips of liner material with a release coating. Collectors could mount up to seven stamps on the strips for storage or display in a collection.

The Juke Box linerless coil stamp was sold in rolls of 10,000 or 30,000. However, because of the large size of the rolls, collectors were offered the option of buying the stamp in strips of seven, already mounted on liner material.

The linerless Fruit Berries coil stamps, like the Flag Over Porch prototype, also were sold only in full rolls. Those ordered from Stamp Fulfill-

306

ment Services in Kansas City, Missouri, were sent along with five storage strips of liner material. Each strip measured 1.25 inches by 7 inches, long enough to hold a strip of seven stamps. This is two more than the typical strip of five stamps, with the plate-number coil stamp in the center, that is saved by PNC collectors.

However, the Postal Service apparently overlooked the fact that because the Fruit Berries coil consisted of four different designs in a repeating pattern — strawberry, blackberry, raspberry, blueberry — the concept of five stamps as the PNC collectible unit didn't apply.

The four-digit cylinder number appears on every 12th stamp, which is always a blackberry. The 11 stamps in between each pair of numbered stamps, including two blackberry stamps, have no numbers. PNC collectors want strips that contain both numbered and unnumbered examples, but many of them also want symmetry. In the case of the Fruit Berries, that requires nine stamps, with a numbered blackberry in the center and a numberless blackberry on either end. The Scott catalog recognizes two options for PNC strips, five stamps and nine stamps, just as it does for the earlier Fruit Berries coil stamps issued on liner paper.

Because the liner strips furnished by Stamp Fulfillment Services were too short to hold strips of nine, dealers and collectors had to improvise. Dealer Stephen G. Esrati reported that one wholesaler was mounting the strips on backing paper he obtained from a roll of 10,000 conventional self-adhesive coil stamps that had gone through an automatic stamp-affixing machine. Another dealer, Robert Rabinowitz, suggested that collectors use the backing from self-adhesive rolls of 100 or 500 registry labels that can be obtained from post offices.

Linn's Stamp News sounded a note of caution about storage strips. "It is still not known if these ... strips are of archival quality, suitable for long-term care of stamps," the publication said. "Therefore, collectors should be cautious about using them to mount their stamps."

The Scott *Specialized Catalogue of U.S. Stamps & Covers* warned of another potential problem for collectors. "The adhesive [on the linerless Fruit Berry coil stamps] is strong and can remove the ink from stamps in the roll," read a footnote. Charles Snee of *Linn's* wrote of buying a strip of linerless Fruit Berries from a local post office, only to find that one of the Blueberry stamps was missing a small portion of its design. The missing portion was found attached to the adhesive side of a Strawberry stamp that had been directly on top of the Blueberry stamp when the strip was part of its original roll.

The stamps created problems for non-collectors, as well. An internal USPS memo addressed to "All Offices" and sent to some post offices in the Midwest in mid-September 2000 noted "that some of our customers returned [Fruit Berries coils] because of difficulty in removing [the] stamps." The memo then asked employees to "share the following information with customers so that stamps can be separated properly."

"Since there is no liner paper to support the [coiling] of stamps, the stamps have to be 'interconnected' so a roll can be formed," the memo said.

"Unlike coil stamps with liner paper, in which adjacent stamps were separated by a complete die cut, the Berries linerless coil stamp was constructed with 'tensile-strength-balanced' die cuts."

This technical description meant that the die cuts are similar to a roulette rather than cut through along the entire length of the die cut, as was the case with the 1999 Berries coils. Thus, when a linerless Berries coil stamp is separated from the roll, small tufts of paper fiber can be seen on either side of the die-cut peak.

"Please tell customers to hold the stamp they intend to use and the stamp next to it, then pull them apart" to avoid tearing stamps, the memo said.

"Also, please ask them to save the small liner paper tab at the beginning of each roll and place it under the leading stamp after each use. This practice would facilitate use and prevent damage to the underlying stamps."

The Designs

The linerless coil stamps depict the same Ned Seidler illustrations of berries that were shown on the Fruit Berries stamps issued in 1999 and earlier in 2000. However, because the new stamps are horizontally rather than vertically arranged, their designs display more of the mottled pinkish surface on which the berries are placed, and more white space to the left of the berries, than do the designs of the earlier versions.

The designs include a black "2000" year date superimposed on the pinkish background in the lower-left corner. The vertically arranged Fruit Berries coil stamps that were issued in 1999 bear that year's date, which is located below the illustration on the left.

Plate numbers on modern U.S. coil stamps almost always are at the bottom of the stamp, parallel to the straight edge. However, on horizontally arranged coil stamps like the linerless Fruit Berries the straight edges are on the left and right sides. On these stamps, the cylinder number combination found on every 12th stamp is along the right-side straight edge, reading bottom to top.

First-day Facts

The linerless Fruit Berries coil stamps were released in conjunction with the June 16-18 National Topical Stamp Show 2000 at the Buffalo Convention Center in Buffalo, New York. There was no official USPS first-day ceremony, although the sponsoring American Topical Association and the Buffalo post office jointly hosted an event.

USPS offered sets of four uncacheted first-day covers, each franked with a different stamp, for $2.16 per set.

10¢ JOSEPH W. STILWELL
DISTINGUISHED AMERICANS SERIES

Date of Issue: August 24, 2000

Catalog Number: Scott 3420

Colors: black, red (PMS 1797) (offset); black (intaglio)

First-Day Cancel: Providence, Rhode Island

First-Day Cancellations: 21,669

Format: Pane of 20, vertical, 5 across, 4 down. Offset and intaglio printing plates of 240 subjects, 15 across, 16 around.

Gum: water activated

Overall Stamp Size: 0.84 by 0.99 inches; 21.34 by 25.15mm

Pane Size: 5.04 by 4.95 inches; 128.02 by 125.73mm

Perforations: 11 (Wista BPA 9070 stroke perforator)

Selvage Markings: "©USPS/2000." ".10/x20/$2.00." "Plate/Position" and diagram. Universal Product Code (UPC) "106600."

Illustrator: Mark Summers of Waterdown, Ontario, Canada

Designer, Art Director and Typographer: Richard Sheaff of Scottsdale, Arizona

Engraver: Chemically engraved by Banknote Corporation of America, Browns Summit, North Carolina

Stamp Manufacturing: Stamps printed by BCA on Goebel 670 offset press and Epikos 5009 intaglio press. Stamps processed by BCA.

Quantity Ordered: 100,000,000

Plate Number Detail: 2 offset plate numbers preceded by the letter B and 1 intaglio plate number in selvage above or below each corner stamp

Plate Number Combination Reported: B11-1

Paper Supplier: Paper Corporation of the United States/Spinnaker Coatings/Ivex

Tagging: phosphored paper

The Stamp

On August 24, the Postal Service launched a new series of definitives with a 10¢ stamp depicting General Joseph W. Stilwell, a prominent U.S. military leader of World War II. The first-day ceremony in Providence, Rhode Island, was one of the opening events of the American Philatelic Society's annual Stampshow.

USPS officials at the outset weren't thinking in terms of a new series, but rather of a redesign of the Great Americans series, which was introduced in 1980 with a 19¢ stamp honoring Sequoyah and went on to become the Postal Service's basic group of small-size, sheet-format definitive stamps of varied denominations.

However, the new stamps, beginning with the 10¢ Stilwell, constituted such a sharp departure in appearance from the Great Americans — they were bicolored, not monochrome, and they incorporated italic type rather than Roman — that collectors concluded that a new series was at hand and called for a new name. The Postal Service accepted their verdict and announced that the set would be called "Distinguished Americans." This meant that the 55¢ Justin Morrill stamp, which had been issued in 1999 as the 63rd face-different entry in the Great Americans series, became in retrospect the last of its line.

The intent behind the Great Americans was to honor not only well-known individuals but also people of significant achievement whose names were less well known to the public. The stamps, printed by intaglio, were simple and free of ornamentation, but over time, as new entries appeared, their appearance underwent subtle changes. In 1990, for example, the designs began including a word or words describing the pictured individual's field of activity.

Ultimately, the Citizens' Stamp Advisory Committee and the Postal Service's part-time art directors "decided the Great Americans needed to be revamped, reworked, redesigned," said Terrence McCaffrey, manager of stamp development and head of stamp design for USPS. "We felt the design format was getting dated and tired, and the type treatment was too varied for consistency's sake. We felt the designs needed a little life and oomph to draw some interest."

One artist who could provide that "life and oomph," the officials agreed, was Mark Summers. Summers is well known for the portraits of literary personalities — some verging on caricature — he has created for the chain bookseller, Barnes & Noble. These images can be found on banners, posters, bags and flyers at Barnes & Noble stores across the country. He uses the scratchboard technique, which, unlike traditional drawing and painting, consists of subtraction, not addition. The artist begins with a completely black surface and scratches away the unwanted color with a pointed tool, leaving the remaining lines and shapes to form the picture.

The committee agreed with McCaffrey's suggestion. Summers was contacted at his home in Waterdown, Ontario, Canada, and gladly enlisted in the redesign project.

310

When USPS unveiled the design of the Stilwell stamp May 30, 2000 — earlier, it had unveiled another definitive in the same design style that honored Claude Pepper — it described them as the first items in what it called "the newly redesigned Great Americans series." But some in the hobby weren't buying the idea.

"It's obvious that it's really something else," *Linn's Stamp News* associate editor Charles Snee wrote in a news story. "While the ... stamp shares some obvious general characteristics of its Great Americans predecessors, such as size and acknowledgment of the honoree's name and significant occupation on the stamp, it is significantly different."

"What is clear is that the two new stamps thus far unveiled are both very different from the last two decades of the Great Americans, and similar enough to be grouped together as part of a new series," wrote Fred Baumann in *Stamp Collector*. "We've already run through the 'Famous' (1940), the 'Prominent' (1965-78) and the 'Great' Americans (1980-99) — perhaps 'Outstanding' Americans should come next."

"In no way can they be seen as an extension of the Great Americans," added *Linn's* editor and publisher Michael Laurence in his column. "This is clearly a whole new definitive series, for which a new name is needed. Michael Schreiber, *Linn's* managing editor, facetiously suggested that we call them the Scratchboard Americans. That's a good descriptor and has a nice ring to it, but I suspect there's a better title." He invited readers to offer suggestions.

Meanwhile, however, the Postal Service had independently arrived at the same conclusion. This resulted from an exchange between Terrence McCaffrey and stamp writers after a talk by McCaffrey in early July at World Stamp Expo 2000 in Anaheim, California. The writers made such a persuasive case for a new series, McCaffrey said, that he took the idea back to CSAC and convinced the members.

On July 27, USPS officially proclaimed the "Distinguished Americans"

These are three of Richard Sheaff's proposals for a new design format for the Great Americans series, using existing scratchboard portraits by Mark Summers of Will Rogers, William Faulkner and James Joyce. In the end, another Sheaff design approach, also using italic type, was adopted, and a new series, "Distinguished Americans," was launched.

series. McCaffrey issued this explanation:

"We have received numerous letters and calls from the collecting community asking us to give the new design format of these stamps a new title. Stamp collectors felt that the change from the one-color Great Americans design to our new bicolor designs warranted a new series.

"In response to these wishes, the members of the Citizens' Stamp Advisory Committee decided to change the name of the series."

The Stilwell stamp has water-activated gum and conventional perforations. It was printed in two colors by Banknote Corporation of America (BCA) by a combination of intaglio (black) and offset (red and black) and issued in panes of 20. Whereas the Great Americans stamps were engraved by human craftsmen, the die for the intaglio portion of the Stilwell stamp (the portrait) was produced using a photochemical etching process. The two Distinguished Americans stamps, for Stilwell and Claude Pepper, were the only intaglio stamps issued by USPS in 2000.

The 10¢ denomination covers no postal rate by itself but is a useful value for making up various higher rates. With a 10¢ face value, the Stilwell stamp replaces a workhorse Great Americans stamp, the 10¢ Red Cloud (Scott 2175), that was issued in 1987 and has been reprinted periodically.

Postal officials intend to issue the Distinguished Americans stamps in a variety of denominations, which was the original plan for the Great Americans series. In later years, however, several new Great Americans stamps bore the prevailing first-class-rate denominations because their advocates were "politically connected," McCaffrey said, and let USPS management know that they wanted the stamps to be used on first-class mail.

The push for a stamp honoring Joseph Stilwell went back to at least 1989, when John Easterbrook, a grandson of the general, began lobbying the Postal Service for it. Some time thereafter, CSAC approved Stilwell as a Great Americans stamp subject. A design was prepared, based on a pencil portrait by Keith Birdsong of Muskogee, Oklahoma, illustrator of several previous U.S. stamps. The design was "banked" by the Stamp Services section for use when postal rates changed and new stamp denominations would be needed. When the Great Americans series was terminated, however, the Birdsong portrait of Stilwell became obsolete.

Joseph Warren Stilwell served with distinction in the U.S. Army for 42 years. He was known for his candor and his willingness to share the hardships of the common soldier.

He was born in 1883 in Palatka, Florida, and graduated from the U.S. Military Academy in 1904. During World War I, he was an intelligence officer with the fourth Army Corps and was awarded the Distinguished Service Medal. He served three tours of duty in China between the two World Wars, becoming fluent in the Chinese language, and was the military attache at the U.S. Embassy in Peking from 1935 to 1939.

Stilwell commanded all U.S. military forces in the China-Burma-India

Theater during World War II. He also served as chief of staff to Generalissimo Chiang Kai-shek, supreme commander of the Chinese theater, and was the first American general to command a Chinese army.

In 1942, Stilwell was sent to aid the Chinese and British troops defending Burma against Japan. When Japan forced the Allies to withdraw from Burma in May 1942, Stilwell led a group of some 100 soldiers and civilians on a daring 140-mile march through the Burmese jungle to safety in India.

In late 1943, Stilwell led two divisions of Chinese troops he had trained in India, and a U.S. long-range penetration group known as "Merrill's Marauders," back into northern Burma to retake it from Japan. The vital Ledo-Burma Road supply line was reopened in January 1945, ending the land blockade of China, and later was renamed the "Stilwell Road."

Political considerations led to Stilwell's recall from command in the China-Burma-India Theater in October 1944. He assumed command of the Tenth Army in Okinawa in June 1945 and was present on the battleship *USS Missouri* when Japan formally surrendered September 2, 1945. He was awarded the Legion of Merit and the Oak Leaf cluster of the Distinguished Service Medal. In 1946, he was appointed commander of the Sixth Army in charge of the Western Defense Command. He died later that year in San Francisco, California.

According to John Easterbrook, his grandson, Stilwell acquired his famous nickname, "Vinegar Joe," when he was in charge of tactics training in the 1930s. After dressing down an officer for trying to bluff his way through a reconnaissance problem, Stilwell was greeted the next morning by a drawing of a vinegar jug tacked to a bulletin board. The jug bore a caricature of him.

"Stilwell liked it so much," Easterbrook wrote, "that he obtained permission to reproduce it and sent it to his friends. From then on, he was 'Vinegar Joe.' "

The Design

Terrence McCaffrey asked some of his art directors to try their hand at devising the new look that was wanted for the series. Sheaff made several design mockups, using existing portraits by Mark Summers to see how they would work, and Howard Paine did the same thing with photographs of William Jennings Bryan and Admiral Chester W. Nimitz. At the end, one of Sheaff's design formats was chosen.

It consists of a head-and-shoulders portrait of the subject against a white background and a hairline partial frame. The name of the subject, in Minion bold italic letters, runs up the left side, outside the frameline. The descriptive words — in Stilwell's case, "General, U.S. Army" — are in Minion Display italic and run down the right side. "USA" and the denomination, in Minion regular, are placed inside the frame.

On the Stilwell stamp, only the portrait, which is black, is printed by intaglio. The rest of the design — the subject's name, in red, and the rest

of the typography and frame, which are black — is printed by offset.

Columnist John Hotchner, writing in *Linn's*, reported a tendency on the part of the offset-printed frameline to shift slightly horizontally, in relation to the engraved portrait, from one pane to another. He credited collector R.C. de Mordaigle of California with spotting the phenomenon.

"Sometimes, with his portraits, Mark [Summers] uses an exaggerated style," said Terrence McCaffrey. "He elongates faces and does unique, clever things to typify that person's character and what he's famous for. We told him we didn't want him to do that with the stamp portraits — that this had to be a little more serious."

Summers based his portrait of Stilwell on a photo by an unknown photographer that was supplied by the Library of Congress. The photo shows the bespectacled, burr-cut officer in his Army uniform with the four stars of a full general, which means it was taken some time after August 1, 1944, when he received his fourth star. It was the same photo on which Keith Birdsong had based his pencil sketch for the unused Great Americans stamp design.

"The technique I use is very laborious, and I find that creating a finished portrait is actually like spending a day with the person," Summers told Kim Frankenhoff of *Stamp Collector*.

He said it takes approximately 40 hours for him to complete a scratchboard portrait. When mistakes happen, he added, they often can be easily remedied.

This pencil portrait of General Stilwell, made by Keith Birdsong of Muskogee, Oklahoma, was made into a Great Americans design in anticipation of a rate change and the need for new stamp denominations. When the Great Americans series was terminated, the design became obsolete.

"Scratchboard is such a ludicrously slow technique that it would take me 15 minutes to make a mistake," he said. "However, if there is a little bump here or there, it just adds personality. I can also go in with a pen and fix each line if need be."

Only two previous U.S. intaglio-printed postage stamps were designed using the scratchboard technique: Paul Breeden's 29¢ Pine Cone self-adhesive definitive of 1993 (Scott 2491) and John Thompson's 32¢ James K. Polk commemorative of 1995 (Scott 2587). In addition, two Duck stamps have been scratchboard-designed: Stanley Stearns' blue geese in 1955 (Scott RW22) and Alderson "Sandy" Magee's Canada geese in 1976 (Scott RW43).

First-day Facts

John F. Walsh, a member of the USPS Board of Governors, dedicated the stamp in a ceremony at Stampshow 2000 in the Providence Convention Center. Speakers were U.S. Senator Jack Reed, Democrat of Rhode Island; Colonel Michael Haith of the Center for Professional and Military Ethics at the U.S. Military Academy at West Point; John Easterbrook, Joseph W. Stilwell's grandson; and Brigadier General James R. Helmly of the U.S. Army. Robert E. Lamb, executive director of the American Philatelic Society, gave the welcome, and Thomas G. Day, district manager for the Postal Service's Southeast New England District, presided.

Honored guests were: Nancy Sherburne, granddaughter of General Stilwell; Mark Summers, the stamp's illustrator; John Hotchner of the Citizens' Stamp Advisory Committee; Leonard O'Leary, postmaster of Providence; David Quaide, historian emeritus for the Merrill's Marauders Association; and Harold Wolf of the China-Burma-India War Veterans Association.

33¢ CLAUDE PEPPER
DISTINGUISHED AMERICANS SERIES

Date of Issue: September 7, 2000

Catalog Number: Scott 3426

Colors: black, red (PMS 186) (offset); black (intaglio)

First-Day Cancel: Washington, D.C.

First-Day Cancellations: 60,689

Format: Pane of 20, vertical, 5 across, 4 down. Offset and intaglio printing plates of 240 subjects, 15 across, 16 around.

Gum: water activated

Overall Stamp Size: 0.84 by 0.99 inches; 21.34 by 25.15mm

Pane Size: 5.04 by 4.95 inches; 128.02 by 125.73mm

Perforations: 11 (Wista BPA 9070 stroke perforator)

Selvage Markings: "©USPS/1999." ".33/x20/$6.60." "Plate/Position" and diagram. Universal Product Code (UPC) "440900."

Illustrator: Mark Summers of Waterdown, Ontario, Canada

Designer, Art Director and Typographer: Richard Sheaff of Scottsdale, Arizona

Engraver: Chemically engraved by Banknote Corporation of America, Browns Summit, North Carolina

Stamp Manufacturing: Stamps printed by BCA on Goebel 670 offset press and Epikos 5009 intaglio press. Stamps processed by BCA.

Quantity Ordered: 56,000,000

Plate Number Detail: 2 offset plate numbers preceded by the letter B and 1 intaglio plate number in selvage above or below each corner stamp

Plate Number Combination Reported: B11-1

Paper Supplier: Paper Corporation of the United States/Spinnaker Coatings/Ivex

Tagging: phosphored paper

The Stamp

In 1990, a majority of members of the House of Representatives sponsored a resolution expressing "the sense of Congress" that a stamp be issued to honor Florida Democrat Claude Pepper, a long-time member of both houses of Congress and a champion of the interests of poor and elderly Americans.

Pepper had died only a year before, and was ineligible for postal recognition under a rule of the Citizens' Stamp Advisory Committee that no one other than a president or former president can be pictured on a stamp until he or she has been dead for 10 years. The House resolution, sponsored by Representative Jim Moody, a Wisconsin Democrat, and co-sponsored by nearly 300 other members, called on CSAC to consider waiving the rule "in light of Pepper's singular and extraordinary career, and the profound impact this historic figure had on American society." A companion bill in the Senate was sponsored by Senator Bob Graham, D-Florida, and at least 27 co-sponsors.

The effort, at the time, was unsuccessful. However, on October 14, 1999, when the Postal Service unveiled its stamp program for the following year, it announced that a 33¢ stamp honoring Pepper would be issued in 2000, the centennial year of his birth. On September 7, 2000, one day before Pepper's 100th birthday and a little more than 11 years after his death, the stamp was issued in Washington, D.C.

It originally had been announced as part of the Great Americans series, although its appearance differed in significant ways from the existing 63 face-different Great Americans stamps. By the time it was released, however, USPS had decided to create a new series of definitives, which it called "Distinguished Americans," of which the Pepper stamp was the second. The first, a 10¢ stamp depicting General Joseph W. Stilwell, was issued two weeks earlier, on August 24, 2000.

The Pepper stamp is a companion to the Stilwell stamp in all basic respects. It is definitive-size, red and black in color, and bears a portrait done in scratchboard by Mark Summers, the Canadian artist who is widely known for his promotional portraits of literary figures commissioned by the Barnes & Noble book chain. Printed by Banknote Corporation of America by a combination of intaglio and offset, it has water-activated gum and conventional perforations and was issued in panes of 20.

A self-described Alabama plowboy, Claude Denson Pepper was born September 8, 1900, on a farm near Dudleyville, Alabama. He graduated from the University of Alabama in 1921 and Harvard Law School in 1924. His political career began in 1928 when he was elected to the Florida legislature.

In 1936, following the death of Florida's senior U.S. senator, Pepper ran for the vacant seat and won. He became a prominent figure on Capitol Hill, enthusiastically backing the New Deal policies of President Franklin D. Roosevelt. Early in World War II, Pepper fought for passage of the Lend-Lease Act that allowed the United States to support the Allied war

One characteristic of intaglio printing is that the inked, engraved image is applied to stamp paper under great pressure, a fact that is obvious on the reverse side of the Claude Pepper stamp, shown here. The reverse shows a permanent impression of the portrait and the "USA 33" where the intaglio printing plate was impressed against the paper. The other portions of the design were printed by offset, which leaves no impression on the reverse. A similar phenomenon can be seen on the 10¢ General Joseph Stilwell stamp, which, like the Pepper stamp, is part of the Distinguished Americans series and was printed by the same processes, except that on the Stilwell stamp the denomination was printed by offset, not intaglio.

effort. Domestically, Senator Pepper sponsored bills for a minimum wage, equal pay for equal work for women, and research programs for cancer and heart disease. He also co-authored legislation establishing the National Cancer Institute.

Criticized for his alleged sympathy for the Soviet Union in the aftermath of World War II, Pepper was defeated for renomination in a bitter primary election campaign in 1950 by a fellow Democrat and one-time protege, Representative George Smathers, who dubbed him "Red Pepper." Smathers won the general election, and Pepper returned to his law practice in offices in Florida and Washington.

In 1962, Pepper was elected to the House of Representatives in a newly formed district in Miami and Miami Beach. He became a nationally known spokesman for the elderly, was an architect of the Medicare program, and sponsored laws that barred compulsory retirement based on age. In 1977 he became the first chairman of the new Select Committee on Aging, but resigned in 1983 to head the powerful Rules Committee.

President George H.W. Bush presented Pepper with the Medal of Freedom, the nation's highest civilian award, May 25, 1989, five days before he died of cancer at age 88. At the time, he was the oldest sitting member of Congress. His body lay in state in the Capitol rotunda, an honor usually accorded presidents and national heroes.

The Design

The Pepper stamp is designed in the style developed for the series by art director Richard Sheaff and used for the series prototype honoring General Joseph W. Stilwell. Mark Summers' head-and-shoulders portrait of Pepper is shown against a white background with a partial frameline. The words "Claude Pepper," in red Minion semibold italic letters, run up the left side, outside the frameline; the word "Senator," in black Minion Display italic, runs down the right side. "USA 33," in black Minion regular, is tucked inside the frame, above Pepper's right shoulder.

The portrait and "USA 33" are printed by intaglio, while the rest of the design is offset-printed. This differs somewhat from the Stilwell stamp, on which the portrait also is intaglio but the "USA" and denomination were printed from the black offset plate.

Columnist John Hotchner, writing in *Linn's Stamp News*, reported a tendency on the part of the offset-printed frameline to shift slightly horizontally, in relation to the engraved portrait and denomination, from one pane to another. The same phenomenon could be found on the Stilwell stamp, Hotchner wrote.

The design of the stamp that was placed on sale is different from the design that USPS released in October 1999. That one incorporated a Mark Summers portrait based on a photograph taken by Diana Walker in January 1988. It had been approved by the Florida-based Claude Pepper Foundation, the board of which included Pepper's brother, Frank Pepper. Postal officials thus assumed the family had seen the design and was satisfied with it, said Terrence McCaffrey, head of stamp design for USPS.

Then, only a few weeks before the scheduled issue date, "I got a phone call from Frank Pepper himself," McCaffrey said. "He said he was very unhappy with the artwork. He said it looked too young" — even though the source photo had been taken only a year before the congressman's death — "and looked 'cartoony,' and he wanted us to change it. I said it had been approved by the Foundation. He said he had never seen it. The Foundation had signed off on it but hadn't shared it with the family!"

McCaffrey told Frank Pepper a new portrait could be drawn, but it would have to be done in a hurry and the family would have to furnish a satisfactory photograph from which Summers could work. This turned out to be one taken in 1984 by Yousuf Karsh, whose photographs of famous people are well known. Kelly Spinks, the Postal Service lawyer in charge of obtaining rights to copyrighted and trademarked material, was able to get quick clearance.

In May 2000 Summers was asked to prepare a new drawing of Pepper from the Karsh photo. He created the new artwork in about 10 days,

This is an early version of the Claude Pepper stamp design, bearing a scratchboard portrait by Mark Summers based on a 1988 photograph by Diana Walker. It is the design that first was released to the public by USPS. Frank Pepper, brother of the congressman, disliked the picture, and at his request, the Postal Service commissioned a new drawing by Summers.

Shown here is the Yousuf Karsh photograph of Claude Pepper on which the final stamp portrait was based.

Summers recalled, and it is that portrait — a three-quarters view of the lawmaker, rather than the full face of the original — that appears on the issued stamp.

The descriptive term next to the portrait is "Senator," even though Pepper served much longer in the House. Representative E. Clay Shaw, a Florida Republican who represents part of the area Pepper had represented, told USPS officials at the first-day ceremony that he objected to the identification. "He was a man of the House," Shaw said.

In fact, an early version of the design did bear the word "Congressman." "We didn't know what to put on it," said McCaffrey. "Then the Foundation suggested that the word should be 'Senator,' because that was his highest rank, even though he was much better known as a congressman."

First-day Facts

S. David Fineman of the USPS Board of Governors dedicated the stamp in a ceremony at the House Cannon Caucus Room on Capitol Hill. The ceremony was delayed by 50 minutes because of a prolonged meeting of House Democrats in the same room.

Speakers were Senators Bob Graham and Connie Mack of Florida and Richard Durbin of Illinois and Representative Ileana Ros-Lehtinen of

Florida. Postmaster General William J. Henderson gave welcoming remarks, and Representative Joseph Moakley of Massachusetts presided. Thomas J. Spulak, chair of the Claude Pepper Foundation, introduced a video presentation.

Another speaker was Israel Putnam, age 98, of Brooksville, Florida. Putnam was present as the winner of a contest sponsored by the Claude Pepper Foundation to find the oldest stamp collector in Florida. He beat out Clarence Reed, 96, of Pembroke Pines; Lucille Fair, 92, of Orlando; and Lieutenant Colonel William Jones, 90, of Winter Park, for the distinction. According to the foundation, Putnam had 40 stamp albums and spent up to 10 hours a day, seven days a week working on his collection. The Foundation flew him to Washington for the first-day ceremony, and invited the other senior stamp collectors to join him in Tallahassee, Florida, for a second-day ceremony for the stamp September 8, the 100th anniversary of Pepper's birth.

The earliest-known prerelease use of a Claude Pepper stamp was on a cover reported to *Linn's Stamp News* by a reader in New York and postmarked August 31, eight days before the official first day of issue.

1¢ AMERICAN KESTREL, 2000 YEAR DATE
FLORA AND FAUNA SERIES

Date of Issue: October 2000

Catalog Number: Scott 3031A

Colors: gray (PMS 7528), black, cyan, magenta, yellow, blue (PMS 293)

First-Day Cancel: none

First-Day Cancellations: none

Format: Panes of 50, vertical, 10 across, 5 down. Offset printing plates of 400 subjects, 2 panes across, 4 panes around.

Gum Type: self-adhesive

Overall Stamp Size: .84 by .99 inches; 21.34 by 25.15mm

Pane Size: 9.25 by 5.63 inches; 234.95 by 143.00mm

Perforations: 11¼ (die-cut simulated perforations) (rotary die cutter)

Selvage Markings: "©1991 USPS." ".01/x50/$.50." "PLATE/POSITION" and diagram.

Illustrator: Michael R. Matherly of Cambridge City, Indiana

Art Director: Joe Brockert (USPS)

Typographer: John Boyd of New York, New York

Stamp Manufacturing: Stamps printed by Banknote Corporation of America, Browns Summit, North Carolina, on Goebel 670 offset press. Stamps processed by BCA.

Quantity Ordered: 500,000,000

Plate Number Detail: 1 set of 6 plate numbers preceded by the letter B in selvage above or below each corner stamp

Plate Number Combinations Reported: B111111, B222222, B333333, B444444, B555555

Paper Supplier: Paper Corporation of the United States/Spinnaker Coatings

Tagging: none

The Stamp

In October 2000, the Postal Service placed on sale a new version of the 1¢ American Kestrel definitive stamp. It did so in anticipation of the 1¢ increase in the first-class postage rate that would take place the following January. There was no advance notice of the stamp and no officially designated first day of issue, and the philatelic press didn't learn of its existence until early December.

The stamp was the fifth major variety to use the basic American Kestrel design. The printer was Banknote Corporation of America, which had not previously produced Kestrels for USPS. BCA's version, a self-adhesive sheet stamp, was distinguishable from prior versions in that the words "American Kestrel" and the year date "2000" below the design are printed in blue. All previous Kestrel stamps have earlier year dates, with the typography in black.

The design first appeared in 1991 on a stamp printed by the American Bank Note Company with water-activated gum and conventional perforations and issued in panes of 100. On that stamp (Scott 2476), the denomination was shown as "01," which at that time was USPS style for denominations below 10¢. In 1995, when additional supplies were needed, the job went to the Bureau of Engraving and Printing, and the denomination was changed to "1¢," the present style (Scott 2477).

Early the following year, the Postal Service issued a conventionally gummed-and-perforated coil version of the Kestrel printed by BEP in rolls of 500 and 3,000 (Scott 3044). And in November 1999, BEP produced a self-adhesive Kestrel with die-cut simulated perforations that was sold in panes of 50 (Scott 3031). It bore a black "1999" year date.

In addition, minor varieties of the Kestrel coil made their appearance in 1999 with larger "1996" year dates and/or different sequences of colors in the plate numbers.

Like all its predecessors, the BCA version of the Kestrel stamp was printed by offset lithography. It was issued in panes of 50. A total of 1.3 billion were ordered.

The Design

The design of the BCA stamp, like that of the previous American Kestrel stamps, features Michael Matherly's acrylic painting of an American kestrel, or sparrow hawk, sitting on a cedar branch.

However, a side-by-side comparison of the new stamp with the other self-adhesive version, by BEP, reveals some subtle differences. BEP used only the four standard process colors, yellow, magenta, cyan and black, to print its Kestrels. BCA used those four plus two more: gray (PMS 7528) for the background, and blue (PMS 293) for the italic "American Kestrel" inscription. The image on the BCA stamp is slightly smaller than that of the BEP stamp, and not quite so sharply defined. The background color of the BEP stamp consists primarily of yellow and magenta dots, while the

The BCA version is the first American Kestrel stamp with microprinting in its design. The letters "USPS," in black, can be found on the vertical branch below the bird's left claw.

more finely screened (300-line) background of the BCA version appears to be made up only of gray ink.

Although all varieties of the American Kestrel stamp have been offset-printed, the BCA version is the first to include microprinting in its design, which is a security feature that USPS normally requires on stamps produced by offset. The letters "USPS" in black can be found on the vertical branch below the bird's left claw.

First-day Facts

The Postal Service didn't announce the issuance of the BCA version or observe an official first day of sale because it considered the stamp to be an established design, rather than a new variety. Collectors, of course, see such matters differently.

NONDENOMINATED (10¢) NEW YORK LIBRARY LION COIL

Date of Issue: November 9, 2000

Catalog Number: Scott 3447

Colors: blue (PMS 5477), beige (PMS 155), brown (402), light gray (417), black

First-Day Cancel: New York, New York

First-Day Cancellations: 18,477

Format: Coils of 10,000, vertical. Gravure printing cylinders of 252 subjects (12 across, 21 around).

Gum Type: self-adhesive

Overall Stamp Size: .870 by .982 inches; 22.09 by 24.94mm

Perforations: 11½ (die-cut simulated perforations) (Comco rotary die cutter)

Illustrator: Nancy Stahl of New York, New York

Designer, Art Director and Typographer: Carl Herrman of Carlsbad, California

Modeler: Donald H. Woo of Sennett Security Products, Chantilly, Virginia

Stamp Manufacturing: Stamps printed for Sennett Security Products by American Packinging Corporation, Columbus, Wisconsin, on Rotomec 3000 gravure press. Stamps processed by Unique Binders, Fredericksburg, Virginia.

Quantity Ordered: 100,000,000

Cylinder Number Detail: 1 group of 5 cylinder numbers preceded by the letter S on every 21st stamp

Cylinder Number Combinations Reported: S11111, S22222

Counting Number Detail: 1 5-digit counting number in magenta on back of liner paper behind every 10th stamp.

Paper Supplier: Ivex

Tagging: untagged

The Stamp

On November 9, the Postal Service issued a nondenominated self-adhesive coil stamp bearing a stylized image of one of the two stone lions that guard the entrance to the New York Public Library on Fifth Avenue in New York City. The stamp was dedicated on the opening day of the Postage Stamp Mega-Event show at New York's Jacob K. Javits Convention Center, a few blocks from the lions and the library.

The Lion stamp sold for 10¢ and bears the service inscription "PRESORTED STANDARD," indicating that it was created for a class of quantity mail called "standard" that formerly was known as third-class bulk mail. Many direct-mail advertisers prefer stamps to printed indicia because of evidence that stamps increase the rate of favorable responses.

Stamps such as this one bear inscriptions describing the mail classification for which they are intended, but have no denominations. They are used under an arrangement collectors call false franking. The user, at the time of mailing, pays the difference between the cost of the stamp and the actual postage charged for the item to which it is affixed, a charge that varies depending on the degree to which the mail is presorted and other factors.

The Postal Service considers service inscriptions such as the "Presorted Standard" of the Lion stamp to be precancels. These stamps are untagged, and mail bearing them bypasses the post office canceling machines.

American Packaging Corporation of Columbus, Wisconsin, printed the Lion stamp for Sennett Security Products by the gravure process in rolls of 10,000. The individual stamps are attached to their backing paper with spaces between, above and below them. Plate numbers appear on the stamps at intervals of 21, and 5-digit counting numbers in magenta are printed on the backing paper at 10-stamp intervals.

A version of the Lion stamp with water-activated gum would be issued at a later date, USPS said.

The Lion stamp supplemented two previous stamps for presorted standard mail that also sold for 10¢. Both were issued in 1998, each with two types of gum: self-adhesive and water-activated. One stamp depicted a portion of the frame and handlebars of a green bicycle. The other was an adaptation of an Eagle and Shield design that first was used in 1991. USPS has a policy of periodic replacement of the designs of its nondenominated service-inscribed coil stamps.

In 1995, USPS had announced that such stamps in the future would comprise three series: American Scenes, for nonprofit mail; American Transportation, for bulk (now standard) mail; and American Culture, for first-class presorted mail. Designs in each series would be changed periodically, USPS said.

The first standard-mail stamp issued under that program, in 1995, depicted a vintage automobile.

The Lion stamp, however, was not announced as part of any of the series. It grew out of a decision by USPS officials to create some different kinds of definitive-stamp designs they described variously as "symbolic" and "federal-looking."

The two lion statues have become an enduring symbol of the New York Public Library since the May 23, 1911, dedication of the massive Beaux-Arts building on Fifth Avenue at 42nd Street in Manhattan. Sculptor Edward Clark Potter crafted the statues from pink Tennessee marble.

Initially, the lions were called Leo Astor and Leo Lenox, after the founders of the library, John Jacob Astor and James Lenox. They have been known affectionately since the 1930s as Patience and Fortitude, references to the traits that New York Mayor Fiorello LaGuardia said New Yorkers needed to have to weather the Great Depression. According to USPS, it is Patience that is shown on the stamp.

The New York Public Library, along with the Astor, Lenox and Tilden Foundations, comprises four research centers in Manhattan and 85 branch libraries spread across the Bronx, Manhattan and Staten Island. This network makes it the largest public library in the United States and the world's largest research library with a circulating collection.

According to the library's Internet Web site (www.nypl.com), more than 10 million people use the library each year, taking advantage of holdings that number nearly 12 million volumes. The collection continues to expand at the rate of some 10,000 items a week.

Among the library's possessions is the Benjamin Miller stamp collection. Portions of the collection were stolen in 1977, but many of the items were recovered, including a 24¢ Jenny airmail invert (Scott C3a).

The Design

Art director Carl Herrman commissioned Nancy Stahl of New York City, a free-lance illustrator, to develop some design ideas for definitive stamps. "I told her to sort of let loose with any idea she thought would work in a small size," he said. "I got back a bunch of felt-tip pen sketches that went in a very free-spirited way, to say the least."

Among the sketches were a buffalo, bridges, an Indian head, cowboys twirling lariats, a cowboy boot, a female figure whom Stahl labeled "Goddess of Recycling," and some architectural and sculptural elements,

Nancy Stahl submitted these illustration ideas for definitive stamps, done in felt-tip pen: an Indian, cowboys, a cowboy boot, a buffalo, bridges and a female figure whom she labeled "Goddess of Recycling." There also are some architectural and sculptural items, including the New York Public Library lion that became a finished stamp.

Stahl's first version of the finished artwork from her computer included an additional column on the right side and the initials NYPL, for New York Public Library, in relief below the statue. These were omitted on the stamp.

including one of the New York Public Library lions. The Citizens' Stamp Advisory Committee liked the lion, and Herrman told the artist to work it up for use on a stamp.

Stahl created the final product on her computer, using Illustrator software. The result was a stylized image of the lion against a dark background, with two columns on the left. Shadows and highlights are rendered in clearly defined shapes.

"She didn't try to make a photograph out of this illustration," Herrman said. "Instead of blending things, she has almost abrupt changes in color, but they're also subtle, so the eye does the blending. She's very skilled and has a terrific sense of design."

The lion and columns are shown in shades of gray and beige against a dark green background. "USA" is lettered in white capitals in the upper-right corner, and "PRESORTED STANDARD" in black capitals across the bottom. The typeface is a variation of Huxley vertical called Chrysler.

328

Stahl's first version of the artwork included an additional column on the right side, just beyond the lion's nose, but the committee felt the design would be improved by its removal.

The words "THE NEW YORK PUBLIC LIBRARY," in small black capitals, were added, on the edge of the ledge below the lion, after the Postal Service had released the design. The addition was requested by representatives of the New York Public Library, who informed the Postal Service that the statues are trademark symbols of the institution and that the library's name had to be displayed along with the image.

"To me, this is one of the nicest of the definitives," Herrman said. "The art has detail, yet it is very simple, and it reproduced beautifully."

Stahl has numerous business clients for whom she creates packaging and corporate identifiers. Her work also has appeared in numerous magazines and on book and CD covers.

She described her working process to *Stamp Collector*. "I still draw an initial sketch, which I then scan in and use as a template," she said. "It functions similarly to tracing paper, where it's used in creating the final design but isn't actually part of the final design.

"Then I output it to see how the colors work and, if necessary, rescan it and keep working with it until I have what I want."

First-day Facts

John F. Walsh, a member of the Board of Governors of USPS, dedicated the Lion stamp in a ceremony at the Javits Center on the first day of the four-day mega-event show. Vinnie Malloy, postmaster and district manager for the Postal Service's New York City district, officiated.

Jackson Taylor, president of the American Stamp Dealers Association, a mega-event sponsor, gave the welcome. Speakers were Nancy Kranich, president of the American Library Association; Dr. Paul LeClerc, president of the New York Public Library; and Lloyd deVries, a director of the American Philatelic Society, another show sponsor.

Stamp Fulfillment Services offered uncacheted first-day covers of the Lion stamp, accompanied by a single 33¢ Flag Over City coil stamp (Scott 3282), for 64¢.

NONDENOMINATED (34¢) FLAG OVER FARM

Date of Issue: December 15, 2000

Catalog Number: Scott 3448

Colors: black, cyan, magenta, yellow

First-Day Cancel: Washington, D.C.

First-Day Cancellations: 178,635 (includes all varieties of nondenominated Flag Over Farm, Statue of Liberty and Flowers stamps)

Format: Pane of 20 stamps, vertical, 5 across, 4 down. Offset printing plates printing 240 subjects per impression (15 across, 16 around).

Gum Type: water-activated

Overall Stamp Size: .84 by .99 inches (21.336 by 25.146mm)

Pane Size: 5.04 by 4.95 inches (128.016 by 125.730mm)

Perforations: 11¼ (Wista stroke perforator)

Selvage Markings: "©2000 USPS." "PLATE/POSITION" and diagram. Universal Product Code (UPC) "100800."

Illustrator: Hiro Kimura of Brooklyn, New York

Designer, Art Director and Typographer: Richard Sheaff of Scottsdale, Arizona

Modeler: Joseph Sheeran of Ashton-Potter (USA) Ltd., Williamsville, New York

Stamp Manufacturing: Stamps printed by Ashton-Potter on offset portion of Stevens Variable Size Security Documents webfed 6-color offset, 3-color intaglio press. Stamps processed by Ashton-Potter.

Quantity Ordered: 25,000,000

Plate Number Detail: 1 set of 4 plate numbers preceded by the letter P in selvage above or below each corner stamp

Plate Number Combinations Reported: P1111

Paper Supplier: Tullis Russell

Tagging: overall tagging

NONDENOMINATED (34¢) FLAG OVER FARM PANE OF 20, SELF-ADHESIVE

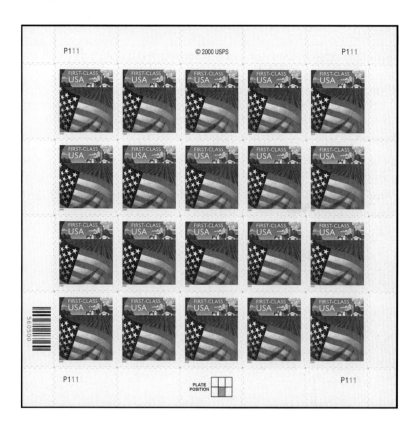

Date of Issue: December 15, 2000

Catalog Number: Scott 3449

Colors: black, cyan, magenta, yellow

First-Day Cancel: Washington, D.C.

First-Day Cancellations: 178,635 (includes all varieties of nondenominated Flag Over Farm, Statue of Liberty and Flowers stamps)

Format: Pane of 20 stamps, vertical, 5 across, 4 down. Offset printing plates printing 240 subjects per impression (15 across, 16 around).

Gum Type: self-adhesive

Overall Stamp Size: .84 by .99 inches (21.336 by 25.146mm)

Pane Size: 5.04 by 4.95 inches (128.016 by 125.730mm)

Perforations: 11¼ (die-cut simulated perforations) (Arpeco die cutter)

Selvage Markings: "©2000 USPS." "PLATE/POSITION" and diagram. Universal Product Code (UPC) "560500." (Check marginal markings)

Illustrator: Hiro Kimura of Brooklyn, New York

Designer, Art Director and Typographer: Richard Sheaff of Scottsdale, Arizona

Modeler: Joseph Sheeran of Ashton-Potter (USA) Ltd., Williamsville, New York

Stamp Manufacturing: Stamps printed by Ashton-Potter on offset portion of Stevens Variable Size Security Documents webfed 6-color offset, 3-color intaglio press. Stamps processed by Ashton-Potter.

Quantity Ordered: 200,000,000

Plate Number Detail: 1 set of 4 plate numbers preceded by the letter P in selvage above or below each corner stamp

Plate Number Combinations Reported: P1111, P2222, P3333

Paper Supplier: Glatfelter/Fasson

Tagging: phosphored paper

NONDENOMINATED (34¢) FLAG OVER FARM
PANE OF 18, ATM-VENDED

Date of Issue: December 15, 2000

Catalog Number: Scott 3450, single stamp; 3450a, pane of 18

Colors: yellow, magenta, cyan, black

First-Day Cancel: Washington, D.C.

First-Day Cancellations: 178,635 (includes all varieties of nondenominated Flag Over Farm, Statue of Liberty and Flowers stamps)

Format: Pane of 18, vertical, arranged vertically 3 across by 6 down, with horizontal peel-off strip between horizontal rows 3 and 4. Gravure printing cylinders printing 30 panes per revolution (5 across, 6 around) manufactured by Southern Graphics System.

Gum Type: self-adhesive

Overall Stamp Size: .870 by .982 inches (20.098 by 24.942mm)

Pane Size: 2.610 by 6.125 inches (66.294 by 155.100mm)

Perforations: 8 (die-cut simulated perforations) (Comco Commander rotary die cutter)

Front Markings: on peel-off strip: "Peel here to fold • Self-adhesive stamps • DO NOT WET," color registration dots and cylinder numbers

Back Markings: "Farm Flag/Eighteen Self-Adhesive Stamps/First-Class Rate." "©USPS 2000." USPS logo. Universal Product Code (UPC). Promotion for www.stampsonline.com web site. Disclaimer of any amount charged over stamps' face value.

Illustrator: Hiro Kimura of Brooklyn, New York

Designer, Art Director and Typographer: Richard Sheaff of Scottsdale, Arizona

Stamp Manufacturing: Stamps printed by Avery Dennison Security Printing Division, Clinton, South Carolina, on a Dia Nippon Kiko 8-station gravure press. Stamps lacquer coated, front and back, die cut, processed and shipped by Avery Dennison.

Quantity Ordered: 300,000,000

Cylinder Number Detail: 1 group of 4 gravure cylinder numbers preceded by the letter V on peel-off strip

Cylinder Number Combination Reported: V1111

Paper Supplier: Avery Dennison Fasson Division

Tagging: phosphor added to lacquer coating applied to front of pane

The Stamps

On December 15, the Postal Service issued a group of nondenominated stamps, selling for 34¢ each, for use with the pending new 34¢ first-class rate. The stamps, in several different designs and formats, were the final U.S. stamp issues of 2000.

The stamps and their date of issue were announced November 20, 2000, after the independent Postal Rate Commission recommended November 13 that the existing 33¢ first-class rate be increased by a penny, but before the USPS Board of Governors had formally accepted the recommendation. The governors took that action December 5 and set a date of January 7, 2001, for the new rate to take effect.

It was the ninth time that USPS had prepared for a rate change by issuing stamps that it had printed and stockpiled long in advance. Because the exact amount of the new rates can't be known ahead of time, such stamps bear no denomination, but are assigned the value of the new first-class rate once it has been determined.

In the past, each new group of nondenominated stamps was distinguished from its predecessors by a letter of the alphabet. The A stamps were issued in 1978 to cover the pending 15¢ rate; the most recent, the H (for Hat) stamps, came out late in 1998, two months before the price of a first-class stamp rose to 33¢.

This time, however, USPS broke with its alphabetic tradition. Instead of the letter I, the new designs were given the inscription "First-Class." That didn't mean that the stamps always would be honored at the first-class rate, Postal Service spokesman Don Smeraldi told *Linn's Stamp News*. Their value would remain at 34¢, he said, and they would have to be supplemented with additional postage the next time the first-class rate was increased.

Among the new designs was one that continued the Postal Service's policy of always having available a first-class-rate definitive that shows the U.S. flag in full color waving over a national landmark or against a generic backdrop. In this case, the background is a farm scene. The design was an appropriate successor to the "Flag Over City" image that was featured on various 33¢ sheet, coil and booklet stamps in 1999, and was the work of the same artist, Hiro Kimura, and art director, Richard Sheaff.

The Flag Over Farm stamp was issued in three formats:

• Pane of 20, with water-activated gum and conventional perforations, printed by offset lithography by Ashton-Potter (USA) Ltd. (Scott 3448). A block of taggant covers the 20 stamps on the pane.

• Pane of 20, self-adhesive, with die-cut simulated perforations, also offset-printed by Ashton-Potter (Scott 3449). The designs of the two Ashton-Potter stamps are identical, as are the selvage markings, with the exception of the Universal Product Code, which has different bar arrangements and UPC numbers on the two panes. The paper is prephosphored.

• Pane of 18, self-adhesive, with die-cut simulated perforations, made for sale through automated teller machines (ATMs). This variety was printed by the gravure process by Avery Dennison Security Products. Like all panes made for ATMs, it has the dimensions and thickness of U.S. currency and is printed on nonphosphored paper. To prevent curling, a lacquer coating was applied to the pane after printing. This coating, on the front, contained the tagging material.

As soon as the Postal Rate Commission approved the new 34¢ first-class rate, the Stamp Services section ordered production of denominated versions of the Flag Over Farm stamps and the other nondenominated stamps that were scheduled for issuance December 15. The denominated versions would be issued early in 2001.

Each of the three preceding increases in the first-class rate — in 1991, 1995 and 1999 — was preceded by issuance of a nondenominated "make-up stamp" with an assigned value equal to the difference between the old and new first-class rates. This time, however, the Postal Service had ample supplies of denominated 1¢ Kestrel stamps for customers to use with their leftover 33¢ stamps, and saw no need to issue a makeup stamp.

The Design

Hiro Kimura of Brooklyn, New York, is an artist who began his professional career designing video game packaging and has gone on to become a successful creator of book covers, magazine art and advertising materi-

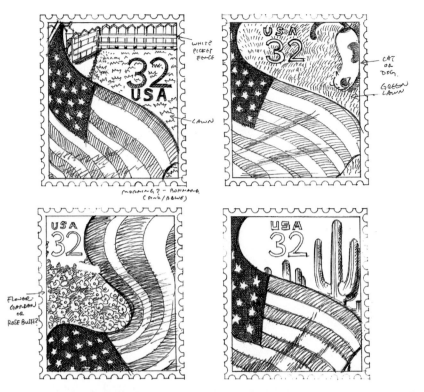

In the process of developing his illustration of a flag over a farm scene, Hiro Kimura made these pencil sketches showing the flag in alternative settings: a suburban yard and garden and a Southwest area with cacti.

al. He characterizes his work as "graphic stylized," and for years his preferred medium was acrylic paint, although he since has turned to computers to create his "painting look."

In 1995, working with art director Richard Sheaff, Kimura sketched numerous American flag designs for use on definitive stamps as needed. Out of them came three finished pieces of art. One became the 33¢ Flag Over City stamp, issued in sheet, booklet and coil formats in 1999. The second, showing a flag in a schoolroom (Flag Over Chalkboard), was used on a 33¢ ATM-vended stamp, also in 1999. The third was the Flag Over Farm image. Kimura created these in the traditional way: paint on canvasboard.

A rippling American flag occupies the lower half of Kimura's Flag Over Farm illustration, with a narrow portion of the flag's blue field curving around to the upper-left corner. Behind it is a farm scene, with neat rows of green crops stretching away to the horizon. A group of rural buildings, including a silo and red barn, is in the distance, and at the top is a blue sky with puffy white clouds. "FIRST-CLASS" and "USA," in a typeface called Gill Sands, is dropped out of this blue background.

336

On both the self-adhesive and conventionally gummed versions of the Flag Over Farm stamp printed by Ashton-Potter, the microprinted letters "USPS" can be found on the white wall of the low farm building, between the two doors.

Single specimens of the three varieties of Flag Over Farm stamp can be easily distinguished from one another.

• A stamp from the pane of 20 with water-activated gum has conventional perforation teeth on all four sides.

• A stamp from the self-adhesive pane of 20 has die-cut simulated perforations on all four sides. These have a relatively fine gauge, defined in the Scott catalogs as 11¼.

• A stamp from the self-adhesive pane of 18 also has die-cut simulated perforations, but of a coarser gauge, listed as 8 by Scott. Furthermore, 14 of the 18 stamps on the pane have a straight edge on either one or two sides.

The stamps from Ashton-Potter's 20-stamp panes, which were printed by offset with a 300-line screen, have a somewhat sharper and clearer look than Avery Dennison's gravure-printed ATM stamp. The "2000" year date beneath the design is small and clear on the offset-printed stamps, larger and heavier on the gravure product.

Because USPS considers offset a somewhat less secure printing method than gravure, it requires stamp printers using offset to incorporate microprinting in the designs as a safeguard against counterfeiting. On Ashton-Potter's two Flag Over Farm varieties, the letters "USPS," in microtype, can be found on the white wall of the low building, between the two doors. There is no microprinting on Avery Dennison's ATM stamp.

The Flag Over Farm stamp wasn't the first Flag definitive to depict a generic rural scene. In 1995, USPS issued a 32¢ ATM stamp with a cut-paper collage by Sabra Fields showing the Stars and Stripes waving over a stylized field and hills (Scott 2919).

First-day Facts

No first-day ceremony was held for the nondenominated rate-change stamps issued December 15. The stamps were placed on sale nationwide. First-day covers were postmarked Washington, D.C.

NONDENOMINATED (34¢) STATUE OF LIBERTY CONVERTIBLE BOOKLET OF 20

Date of Issue: December 15, 2000

Catalog Number: Scott 3451, single stamp; 3451a, pane of 20

Colors: yellow, magenta, cyan, black

First-Day Cancel: Washington, D.C.

First-Day Cancellations: 178,635 (includes all varieties of nondenominated Statue of Liberty, Flowers and Flag Over Farm stamps)

Format: Convertible booklet pane of 20, horizontal, 4 across, 5 down, with vertical peel-off strip between second and third vertical rows. Gravure printing cylinders printing 24 panes per revolution (3 across, 8 around) manufactured by Southern Graphics Systems.

Gum Type: self-adhesive

Overall Stamp Size: .982 by .870 inches; 24.948 by 22.098mm

Pane Size: 4.125 by 4.350 inches; 104.78 by 110.49mm

Perforations: 11 (die-cut simulated perforations) (Comco Commander rotary die cutter). Cover scored for folding.

Selvage Markings: "Peel here to fold • Self-adhesive stamps • DO NOT WET" • © 2000 USPS" plus cylinder numbers on peel-off strip

Back Markings: "The Statue/of Liberty/Twenty/Self-adhesive/Stamps/First-Class Rate" on front of cover. Promotion for www.stampsonline.com web site and Universal Product Code (UPC) on back of cover.

Photographer: Paul Hardy of New York, New York

Designer, Art Director and Typographer: Derry Noyes of Washington, D.C.

Stamp Manufacturing: Stamps printed by Avery Dennison Security Division, Clinton, South Carolina, on an 8-color Dia Nippon Kiko webfed gravure press. Stamps processed by Avery Dennison.

Quantity Ordered: 1,500,000,000 stamps

Cylinder Number Detail: 1 set of 4 cylinder numbers preceded by the letter V on peel-off strip.

Cylinder Number Combinations Reported: V1111, V2222

Paper Supplier: Fasson Division of Avery Dennison

Tagging: phosphored paper

NONDENOMINATED (34¢) STATUE OF LIBERTY VENDING BOOKLET OF 20

Date of Issue: December 15, 2000

Catalog Number: Scott 3451, single stamp; 3451b, pane of 4; 3451c, pane of 6

Colors: yellow, magenta, cyan, black

First-Day Cancel: Washington, D.C.

First-Day Cancellations: 178,635 (includes all varieties of nondenominated Statue of Liberty, Flowers and Flag Over Farm stamps)

Format: Vending booklet of 20, horizontal, 10 across by 2 down, in 4 segments: 4 (2 by 2), 6 (3 by 2), 6 (3 by 2) and 4 (2 by 2). Gravure printing cylinders of 480 (24 across, 20 around) printing 24 panes per revolution.

Gum Type: self-adhesive

Overall Stamp Size: .982 by .870 inches; 24.948 by 22.098mm

Pane Size: 10.375 by 1.740 inches; 263.530 by 44.196mm

Perforations: 11 (die-cut simulated perforations) (Comco Commander rotary die cutter). Cover scored for folding.

Selvage Markings: none

Back Markings: "The Statue/of Liberty/Twenty/Self-adhesive/Stamps/First-Class Rate" on front of cover. "© 2000 USPS," USPS logo, Universal Product Code and promotion for www.stampsonline.com web site on back cover.

Photographer: Paul Hardy of New York, New York

Designer, Art Director and Typographer: Derry Noyes of Washington, D.C.

Stamp Manufacturing: Stamps printed by Avery Dennison Security Division, Clinton, South Carolina, on an 8-color Dia Nippon Kiko webfed gravure press. Stamps processed by Avery Dennison.

Quantity Ordered: 200,000,000 stamps

Cylinder Number Detail: 1 set of 4 cylinder numbers preceded by the letter V on right-end stamp on bottom row of 10

Cylinder Number Combination Reported: V1111

Paper Supplier: Fasson Division of Avery Dennison

Tagging: phosphored paper

NONDENOMINATED (34¢) STATUE OF LIBERTY COIL (WATER-ACTIVATED GUM), ROLL OF 3,000

Date of Issue: December 15, 2000

Catalog Number: Scott 3452

Colors: yellow, magenta, cyan, black

First-Day Cancel: Washington, D.C.

First-Day Cancellations: 178,635 (includes all varieties of nondenominated Statue of Liberty, Flowers and Flag Over Farm stamps)

Format: Coil of 3,000, vertical. Gravure cylinders printing 432 stamps per revolution (24 by 18)

Gum Type: water-activated

Overall Stamp Size: .87 by .96 inches; 22.1 by 24.4mm

Perforations: 9¾

Photographer: Paul Hardy of New York, New York

Designer, Art Director and Typographer: Derry Noyes of Washington, D.C.

Stamp Manufacturing: Stamps printed by Bureau of Engraving and Printing on 7-color Andreotti gravure press (601)

Quantity Ordered: 200,000,000

Cylinder Number Detail: 1 set of 4 numbers on every 24th stamp

Cylinder Number Combination Reported: 1111

Counting Number Detail: 1 4-digit counting number in aqua on back of every 20th stamp

Tagging: phosphored paper

NONDENOMINATED (34¢) STATUE OF LIBERTY COIL (SELF-ADHESIVE), ROLL OF 100

Date of Issue: December 15, 2000

Catalog Number: Scott 3453

Colors: yellow, magenta, cyan, black

First-Day Cancel: Washington, D.C.

First-Day Cancellations: 178,635 (includes all varieties of nondenominated Statue of Liberty, Flowers and Flag Over Farm stamps)

Format: Coil of 100, vertical. Gravure cylinders printing 480 stamps per revolution (24 by 20)

Gum Type: self-adhesive

Overall Stamp Size: .87 by .96 inches; 22.1 by 24.4mm

Perforations: 10 (die-cut simulated perforations)

Photographer: Paul Hardy of New York, New York

Designer, Art Director and Typographer: Derry Noyes of Washington, D.C.

Stamp Manufacturing: Stamps printed by Bureau of Engraving and Printing on 7-color Andreotti gravure press (601)

Quantity Ordered: 1,000,000,000

Cylinder Number Detail: 1 set of 4 numbers on every 24th stamp

Cylinder Number Combination Reported: 1111

Tagging: phosphored paper

The Stamps

An American icon, the Statue of Liberty, is featured on the second set of nondenominated stamps that was placed on sale by the Postal Service December 15. The stamps were assigned a face value of 34¢ and were intended as a stopgap issue for use immediately after the pending increase in the first-class rate took effect.

Like the Flag Over Farm stamps described in the preceding chapter, the Statue of Liberty stamps differ from previous nondenominated stamps intended for first-class mail in that they bear the inscription "First-Class" instead of a letter of the alphabet.

Two printers produced the Statue of Liberty stamps in four formats, resulting in three collectible varieties of single stamps. All varieties were printed by the gravure process. They were:

• Pane (convertible booklet) of 20 horizontally arranged stamps, self-adhesive, four across by five down, with a vertical peel-off strip and scoring to allow the pane to be folded. The stamp (Scott 3451) was printed by Avery Dennison Security Printing Division. The four-digit cylinder number combination is printed on the peel-off strip.

• The same stamp as above, in a vending-machine booklet of 20. The booklet pane, 10 across by two down, is divided into segments of four, six, six and four stamps. It is folded in the middle, between the two six-stamp segments, and the four-stamp segments on each end are folded inside, making a flat palm-sized packet. The cylinder-number combination is printed on the bottom-right corner stamp, below the frameline on the right side, opposite the "2000" year date.

• Coil of 3,000 vertically arranged stamps, with water-activated gum and conventional perforations (Scott 3452). A four-digit cylinder number appears on every 24th stamp and an aqua four-digit counting number is on the back of every 20th stamp. The Bureau of Engraving and Printing produced the stamps.

• Coil of 100 vertically arranged stamps, self-adhesive (Scott 3453). The stamps abut each other on the coil, with no backing paper visible between, above or below them. A four-digit cylinder number is found on every 24th stamp. There are no counting numbers on the back. Again, BEP was the printer.

The two coil varieties were the only postage stamps issued in 2000 to be printed by the Bureau of Engraving and Printing. BEP, located a few blocks from USPS headquarters in Southeast Washington, D.C., once was the exclusive manufacturer of U.S. postage stamps. Today, the task has

Both Tom Engeman's illustration of the Statue of Liberty, shown here on a 32¢ stamp of 1997, and Paul Hardy's photograph used on the 2000 stamps show the statue's head and torch from a similar angle. However, the photograph is cropped to include the tablet of law in the statue's left hand, a feature designer Derry Noyes considered important.

largely been taken over by private-sector companies.

Individual Statue of Liberty stamps from the two varieties of booklet are indistinguishable from each other except in two instances. A stamp with die-cut simulated perforations on all four sides can come only from the interior of the convertible booklet, and a stamp with cylinder numbers at the bottom can come only from the vending-machine booklet.

The Statue of Liberty stamp in vending-booklet format is the fourth U.S. booklet stamp that can be found with plate numbers printed on the stamp itself. The first three were the Yellow Rose of 1996 (Scott 3049), printed by Stamp Venturers, and the Statue of Liberty stamp of 1997 (Scott 3122) and Flag Over City stamp of 1999 (Scott 3278), both printed by Avery Dennison.

The design of the Statue of Liberty stamp in its horizontally arranged version was made public by USPS August 23, 2000, at a meeting of Terrence McCaffrey, head of stamp design, with stamp journalists at Stampshow 2000 in Providence, Rhode Island.

Stamp dealer and columnist Robert Rabinowitz, writing in *Linn's Stamp News*, reported that there are two different types of the "2000" year date in the lower-left corner of the self-adhesive coil version of the stamp. However, no reference is made to the difference in the Scott *Specialized Catalogue of U.S. Stamps & Covers*.

On some stamps, the "2000" appears gray-black and has thin digits, while on other stamps the "2000" is intense black and has thick digits, Rabinowitz wrote. Both date types appear on stamps printed from cylinder number combination 1111, the only combination used for the self-adhesive coils.

Bureau of Engraving and Printing representatives denied that the two date types came about because the set of four cylinders, one for each of the process colors, that was used to print the stamps was replaced with another set using the same four numbers. Their explanation, Rabinowitz wrote, was that while the initial printing was taking place, the year dates on some of the stamps were judged to be too light. The Bureau then applied another thin layer of chrome on the copper cylinder that applied the black ink. This resulted in a much darker year date, and also one that was slightly longer — approximately 1.5mm, compared to 1.3mm.

The two different types of "2000" year date on nondenominated Statue of Liberty self-adhesive coil stamps are shown here. The date on the left stamp (shown cropped) is gray-black and has thin digits, while the date on the right stamp (also cropped) is intense black and has thick digits.

The Statue of Liberty, or its head or torch, has been prominently featured on more than two dozen U.S. stamps, envelopes and postal cards. However, the December 15 stamps were the first to display a photograph of the monument. The statue made its U.S. postal debut on the 15¢ value of the 1922-26 series (Scott 566), and was shown most recently in 1999 on one of the 15 stamps in the Celebrate the Century pane commemorating the 1970s. Kazuhiko Sano's illustration for that stamp depicted Liberty against a backdrop of exploding fireworks, evoking the July 4, 1976, celebration of the U.S. Bicentennial in New York Harbor.

In 1985 and 1986 the Postal Service issued two stamps linked to the statue's centennial. The first (Scott 2147) honored Frederic Auguste Bartholdi, the sculptor; the second (Scott 2224), part of a joint issue with France, commemorated the anniversary of its dedication.

The Design

The Statue of Liberty stamp was the product of a continuing effort by the Postal Service's contractual art directors to keep a supply of designs for definitive and special stamps in reserve for use when needed.

Such designs often incorporate patriotic themes, and with this thought in mind art director Derry Noyes obtained some stock photographs of the Statue of Liberty. She was particularly attracted to one photo, supplied by The Stock Market, for its color and strong silhouette. The photographer, Paul Hardy, made his shot in 1996 from near the statue's feet on Liberty Island, looking up at the head, crown and uplifted torch. The shadows on the statue's green copper skin are deep blue, as is the sky overhead. Hardy used a Pentax 6x7 camera with a 500mm lens.

Noyes adapted the photo for use as a definitive-size stamp in horizontal format, cropping it at the waist so that the picture included not only the head, crown, right arm and torch, but also the tablet of law that Liberty grips in her left hand.

The art director said she probably was influenced to include the tablet by the case of Elian Gonzalez, the Cuban child who was reunited with his father and repatriated amid much controversy in 2000. Noyes' husband, Gregory Craig, a Washington, D.C., lawyer, represented Elian's father in the accompanying litigation.

"I was struck at the time by how the Cubans don't have the rule of law in their country, and we rely on it so much in our country," Noyes said. "I think that's why I included that [tablet] in the design. We sort of take it for granted, and I thought, 'Well, it's a fresh look for the Statue of Liberty, which we've done so many times.' "

Noyes inserted the inscription "USA/FIRST-/CLASS," in dropout white Clarendon type, in the lower-left corner of the design.

Her horizontal layout was used for the stamps in the two booklet formats. For coil use, a vertical layout was required, and the photo was reduced in size and recropped for that purpose. Slightly more of the waist area of the statue is seen in the vertical version.

Varieties

The convertible booklet of 20 of the Statue of Liberty stamp is known without die-cut simulated perforations (Scott 3451d). Imperforate specimens of the self-adhesive coil stamp also have been found (Scott 3453a).

First-day Facts

No first-day ceremony was held for the nondenominated rate-change stamps issued December 15. The stamps were placed on sale nationwide. First-day covers were postmarked Washington, D.C.

NONDENOMINATED (34¢) FLOWERS (4 DESIGNS) CONVERTIBLE BOOKLET OF 20

Date of Issue: December 15, 2000

Catalog Numbers: Scott 3454-3457, single stamps, die-cut 10¼ by 10¾; 3457a, same stamps, block of 4; 3457e, double-sided pane of 20, 5 3457a; 3458-3461, single stamps, die-cut 11½ by 11¾; 3461a, same stamps, block of 4; 3461b, double-sided pane of 20, 2 3461a, 3 3457a; 3461c, double-sided pane of 20, 2 3457a, 3 3461a

Colors: magenta, yellow, cyan, black

First-Day Cancel: Washington, D.C.

First-Day Cancellations: 178,635 (includes all varieties of nondenominated Flowers, Statue of Liberty and Flag Over Farm stamps)

Format: Convertible booklet pane of 20, vertical. Stamps on both sides, 8 (2 across by 4 down) plus label (booklet cover) on one side, 12 (2 across by 6 down) on other side, with 2 horizontal peel-off strips on each side.

348

Gravure printing cylinders of 192 (16 across, 12 around), cover side; 288 (16 across, 18 around), all-stamp side.

Gum Type: self-adhesive

Overall Stamp Size: 0.870 by 0.982 inches; 22.09 by 24.94mm

Pane Size: 1.7400 by 6.2083 inches; 44.19 by 157.69mm

Perforations: 10¼ by 10¾ or 11½ by 11¾ (die-cut simulated perforations) (Comco custom die-cutter)

Selvage Markings: "© 2000 USPS • Peel here to fold • Self-adhesive stamps • DO NOT WET" on first peel-off strip on all-stamp side; "• Peel here to fold • Self-adhesive stamps • © 2000 USPS" plus cylinder numbers on second peel-off strip on all-stamp side.

Back Markings: "4 Flowers/Twenty/Self-adhesive/Stamps/First-Class Rate/© 2000 USPS" and Universal Product Code (UPC) on label (booklet cover).

Photographer: Robert Peak of Winter Park, Florida

Designer, Art Director and Typographer: Derry Noyes of Washington, D.C.

Modeler: Donald Woo of Sennett Security Products of Chantilly, Virginia

Stamp Manufacturing: Stamps printed for Sennett Security Products by American Packaging Corp. of Columbus, Wisconsin, on Rotomec 3000 gravure press. Stamps finished by Unique Binders of Fredericksburg, Virginia.

Quantity Ordered: 1,500,000,000 stamps

Cylinder Number Detail: 1 set of 4 cylinder numbers preceded by the letter S on 1 peel-off strip.

Cylinder Number Combination Reported: S1111

Paper Supplier: Paper Corporation of the United States/Spinnaker Coatings

Tagging: phosphored paper with phosphate blocker applied to the label (booklet cover) portion of the pane

NONDENOMINATED (34¢) FLOWERS (4 DESIGNS)
VENDING BOOKLET OF 20

Date of Issue: December 15, 2000

Catalog Numbers: Scott 3454-3457, single stamps; 3457a, block of 4; 3457b, booklet segment of 4; 3457c, booklet segment of 6, 3456, 3457, 2 each 3454-3455; 3457d, booklet segment of 6, 3454, 3455, 2 each 3456-3457; BK158, vending booklet containing 3457b, 3457c, 3457d

Colors: magenta, yellow, cyan, black

First-Day Cancel: Washington, D.C.

First-Day Cancellations: 178,635 (includes all varieties of nondenominated Flowers, Statue of Liberty and Flag Over Farm stamps)

Format: Vending booklet of 20, vertical, 2 across by 10 down, in 4 segments: 4 (2 by 2), 6 (2 by 3), 6 (2 by 3) and 4 (2 by 2). Gravure printing cylinders of 480 (24 across, 20 around) printing 24 panes.

Gum Type: self-adhesive

Overall Stamp Size: .870 by .982 inches; 22.09 by 24.94mm

Pane Size: 1.739 by 10.375 inches; 44.17 by 263.52mm

Perforations: 10¼ by 10¾ (die-cut simulated perforations) (Comco custom die-cutter)

Selvage Markings: none

Back Markings: "4 Flowers/Twenty Self-adhesive/Stamps/First-Class Rate/" on front cover. "© 2000 USPS," USPS logo, Universal Product Code (UPC) and promotion for www.stampsonline.com web site on back cover.

Photographer: Robert Peak of Winter Park, Florida

Designer, Art Director and Typographer: Derry Noyes of Washington, D.C.

Modeler: Donald Woo of Sennett Security Products of Chantilly, Virginia

Stamp Manufacturing: Stamps printed for Sennett Security Products by American Packaging Corp. of Columbus, Wisconsin, on Rotomec 3000 gravure press. Stamps finished by Unique Binders of Fredericksburg, Virginia.

Quantity Ordered: 200,000,000 stamps

Cylinder Number Detail: 1 set of 4 cylinder numbers preceded by the letter S on back of backing paper, behind top 4-stamp segment

Cylinder Number Combination Reported: S1111

Paper Supplier: Paper Corporation of the United States/Spinnaker Coatings

Tagging: phosphored paper

NONDENOMINATED (34¢) FLOWERS (4 DESIGNS), COIL

Date of Issue: December 15, 2000

Catalog Numbers: Scott 3462-3465, single stamps; 3465a, strip of 4

Colors: black, cyan, magenta, yellow

First-Day Cancel: Washington, D.C.

First-Day Cancellations: 178,635 (includes all varieties of nondenominated Flowers, Statue of Liberty and Flag Over Farm stamps)

Format: Coil of 100, vertical. Gravure cylinders printing 384 subjects per revolution (16 by 24) manufactured by Acitronics.

Gum Type: self-adhesive

Overall Stamp Size: .870 by .965 inches; 22.10 by 24.51mm

Perforations: 8½ (die-cut simulated perforations) (George Schmitt & Co. rotary die cutter)

Photographer: Robert Peak of Winter Park, Florida

Designer, Art Director and Typographer: Derry Noyes of Washington, D.C.

Stamp Manufacturing: Stamps printed by Guilford Gravure, Guilford, Connecticut, for Banknote Corporation of America, Browns Summit, North Carolina, on Cerrutti R118 gravure press. Stamps finished by Guilford Gravure.

Quantity Ordered: 500,000,000

Cylinder Number Detail: 1 set of 4 cylinder numbers preceded by the letter B on every 12th stamp

Cylinder Number Combination Reported: B1111

Paper Supplier: Paper Corporation of the United States/Spinnaker Coatings

Tagging: phosphored paper

The Stamps

The third set of nondenominated stamps placed on sale by the Postal Service December 15 in anticipation of the pending new 34¢ first-class rate incorporated four different flower designs arranged se-tenant in three formats. A total of 12 major collectible varieties resulted.

Although many previous U.S. stamps had depicted flowers, a popular subject with postal customers, these were the first to use photographs rather than illustrations. The four pastel-colored flowers — not identified on the stamps themselves — are the freesia, Asian hybrid lily, cymbidium orchid and longiflorum lily.

All the stamps are self-adhesives, with die-cut simulated perforations, and were printed by the gravure process on phosphored paper. The formats are:

• Vending-machine booklet of 20, printed by American Packaging Corporation for Sennett Security Products. The booklet pane is two stamps across by 10 stamps down. Each stamp has either one or two straight edges. The top pair of stamps is longiflorum lily and cymbidium orchid, the pair beneath it is freesia and Asian hybrid, and these pairings alternate to the bottom of the pane, which is divided into segments of four, six, six and four stamps (Scott 3454-3457). The pane is folded in the middle, between the two six-stamp segments, and the four-stamp segments on each end are folded inside, making a flat palm-sized packet.

The gauge of the die-cut simulated perfs is 10¼ by 10¾. The four

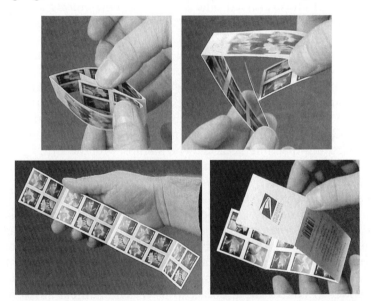

The 20-stamp nondenominated Four Flowers vending booklet differs somewhat from previous booklets of U.S. self-adhesive stamps. The booklet is sold neatly folded into a flat palm-sized packet. The four-stamp segments on each end are folded inside (upper left) and held together with several spots of light adhesive. Once opened (upper right), the booklet extends into one unit more than 10¼ inches long (lower left). There are no plate numbers on the stamps or on interior selvage; instead they are found printed across the top of the reverse of the booklet, on the paper backing the upper four-stamp segment.

cylinder numbers, preceded by the letter S for Sennett, are not on the stamps or interior selvage, but are printed across the top of the reverse of the booklet.

• Two-sided pane (convertible booklet) of 20, 12 stamps on one side, eight on the other, printed by American Packaging Corporation for Sennett Security Products. The stamps are arranged in blocks of four, in this order: longiflorum lily, cymbidium orchid, freesia, Asian hybrid. On one side are three blocks of four, separated by horizontal peel-off strips, one of which has the cylinder-number combination, preceded by the letter S. On the other side are two blocks of four plus the booklet cover, which actually is a large peelable label. A phosphor blocker was applied to the cover to prevent its use as a "stamp." As with the vending-machine booklet, all the stamps have either one or two straight edges.

After the convertible booklets were issued, collector Gregg Greenwald of Wisconsin discovered that some panes existed with different die cutting on the two sides. On normal panes, the die cuts on both sides measure10¼ by 10¾, the same as the stamps in the vending-machine booklet. Other panes, however, have 11½ by 11¾ die-cutting on the side containing eight stamps and normal die cutting on the 12-stamp side, while on still other panes, the situation is reversed: The 11½ by 11¾ die-cutting is on the side with 12 stamps, while the normal 10¼ by 10¾ die cuts are on the eight-stamp side.

The discovery required Scott to revise catalog numbers it had assigned only a few weeks earlier, to conform to a recently adopted policy that stamps of the same design having perf or die-cutting differences of ½ gauge or more would be assigned separate major catalog numbers. The stamps with the normal 10¼ by 10¾ die cuts retained their original numbers (3454-3457), which also are the numbers assigned to single stamps from the vending-machine booklet. The stamps with the 11½ by 11¾ die cuts were given the Scott numbers 3458-3461.

• Coil of 100, printed by Guilford Gravure for Banknote Corporation of America and finished by BCA. The order of the stamps on the coil is: freesia, Asian hybrid lily, cymbidium orchid and longiflorum lily. The stamps abut each other on the backing paper with no spaces between, above or below them. The four-digit cylinder number combination, preceded by the letter B for BCA, appears on every 12th stamp, which is always a cymbidium orchid. Many collectors of plate number coils, or PNCs, opted to collect these coil stamps in symmetrical strips of nine, with the plate-number stamp in the center and a non-numbered cymbidium orchid stamp on either end.

As soon as the Postal Rate Commission approved the new 34¢ first-class rate, the Stamp Services section ordered production of denominated versions of the Flowers stamps and the other nondenominated stamps that were scheduled for issuance December 15. The denominated versions were issued early in 2001.

The Design

Derry Noyes, a Postal Service art director, asked photographer Robert Peak of Winter Park, Florida, to make a set of photographs of flowers that could be adapted for stamp use as needed. "We thought photographing flowers would be a nice new twist for the Postal Service because we had never used flower photos before," Noyes said.

Peak's name was suggested by Michael Brock, a graphic designer and member of the Citizens' Stamp Advisory Committee. The photographer's father, also named Robert Peak, was an illustrator who had created the artwork for several U.S. stamps in the past, including the 24 commemoratives and airmails issued in 1983 and 1984 for the Olympic Games, as well as the Auto Racing stamped envelope of 1978.

Peak brought an assortment of flowers to his studio and photographed them. These included several varieties besides the four finally selected for stamp designs, including an iris, daisy and sunflower. Noyes tried some of these additional photos as stamps, as well.

Shown above and below are several of Robert Peak's flower photos, adapted by Derry Noyes for Love stamp use in convertible booklets and/or on booklet covers. None of these flower images appeared on the four issued definitive stamps.

Noyes adapted Peak's photograph of a cymbidium orchid as a horizontally arranged Love stamp for convertible-booklet use and also as a booklet cover. Ultimately, the photo was used on a vertically arranged definitive.

This proposed layout for a convertible booklet of definitive stamps incorporated five of Peak's photographs: the four that finally were chosen, plus a yellow daisy that wasn't used.

"I presented them to the committee as Love stamps, thinking that might be a possible use for the photos," Noyes said. "I presented them as sheets, as booklets, every way I could think of. It's my style. I try out all the different possibilities. We're always looking for Love stamps, but Cathy [Caggiano, in charge of stamp acquisition and distribution] also needed designs for regular use, and these ended up being definitives."

Each of the four stamps, as issued, has a distinctive background color. For the longiflorum lily, it is purple; the cymbidium orchid, yellow-brown; the freesia, blue-green; the Asian hybrid, dark reddish-brown.

A comparison of the booklet and coil stamps shows that the printing on the coil versions is somewhat crisper and clearer than on the booklets. The year date "2000" is slightly wider on the booklet stamps and has rounder zeroes than on the coils.

In the booklets, the words "first-class usa," in dropout white Garamond italic letters, are outlined in black on three of the four stamps. On the fourth stamp, the freesia, there is no outline. In the coils, however, the lettering is outlined on all four stamps, including the freesia.

First-day Facts

No first-day ceremony was held for the nondenominated rate-change stamps issued December 15. The stamps were placed on sale nationwide. First-day covers were postmarked Washington, D.C.

356

REVISED DEFINITIVES

Nondenominated (33¢) H Stamp, Pane of 20

The nondenominated H (Hat) stamp was issued in numerous formats November 9, 1998, in advance of the increase in the first-class postage rate from 32¢ to 33¢ scheduled for January 10, 1999. One of those formats was a flat pane (convertible booklet) of 20 self-adhesive stamps printed by Avery Dennison Security Printing Division. The stamps had die-cut simulated perforations listed in the Scott *Specialized Catalogue of U.S. Stamps & Covers* as gauging 11¼. Later, a variety of the stamp was found with die cuts gauging 11. Scott assigned the new variety the minor-letter designation 3268b, which previously had been assigned to a pane of 20, and redesignated the pane of 20 3268c.

22¢ Uncle Sam, pane of 20

A vertical die-cut variety of the 22¢ Uncle Sam self-adhesive stamp issued in panes of 20 (Scott 3259) was found late in 2000 by Daniel Sherwood, a collector from New York. The stamp, issued November 9, 1998, was printed by American Packaging Corporation for Sennett Security Products and finished by Unique Binders of Fredericksburg, Virginia.

Normal stamps on the pane have die-cut simulated perforations measuring 10.8 on all four sides. The variety stamps are 10.8 horizontally by 10.5 vertically.

The variation is found only on the five stamps of a single horizontal row on a pane. The affected row can be any one of the horizontal rows — first, second, third or fourth.

Sherwood told *Linn's Stamp News* he discovered the variety when he was trying to assemble 20 used Uncle Sam stamps by affixing them to the backing paper of an Uncle Sam pane from which all the stamps had been removed, leaving the selvage intact. "But the attempt ended in dismal failure when the stamps didn't fit on the backing paper," Sherwood told *Linn's*. The misfits occurred because some of the stamps he was using had the different gauge of vertical "perfs."

In the 2002 Scott *Specialized Catalogue of U.S. Stamps & Covers*, the variety is listed as 3259a.

The die cuts of the 22¢ Uncle Sam variety on the left measure 10.5 vertically by 10.8 horizontally, while the normal stamp on the right measures 10.8 on all four sides.

$15 MIGRATORY BIRD HUNTING (DUCK) STAMP 2000-2001

Date of Issue: June 30, 2000

Catalog Number: Scott RW67

Colors: Face: magenta, yellow, cyan, black (offset), black (intaglio). Back: black (offset).

First-Day Cancel: July 1, 2000, Washington, D.C.; artist's hometown event, July 22, 2000, Elyria, Ohio

Format: Panes of 20, horizontal, 5 across, 4 down. Offset printing plates of 80 subjects (8 across, 10 around); intaglio printing sleeves of 160 subjects (8 across, 20 around); flexographic back plate of 80 subjects (8 across, 10 around).

Gum Type: water-activated

Overall Stamp Size: 1.96 by 1.41 inches

Pane Size: 10.220 by 7.045 inches

Perforations: 11¼ (Eureka stroke perforator)

Selvage Markings: " 'DAWN OF A NEW MILLENNIUM'/ARTIST: ADAM GRIMM," "DEPARTMENT OF THE INTERIOR/20 X $15.00," repeated four times in selvage. "PLATE/POSITION" and diagram. Duck silhouettes in each of four process colors and one engraved color, repeated twice in selvage.

Back Inscription (printed on top of gum): "INVEST IN AMERICA'S FUTURE/BUY DUCK STAMPS AND/SAVE WETLANDS/SEND IN OR REPORT ALL/BIRD BANDS TO/1-800-327-BAND/IT IS UNLAWFUL TO HUNT WATERFOWL OR USE THIS STAMP/AS A PASS TO A NATIONAL WILDLIFE REFUGE UNLESS/YOU SIGN YOUR NAME IN INK ON THE FACE OF THIS STAMP."

Stamp Artist: Adam Grimm of Elyria, Ohio

Stamp Design, Typography and Modeling: Brian Thompson, Bureau of Engraving and Printing

Engravers: Christopher Madden, BEP, picture; John Smith Jr., BEP, lettering

Stamp Manufacturing: Stamps printed by BEP on the 4-color offset, 3-color intaglio webfed F press (801)

Quantity Ordered: 1,200,000

Sleeve Number: 1 6-digit intaglio sleeve number printed in selvage above or below each corner stamp

Sleeve Number Reported: 199119

Paper Supplier: Glatfelter/Spinnaker Coating

Tagging: untagged

$15 MIGRATORY BIRD HUNTING (DUCK) STAMP 2000-2001 (SELF-ADHESIVE)

Date of Issue: June 30, 2000

Catalog Number: Scott RW67A

Colors: Front: magenta, yellow, cyan, black (offset), black (intaglio). Back: black (offset).

First-Day Cancel: July 1, 2000, Washington, D.C.; artist's hometown event, July 22, 2000, Elyria, Ohio

Format: Sold in single-stamp panes. Offset printing plates of 24 subjects (3 across, 8 around) and intaglio printing sleeves of 48 subjects (3 across, 16 around).

Gum Type: self-adhesive

Overall Stamp Size: 1.96 by 1.41 inches

Pane Size: 6.14 by 2.60 inches

Perforations: 11¼ (die-cut simulated perforations) (Goebel stroke die cutter)

Selvage and Back Markings: see illustrations above

Stamp Artist: Adam Grimm of Elyria, Ohio

Stamp Design, Typography and Modeling: Brian Thompson, Bureau of Engraving and Printing

Engravers: Christopher Madden, BEP, picture; John Smith Jr., BEP, lettering

Stamp Manufacturing: Stamps printed by BEP on the 4-color offset, 3-color intaglio webfed F press (801)

Quantity Ordered: 2,800,000	
Sleeve Number: none	
Paper Supplier: Glatfelter/Spinnaker Coating	
Tagging: untagged	

The Stamps

Adam Grimm, a 21-year-old artist who had been drawing and painting since childhood, became the youngest winner in the history of the federal duck stamp contest when his oil painting of a male mottled duck took first place in the November 2-4, 1999, judging at the Department of the Interior in Washington, D.C.

As a result, the Elyria, Ohio, resident's artwork was depicted on the duck stamp that went on sale June 30, 2000, for a one-year period.

Grimm was a junior at the Columbus, Ohio, College of Art and Design when he got the telephone call from Washington that in an instant elevated him to the top rank of wildlife artists. The call prompted a swift and easy decision to drop out of school, where only a few of the instructors had understood his passion for painting birds, and devote full time to that passion.

His parents, Len and Jane Grimm, "had said the only way they would support my leaving school and trying to do the wildlife art thing on my own without getting a degree was — it was kind of like they were really reaching high — 'If you won the federal duck stamp contest,' " Grimm told *The Yearbook.* "I just laughed and said, 'It looks like I'm stuck here.'

"Now, if I can do this [hunt and paint] for the rest of my life, I'll be a happy man. There's not much else I'd rather be doing."

Adam Grimm, shown here in one of the Lake Erie marshes where he goes often to hunt and sketch waterfowl.

This is Adam Grimm's backlit oil painting of a mottled duck on the surface of a pond that won the 1999 duck stamp contest and was reproduced on the 2000-2001 federal duck stamp.

361

The duck stamp, officially known as the Migratory Bird Hunting and Conservation stamp, costs $15 and is issued by the Fish and Wildlife Service, a branch of the Interior Department, to raise money to buy waterfowl habitat. A newly designed duck stamp has been issued each year since 1934, when the first one, with a face value of $1, appeared.

Each year a current stamp must be purchased by waterfowl hunters over 16 years of age. Duck stamps also are popular with stamp collectors, wildlife artists and conservationists. The stamps are sold at post offices, national wildlife refuges and some national retail chain stores and sporting-goods stores.

Ninety-eight cents of each duck stamp dollar goes to buy wetlands habitat for the National Wildlife Refuge System, which includes 514 national wildlife refuges and 37 wetlands management districts. To date, more than $500,000,000 raised from duck stamp sales has been used to acquire some 5,000,000 acres for the system.

The Fish and Wildlife Service produced two varieties of the 2000 stamp, each with the same design. One has conventional perforations and water-activated gum and was distributed in panes of 20. The other is a self-adhesive with die-cut simulated perfs and was issued on a piece of dollar-sized backing paper from which the buyer could peel it and affix it to his or her hunting license.

Issuance of the self-adhesive version in 2000 concluded a successful three-year trial of that format that began in 1998. Both versions were printed by a combination of offset lithography and intaglio by the Bureau of Engraving and Printing, which has been the sole producer of duck stamps since their beginning.

The pane of 20, five across by four down, was a new layout for the conventionally gummed version. Since 1959, duck stamps had been distributed in panes of 30, five across by six down, with a set of plate numbers in one corner. The 20-stamp pane has four sets of plate numbers, one set above or below each of the four corner stamps.

The duck stamp office said the change to a 20-stamp pane was made so more collectors might be able to purchase the entire pane, "now a $300 product, rather than the old format, which was a $450 product."

"Also, there is less waste when breaking a sheet [pane] into plate blocks and plate singles," the explanation continued. "The sheet stamp scrap creates an inventory nightmare."

The selvage of the 2000 stamp pane contains the name of the artist, Adam Grimm, and the title of his artwork, "Dawn of a New Millennium." No previous duck stamp's pane had displayed such information. Also in the selvage are a plate-position diagram, "U.S. Department of the Interior," "20 x $15.00," and five duck silhouettes printed in the different inks used to print the stamp: the four offset process colors, magenta, yellow, cyan and black, plus the intaglio black. The effect of the silhouettes is similar to a printer's color bar, but with little ducks instead of rectangles.

The duck stamp contest is the only federally sponsored art competition.

Winning artists receive no prize money, but the professional recognition is extremely valuable, and they also stand to earn hundreds of thousands of dollars from the sale of limited-edition prints of their artwork to collectors and licensed products bearing the image of their stamp designs.

Each year, competitors are given a list of the species from which to select their subjects. In even-numbered years, the list contains familiar American waterfowl that have been depicted on duck stamps in the past. In odd-numbered years, the list comprises a dwindling number of species that never have been shown before. In the 1999 competition, that number was reduced to two: the black scoter and the mottled duck.

Of the 243 artists who paid the $100 entry fee to compete in the 1999 contest, 135 chose the mottled duck as their subject and 108 chose the black scoter. In 2001, because Grimm's victory "retired" the mottled duck, competitors will be allowed to paint only the black scoter.

The mottled duck (Anas fulvigula), a close relative of the mallard and the black duck, resides in the fresh and brackish waters and marshes of southern Texas and southern Louisiana, feeding on aquatic plants, mollusks, insects, crustaceans and fish. A geographical variation called the Florida duck is found in most of the Florida peninsula. Slightly smaller than a mallard, the mottled duck has plumage of dusky brown. Its most colorful feature is an iridescent purplish-blue speculum, or patch of color, edged with narrow white bars, on the trailing edge of each wing. The male's bill is bright yellow, the female's olive-drab to orange.

Out of a possible 25 points in the final round of judging, Grimm's entry scored 20, as did a pair of black scoters in flight painted in acrylic by Terry Doughty of Brookfield, Wisconsin. After a tie-breaking vote, Grimm's work edged out Doughty's, 22-20. Beginning with a three-way tie, third place ultimately went to Paco Young of Bozeman, Montana, for his acrylic painting of a pair of mottled ducks on the wing.

This acrylic painting of a pair of black scoters in flight by Terry Doughty of Brookfield, Wisconsin, finished a close second to Adam Grimm's winning painting in the 1999 federal duck stamp competition.

Paco Young of Bozeman, Montana, took third place in the 1999 competition with this acrylic painting of two mottled ducks on the wing.

The judges were F. Burton Sellers, senior vice president of the International Federation of Philately and a past president of the American Philatelic Society; Matt Connally, former executive vice president of Ducks Unlimited; Betty Lou Fegely, chairwoman of the Outdoor Writers Association of America; Sara Gilbert, editor of *U.S. Art* magazine; and Wayne Trimm, an ornithologist.

It had been announced that Vice President Al Gore, then in the midst of his campaign for president, would be present and personally announce the winner at the conclusion of the judging, but Gore didn't show up.

"The relatively low scores reflect the tough grading standards of this year's judging panel," wrote duck stamp expert and dealer Bob Dumaine in *Linn's Stamp News.* "...The artwork in the finals all was excellent, and the voting was so close that any wavering of the judges' voting could have changed the result.

"A possible factor in the low scores was the difficulty of acquiring models for these obscure and much-maligned so-called ugly ducks."

With his win at age 21, Grimm replaced Jim Hautman as the youngest champion ever. Hautman won at age 25 in 1988 and went on to win the 1994 and 1998 contests as well, recording, in each of the latter two years, a perfect score of 25 in the final judging — the only two times that has been done.

Hautman is one of three brothers who have dominated the duck stamp competition for over a decade. Both Jim and brother Robert, who won in 1996, were ineligible for the 1999 contest under a rule that excludes winners for the following three years. The oldest brother, Joe, who placed first in 1991, finished seventh in 1999.

Grimm was the first person to win the contest after placing in the federal junior duck stamp design contest (he finished fourth in 1996) and the first to win after attending a duck stamp artists' workshop sponsored by the Fish and Wildlife Service. The workshop, held in August 1999 at the Beartooth School of Art in Big Timber, Montana, included instruction by two previous federal duck stamp winners, Daniel Smith (1987) and Bruce Miller (1992). Grimm had brought along his unfinished painting of the mottled duck, and both Smith and Miller gave him tips for some minor improvements. A few weeks later, their student's painting would outscore their own entries in the 1999 contest.

The 1999 competition was Grimm's third attempt at the big prize. In 1997 his painting of a pair of mottled ducks had taken 16th place. The following year, he moved up to eighth place with a painting of a green-winged teal.

"I had done a lot of research on mottled ducks because I wanted to have the habitat and the anatomy correct," Grimm said. "I talked to biologists down in southern Texas, experts on mottled ducks. When I got 16th place I was really excited. I thought, 'Well, I didn't do too bad. All that work must have really paid off.'

"The next year, with the green-winged teal, I did the same thing, a lot of research. My paintings were getting better, too, from the standpoint of realism. They were becoming more the painting style the judges look for."

The November 4, 1999, telephone call notifying Grimm, in Columbus, of his victory came from Jamie Clark, director of the Fish and Wildlife Service. In his response, heard via speakerphone by the audience in the Department of the Interior auditorium, the artist dedicated the win to his late grandfather, Elmer Grimm, who had died the previous spring.

"My grandpa was by far my biggest fan, my biggest supporter," Adam Grimm explained later. "I don't think there ever was a doubt in his mind that I would one day win this competition. He bought my very first pencil drawing when I was 11 or 12. He said, 'I think you're good enough now. You ought to get paid for your artwork.' That was when I started thinking, 'Gosh, that would be really cool if I could make some money doing this.' "

Grimm's federal contest win ensured that he would do exactly that. To publish his limited-edition prints he chose Steiner Prints of San Francisco, California, owned by Robert Steiner, whose painting of a Barrow's goldeneye was featured on the 1998 U.S. duck stamp. Since then, Grimm has won commissions to illustrate the 2000 Alaska and 2001 Washington state duck stamps. When Grimm spoke with *The Yearbook*, he had just finished a five-foot-long painting of old squaw ducks in flight, which he planned to offer for sale, and was busy on a four-foot-long painting of pintails. His studio is, as it always has been, his parents' kitchen in Elyria, with the kitchen table serving as an easel.

With the 2000 stamp, the federal duck stamp office announced a change in marketing policy. Beginning July 1, 2000, gummed examples of the annual stamps no longer were available from that office, either in Washington or at the office's booths at stamp shows. The sale of duck stamps from the previous two years also was discontinued. The office now handles only the current self-adhesive stamp, artist-signed examples of the same, and licensed products (such as shirts and caps) bearing images of the federal duck stamp.

Some collectors found that their local post offices didn't carry the 2000 gummed stamp, either. As happened in 1998 and 1999, many small offices ordered only one version in order to hold down the dollar amount of their stamp inventory. The stamp of choice usually was the self-adhesive, because it was easier to handle and the back of its backing paper was barcoded to simplify inventory concerns.

This left those collectors with no other way to obtain the gummed variety of the duck stamp than by ordering it from USPS Stamp Fulfillment Services or finding a post office with a philatelic window. They might not have to concern themselves with this particular problem in the future, however. In April 2001, Robert C. Lesino, chief of the federal duck stamp office, wrote in a letter to collectors:

"Future cost-cutting measures may require the elimination of the gummed traditional stamp and/or the stamp as an engraved product. We are working with the Bureau of Engraving and Printing to keep quality and tradition, but to reduce costs."

The Design

Adam Grimm's dramatically backlit painting shows a rear view of a mottled duck standing erect on the water, its wings outstretched and its tail and feet out of sight below the surface. Although the Fish and Wildlife Service originally described the bird as "poised for takeoff," Grimm says it actually is flapping its wings to rid its feathers of excess water. Golden light illuminates the upper part of the right wing and the edge of the head and neck and shines through the extended feathers of the left wing. The blurry ripples in the background are a soft golden color.

Bob Dumaine pointed out that the 2000 duck stamp is the first ever to show its subject from behind. The pose is one that Grimm "borrowed" from a sighting he had made earlier in 1999 of a hen blue-winged teal while he was on a hunting trip with his father to South Dakota. Its strength is that it shows a rather unattractive bird in a highly attractive way.

"It was late spring, early in the morning, and I saw this teal rise up and flap her wings," Grimm recalled. "I couldn't catch her with a camera — she was quite a ways off — but I just got this image in my head of what it would look like if I could have held her in that pose with the sunlight coming from behind her. She's a brown duck and the light would be a kind of orangeish gold, and I thought, 'Wow, that would be a really cool painting.'

"I immediately started thinking about it for a stamp picture, because it's good to do single birds, and I was trying to come up with an idea for something to do with the mottled duck, which is a brown duck, too. I went back and did a few sketches. The very first sketch I did was actually the design I ended up with. I drew a little arrow to show the direction of the light, just to help me remember the initial idea."

This is the first pencil sketch made by Adam Grimm after getting the idea of painting a mottled duck in the same pose in which he had seen a female blue-winged teal. It became the basis for the artwork that won the 1999 federal duck stamp competition. Grimm drew the arrow that appears outside the upper-right corner of the sketch to show the direction of the light, "just to help me remember the initial idea," he said. The words beneath the sketch are a note he wrote after talking on the phone with Robert C. Lesino, chief of the federal duck stamp office, about his contest entry from the previous year.

Grimm turned to the research on mottled ducks he had done two years earlier. At that time he had sought the help of a hunter friend, Bob Taylor of Harlingen, Texas, who sent him frozen specimens of several varieties of ducks, including a male mottled duck. Another friend, a local taxidermist, mounted the birds for him, and he used the mottled duck as reference for details of anatomy and feathers. The painting took about 2½ weeks to complete.

"I always said I didn't want to do something that would look like somebody else's," Grimm said. "I didn't want people to think, 'Oh, he just copied a Hautman painting or Will Goebel's painting [the 1995 contest winner]. I wanted it to be my own individual thing."

The stamp, like all duck stamps in recent years, was printed by a combination of intaglio and four-color offset lithography. The offset printing with which the basic illustration is reproduced is supplemented by densely engraved black intaglio lines that give texture and depth to the duck's body, head, neck and wings, as well as the ripples at the point where the body meets the water. The black lettering across the top and down the right side also is engraved.

Most previous duck stamps have had white borders around the central illustration. The 2000 stamp represented a sharp departure from the tradition. Its border and the pane selvage are purple, a color blended from the process colors used on the offset portion of BEP's F press. Against this background, the black typography on the stamps and selvage, including the unusually small plate numbers, is somewhat difficult to read.

The duck stamp office's decision to color the stamp's borders found a strong critic in Bob Dumaine. The image of the stamp "is very bright," Dumaine wrote in *Linn's*, "but because of the purple-everywhere design, the stamp to me actually looks dull.

"Additionally, when stamps are separated from each other, the perforation tips show white paper fiber, giving the stamp a shabby appearance.

"When you glance at the issued stamp, all you see is the purple instead of the elegant design. The bright border distracts from the beauty of the mottled duck painting and diminishes the effectiveness of the design, which itself is very strong.

"I feel the design would have been better presented with normal white borders. ... I hope this unfortunate color choice will be only a one-year catastrophe and a sole monument of how poor use of border color can ruin a great duck stamp design."

On the other hand, the purple stamp borders and selvage did give Adam Grimm an opportunity to create a unique kind of remarque.

A remarque is a small illustration added by the artist to a stamp or print to personalize it. Such enhancements, for which the artist charges extra, are prized by many collectors and add to the collectible value of the item. Working with plate blocks of six Mottled Duck stamps, Grimm first used an eraser to create a cloud pattern in the selvage, then painted a flock of

Artist Adam Grimm created this unusual remarque in the selvage of a duck stamp plate block by erasing some of the purple color to create a cloud pattern, then painting a flock of mottled ducks in flight across the clouds. Grimm then signed the selvage in the upper-left corner. *(Plate block photo courtesy of Bob Dumaine)*

mottled ducks flying against the clouds. He had hit on the device by accident, after he had tried to erase a lightly penciled sketch line in the selvage and found that the eraser took the purple color off as well.

"Bob Dumaine loved it and the collectors seemed to like it a lot, so he said, 'Do some more for me with the clouds,'" Grimm said. "I said to him, 'Hey, Bob, you don't like that purple selvage, but it sure would have been hard erasing clouds on white paper.'"

First-day Facts

The Federal Duck Stamp Office held the first-day-of-sale and signing ceremony for the 2000 stamps at the National Postal Museum in Washington, D.C., June 30, one day before the stamps went on sale nationwide.

Adam Grimm was on hand to sign autographs. A special pictorial cancellation designed by Grimm was available for the event.

As in the past, a second "artist's hometown" ceremony was held. The date was July 22 and the place was Elyria Catholic High School in Grimm's hometown of Elyria, Ohio. Grimm graduated from the school in 1997.

Hometown ceremony cacheted covers franked with the 2000 $15 federal duck stamp were available for purchase for $25. The covers were signed by Grimm and bore a special cancel provided by the U.S. Postal Service. All profits from the sale of the covers were donated in Grimm's name to the Willow Point Wildlife Area restoration project managed by the Ohio Division of Wildlife.

20¢ UNIVERSITY OF UTAH POSTAL CARD
HISTORIC PRESERVATION SERIES

Date of Issue: February 28, 2000

Catalog Number: Scott

Colors: magenta, yellow, cyan, black

First-Day Cancel: Salt Lake City, Utah

First-Day Cancellations: 14,230

Format: Cards printed in 80-subject sheet but available only as single-cut cards. Offset printing plates of 80 subjects (8 across, 10 down).

Size: 5.5 by 3.5 inches

Marking: "©USPS 1999." Recycled logo followed by "recycled."

Illustrator: Allen Garns of Mesa, Arizona

Designer, Art Director and Typographer: Ethel Kessler of Bethesda, Maryland

Card Manufacturing: Cards printed by the Government Printing Office in Washington, D.C., on a 5-color MAN Roland sheetfed offset press. Cards processed and shipped by GPO.

Quantity Ordered: 6,000,000

Paper Type: 22-pound bright white

Tagging: vertical bar to right of stamp

The Card

On February 28, the Postal Service marked the 150th anniversary of the founding of the University of Utah by issuing a 20¢ postal card in the Historic Preservation series.

The card depicts the neoclassical John R. Park Building on the university campus. Designed by the architectural firm of Cannon, Fetzer and Hansen of Salt Lake City and completed in 1914, the Park Building is one

of several historic structures located around Presidents Circle, which was placed on the National Register of Historic Places in 1978.

The only previous card in the series to honor a Utah institution was the fourth, in 1980, which depicted Salt Lake Temple (Scott UX83). In recent years, the Historic Preservation series has been used mostly to honor colleges and universities as they reach significant milestones.

In keeping with USPS policy established in 1999, the University of Utah card was offered for general sale only at post offices in Utah. It also was available at philatelic centers around the country and through Stamp Fulfillment Services in Kansas City, Missouri. Like other postal cards, it sold for a penny over its face value, a charge that USPS justifies as defraying the cost of production.

The University of Utah, in Salt Lake City at the foot of the Wasatch Mountains, was among the first universities established west of the Missouri River. (Willamette University in Salem, Oregon, founded in 1842 and honored with a Historic Preservation postal card in 1992, is the oldest.) It was founded February 28, 1850, as "the University of Deseret," only three years after Mormon settlers arrived at the Valley of the Great Salt Lake. Its name was changed to its present name in 1892. Today, it serves some 26,000 students from 50 states and more than 100 countries, offering undergraduate, graduate and professional programs in 15 colleges and professional schools.

The Design

The Park Building's prominence on campus and its status as a building on the National Register of Historic Places made it the natural design subject for the card. Art director Ethel Kessler first tried developing a design using photographs of the building, "which would have been a typical way to go," she said, "but it didn't do anything for me."

Among the visual research material Kessler had received via PhotoAssist, the Postal Service's research firm, was a set of the original pre-1914 architectural drawings of the Park Building by Cannon, Fetzer and Hansen. Many of the clients of Kessler's design business have been architects and space planners, and she has had considerable experience working with their graphic renderings. Now, looking at a west elevation of the

370

Allen Garns made this preliminary version of the art for the imprinted stamp, using pastels to color an architect's west elevation of the building and provide the "soft edge" that was retained on the finished picture.

building, she decided to take "a very different approach from what any of the postal cards had been before."

To execute her idea, Kessler called on Allen Garns, an illustrator from Mesa, Arizona, whose work in light, shadow and space she recently had discovered and admired. Working directly on the architect's drawing, Garns used pastels to add color and shading to the building's walls, windows and cupola and created a cloud-filled blue sky overhead. He removed the lettering from the drawing and added an olive-brown "soft edge" frame to the horizontal rectangular design, and the result, Kessler said, "was like a beautiful little painting."

Kessler superimposed the year dates "1850-2000" on the imprinted stamp, just below the columned entrance to the building. It was a last-minute addition; the image released in advance by USPS didn't include the dates. The inscription "UNIVERSITY OF UTAH 20 USA," in black Garamond capitals, appears beneath the stamp.

First-day Facts

M. Richard Porras, chief financial officer and executive vice president of USPS, and J. Bernard Machen, president of the University of Utah, dedicated the card in a ceremony in the foyer of the Park Building that the university also billed as its birthday party. Honored guests were Stephen L. Johnson, USPS Salt Lake City district manager for customer service and sales, and Ralph Hamilton, Salt Lake City's postmaster. A cake was cut and the university band performed.

The earliest-known use of a University of Utah card was February 23, five days before the official first day of issue.

20¢ RYMAN AUDITORIUM POSTAL CARD
HISTORIC PRESERVATION SERIES

Ryman Auditorium, Nashville, Tennessee

Date of Issue: March 18, 2000

Catalog Number: Scott UX313

Colors: magenta, yellow, cyan, black

First-Day Cancel: Nashville, Tennessee

First-Day Cancellations: 12,690

Format: Cards printed in 80-subject sheet but available only as single-cut cards. Offset printing plates of 80 subjects (8 across, 10 down).

Size: 5.5 by 3.5 inches; 139.59 by 88.83mm

Marking: "©USPS 1999." Recycled logo followed by "recycled."

Illustrator: Mike Summers of Nashville, Tennessee

Designer, Art Director and Typographer: Richard Sheaff of Scottsdale, Arizona

Card Manufacturing: Cards printed by the Government Printing Office in Washington, D.C., on a 5-color MAN Roland sheetfed offset press. Cards processed and shipped by GPO.

Quantity Ordered: 6,000,000

Paper Type: 22-pound bright white

Tagging: vertical bar to right of stamp

The Card

When Postmaster General Marvin T. Runyon, a former Tennessee resident, suggested to the Citizens' Stamp Advisory Committee that it endorse a stamp to commemorate the 75th anniversary of Nashville's Grand Ole Opry in 2000, CSAC informed him that its guidelines precluded stamps for 75th anniversaries.

Runyon then asked the committee to consider approving a postal card in the Historic Preservation series to honor the Ryman Auditorium in Nashville, which had been the home of the Opry for more than 30 years and was called "the mother church of country music." CSAC agreed, and the card was issued March 18.

The Ryman Auditorium card was the first in the Historic Preservation series to honor a Tennessee landmark. Six million were issued, with sale of the card limited to post offices in Tennessee and philatelic centers around the country and through Stamp Fulfillment Services in Kansas City, Missouri, the Postal Service's mail-order headquarters.

A three-week tent revival in Nashville in 1885, conducted by Samuel Porter Jones, a fiery evangelical preacher, was the catalyst for the building's construction. Among those converted was a wealthy owner and captain of Cumberland River steamboats, Thomas Ryman. He vowed to build a hall so "that Sam Jones will never have to preach in a tent again." Ground was broken in 1889 for his Union Gospel Tabernacle, which was constructed at a cost of approximately $130,000 and was opened in 1892. The original name remains carved in a stone panel above the front entrance.

In 1897 a balcony was added — the Confederate Gallery — to accommodate a reunion of Confederate soldiers. Four years later, at the behest of the Women's League of Nashville, a stage was built so that a touring production of the opera *Carmen* could be booked into the tabernacle. Until then, events had been presented in the round.

Ryman died in 1904, and the Rev. Jones, officiating at the funeral, proposed that the name of the building be changed to the Ryman Auditorium. All 4,000 mourners reportedly rose to their feet in approval. As one of the largest auditoriums in the Southeast, the Ryman hosted a wide variety of concerts, lectures and stage productions, in addition to revival meetings. Then, in 1943, it became the home of the Grand Ole Opry.

The Opry originated in 1925, wrote Gerald Nachman in his book *Raised on Radio*, when the National Life and Accident Insurance Company built a 1,000-watt radio station in downtown Nashville with the call letters WSM, standing for "We Shield Millions," and began broadcasting a weekly show of music by country fiddlers, pickers and singers. A harmonica player on an early show told the audience: "Our program can't be called grand opera. But, folks, I don't see why we can't call it 'opry.' So from now on we will be presenting Grand Ole Opry." The down-home handle stuck.

From its home studio, the show moved to a theater, then to the Dixie Tabernacle, then to the War Memorial Auditorium, and finally, in 1943, to Ryman Auditorium. It broadcast from the Ryman until 1974, when it moved to new theme-park headquarters at Opryland USA. During that time, country legends like Hank Williams, Roy Acuff, Patsy Cline and Minnie Pearl performed on the Ryman stage before wooden pews packed with fans and a radio audience of millions.

When the Opry left, the Ryman was vacant. It was used as a backdrop in the films *Nashville, Coal Miner's Daughter* and *Sweet Dreams*. In 1993 the diversified entertainment company Gaylord Entertainment began an $8.5 million renovation of the Ryman, and it reopened in June 1994 as a premier performance hall, seating 2,100 in the pews, with a museum of country music.

The building was placed on the National Register of Historic Places in 1971 and was designated a National Historic Landmark in 2001.

The Design

To illustrate the card, designer and art director Richard Sheaff chose an existing piece of art: an oil on canvas painting of Ryman Auditorium as it appeared shortly after its construction as the Union Gospel Tabernacle. The red brick building is shown in dramatic perspective, with its elaborate roofline decoration (a feature that, unfortunately, has been lost). A horse and carriage moves along the unpaved street in front of the building, with a barefoot boy running behind, rolling a hoop. On the side of the carriage is painted the name of the H.W. Buttorff Company, a firm that did business with Captain Ryman's shipping company, although the name isn't legible in the image on the postal card. Pedestrians in period costume are seen on the brick sidewalks.

"It's a lovely period image from the turn of the century," Sheaff said. "It was so perfect that we gave no thought to having a new piece of art prepared."

The art was created for Gaylord Entertainment in conjunction with the

Mike Summers referred to this early photograph of the Union Gospel Tabernacle (Ryman Auditorium), circa 1904, in making his oil painting that was reproduced on the postal card.

This is the refurbished Ryman Auditorium as it looks today.

opening of the refurbished auditorium in 1994. The artist was Mike Summers of Nashville, who at the time was a senior designer and illustrator for Gaylord and now has his own design studio. The painting, 84 by 60 inches in size, hangs on a landing in the staircase to the balcony in a new portion of the Ryman, on what formerly was an exterior wall but now is inside the building. Summers' reference material included a rare early photograph, circa 1904, now in the collection of the Nashville Public Library, which shows the building from exactly the same angle, although the streets and sidewalks are empty.

Sheaff placed "USA," in blue Frutiger type, and "20," in ITC Officina Sans Bold, in the upper-right corner of the picture. The words "Ryman Auditorium, Nashville, Tennessee" are in a single line of green Frutiger beneath the frameline.

First-day Facts

Deborah K. Willhite, USPS senior vice president for government relations and public policy, dedicated the card in a ceremony at the Ryman Auditorium. Regular admission charges to the auditorium were waived for a brief period to enable the public to attend.

Bill Anderson, a Grand Ole Opry member, was the principal speaker. Paul T. Couch, general manager of Ryman Auditorium, gave the welcome, and Eddie Perez, Nashville's postmaster, presided. Lorrie Morgan, another member of the Grand Ole Opry, provided a singing interlude. Mike Summers, whose painting is reproduced on the card, was a special guest.

20¢ WILE E. COYOTE AND ROAD RUNNER PICTURE POSTAL CARD LOONEY TUNES SERIES

Date of Issue: April 26, 2000

Price: $6.95 for book of 10 cards

Catalog Number: Scott UX314, single card; UX314a, book of 10 cards

Colors: magenta, cyan, yellow, black

First-Day Cancel: Phoenix, Arizona

First-Day Cancellations: 154,903 (includes Wile E. Coyote and Road Runner stamp)

Format: Book of 10 stamped cards, with microperforations to permit removal of individual cards. Offset printing plates of 30 subjects for cards. Offset plates of 12 subjects for book covers.

Size of Card: 6.00 by 4.25 inches

Size of Book: 6.75 by 4.25 inches

Card Markings: On address side of each card: "THE 2000 WILE E. COYOTE & ROAD RUNNER STAMP." "©USPS 2000." "LOONEY TUNES, characters, names and all related indicia are trademarks of Warner Bros. © 2000."

Cover Markings: On inside of front cover: "When Bugs Bunny was named/ambassador for STAMPERS®—the/coolest group of collectors around —/he knew it would be big. After all,/he is Bugs./But now the Looney Tunes series has/gone truly wild, as America's favorite/speed demon, Road Runner, and his/persistent predator, Wile E. Coyote,/slow down just long enough to be/captured on a fabulous new stamp./So get

376

moving and start collecting./Stamps are the fast way to fun." On outside of back cover: "UNITED STATES/POSTAL SERVICE®" and logo. "©2000 U.S. Postal Service. All rights Reserved. To obtain additional information/on Commemorative Stamps and Stamp Products available from the U.S. Postal Service/please write to: Information Fulfillment, USPS, PO Box 219424, Kansas City, MO 64121-9494./LOONEY TUNES, characters, names, and all related indicia are trademarks of Warner Bros. ©2000."

Illustrator and Designer: Ed Wleczyk, Warner Bros., Los Angeles, California

Character Art: Frank Espinosa, Warner Bros.

Concept: Brenda Guttman, Warner Bros.

Art Director: Terrence McCaffrey, USPS

Card Manufacturing: Cards printed for Banknote Corporation of America (BCA), Browns Summit, North Carolina, by PBM Graphics, Greensboro, North Carolina, on a Komori Lithrone offset press. Die-cut microperforations applied with a Bobst rotary die-cutter.

Quantity Ordered: 100,000 books (1,000,000 cards)

Paper Type: Domtar 10 point C1S, coated on one side

Tagging: Vertical bar to right of stamp

The Card

When the Postal Service issued its 33¢ Wile E. Coyote and Road Runner commemorative stamp April 26 in Phoenix, Arizona, it also issued a 20¢ picture postal card, just as it had done with the three previous stamps in the Looney Tunes series.

Once again the stamp design is reproduced in the card's imprinted stamp, with only the denomination changed. The design also is printed in enlarged form on the picture side, without typography.

Like its predecessors in the series, the Coyote and Road Runner card was offset printed and bound in books of 10 cards, with microperforations to facilitate their removal. The image on the front cover of the book is the same as that on the picture side of the card, but slightly larger.

USPS sold the book for $6.95, or 69.5¢ per card, by mail order and through self-service postal stores. The price was the same as USPS had charged in 1999 for the Daffy Duck stamped card book.

The Coyote-Road Runner card was printed by PBM Graphics of Greensboro, North Carolina, as a subcontractor for Banknote Corporation of America, on a Komori Lithrone offset press. BCA delivered a total of 1 million cards to the Postal Service, compared to the 2,255,500 Daffy Duck cards that USPS had ordered the year before from Ashton-Potter (USA) Ltd.

The Design

The design used for the card's imprinted stamp and picture side is the illustration devised by Warner Bros. artists Ed Wleczyk and Frank

377

Espinosa for the postage stamp. It shows Road Runner perched on top of a rural mailbox beside a stretch of desert road, a mailbag slung around his neck. He is holding out an envelope addressed to Wile E. Coyote, who lies prone on the ground, a look of frustration on his face, his right paw extended upward to accept his mail. On Wile E.'s back is the sputtering rocket pack that has, naturally, malfunctioned and spoiled his plan to hurtle down on his quarry from above.

The image on the imprinted stamp is virtually identical to that of the self-adhesive postage stamp, except that the denomination that is formed by clouds in the sky is "20" instead of "33" and there is no "2000" date beneath the frameline. Because BCA's subcontractor had to use a 150-line screen for the card stock rather than the much finer 350-line screen that BCA itself used to print the stamp, the image on the stamped card is much less detailed.

First-Day Facts

For information on the first-day ceremony, see the chapter on the Wile E. Coyote and Road Runner stamps.

ADOPTION PICTURE POSTAL CARD

Date of Issue: May 10, 2000

Price: $6.95 for book of 10 cards

Catalog Number: Scott UX315, single card; UX315a, book of 10 cards

Colors: magenta, cyan, yellow, black

First-Day Cancel: Los Angeles, California

First-Day Cancellations: 137,903 (includes Adoption stamp)

Format: Book of 10 stamped cards, with microperforations to permit removal of individual cards. Offset printing plate of 30 subjects for cards and 12 subjects for book covers.

Size of Card: 6.00 by 4.25 inches

Size of Book: 6.75 by 4.25 inches

Card Markings: On address side of each card: "Adoption stamp,/Issued in 2000." "©2000 USPS."

Cover Markings: On front cover: "Adopting a CHILD/Creating a WORLD/Shaping a LIFE/Building a HOME." "The U.S. Postal Service/Ready-to-Mail Postal Cards." On back cover: "UNITED STATES/POSTAL SERVICE®" and logo. "©2000 U.S. Postal Service. All Rights Reserved. To obtain additional information/on Commemorative Stamps and Stamp Products available from the U.S. Postal Service/please write to: Information Fulfillment, USPS, PO Box 219424, Kansas City, MO 64121-9424."

Illustrator, Designer and Typographer: Greg Berger of Bethesda, Maryland

Art Director: Ethel Kessler of Bethesda, Maryland

Card Manufacturing: Cards printed for Banknote Corporation of America

(BCA), Browns Summit, North Carolina, by PBM Graphics, Greensboro, North Carolina, on a Komori Lithrone offset press. Die-cut microperforations applied with a Bobst rotary die-cutter.

Quantity Ordered: 100,000 books (1,000,000 cards)

Paper Type: Domtar 10 point C1S, coated on one side

Tagging: Vertical bar to right of stamp

The Card

On May 10, in Beverly Hills, California, the Postal Service issued a 20¢ picture stamped card promoting adoption. The card was a companion to a 33¢ commemorative stamp issued at the same time and place.

The card reproduces the stamp design in its own imprinted stamp and displays a modified version of the stamp design on its picture side. It was sold in books of 10 cards for $6.95, or 69.6¢ for each 20¢ card.

PBM Graphics of Greensboro, North Carolina, printed the cards and covers as a subcontractor to Banknote Corporation of America, using a Komori Lithrone offset press. Die-cut microperforations were applied to facilitate the removal of individual cards from the books.

The Design

Greg Berger's design for the imprinted stamp on the Adoption card is the same as that of the Adoption stamp that he also designed, except that the denomination is 20¢ instead of 33¢ and there is no tiny "2000" year-of-issue just outside the lower part of the right frameline.

The picture side of the card is an enlarged version of that same basic image, arranged vertically, but with changes in the portions outside the central vignette. On the stamp, the inscriptions "Creating a WORLD," "Adopting a CHILD," "Shaping a LIFE" and "Building a HOME" surrounding the vignette are in black and colored letters on a white background. On the card, the first three of those inscriptions are superimposed on simple blocks of color — green, red and orange, respectively — with the capitalized words in dropout white. The fourth inscription, "Building a HOME," is on a wider strip across the bottom of the card that replicates some of the visual elements of the central image: the moon, stars and planets against a night sky on the left; the cottage on a green hilltop in the center, and the daytime sun with puffy clouds on the right.

Berger also designed the book cover. The front incorporates the same design elements as the picture side of the card, but is arranged horizontally rather than vertically. The back shows the stick-figure dog from the stamp illustration against a broad band of green, while along the bottom is a strip of dark blue bearing a moon, stars and planets similar to those on the stamp.

First-Day Facts

For details of the first-day sale, see the chapter on the Adoption stamp.

20¢ MIDDLEBURY COLLEGE POSTAL CARD
HISTORIC PRESERVATION SERIES

Old Stone Row, Middlebury College, Vermont

Date of Issue: May 19, 2000

Catalog Number: Scott UX316

Colors: magenta, yellow, cyan, black

First-Day Cancel: Middlebury, Vermont

First-Day Cancellations: 13,586

Format: Cards printed in 80-subject sheet but available only as single-cut cards. Offset printing plates of 80 subjects (8 across, 10 down).

Size: 5.5 by 3.5 inches

Marking: "©USPS 1999." Recycled logo followed by "recycled."

Illustrator: Arnold Holeywell of Warrenton, Virginia

Designer and Art Director: Howard Paine of Delaplane, Virginia

Typographer: Tom Mann of Vancouver, Washington

Card Manufacturing: Cards printed by the Government Printing Office in Washington, D.C., on a 5-color MAN Roland sheetfed offset press. Cards processed and shipped by GPO.

Quantity Ordered: 4,000,000

Paper Type: 22-pound bright white

Tagging: vertical bar to right of stamp

The Card

On May 19, the Postal Service issued a 20¢ postal card in the Historic Preservation series to commemorate the 200th anniversary of Middlebury College in Middlebury, Vermont.

The card depicts the east side of Old Stone Row, a group of three 19th-century stone buildings on the campus. The buildings are on the National

Register of Historic Places, a status that was a direct result of college officials' desire for postal commemoration of the institution's anniversary.

Late in 1996, the committee planning the bicentennial decided to ask for a stamp, and Adrianne Tucker, the college's public affairs coordinator and assistant to public affairs director Phil Benoit, was assigned to the project. She learned, as representatives of many other colleges before her have done, that USPS recognizes college and university anniversaries only with postal cards in the Historic Preservation series, and that a building, to qualify, must be on the National Register. Middlebury had no buildings so listed at the time.

The college set out to rectify the situation. Hugh Henry, an architectural historian from Chester, Vermont, was hired to help prepare an application. It was decided not to focus exclusively on the oldest building on campus — Painter Hall (1812-1816), which also is the oldest college building in Vermont — but to seek recognition for two other buildings as well: Old Chapel (1834-1836), which stands next to Painter, and Starr Hall (1861, rebuilt in 1865 after a fire), the third building in Old Stone Row.

Historians consider the buildings significant because they embody the architectural characteristics of the early 19th-century stone mill building type, as adapted to educational purposes. Old Stone Row has been called one of the best surviving examples of the linear row of architecturally unified college buildings that originated at Yale University in the 18th century.

In June 1997, Middlebury completed its application for historic status for the buildings and submitted it to the Vermont Division of Historic Preservation for state-level approval, a required first step. That approval came the following month, and on September 18, 1997, the U.S. National Park Service announced that Old Stone Row officially had been placed on the National Register of Historic Places. With that done, a letter was sent to the Citizens' Stamp Advisory Committee signed by John M. McCardell Jr., president of the college, asking for a postal card for the bicentennial. CSAC agreed, and USPS announced the card October 14, 1999, when it unveiled its 2000 commemorative stamp program.

The card was the second in the Historic Preservation series to honor a Vermont institution. In 1991 USPS had issued a 19¢ card (Scott UX159) commemorating the 200th anniversary of the University of Vermont at Burlington and picturing the Old Mill, an early campus structure that got its name from its resemblance to the brick mill buildings that housed New England's rapidly expanding textile industry.

In keeping with USPS policy established in 1999, the Middlebury College card was offered for general sale only at post offices in Vermont. It also was available at philatelic centers around the country and through Stamp Fulfillment Services in Kansas City, Missouri. Like other postal cards, it sold for a penny over its face value, a charge that USPS justifies as defraying the cost of production.

The card had a printing of only 4 million, compared to the print runs of 6 million ordered for previous Historic Preservation cards since the end of 1998. Before that, quantities ordered were much larger. The 1998 Northeastern University and Brandeis University cards had printings of 21 million each. Stamp Fulfillment Services listed the Middlebury College card "sold out" in its Summer 2001 *USA Philatelic* catalog, while several older commemorative postal cards remained available.

Middlebury College received its charter November 1, 1800, and held its first class five days later. It is the oldest operating institution of higher education in Vermont and second in terms of charter date to the University of Vermont, which was chartered November 3, 1791.

The Design

Howard Paine, designer of the Middlebury College card, chose as his illustrator Arnold Holeywell, of Warrenton, Virginia, an old friend and associate. Holeywell's artistic career dates to the 1950s, when he produced cover and story illustrations for *Field & Stream* magazine. In 1967, he became assistant art director of Time-Life Books. Now retired and a well-known architectural artist, he travels widely, painting old-time gas stations and general stores — buildings on the brink of extinction.

Holeywell was familiar with the Middlebury campus, having spent time there after World War II visiting former Army friends who had enrolled at the college. To create his gouache painting of Old Stone Row, he worked from an assortment of photographs and engravings obtained from the college by PhotoAssist, the Postal Service's research firm.

The artist's principal visual reference, on which the angle and perspective of the painting are based, was a color photo of the east side of Old Stone Row by Tad Merrick, a professional photographer in Middlebury. The season is winter, with the trees leafless and patches of snow on the ground — patches that Holeywell enlarged somewhat in his painting. The

In this source photograph used by Arnold Holeywell for his painting, tree branches partly obscure the buildings of Old Stone Row. Holeywell artistically "pruned" the trees so the buildings could be clearly seen. (Photo by Tad Merrick)

light gray of the stone walls, with a yellowish cast, predominates, while a blue sky and red chimneys provide a touch of color.

Painter Hall is on the right side of the painting, Old Chapel in the middle and Starr Hall on the left. Holeywell used artistic license to relocate some of the branches that in the photograph obstructed the view of the Old Chapel clock tower. "Basically it's what was there, but the branches are just moved a little bit one way or the other," he said.

The words "Old Stone Row, Middlebury College, Vermont" appear beneath the imprinted stamp.

First-day Facts

Philip Dennis, district manager for the USPS Springfield District, dedicated the card in a ceremony in front of Old Chapel on the Middlebury campus.

The principal speaker was Robert T. Stafford, Middlebury '35, a former governor, U.S. representative and U.S. senator from Vermont. John M. McCardell Jr., president of Middlebury, and Nicholas R. Clifford, a Middlebury trustee and co-chair of the college's bicentennial commission, gave the welcome. Celeste G. Planzo, manager of marketing for the USPS Springfield District, presided. Honored guests were Randall Waters, Middlebury postmaster; James H. Douglas, Middlebury '72, treasurer of the state of Vermont; John Tenny, chair of the Middlebury Board of Selectmen; and Betty Wheeler, Middlebury town manager.

20¢ STARS AND STRIPES PICTURE POSTAL CARDS (20 DESIGNS)

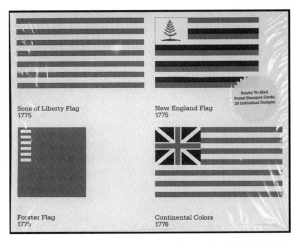

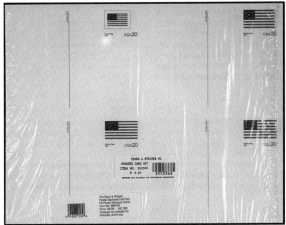

Date of Issue: June 14, 2000

Price: $8.95 for set of 20 cards

Catalog Numbers: Scott UX317-UX336, single cards; UX320a, UX324a, UX328a, UX332a, UX336a, sheets of 4 cards each

Colors: black, red (PMS 193), blue (PMS 281), green (PMS 356), brown (PMS 126)

First-Day Cancel: Baltimore, Maryland

First-Day Cancellations: 1,121,071 (includes Stars and Stripes stamps)

Format: Cards are in sheets of 4, with microperforations to permit separation. Cards are sold in shrink-wrapped sets of 5 sheets. Offset printing plates printing 8 sheets per impression, 4 across by 2 down.

Size of Cards: 5.50 by 4.25 inches

Size of Sheets: 11.0 inches by 8.5 inches

Card Markings: On address side of each card, "©2000 USPS."

Designer, Typographer and Art Director: Richard Sheaff of Scottsdale, Arizona

Modeler: Joseph Sheeran, Ashton-Potter (USA) Ltd., Williamsville, New York

Card Manufacturing: Cards printed by Partners Press, Kenmore, New York, for Ashton-Potter (USA) Ltd. on Heidelberg Speedmaster 6-color sheetfed offset press. Cards processed by Ashton-Potter.

Quantity Ordered: 2,000,000 cards (100,000 sets of 5 sheets of 4)

Paper Supplier: Carolina 10 point C1S, (coated on one side)

Tagging: vertical block to right of stamped image

The Cards

On June 14, the Postal Service issued a set of 20 picture postal cards to accompany the pane of 20 Stars and Stripes stamps it issued the same day. The cards and stamps, part of the Classic Collection series, had their first-day sale in Baltimore, Maryland.

The cards were produced in sheets, 11 by 8.5 inches in dimension, each containing four different varieties, and were sold in shrink-wrapped packs containing all five sheets for $8.95, or just under 45¢ for each 20¢-face-value card. They were printed by Partners Press of Kenmore, New York, as a subcontractor to Ashton-Potter (USA) Ltd., on a Heidelberg Speedmaster offset press.

In this format, the individual cards measure 5.5 by 4.25 inches each, which is somewhat more nearly square than the dimensions of U.S. stamped cards that are sold individually or bound in books.

Cards sold in sheet form can be used by quantity mailers, who are able to imprint messages and addresses on them using a laser printer or photocopying machine. USPS required the manufacturer to use heat-resistant inks that wouldn't deface the card at the high temperatures generated by a laser printer.

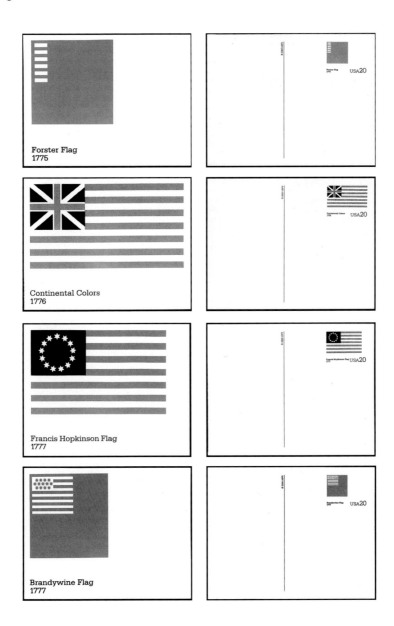

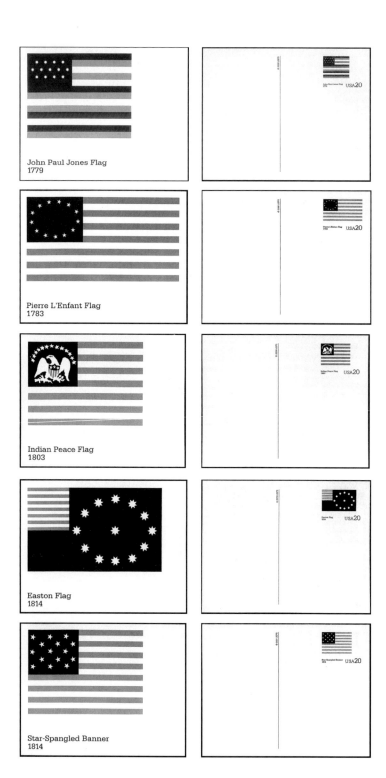

John Paul Jones Flag
1779

Pierre L'Enfant Flag
1783

Indian Peace Flag
1803

Easton Flag
1814

Star-Spangled Banner
1814

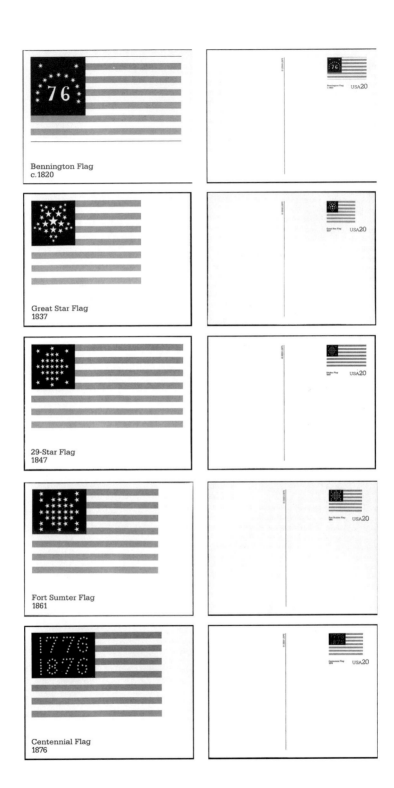

Bennington Flag
c.1820

Great Star Flag
1837

29-Star Flag
1847

Fort Sumter Flag
1861

Centennial Flag
1876

389

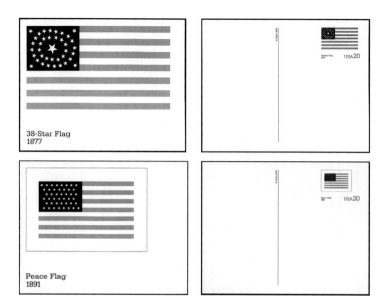

38-Star Flag
1877

Peace Flag
1891

Each sheet comprises four flags from one of the horizontal rows of four stamps on the stamp pane. For example, the flags shown on the top row of stamps — Sons of Liberty, New England, Forster and Continental Colors — comprise one sheet of four stamped cards.

The Stars and Stripes stamps were conceived and designed by Richard Sheaff, one of the Postal Service's contractual art directors, as a way to show the evolution of the present 50-star Old Glory. The historic flags depicted on the stamps and, by extension, on the stamped cards were chosen with the help of Whitney Smith, author and executive director of the Flag Research Center in Winchester, Massachusetts.

As with all stamps in the Classic Collection series, the Stars and Stripes stamps had text printed on the back conveying a brief description of the flag shown on the front. In each previous instance in which a Classic Collection stamp set was accompanied by matching postal cards in a booklet — Legends of the West, Civil War, Comic Strip Classics and Centennial Olympics — as well as the Legends of Baseball cards issued just 22 days later, the verso text on the stamps was reproduced on the address sides of the postal cards. However, this wasn't done with the Stars and Stripes cards, and the message portions of the cards were left clear.

The Designs

The cards reproduce the 20 flags shown on the Stars and Stripes stamps. The imprinted stamps on the address sides are almost exact replicas of their stamp counterparts, except that the denomination is 20 rather than 33 and there is no tiny "2000" year-of-issue beneath the designs on the left. The same images are shown in enlarged form on the picture sides, but without the "USA" and denomination.

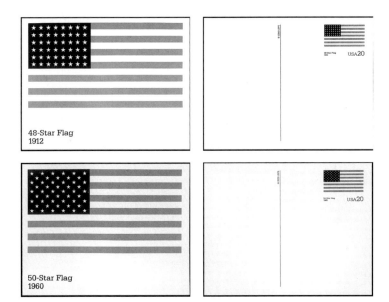

48-Star Flag
1912

50-Star Flag
1960

Banknote Corporation of America printed the stamps in solid colors, without screening. For the postal cards, however, Partners Press used a 250-line screen. Red, blue and black were the predominant colors, with green and brown used only for the pine-tree canton emblem on the New England flag.

First-Day Facts

For details on the first-day sale, see the chapter on the Stars and Stripes stamps.

20¢ LEGENDS OF BASEBALL
PICTURE POSTAL CARDS (20 DESIGNS)
CLASSIC COLLECTION SERIES

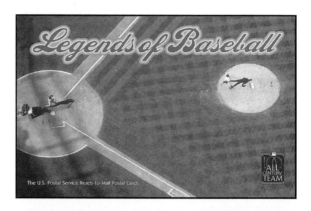

Date of Issue: July 6, 2000

Price: $8.95 for book of 20 cards

Catalog Numbers: Scott UX337-UX356, single cards; UX356a, book of 20 cards

Colors: black, cyan, magenta, yellow

First-Day Cancel: Atlanta, Georgia

First-Day Cancellations: 1,214,413 (includes Legends of Baseball stamp)

Format: Book of 20 stamped cards, with microperforations to permit removal of individual cards. Offset printing plates of 20 subjects, 5 across by 4 down, for cards. Offset plates of 10 subjects for book covers.

Size of Card: 6.00 by 4.25 inches

Size of Book: 6.75 by 4.25 inches

Card Markings: On address side of each card: "©2000 USPS." On individual cards: "TY COBB/Known for his aggressive style at the plate and on the base/paths, Ty Cobb may have been the greatest all-around player/in Major League Baseball®. In his 24-year career, 22 with the/Detroit Tigers™, the 'Georgia Peach' won 9 straight American/League™ batting titles." "CHRISTY MATHEWSON/In 1901, 21-year-old Christy Mathewson won 20 games for/the New York Giants™. With his 'fadeaway' pitch, he posted/three consecutive 30-victory seasons and in the 1905 World/Series® threw three shutouts in only six days." "EDDIE COLLINS/Eddie 'Cocky' Collins played the game of baseball for 25/seasons, a 20th-century record for nonpitchers. His brilliant/baserunning and batting helped four teams win World/Championships." "JACKIE ROBINSON/Jackie Robinson broke the Major League Baseball® color barrier/when he came to the Brooklyn Dodgers™ in 1947. Two years/later, he hit a league-leading .342, drove in 124 runs, and was/voted the Most Valuable Player in the National League™." "ROBERTO CLEMENTE/The first Hispanic elected to the Hall of Fame™, Roberto/Clemente was admired for his superb hitting, rifle-like arm,/and philanthropic spirit. He helped the Pittsburgh Pirates™ win two World Championships." "WALTER JOHNSON/Walter 'Big Train' Johnson used a sweeping sidearm motion/to fire fastballs over home plate. In his 21-year career with the/Washington Senators™, he fanned 3,509 batters, won 417/games, and pitched a record 110 shutouts." "BABE RUTH/Babe Ruth was the most celebrated athlete of his time. Before/beginning play with the New York Yankees™ in 1920, the/'Sultan of Swat' was a successful pitcher for the Boston Red/Sox™. In 1927, he hit a record-setting 60 homers." "MICKEY COCHRANE/Mickey Cochrane sparked the Philadelphia Athletics'/championship teams of 1929-1931 with his potent bat, skill/behind the plate, and fierce, competitive spirit." "ROGERS HORNSBY/Rogers Hornsby was the most impressive right-handed/hitter in the history of the game. He won seven batting/championships (six in a row) and managed the 1926/St. Louis Cardinals™ to their first World Championship." "PIE TRAYNOR/Rated as one of the finest third basemen of all time, the/Pittsburgh Pirates' Pie Traynor had a defensive prowess/that often overshadowed his strong hitting. His nickname/reportedly came from a childhood fondness for pastry." "JIMMIE FOXX/One of the top Major League Baseball® sluggers of all time,/Jimmie Foxx hit 30 or more home runs for 12 seasons in a/row. Foxx won the Triple Crown for the Philadelphia Athletics™/in 1933, leading the American League™ in home runs, batting,/and RBIs." "CY YOUNG/Denton True Young, nicknamed Cy (short for 'Cyclone'), won/511 games in his 22-year Major League Baseball® career—/almost 100 more than any other pitcher. A durable athlete,/Young pitched an astonishing 749 complete games." "TRIS SPEAKER/Tris Speaker revolutionized outfield play by positioning/himself in shallow center field. As a result, this Cleveland/Indian recorded more assists than any other outfielder in the/long history of Major League/Baseball™." "LEFTY GROVE/One of the finest left-handed pitchers in the history of Major/League Baseball®, Lefty Grove went 31-4 for the 1931/Philadelphia Athletics™. In the process, he put together a/16-game winning streak." "LOU GEHRIG/First baseman for the New York Yankees™, Lou Gehrig played in/2,130 consecutive games. In 1934 the 'Iron Horse' led the/American League™ in batting average (.363), home runs (49),/and RBIs (165)." "DIZZY DEAN/Dizzy Dean, fastball-throwing member of the St. Louis/Cardinals' 'Gas House Gang,' was a legend in his own time,/once holding the modern single-game record of 17 strike-/outs. In 1934 he and brother Paul led the Cardinals to the/World Championship." "JOSH GIBSON/Among the biggest draws in the Negro Leagues, popular Josh/Gibson is generally considered one of the most prodigious/power hitters in the history of professional baseball." "HONUS WAGNER/The Pittsburgh Pirates' star shortstop, Honus Wagner/also was a league-leading batter and base stealer. The 'Flying/Dutchman' enjoyed 15 consecutive .300 seasons, 8 as the/National League™ batting champ." "SATCHEL PAIGE/A legend after two decades in the Negro Leagues, pitcher/Satchel Paige signed with the Cleveland Indians™ in 1948. At/age 42, this 'veteran-rookie' helped his team win the/American League™ pennant."

Cover Markings: On front cover: "Legends of Baseball/The U.S. Postal Service Ready-to-Mail Postal Cards." On back cover: "Legends of Baseball" and All-Century Team logo. "UNITED STATES/POSTAL SERVICE®" and logo. "©2000 U.S. Postal Service. All rights reserved. To obtain additional information on/Commemorative Stamps and Stamp Products available from the U.S. Postal Service please write to:/Information Fulfillment, USPS, PO Box 219424, Kansas City, MO 64121-9424." On inside of front cover: "HEY FANS! CATCH THIS ALL-STAR OFFER!" and promotion for Legends of Baseball stamps and stamped cards. On inside of back cover: "Major League Baseball trademarks and copyrights are used with permission/of Major League Baseball Properties, Inc./www.majorleague-baseball.com." "Cover photograph ©Yann Arthus-Bertrand/CORBIS/ Stamp illustrations by Joseph Saffold."

Illustrator: Joe Saffold of Savannah, Georgia

Art Director, Designer and Typographer: Phil Jordan of Falls Church, Virginia

Modeler: Joseph Sheeran of Ashton-Potter (USA) Ltd., Williamsville, New York

Card Manufacturing: Cards printed for Ashton-Potter (USA) Ltd. by Partners Press, Kenmore, New York, on Heidelberg 6-color offset press. Cards bound into books by Quality Bindery Services, Buffalo, New York. Books finished and shipped by Ashton-Potter.

Quantity Ordered: 105,000 books (2,100,000 cards)

Paper Type: Manchester 10 point C1S (coated on one side)

Tagging: vertical bar to right of stamp

The Cards

On July 6, in Atlanta, Georgia, the Postal Service issued a book containing 20 different picture stamped cards, each featuring a member of the National Baseball Hall of Fame in Cooperstown, New York. The cards are companion pieces to a pane of 20 Legends of Baseball stamps that were issued the same day.

JACKIE ROBINSON
Jackie Robinson broke the Major League Baseball® color barrier when he came to the Brooklyn Dodgers™ in 1947. Two years later, he hit a league-leading .349, drove in 791 runs, and was voted the Most Valuable Player in the National League™.

EDDIE COLLINS
Eddie "Cocky" Collins played the game of baseball for 25 seasons, a 20th-century record for nonpitchers. His brilliant baserunning and batting helped four teams win World Championships.

CHRISTY MATHEWSON
In 1901, 21-year-old Christy Mathewson won 20 games for the New York Giants™. With his "fadeaway" pitch, he posted three consecutive 30-victory seasons and in the 1905 World Series™ threw three shutouts in only six days.

TY COBB
Known for his aggressive style at the plate and on the base paths, Ty Cobb may have been the greatest all-around player in Major League Baseball®. In his 24-year career, 22 with the Detroit Tigers™, the "Georgia Peach" won 9 straight American League™ batting titles.

Each of the 20 players had been nominated for a spot on Major League Baseball's All-Century Team, chosen by baseball fans and a specially appointed committee in 1999. To obtain rights to depict the images and names of the players and team uniforms, the Postal Service agreed to depict the All-Century Team logo in the stamp selvage and on the cover of the booklet containing the cards.

The cards were manufactured by Ashton-Potter (USA) Ltd. of Williamsville, New York, which also had printed the stamps. Ashton-Potter subcontracted the card work to Partners Press of Kenmore, New York, which printed the cards and booklet covers on a Heidelberg Speedmaster sheetfed six-color offset press. Microperfing to facilitate the removal of the cards from their books was done on the press.

Two plates with 20 card-sized subjects were used for the cards, one for the address sides, one for the picture sides, with each 22- by 37-inch sheet going through the press twice, once for each side. A third and fourth plate printed 10 sets of booklet covers, outsides on one pass, insides on the second pass.

The four standard process colors were used to print the cards and covers. A fifth ink station on the Heidelberg tagged the cards on the address sides. For the covers and the picture sides of the cards, one station applied a scuff-resistant acrylic coating.

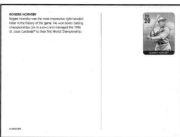

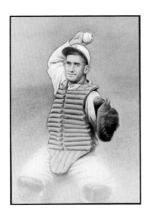

MICKEY COCHRANE
Mickey Cochrane sparked the Philadelphia Athletics' championship teams of 1929–1931 with his potent bat, skill behind the plate, and fierce, competitive spirit.

© 2000 USPS

BABE RUTH
Babe Ruth was the most celebrated athlete of his time. Before beginning play with the New York Yankees™ in 1920, the "Sultan of Swat" was a successful pitcher for the Boston Red Sox™. In 1927, he hit a record-setting 60 homers.

© 2000 USPS

WALTER JOHNSON
Walter "Big Train" Johnson used a sweeping sidearm motion to fire fastballs over home plate. In his 91-year career with the Washington Senators™, he fanned 3,509 batters, won 417 games, and pitched a record 110 shutouts.

© 2000 USPS

ROBERTO CLEMENTE
The first Hispanic elected to the Hall of Fame™, Roberto Clemente was admired for his superb hitting, rifle-like arm, and philanthropic spirit. He helped the Pittsburgh Pirates™ win two World Championships.

© 2000 USPS

LEFTY GROVE
One of the finest left-handed pitchers in the history of Major League Baseball®, Lefty Grove went 31-4 for the 1931 Philadelphia Athletics™. In the process, he put together a 16-game winning streak.

© 2001 USPS

TRIS SPEAKER
Tris Speaker revolutionized outfield play by positioning himself in shallow center field. As a result, this Cleveland Indian recorded more assists than any other outfielder in the long history of Major League Baseball®.

© 2001 USPS

CY YOUNG
Denton True Young, nicknamed Cy (short for "Cyclone"), won 511 games in his 22-year Major League Baseball® career—almost 100 more than any other pitcher. A durable athlete, Young pitched an astonishing 749 complete games.

© 2001 USPS

JIMMIE FOXX
One of the top Major League Baseball® sluggers of all time, Jimmie Foxx hit 30 or more home runs for 12 seasons in a row. Foxx won the Triple Crown for the Philadelphia Athletics™ in 1933, leading the American League™ in home runs, batting, and RBIs.

© 2001 USPS

398

PIE TRAYNOR
Rated as one of the finest third basemen of all time, the
Pittsburgh Pirates' Pie Traynor had a defensive prowess
that often overshadowed his strong hitting. His nickname
reportedly came from a childhood fondness for pastry.

SATCHEL PAIGE
A legend after two decades in the Negro Leagues, pitcher
Satchel Paige signed with the Cleveland Indians™ in 1948. At
age 42, the "veteran-rookie" helped his team win the
American League™ pennant.

HONUS WAGNER
The Pittsburgh Pirates' star shortstop, Honus Wagner
also was a league-leading batter and base stealer. The "Flying
Dutchman" enjoyed 15 consecutive .300 seasons, 8 as the
National League™ batting champ.

JOSH GIBSON
Among the biggest draws in the Negro Leagues, popular Josh
Gibson is generally considered one of the most prodigious
power hitters in the history of professional baseball.

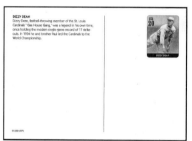

Ashton-Potter sent the cards to Quality Bindery Services in Buffalo to be bound into books. The books then were returned to the prime contractor for final trimming, examination and shrink-wrapping.

On the address side of each card appears the same thumbnail biography that appears on the back of that particular player's stamp on the stamp pane. Unlike the stamp biographies, however, those on the cards are sprinkled with the ® symbol, which appears after each reference to a registered name such as Major League Baseball and the World Series, and the ™ (trademark) symbol, after each reference to the National League, American League, Hall of Fame or an individual team.

There are some inconsistencies in the team names, however. For instance, the name "St. Louis Cardinals" is followed by a ™ on the Rogers Hornsby card, but lacks a ™ on the Dizzy Dean card. A ™ accompanies the obsolete name "Philadelphia Athletics" on the Lefty Grove and Jimmie Foxx cards, but not on the Mickey Cochrane card.

The Designs

Each card reproduces on its imprinted stamp the image that appears on the corresponding stamp, except that the denomination is 20¢ instead of 33¢ and there is no tiny "2000" year-of-issue date beneath the bottom left frameline.

The same pictures fill the picture sides of the cards, with no typography. At this size, the quality of Joe Saffold's paintings of the players, with their crisp outlines, soft, semi-photographic facial features and pastel backgrounds, can be fully appreciated.

Because the aspect ratio of the picture sides is different from that of the stamps, the cards display more of the paintings at the top and/or bottom than do the stamps. For instance, catcher Mickey Cochrane's knee protectors, Cy Young's stockings and the tip of Babe Ruth's bat are visible on the cards, but are cropped out of the stamp pictures. On the other hand, more of Josh Gibson can be seen on the stamp than on the card.

The cover of the book containing the cards was designed by Phil Jordan, who was the art director and designer of the stamps. Its front reproduces an overhead photograph of a baseball diamond. In the photo, the pitcher is in a defensive stance after delivering a pitch to the batter, who is shown in mid-swing. The catcher and umpire are shown behind the plate. PhotoAssist obtained the photo from the Corbis picture archive, which identified the photographer as Yann Arthus-Bertrand, a resident of Paris, France. Corbis' records indicate that the stadium was in New York — a company official says he believes it is Yankee Stadium, rather than Shea Stadium — but contain no other information as to the identity of the individuals or teams in the picture, or the date of the photograph. The back of the book of cards shows a portion of the same photo, with miniature reproductions of the 20 imprinted stamps superimposed on it.

In an unusual step, USPS printed the words "Stamp Illustrations by Joseph Saffold" inside the back cover. Only on rare occasions are stamp designers and illustrators identified on anything physically connected to the stamp or postal stationery on which they worked.

First-Day Facts

For information on the first-day sale of the postal cards, see the chapter on the Legends of Baseball stamps.

20¢ DEER PICTURE POSTAL CARDS (4 DESIGNS)

Date of Issue: October 12, 2000

Price: $8.95 for set of 20 cards

Catalog Numbers: Scott UX357-UX360, single cards; UX360a, sheet of 4 different cards

Colors: gold (PMS 871), blue (PMS 541), red (PMS 1807), purple (PMS 2613), green (PMS 349)

First-Day Cancel: Rudolph, Wisconsin

First-Day Cancellations: 40,811

Format: Cards are in sheets of 4, with microperforations to permit separation. Cards are sold in shrink-wrapped sets of 5 sheets. Offset printing plates printing 4 sheets (16 cards), 2 sheets across by 2 down.

Size of Cards: 5.50 by 4.25 inches

Size of Sheets: 11.0 inches by 8.5 inches

Card Markings: On address side of each card, "©2000 USPS."

Designer and Typographer: Tom Nikosey of Canoga Park, California

Art Director: Carl Herrman of Carlsbad, California

Modeler: Joseph Sheeran, Ashton-Potter (USA) Ltd., Williamsville, New York

Card Manufacturing: Cards printed by Sterling Sommer, Tonawanda, New York, for Ashton-Potter (USA) Ltd. on Akiyama 628 6-color sheetfed offset press. Cards processed by Ashton-Potter.

Quantity Ordered: 2,000,000 cards (100,000 sets of 5 sheets of 4)

Paper Supplier: Manchester 10 point C1S (coated on one side)

Tagging: vertical block to right of stamped image

The Cards

On April 4, 2000, USPS announced that the traditional and contemporary Christmas stamps that were issued in 1999 would be made available again for the 2000 holiday season "in a move to continue prudently managing inventories."

It would be the first year since Christmas stamps were introduced in 1962 that a year would go by without a new design. New designs intended for issuance in 2000 had been unveiled, but they would be postponed, USPS said.

"Rather than printing new holiday designs for 2000, we believe it is a good business decision to exhaust our current inventories of 1999 holiday stamps and supplement them with a small reprint of one design," said James Tolbert, executive director of Stamp Services.

The issue that USPS chose to reprint turned out to be 1999's set of four contemporary Christmas stamps, showing a stylized leaping deer printed in gold with backgrounds of four different colors. Postal officials asserted that the decision not to issue new holiday stamps saved the agency some $4 million.

The year 2000 wasn't a blank as far as new holiday postage was concerned, however. The June 15 *Postal Bulletin*, an internal USPS publication, contained the surprise news that a set of four different 20¢ picture stamped cards would be issued for the Yule season.

Placed on sale October 12, the cards reproduce on their imprinted stamps and their picture sides the leaping deer stamp design of 1999, and feature the same four background colors that were used on the stamps: deep red, royal blue, green and purple.

Although these were the first U.S. postal cards created especially for the Christmas holiday season, they were not the first such postal stationery. In 1988, USPS issued a 25¢ Snowflake stamped envelope in red and green with the inscription "Holiday Greetings!" (Scott U613).

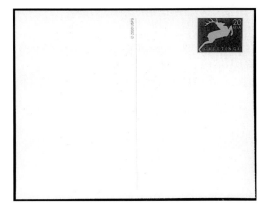

Sterling Sommer printed the Deer cards by the offset process for the contractor, Ashton-Potter (USA) Ltd. Ashton-Potter cut the 19- by 24-inch printed sheets into distribution sheets containing four cards — one of each variety — and microperfed them for easy separation. USPS sold the sheets in shrink-wrapped packages of five each for $8.95, making the individual card price just under 45¢, against a face value of 20¢.

The printer's Akiyama press has six color stations. For the address sides of the cards, five stations were used to apply the colors and the sixth applied the phosphorescent taggant. On the picture sides, the sixth station applied a scuff-resistant transparent acrylic coating.

The Designs

Tom Nikosey of Canoga Park, California, illustrated and designed the Deer stamped cards and the earlier Deer stamps. Nikosey's previous graphic design credits included the logos for Super Bowl XVII, XX, XXII and XXV, the Grammy Awards and Tony Awards, the San Diego Padres baseball team and several musical groups. For the Postal Service, he also had designed the header for the pane of 20 All Aboard! commemorative stamps issued in 1999.

The deer image was inspired by an illustration of a metal typecast ornament, dating to the 1930s, that Nikosey found in two old printers' catalogs. The ornaments were in the public domain and presented no copyright problem for USPS.

Sterling Sommer printed the four background colors on the cards and imprinted stamps as solid blocks of color, without screening. The metallic-gold deer silhouette, typography and lettering, also unscreened, were printed over the background colors.

First-Day Facts

The Deer cards officially were placed on sale October 12 at Rudolph, Wisconsin, the community where the 1999 dedication of the Deer stamps had taken place. This time, there was no official first-day ceremony.

An accounting error at Stamp Fulfillment Services resulted in the sale of 580 20-card packs of Deer cards on August 17, 56 days before the official issue date. Don Smeraldi, a spokesman for USPS, told *Linn's Stamp News* that only four or five of these were sold to individual customers, with the others going to the Postal Service's international stamp agencies. These agencies were told that the cards weren't to be sold until October 12, Smeraldi said.

The spokesman explained that, because the 33¢ Deer stamps of 1999 still were on sale, "the person at Stamp Fulfillment Services who enters account information for a given issue assumed that the Deer postal cards were part of the Deer stamp account and entered the cards as being available for sale starting in August." The individual wasn't aware that there was an official first-day release date set for the Deer cards, Smeraldi said.

Linn's received and illustrated a red Deer card sent to the publication's Charles Snee by Robert Bellinger of California and machine-canceled September 9 in Marina Del Rey, California. Bellinger reported in his message on the card that he had received a pack of cards from Stamp Fulfillment Services on August 23.

2000-2001 DUCK STAMP SOUVENIR CARD
U.S. FISH AND WILDLIFE SERVICE

Date of Issue: June 30, 2000

Catalog Number: none

Colors: Offset: magenta, yellow, cyan, black (duck stamp illustration); black (back text). Foil stamp: gold (agency seals). On face, stamp illustration and frame: clear varnish.

First-Day Release: Washington, D.C.

Size: 10 by 8 inches

Designer and Modeler: Brian Thompson, Bureau of Engraving and Printing

Card Stock: white, Poseidon perfect

Card Manufacturing: cards printed by Bureau of Engraving and Printing on a 6-color sheetfed Heidelberg offset press for stamp replica and lettering and Kluge letterpress for foil stamping.

Quantity: 7,000 (750 numbered)

The Card

For the 14th consecutive year — and, as it turned out, the final year — the U.S. Fish and Wildlife Service's federal duck stamp office on June 30,

2000, issued a souvenir card bearing an enlarged replica of the current year's stamp. All proceeds, after deduction of printing and marketing costs, went to buy wetlands for the National Wildlife Refuge System.

In a letter to collectors in April 2001, Robert C. Lesino, chief of the duck stamp office, announced: "I have directed the Bureau of Engraving and Printing not to print any souvenir cards [depicting the 2001 duck stamp]. The numbered, mint and canceled cards are not a profitable product for us to carry and sell. They are being discontinued in their entirety."

The 2000 card, printed by offset by the Bureau of Engraving and Printing, depicts the 2000-2001 stamp against a marbled pinkish background. The stamp's design is based on Adam Grimm's oil painting that won the annual federal duck stamp competition in 1999. The painting shows a male mottled duck standing upright in the water and flapping its wings. On the front, the card reproduces the signatures and agency seals or logos of Bruce Babbitt, secretary of the Interior, and Jamie Rappaport Clark, director of the Fish and Wildlife Service. It also carries a replica of Adam Grimm's signature. Textual material is printed on the reverse.

Seven thousand cards were printed. These cards, which came with a specimen of the $15 duck stamp, were sold for varying prices by the Fish and Wildlife Service. A $5 shipping fee was charged for all orders.

The least expensive items were 5,250 cards without serial numbers or cancellations, which cost $22 each. With these, the duck stamp was included separately in a glassine envelope.

The remaining 1,750 cards each had a duck stamp and a 33¢ postage stamp affixed. The stamps were tied with a Grimm-designed cancellation from Washington, D.C., where the card had its first-day sale June 30.

Of the canceled cards, 1,000 bore no numbers and sold for $26 each, and 750 were numbered in gold and sold for $150 each (numbers 1 through 10), $75 each (numbers 11 through 100) or $50 each (101 through 750). Unnumbered cards could be obtained with the autograph of the artist for an additional $2.

VARIETIES

Canal Boat Coil Stamp

A large imperforate strip of the 10¢ Canal Boat coil stamp of 1987 (Scott 2257, error listed as 2257e) was found in 2000. The strip featured 53 specimens without perforations. The left end of the strip had torn perfs, while the right end was imperforate.

The roll that yielded the imperforate stamps apparently was used by the original owner up to the imperforate portion. Afterward, the strip was placed in a 35-millimeter camera film tube as part of a large accumulation of coil stamps. No further details on its ownership or discovery are available.

The Canal Boat coil was printed by the Bureau of Engraving and Printing on its B press and issued April 11, 1987, with large block tagging. Later it was printed on other BEP presses with overall tagging or on phosphored paper. The error strip has large block tagging and a plate number 1 on the 50th stamp.

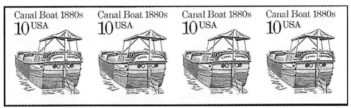

Shown here is an imperforate strip of four 10¢ Canal Boat coil stamps. They are from a larger imperforate strip of 53 stamps.

5¢ Overrun Countries (Austria) Stamp

News of a new double-impression error of a United States stamp was made public in May 2000. The stamp is the 5¢ Austria flag stamp (Scott 919) from the 1943-44 Overrun Countries set, which was printed by the American Bank Note Company by a combination of intaglio (frames) and offset letterpress (flags and country names).

The "AUSTRIA" inscription printed in red just below the flag is doubled, although the red portion of the flag is not doubled. U.S. stamp specialist Ken Lawrence gave this assessment of the variety to *Linn's Stamp News*:

"Two different relief plates were used for the flag and the country inscription. The American Bank Note Company had four stations for offset printing. If fewer than four different colors were used, one color could be used at two different stations. This explains why the red of the Austrian flag is not doubled, while the country name is."

The stamp was given a Philatelic Foundation certificate of authenticity dated September 28, 1999. The Scott *Specialized Catalogue of U.S. Stamps & Covers* lists the error as 919a.

Shown here are the Austria and Czechoslovakia stamps of the 1943-44 Overrun countries series with the country inscriptions doubled.

5¢ Overrun Countries (Czechoslovakia) Stamp

A report on the double-impression Austria stamp described above was published in *Linn's Stamp News* June 26, 2000, and prompted a Michigan collector to re-examine one of his own Overrun Countries stamps, a Czechoslovakia stamp that also had the country name doubled.

The collector then sent the stamp, which he had owned for about 10 years, to the American Philatelic Expertizing Service. The APES certified the stamp as an authentic double impression October 12, 2000. It is listed in the Scott catalog as 910a.

20¢ Blue Jay Booklet Stamp

The first known fully imperforate booklet pane of 10 of the 20¢ Blue Jay definitive of 1995 was reported by its owner, collector-dealer Harold Kass of New Jersey. The booklet stamp, which has water-activated gum and conventional perforations, was produced by Stamp Venturers. It is listed in the Scott U.S. specialized catalog as 2483b.

22¢ Girl Scouts Stamp

The existence of a complete 50-stamp pane of the 22¢ Girl Scouts commemorative of 1987 that is missing its two intaglio colors, red and black, was made public in the May 2000 issue of the *Vermont Philatelist*, the official publication of the Vermont Philatelic Society.

The stamp was printed by a combination of offset and intaglio by the Bureau of Engraving and Printing and depicts all or portions of 14 merit badges. The engraved portions on a normal stamp make up certain details and highlights on some of the badges, and their absence is hard to detect without comparing an error stamp to a normal one.

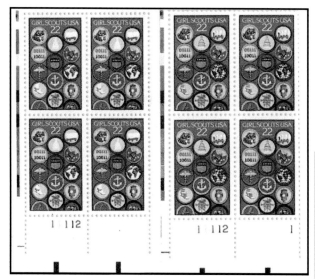

Left, a plate number block of four 22¢ Girl Scouts stamps missing the engraved black and red. A normal plate number block is shown on the right above.

This previously discovered error in the Girl Scouts stamp is the opposite counterpart of the new one. It has the engraved portions but lacks the offset printing.

An anonymous Vermont collector purchased the pane shortly after the stamp was issued in March 1987 but did not discover the printing flaw until the fall of 1999, when he was breaking down a number of stamp panes for postage. The error pane was submitted to the American Philatelic Expertizing Service by the stamp firm of Robert A. Siegel and received a certificate of authenticity dated March 9, 2000. It is listed in the Scott U.S. specialized catalog as 2251b.

A previously discovered error in the stamp, Scott 2251a, is the opposite counterpart of the new one. It lacks all five offset colors and displays only the small red and black engraved portions.

25¢ Ernest Hemingway Stamp

For 11 years, no error in the printing of the 1998 25¢ Ernest Hemingway stamp in the Literary Arts series had been reported. Early in 2000, however, the existence of the stamp minus its horizontal perforations came to light. Error collector Harold Kass told *Stamp Collector* there are only 12 vertical pairs, from a single pane of 50, without horizontal perfs. Such a pair is listed in the Scott U.S. specialized catalog as 2418a.

Above, the front and back of a normal 1955 duck stamp; below, the error copy with the printing on the gum side inverted.

$2 Duck Stamp of 1955

For nearly 45 years an inverted back inscription on a federal duck stamp went unnoted. Then, in 2000, a mint specimen of the 1955 duck stamp, depicting blue geese in flight, was reported with the black printing on the gum side upside down. This printed portion instructs the hunter to sign the front of the stamp in order to make his current license valid. The variety, which originated in California and was sold to a collector on the East Coast, is listed in the Scott U.S. specialized catalog as RW22a.

Breast Cancer Stamp Sales Extended

President Bill Clinton signed a bill July 28, 2000, extending the sale of the Breast Cancer Research semipostal stamp of 1998 for an additional two years. The Postal Service had planned to withdraw it from sale July 29, 2000, two years after its date of issue, as provided in the original law authorizing the stamp. The nondenominated self-adhesive stamp sells for 40¢, with the difference between that amount and the current first-class postage rate being used for breast cancer research.

The legislation was sponsored by Senator Dianne Feinstein, D-California, author of the 1997 law that directed USPS to issue the nation's first charity stamp with breast cancer research as the beneficiary.

In August 2000, USPS ordered 85 million additional Breast Cancer stamps printed, bringing the total production of the stamp as of that date to 416.7 million.

The law extending the stamp's life also gives the U.S. Postal Service authority to determine which causes are "in the national public interest and appropriate" to be the beneficiaries of future semipostal stamps. The action headed off what threatened to be a flood of bills in Congress ordering semipostals for one or another worthy cause. USPS also was given sole control over the number of different semipostal stamps that can be on sale simultaneously.

GAO Deems Breast Cancer Stamp A Success

According to an April 28, 2000, report by the General Accounting Office, the Breast Cancer stamp "has been an effective fund-raiser." At that point, sales of the stamp had generated some $12.5 million for breast cancer research.

But the congressional watchdog agency also expressed some criticism of USPS. "It was not clear precisely how much it cost to develop and sell the [semipostal stamp] because there were costs that the service did not track," the GAO said. "Postal officials said the costs not tracked were inconsequential or immaterial, and it would have been too expensive to track these costs."

GAO found that the cost to USPS of printing the stamp was $21 per 1,000 stamps. This compares to a cost of about $7.50 per 1,000 to print a typical self-adhesive commemorative stamp.

However, the semipostal had $482,000 in expenses that were unique, GAO said. These included the costs of reprogramming sales window automation devices (scanners), a flyer, customer sales receipts, reconfiguring vending machines, self-service packaging and legal fees.

Changes at CSAC

Television talk show host Larry King was named to the Citizens' Stamp

Advisory Committee by Postmaster General William J. Henderson December 22, 2000.

In the USPS press release announcing King's appointment, Henderson said: "Larry King brings to [the committee] years of experience working with some of our country's greatest scholars, inspirational leaders, politicians and entertainers. His unique talents and perspective will help the committee ensure that the U.S. commemorative stamp program continues to celebrate American history and culture in an inspiring and educational way."

Irma Zandl, a youth marketing expert who joined CSAC in May 1993, resigned from the panel after the June 2000 meeting. "I feel the way that the program is going I don't know how relevant stamps are to youth in an age of e-mail," Zandl told *Linn's Stamp News* in an interview.

Caggiano Replaces Tolbert At Stamp Services

On October 26, 2000, James C. Tolbert was removed as executive director of stamp services for the Postal Service and replaced by Catherine Caggiano, the manager of stamp acquisition. Tolbert had held the job since Azeezaly S. Jaffer was promoted in 1999 to vice president of public affairs and communications. He was assigned new duties as a special assistant to Deborah Willhite, senior vice president for government relations and public policy.

Pacific Coast Rain Forest Pane Tops Linn's Poll

The Pacific Coast Rain Forest set of 10 self-adhesive stamps was the overall favorite in *Linn's* 2000 United States Stamp Popularity Poll.

For the second year in a row, *Linn's* readers chose a se-tenant issue from the two-year-old Nature of America series as their favorite U.S. stamp issue. In the 1999 poll, the 33¢ Sonoran Desert stamps — the first issue in the series — captured top honors in the overall-favorite category.

The Rain Forest set received 468 votes. Runners-up were The Stars and Stripes Classic Collection pane of 20 stamps, 394, and the Legends of Baseball Classic Collection pane of 20, 384.

Other categories and the top three finishers were:

Commemoratives, best design: Pacific Coast Rain Forest, The White House, California Statehood.

Commemoratives, worst design: Louise Nevelson, Adoption, Summer Sports.

Commemoratives, most important: Distinguished Soldiers, The White House, The Stars and Stripes.

Commemoratives, least necessary: Wile E. Coyote and Road Runner, Summer Sports, Stampin' the Future.

Definitives/specials, best design: Grand Canyon, Four Flowers, Statue of Liberty.

Definitives/specials, worst design: Lion Statue, Flag Over Farm, Grand Canyon.

Definitives/specials, most important: Statue of Liberty, Joseph W. Stilwell, Grand Canyon.

Definitives/specials, least necessary: Fruit Berries linerless, Lion Statue, Coral Pink Rose.

Postal stationery, best design: Ryman Auditorium card, Middlebury College card, Legends of Baseball cards.

Postal stationery, worst design: Adoption card, Deer Greetings cards, Coyote and Road Runner card.

Postal stationery, most important: The Stars and Stripes cards, Adoption card, Legends of Baseball cards.

Postal stationery, least necessary: Coyote and Road Runner card, Deer Greetings cards, Legends of Baseball cards.

PLATE NUMBER COILS, SHEET, BOOKLET AND SELF-ADHESIVE STAMPS

Changes to the plate number listings that appeared in the 1999 *Linn's U.S. Stamp Year-book*, as well as all new listings, are shown in bold typeface.

Water-activated adhesive
Transportation coils (not precanceled)

Scott number	Stamp	Plate number	Tagging type
1897	1¢ Omnibus (1983)	1, 2, 3, ,5, 6	overall
2225	1¢ Omnibus (1986)	1, 2	block
2225a	1¢ Omnibus (1991)	2, 3	untagged[2]
2225a	1¢ Omnibus (1997)	3	untagged[19]
1897A	2¢ Locomotive (1982)	2, 3, 4, 6, 8, 10	overall
2226	2¢ Locomotive (1987)	1	block
2226a	2¢ Locomotive (1993)	2	untagged
2226a	2¢ Locomotive (1997)	2	untagged[20]
1898	3¢ Handcar (1983)	1, 2, 3, 4	overall
2252	3¢ Conestoga Wagon (1988)	1	block
2252a	3¢ Conestoga Wagon (1992)	2, 3, 5, 6	untagged[15]
2123	3.4¢ School Bus (1985)	1, 2	overall
1898A	4¢ Stagecoach (1982)	1, 2, 3, 4, 5, 6	overall
2228	4¢ Stagecoach (1986)	1	block
2228a	4¢ Stagecoach (1990)	1	overall
2451	4¢ Steam Carriage (1991)	1	overall
2451b	4¢ Steam Carriage (1991)	1	untagged
2124	4.9¢ Buckboard (1985)	3, 4	overall
1899	5¢ Motorcycle (1983)	1, 2, 3, 4	overall
2253	5¢ Milk Wagon (1987)	1	block
2452	5¢ Circus Wagon (1990)	1	overall
2452	5¢ Circus Wagon (1997)	2	untagged
2452	5¢ Circus Wagon (1999)	S2	untagged
2452a	5¢ Circus Wagon (1991)	1	untagged
2452B	5¢ Circus Wagon (gravure) (1992)	A1, A2, A3	untagged
2452D	5¢ Circus Wagon (gravure) (1995)	S1, S2	untagged[12]
1900	5.2¢ Sleigh (1983)	1, 2, 3, 5	overall
2125	5.5¢ Star Route Truck (1986)	1	block
1901	5.9¢ Bicycle (1982)	3, 4	overall
2126	6¢ Tricycle (1985)	1	block
2127	7.1¢ Tractor (1987)	1	block
1902	7.4¢ Baby Buggy (1984)	2	block
2128	8.3¢ Ambulance (1985)	1, 2	overall

414

Scott number	Stamp	Plate number	Tagging type
2129	8.5¢ Tow Truck (1987)	1	block
1903	9.3¢ Mail Wagon (1981)	1, 2, 3, 4, 5, 6	overall
2257	10¢ Canal Boat (1987)	1	block
2257a	10¢ Canal Boat (1991)	1	overall
2257b	10¢ Canal Boat (1992)	1, 2, 3, 4	prephosphored[1]
2257**c**	10¢ Canal Boat (1999)	5	prephosphored[25]
2130	10.1¢ Oil Wagon (1985)	1	block
1904	10.9¢ Hansom Cab (1982)	1, 2	overall
1905	11¢ Caboose (1984)	1	block
2131	11¢ Stutz Bearcat (1985)	1, 2, 3, 4	overall
2132	12¢ Stanley Steamer (1985)	1, 2	overall
2133	12.5¢ Pushcart (1985)	1, 2	block
2134	14¢ Iceboat (1985)	1, 2, 3, 4	overall
2134b	14¢ Iceboat (1986)	2	block
2260	15¢ Tugboat (1988)	1, 2	block
2260a	15¢ Tugboat (1988)	2	overall
1906	17¢ Electric Auto (1981)	1, 2, 3, 4, 5, 6, 7	overall
2135	17¢ Dog Sled (1986)	2	block
2262	17.5¢ Racing Car (1987)	1	block
1907	18¢ Surrey (1981)	1, 2, 3, 4, 5, 6, 7, 8, 9, 10, 11, 12, 13, 14, 15, 16, 17, 18	overall
1908	20¢ Fire Pumper (1981)	1, 2, 3, 4, 5, 6, 7, 8, 9, 10, 11, 12, 13, 14, 15, 16	overall
2263	20¢ Cable Car (1988)	1, 2	block
2263b	20¢ Cable Car (1990)	2	overall
2463	20¢ Cog Railway (1995)	1, 2	prephosphored
2464	23¢ Lunch Wagon (1991)	2, 3, 4, 5	prephosphored[17]
2136	25¢ Bread Wagon (1986)	1, 2, 3, 4, 5	block
2466	32¢ Ferryboat (1995)	2, 3, 4, 5	prephosphored[13]
2468	$1 Seaplane (1990)	1	overall[28]
2468b	$1 Seaplane (1993)	3	prephosphored[1]
2468bc	$1 Seaplane (1998)	3	prephosphored[19]

Transportation coils (precanceled or service-inscribed)

Scott number	Stamp	Plate number	Tagging type
2123a	3.4¢ School Bus (1985)	1, 2	untagged
1898Ab	4¢ Stagecoach (1982)	3, 4, 5, 6	untagged
2124a	4.9¢ Buckboard (1985)	1, 2, 3, 4, 5, 6	untagged
2453	5¢ Canoe (1991)	1, 2, 3	untagged
2454	5¢ Canoe (gravure) (1991)	S11	untagged

Scott number	Stamp	Plate number	Tagging type
1900a	5.2¢ Sleigh (1983)	1, 2, 3, 4, 5, 6	untagged
2254	5.3¢ Elevator (1988)	1	untagged
2125a	5.5¢ Star Route Truck (1986)	1, 2	untagged
1901a	5.9¢ Bicycle (1982)	3, 4, 5, 6	untagged
2126a	6¢ Tricycle (1985)	1, 2	untagged
2127a	7.1¢ Tractor (1987)	1	untagged[3]
2127b	7.1¢ Tractor (1989)	1	untagged[4]
1902a	7.4¢ Buggy (1984)	2	untagged
2255	7.6¢ Carreta (1988)	1, 2, 3	untagged
2128a	8.3¢ Ambulance (1985)	1, 2, 3, 4	untagged
2231	8.3¢ Ambulance (1986)	1, 2	untagged
2256	8.4¢ Wheel Chair (1988)	1, 2, 3	untagged
2129a	8.5¢ Tow Truck (1987)	1, 2	untagged
1903a	9.3¢ Mail Wagon (1981)	1, 2, 3, 4, 5, 6, 8	untagged
2457	10¢ Tractor Trailer (1991)	1	untagged
2458	10¢ Tractor Trailer (gravure) (1994)	11, 22	untagged
2130a	10.1¢ Oil Wagon (1985)	1, 2	untagged[5]
2130a	10.1¢ Oil Wagon (1988)	2, 3	untagged[6]
1904a	10.9¢ Hansom Cab (1982)	1, 2, 3, 4	untagged
1905a	11¢ Caboose (1984)	1	untagged[7]
1905a	11¢ Caboose (1991)	2	untagged
2132a	12¢ Stanley Steamer (1985)	1, 2	untagged
2132b	12¢ Stanley Steamer (1987)	1	untagged
2133a	12.5¢ Pushcart (1985)	1, 2	untagged
2258	13¢ Patrol Wagon (1988)	1	untagged
2259	13.2¢ Coal Car (1988)	1, 2	untagged
2261	16.7¢ Popcorn Wagon (1988)	1, 2	untagged
1906a	17¢ Electric Auto (1981)	1, 2, 3, 4, 5, 6, 7	untagged
2262a	17.5¢ Racing Car (1987)	1	untagged
2264	20.5¢ Fire Engine (1988)	1	untagged
2265	21¢ Railroad Mail Car (1988)	1, 2	untagged
2266	24.1¢ Tandem Bicycle (1988)	1	untagged

Flag coil series

Scott number	Stamp	Plate number	Tagging type
1891	18¢ Sea to Shining Sea (1981)	1, 2, 3, 4, 5, 6, 7	block
1895	20¢ Over Supreme Court (1981)	1, 2, 3, 4, 5, 6, 8, 9, 10, 12, 13, 14	block
1895e	20¢ Over Supreme Court precanceled (1984)	14	untagged

Scott number	Stamp	Plate number	Tagging type
2115	22¢ Over Capitol Dome (1985)	1, 2, 3, 4, 5, 6, 7, 8, 10, 11,12, 13,14, 15, 16, 17, 18, 19, 20, 21, 22	block
2115a	22¢ Over Capitol Dome (1987)	T1	prephosphored
2280	25¢ Over Yosemite (1988)	1, 2, 3, 4, 5, 7, 8, 9	block
2280	25¢ Over Yosemite (1989)	1, 2, 3, 5, 6, 7, 8, 9, 10, 11, 12, 13, 14, 15	prephosphored
2523	29¢ Over Mount Rushmore (1991)	1, 2, 3, 4, 5, 6, 7, 8, 9	prephosphored
2523A	29¢ Over Mount Rushmore (1991) (gravure)	A111111, A222211	prephosphored
2609	29¢ Over the White House (1992)	1, 2, 3, 4, 5,6, 7, 8, 9, 10, 11, 12, 13, 14, 15, 16, 18	prephosphored
2913	32¢ Over the Porch (1995)	11111, 22221, 22222, 22322, 33333, 34333, 44444, 45444, 66646, 66666, 77767, 78767, 91161, 99969	prephosphored[14]
2914	32¢ Over the Porch (1995)	S11111	prephosphored[12]
3280	33¢ Flag Over City (1999)	1111, 2222	prephosphored
3280a	33¢ Flag Over City (1999)	**3333**	prephosphored

Nondenominated rate-change coil stamps

Scott number	Stamp	Plate number	Tagging type
2112	D (22¢) Eagle (1985)	1, 2	block
O139	D (22¢) Official (1985)	1	block
2279	E (25¢) Earth (1988)	1111, 1211, 1222, 2222	block
2518	F (29¢) Flower (1991)	1111, 1211, 1222, 2211, 2222	prephosphored
2893	G (5¢) Old Glory nonprofit (1995)	A11111, A21111	untagged
2888	G (25¢) Old Glory presort (1994)	S11111	prephosphored
2889	G (32¢) Old Glory (1994)	1111, 2222	prephosphored
2890	G (32¢) Old Glory (1994)	A1111, A1112, A1113, A1211, A1212, A1222, A1311, A1313, A1314, A1324, A1417, A1433, A2211, A2212, A2213, A2214, A2223, A2313, A3113, A3114, A3314, A3315, A3323, A3324, A3423, A3426, A3433, A3435, A3436, A4426, A4427, A4435, A5327, A5417, A5427, A5437	prephosphored
2891	G (32¢) Old Glory (1994)	S1111	prephosphored[11]
2892	G (32¢) Old Glory (1994)	S1111, S2222	prephosphored
3264	(33¢) H (Hat) (1998)	1111, 3333, **3343**, 3344, 3444	prephosphored[25, 26]

Scott number	Stamp	Plate number	Tagging type
3265	(33¢) H (Hat) (1998)	1111, 1131, 1141, 2222, 3333	prephosphored[21]
3266	(33¢) H (Hat) (1998)	1111	prephosphored[21, 22, 23, 27]
3452	**(34¢) Statue of Liberty**	**1111**	**prephosphored**

Miscellaneous coil stamps

Scott number	Stamp	Plate number	Tagging type
3044	1¢ Kestrel (1996)	1111	untagged[29]
3044	1¢ Kestrel (1996-99)	1111	untagged[30]
3044a	1¢ Kestrel (1999)	1111, **2222**	untagged[31]
3045	2¢ Woodpecker	**11111, 22222**	untagged
2149	18¢ Washington (1985)	1112, 3333	block
2529	19¢ Fishing Boat (1991)	A1111, A1112, A1212, A2424	prephosphored
2529a	19¢ Fishing Boat (1993)	A5555, A5556, A6667, A7667, A7679, A7766, A7779	prephosphored
2529c	19¢ Fishing Boat (1994)	S11	prephosphored
2005	20¢ Consumer Education (1982)	1, 2, 3, 4	overall
O135	20¢ Official (1983)	1	block
2150	21.1¢ Letters (1985)	111111, 111121	block
2281	25¢ Honey Bee (1988)	1, 2	block
2525	29¢ Flower (1991)	S1111, S2222	prephosphored
2526	29¢ Flower (1992)	S2222	prephosphored
3302-05	33¢ Berries (Blackberry, 1999)	B1111, B1112, B2211, B2221, B2222	prephosphored
CVP31 and CVP31a	variable-rate coil (1992)	1	prephosphored[8]
CVP31b and CVP31c	variable-rate coil (new font) (1994)	1	prephosphored[8]
CVP32	variable-rate coil (1994)	A11	prephosphored
CVP33	variable-rate coil (1996)	11	prephosphored

Miscellaneous precanceled (service-inscribed) coils

Scott number	Stamp	Plate number	Tagging type
2902	(5¢) Butte (1995)	S111, S222, S333	untagged[12]
2903	(5¢) Mountains (1996)	11111	untagged
2904	(5¢) Mountains (1996)	S111	untagged
2602	(10¢) Eagle & Shield (1991) "Bulk Rate USA"	A11111, A11112, A12213, A21112, A21113, A22112, A22113, A32333, A33333, A33334, A33335, A34424, A34426, A43324, A43325,	untagged

Scott number	Stamp	Plate number	Tagging type
2602	(10¢) Eagle & Shield (1991) "Bulk Rate USA" (continued)	A43326, A43334, A43335, A43426, A53335,A54444, A54445, A77777, A88888, A88889, A89999, A99998, A99999, A1010101010, A1011101010, A1011101011, A1011101012, A1110101010, A1110101011, A1110111110, A1111101010, A1111111010, A1211101010, A1411101010, A1411101011, A1412111110, A1412111111	
2603	(10¢) Eagle & Shield "USA Bulk Rate" (1993)	11111, 22221 22222, 33333, 44444	untagged[9]
2603b	**(10¢) Eagle & Shield "USA Bulk Rate" (1993)**	**11111, 22221 22222**	tagged error
2604	(10¢) Eagle & Shield (gold) "USA Bulk Rate" (1993)	S11111, S22222	untagged[16]
3270	(10¢) Eagle & Shield "USA Presorted Std" (1998)	11111	untagged
3270a	(10¢) Eagle & Shield "USA Presorted Std" (1998)	**22222**	untagged
2905	(10¢) Auto (1995)	S111, S222, S333	untagged[12]
3229	(10¢) Green Bicycle (1998)	S111	untagged[23, 25]
2908	(15¢) Tail Fin (1995)	11111	untagged
2909	(15¢) Tail Fin (1995)	S11111	untagged[12]
2149a	18¢ Washington (1985)	11121, 33333, 43444	untagged[10]
2150a	21.1¢ Letters (1985)	111111, 111121	untagged
2605	23¢ Flag Presort (1991)	A111, A112, A122, A212, A222, A333	untagged
2606	23¢ USA Presort (1992) (dark blue)	A1111, A2222, A2232, A2233, A3333, A4364, A4443, A4444, A4453	untagged
2607	23¢ USA Presort (1992) (light blue)	1111	untagged[2]
2608	23¢ USA Presort (1993) (violet blue)	S111	untagged
2911	(25¢) Jukebox (1995) "Presorted First-Class"	111111, 212222, 222222, 33222	untagged
2912	(25¢) Jukebox (1995) "Presorted First-Class"	S11111, **S22222**	untagged[12]
3208	(25¢) Diner "Presorted First-Class"	S11111	untagged[23, 25]

Self-adhesive coil stamps

Scott number	Stamp	Plate number	Tagging type
2902B	(5¢) Butte (1996)	S111	untagged[12]
2904A	(5¢) Mountains (1996)	V222222, V333323, V333333, V333342, V333343	untagged[12]

Scott number	Stamp	Plate number	Tagging type
2904B	(5¢) Mountains (1997)	1111	untagged[11, 21, 23, 24]
3207A	(5¢) Wetlands (1998)	1111, **2222, 3333, 4444, 5555**	untagged[11, 21, 22, 23]
2906	(10¢) Auto (1996)	S111	untagged[12]
2907	(10¢) Eagle & Shield (1996)	S11111	untagged[12]
3228	(10¢) Green Bicycle (1998)	111, 221, 222, 333, 344, 444, 555, 666, 777, 888, 999	untagged[21, 23, 24]
3271	(10¢) Eagle & Shield "USA Presorted Std" (1998)	11111, **22222**	untagged[21, 22, 24]
3271a	(10¢) Eagle & Shield "USA Presorted Std" (1998)	**33333**	untagged[21, 22, 24]
3271b	(10¢) Eagle & Shield "Presorted Std"	11111	tagged error[21, 22, 24]
2910	(15¢) Tail Fin (1996)	S11111	untagged[12]
3053	20¢ Blue Jay (1996)	S1111	prephosphored
3055	20¢ Pheasant (1998)	1111, **2222**	prephosphored[21]
3263	22¢ Uncle Sam (1998)	1111	prephosphored[21]
3263	22¢ Uncle Sam (1999)	11111	prephosphored[21]
2912A	(25¢) Jukebox (1997) "Presorted First-Class"	**S11111**, S22222	untagged[21, 22, 23, 24, 27]
2912B	(25¢) Jukebox (1997) "Presorted First-Class"	**11111**, 22222	untagged[21, 22, 23, 24, 27]
3132	(25¢) Jukebox (1997)	M11111	untagged
3208A	(25¢) Diner "Presorted First-Class"	11111, 22211, 22222, 33333, 44444	prephosphored untagged[21, 22, 23, 24, 27]
2480	29¢ Pine Cone (1993)	B1	prephosphored
2799-2802	29¢ Christmas Contemp. (1993)	V1111111	prephosphored
2598	29¢ Eagle (1994)	111	prephosphored
2599	29¢ Statue of Liberty (1994)	D1111	prephosphored
2813	29¢ Sunrise Love (1994)	B1	prephosphored
2873	29¢ Christmas Santa (1994)	V1111	prephosphored
2886	G (32¢) Old Glory self-adhesive (1994)	V11111	prephosphored
2492	32¢ Pink Rose (1995)	S111	prephosphored
2495-95A	32¢ Peach/Pear (1995)	V11111	prephosphored
2915	32¢ Flag Over Porch (1995)	V11111	prephosphored
2915A	32¢ Flag Over Porch (1996)	**11111, 22222, 23222, 33333, 44444, 45444, 55555, 66666, 78777, 87888, 87898, 88888, 88898, 89878, 89888, 89898, 89899, 97898, 99899, 99999,** 11111A, 13211A, 13231A, 13311A, 22222A, 33333A, 44444A, 55555A, 66666A, 77777A, 78777A, 88888A	prephosphored[1, 2]

Scott number	Stamp	Plate number	Tagging type
2915B	32¢ Flag Over Porch (1996)	S11111	prephosphored[12]
2915C	32¢ Flag Over Porch (1996)	55555, 66666	prephosphored
2915D	32¢ Flag Over Porch (1997)	11111	prephosphored
3133	32¢ Flag Over Porch (1997)	M11111	prephosphored
3014-17	32¢ Santa/Children & Toys (1995)	V1111	prephosphored
3018	32¢ Midnight Angel (1995)	B1111	prephosphored
3054	32¢ Yellow Rose (1997)	1111, 1112, 1122, 2222, 2223, 2233, 2333, 3344, 3444, 4455, 5455, 5555, 5556, 5566, 5666, 6666 6677, 6777, 7777, 8888	prephosphored[1, 2]
3281	33¢ City Flag coil (large date)	6666, 7777, 8888, 9999, 1111A, 2222A, 3333A, 4444A, 5555A, 6666A, 7777A, 8888A, 1111B, 2222B	
3281c	**33¢ City Flag coil (small date)**	**1111, 2222, 3333, 3433, 4443, 4444, 5555, 9999A**	
3282	33¢ Flag City (1999)	1111, 2222	prephosphored
3302-05	33¢ Four Fruit Berries (1999)	B1111, B1112, B2211 B2221, B2222	prephosphored[1, 2]
3404-07	33¢ Four Fruit Berries (2000) linerless	G1111	prephosphored
3447	**(10¢) Lion Statue (2000)**	**S11111, S22222**	**untagged**
3453	**(34¢) Statue of Liberty (2000)**	**1111**	**prephosphored**
3462-65	**(34¢) Four Flowers**	**B1111**	**prephosphored**

Test stamps

Scott number	Stamp	Plate number	Tagging type
Unassigned	For Testing Purposes Only black on blue printing paper (1996)	1111	untagged[12, 18]
Unassigned	For Testing Purposes Only black on white (1996)	V1	untagged
Unassigned	**For Testing Purposes Only self-adhesive ATM booklet straight-line die cut**	**V1**	**untagged**
Unassigned	**For Testing Purposes Only self-adhesive ATM booklet serpentine die cut gauge 7.8**	**V1**	**untagged**
Unassigned	**For Testing Purposes Only (blue temple) self-adhesive ATM booklet**	**V1**	**untagged**
Unassigned	**Eagle Over Forest (World Stamp Expo 2000)**	**S1111**	**untagged**
Unassigned	**Eagle linerless coil (1997)**	**1111**	**untagged**

Plate number coil notes

1 *Shiny gum*
2 *Plate number 3 shiny and dull gum*
3 *Service inscribed in black "Nonprofit Org."*
4 *Service inscribed in black "Nonprofit Org. 5-Digit ZIP+4"*
5 *Service inscribed in black "Bulk Rate" (between two lines)*
6 *Service inscribed in red "Bulk Rate Carrier Route Sort"*
7 *Has two black precancel lines*
8 *Shiny gum and dull gum*
9 *22222 shiny and dull gum, 33333 dull gum*
10 *11121 shiny gum, 33333 and 43444 dull gum*
11 *Rolls of 3,000 and 10,000 have back numbers*
12 *Has back numbers*
13 *2 and 4 shiny gum, 3, 4 and 5 low gloss and shiny gum*
14 *22221 shiny only and 11111, 22222 shiny and low gloss gum; others low-gloss gum only*
15 *2 dull gum, 3 dull and shiny gum, 6 shiny gum*
16 *S22222 has back numbers*
17 *Plate number 2 dull gum, 3 shiny dull, 4 shiny*
18 *Tagged paper printed with three layers of opaque white*
19 *3 low-gloss gum*
20 *Shiny gum, new white paper on 2¢ Locomotive*
21 *Die cut, equivalent to perf 10*
22 *Stamps spaced on backing paper*
23 *Back numbers, can be both top and bottom*
24 *Self-adhesive*
25 *Water-activated gum*
26 *Roll of 100, has shinier gum, plate numbers (1111) nearly touch "st-Cl" of "First-Class" on roll of 100, 1998 is ½mm farther to right of perforations as compared to roll of 3,000*
27 *Rounded corners (all four) are found only on spaced self-adhesive stamps*
28 *New white paper and shinier gum on $1 Seaplane with plate number 3*
29 *Process-color plate number digits ordered black, yellow, cyan and magenta*
30 *Process-color plate number digits ordered black, cyan, yellow and magenta*
31 *Process-color plate number digits ordered yellow, magenta, cyan and black*

Great Americans sheet stamps

Scott number	Stamp	Plate number	Perf type	Tagging type
1844	1¢ Dix	1 floating	bull's-eye	block
1844c	1¢ Dix	1, 2 floating	L perf	block
2168	1¢ Mitchell	1	bull's-eye	block
1845	2¢ Stravinsky	1, 2, 3, 4, 5, 6	electric-eye	overall
2169	2¢ Lyon	1, 2	bull's-eye	block
2169a	2¢ Lyon	3	bull's-eye	untagged
1846	3¢ Clay	1, 2	electric-eye	overall
2170	3¢ White	1, 2, 3	bull's-eye	block
2170a	3¢ White	4	bull's-eye	untagged[17]
1847	4¢ Schurz	1, 2, 3, 4	electric-eye	overall
2171	4¢ Flanagan	1	bull's-eye	block
2171a	4¢ Flanagan	1, 2	bull's-eye	untagged
1848	5¢ Buck	1, 2, 3, 4	electric-eye	overall
2172	5¢ Black	1, 2	bull's-eye	block
2173	5¢ Munoz	1	bull's-eye	overall

Scott number	Stamp	Plate number	Perf type	Tagging type
2173a	5¢ Munoz	2	bull's-eye	untagged
1849	6¢ Lippmann	1 floating	L perf	block
1850	7¢ Baldwin	1 floating	L perf	block
1851	8¢ Knox	3, 4, 5, 6	L perf	overall
1852	9¢ Thayer	1 floating	L perf	block
1853	10¢ Russell	1 floating	L perf	block
2175	10¢ Red Cloud	1	bull's-eye	block
2175a	10¢ Red Cloud	1, 2	bull's-eye	overall
2175c	10¢ Red Cloud	2	bull's-eye	prephosphored[17]
2175d	10¢ Red Cloud	2	bull's-eye	prephosphored[18]
1854	11¢ Partridge	2, 3, 4, 5	L perf	overall
1855	13¢ Crazy Horse	1, 2, 3, 4	electric-eye	overall
1856	14¢ Lewis	1 floating	L perf	block
2176	14¢ Howe	1, 2	bull's-eye	block
2177	15¢ Cody	1, 3	bull's-eye	block
2177a	15¢ Cody	2, 3	bull's-eye	overall
2177b	15¢ Cody	1	bull's-eye	prephosphored
1857	17¢ Carson	1, 2, 3, 4, 13, 14, 15, 16	electric-eye	overall
2178	17¢ Lockwood	1, 2	bull's-eye	block
1858	18¢ Mason	1, 2, 3, 4, 5, 6	electric-eye	overall
1859	19¢ Sequoyah	39529, 39530	electric-eye	overall
1860	20¢ Bunche	1, 2, 3, 4, 5, 6, 7, 8, 10, 11, 13	electric-eye	overall
1861	20¢ Gallaudet	1, 2, 5, 6, 8, 9	electric-eye	overall
1862	20¢ Truman	1 floating	L perf	block
1862a	20¢ Truman	2	bull's-eye	block
1862b	20¢ Truman	3	bull's-eye	overall
1862d	20¢ Truman	4	bull's-eye	prephosphored[18]
2179	20¢ Apgar	B1, B2, B3	bull's-eye	prephosphored
2180	21¢ Carlson	1	bull's-eye	block
1863	22¢ Audubon	1 floating	L perf	block
1863d	22¢ Audubon	3	bull's-eye	block
2181	23¢ Cassatt	1	bull's-eye	block
2181a	23¢ Cassatt	1, 2	bull's-eye	overall
2181b	23¢ Cassatt	2, 3	bull's-eye	prephosphored[19]
2182	25¢ London	1, 2	bull's-eye	block
2183	28¢ Sitting Bull	1	bull's-eye	block
2184	29¢ Warren	S1, S2 (six positions)	bull's-eye	prephosphored
2185	29¢ Jefferson	S1, S2 (six positions)	bull's-eye	prephosphored

Scott number	Stamp	Plate number	Perf type	Tagging type
1864	30¢ Laubach	1 floating	L perf	block
1864a	30¢ Laubach	2	bull's-eye	block
1864b	30¢ Laubach	2	bull's-eye	overall
2933	32¢ Hershey	B1, B2	bull's-eye	prephosphored
2934	32¢ Farley	**B1**	bull's-eye	prephosphored
2935	32¢ Luce	B1	bull's-eye	prephosphored
2936	32¢ Wallaces	P1	bull's-eye	prephosphored
1865	35¢ Drew	1, 2, 3, 4	electric-eye	overall
2186	35¢ Chavez	S1, S2 (six positions)	L perf	prephosphored
1866	37¢ Millikan	1, 2, 3, 4	electric-eye	overall
1867	39¢ Clark	1 floating	L perf	block
1867c	39¢ Clark	2	bull's-eye	block
1868	40¢ Gilbreth	1 floating	L perf	block
1868a	40¢ Gilbreth	2	bull's-eye	block
2187	40¢ Chennault	1	bull's-eye	overall
2187a	40¢ Chennault	2	bull's-eye	prephosphored[17]
2188	45¢ Cushing	1	bull's-eye	block
2188a	45¢ Cushing	1	bull's-eye	overall
2938	46¢ Benedict	1	bull's-eye	prephosphored
1869	50¢ Nimitz	1, 2, 3, 4	L perf	overall[18]
1869a	50¢ Nimitz	1, 2	bull's-eye	block
1869d	50¢ Nimitz	2, 3	bull's-eye	overall
1869e	50¢ Nimitz	3	bull's-eye	prephosphored[17]
2189	52¢ Humphrey	1, 2	bull's-eye	prephosphored[20]
2940	55¢ Hamilton	B1, B2, **B3**	bull's-eye	prephosphored
2190	56¢ Harvard	1	bull's-eye	block
2191	65¢ Arnold	1	bull's-eye	block
2192	75¢ Willkie	1	bull's-eye	prephosphored[17]
2942	77¢ Breckinridge	B1, **B2**	die-cut	prephosphored
2943	78¢ Paul	B1, B2	bull's-eye	prephosphored
2193	$1 Revel	1	bull's-eye	block
2194	$1 Hopkins	1	bull's-eye	block
2194b	$1 Hopkins	1	bull's-eye	overall
2194d	$1 Hopkins	2	bull's-eye	prephosphored[17]
2195	$2 Bryan	2	bull's-eye	block
2196	$5 Bret Harte	1	bull's-eye	block
2196b	$5 Bret Harte	2	bull's-eye	prephosphored

Great Americans sheet stamps notes

17 Shiny gum and dull gum
18 Shiny gum
19 Plate number 3 shiny gum
20 Plate number 1 shiny and dull gum, plate number 2 shiny gum

General notes

Plate positions: Floating plate number positions are left or right, either blocks of six or strips of 20 (number must be centered in selvage in a block of six). All other plate number positions consist of upper left, upper right, lower left and lower right, with the following exceptions: 29¢ Warren, 29¢ Jefferson and 35¢ Chavez, which have positions of upper left, center upper right, upper right, lower left, center lower right and lower right. (Traditional corners have plate numbers to the side of the stamps; center positions have plate numbers above or below stamps.)

Tagging types

Block: tagging block centered over design of stamp; no tagging in selvage.

Overall: tagging applied to entire pane, often leaving an untagged strip at outer edge of large margin selvage.

Prephosphored: paper that has phosphorescent taggant applied to the paper by the paper supplier prior to printing. On some stamps, under shortwave UV light, the appearance of the phosphorescent tagging is smooth and even (surface taggant), while on others, the taggant appears mottled (embedded taggant). Examples that exhibit both are the 10¢ Red Cloud, 23¢ Cassatt, 40¢ Chennault, 52¢ Humphrey, 75¢ Willkie and $1 Hopkins from the Great Americans and the 23¢ Lunch Wagon, 29¢ Flag Over Mount Rushmore and the variable-denomination coil (Scott 31, 31a, 31b and 31c) from the plate number coils.

Self-adhesive panes

Scott number	Stamp	Denomination	Total value	Number of subjects	Date of issue	Plate numbers	Notes
3031	Kestrel	1¢	$0.50	50	11/19/99	1111, 2222, 2322, 4444, 5555, 5655, 6666, 6766, 7777, 8888, 9999, **1111A, 2222A, 3222A, 3322A, 4322A, 4333A, 4433A, 5433A, 5544A, 5644A, 6755A, 6766A, 7777A, 8888A, 9999A, 1111B, 2222B, 3333B, 4444B, 5555B**	15
3031A	**Kestrel**	**1¢**	**$0.50**	**50**	**10/2000**	**B111111, B222222, B333333, B444444, B555555**	
3048a	Blue Jay	20¢	$2.00	10	8/2/96	S1111, S2222	10, 14
3050a	Pheasant	20¢	$2.00	10	7/31/98	V1111, V2222, V2232, V2332, V2333, V2342, V2343, V3232, V3233, V3243, V3333	14
3259	Uncle Sam	22¢	$4.40	20	11/9/98	S1111	15
2431a	Eagle & Shield	25¢	$4.50	18	11/10/89	A1111	1, 2, 3

425

Scott number	Stamp	Denomination	Total value	Number of subjects	Date of issue	Plate numbers	Notes
2489a	Red Squirrel	29¢	$5.22	18	6/25/93	D11111, D22211, D22221, D22222, D23133	3
2490a	Red Rose	29¢	$5.22	18	8/19/93	S111	3, 4
2491a	Pine Cone	29¢	$5.22	18	11/5/93	B1, B2, B3, B4, B5, B6, B7, B8, B9, B10, B11, B12, B13, B14, B15, B16	5
2595a	Eagle & Shield	29¢	$4.93	17	9/25/92	B1111-1, B1111-2, B2222-1, B2222-2, B3333-1, B3333-3, B3434-1, B3434-3, B4344-1, B4344-3, B4444-1, B4444-3	3, 6, 7
2596a	Eagle & Shield	29¢	$4.93	17	9/25/92	D11111, D21221, D22322, D32322, D32332, D32342, D42342, D43352, D43452, D43453, D54561, D54563, D54571, D54573, D54673, D61384, D65784	3, 6, 7
2597a	Eagle & Shield	29¢	$4.93	17	9/25/92	S1111	3, 6, 7
2598a	Eagle	29¢	$5.22	18	2/4/94	M111, M112	5
2599a	Statue of Liberty	29¢	$5.22	18	6/24/94	D1111, D1212	5
2802a	Christmas	29¢	$3.48	12	10/28/93	V111-1111, V222-1222, V222-2112, V222-2122, V222-2221, V222-2222, V333-3333	5
2813a	Sunrise Love	29¢	$5.22	18	1/27/94	B111-1, B111-2, B111-3, B111-4, B111-5, B121-5, B221-5, B222-4, B222-5, B222-6, B333-5, B333-7, B333-8, B333-9, B333-10, B333-11, B333-12, B333-14, B333-17, B334-11, B344-11, B344-12, B344-13, B434-10, B444-7, B444-8, B444-9, B444-10, B444-13, B444-14, B444-15, B444-16, B444-17, B444-18, B444-19, B555-20, B555-21	5
2873a	Christmas	29¢	$3.48	12	10/20/94	V1111	5
2886a	G	(32¢)	$5.76	18	12/13/94	V11111, V22222	5
2492a	Pink Rose	32¢	$6.40	20	6/2/95	S111, S112, S333, S444, S555	5, 9, 10
2494a	Peach/Pear	32¢	$6.40	20	7/8/95	V11111, V11122, V11131, V11132, V11232, V12131, V12132, V12211, V12221, V12232, V22212, V22221, V22222, V33142, V33143, V33243,	5, 9, 10

Scott number	Stamp	Denomination	Total value	Number of subjects	Date of issue	Plate numbers	Notes
2494a	Peach/Pear (continued)					V33323, V33333, V33343, V33353, V33363, V33453, V44424, V44434, V44454, V45434, V45464, V54365, V54565, V55365, V55565	
2920a	Flag Over Porch	32¢	$6.40	20	4/18/95	V12211, V12212, V12312, V12321, V12322, V12331, V13322, V13831, V13834, V13836, V22211, V23322, V23422, V23432, V23522, V34743, V34745, V36743, V42556, V45554, V56663, V56665, V56763, V57663, V65976, V78989	5, 9, 10 11, 16
2920c	Flag Over Porch	32¢	$6.40	20	4/18/95	V11111	16
2920De	Flag Over Porch	32¢	$3.20	10	1/20/96	V11111, V12111, V23222, V31121, V32111, V32121, V44322, V44333, V44444, V55555, V66666, V66886, V67886, V68886, V68896, V76989, V77666, V77668, V77766, V77776, V78698, V78886, V78896, V78898, V78986, V78989, V89999	10
2949a	Love Cherub	(32¢)	$6.40	20	2/1/95	B1111-1, B2222-1, B2222-2, B3333-2	16
3011a	Santa/Children with Toys	32¢	$6.40	20	9/30/95	V1111, V1211, V1212, V3233, V3333, V4444	5, 16
3012a	Midnight Children	32¢	$6.40	20	10/19/95	B1111, B2222, B33333	5, 10, 16
3030a	Love Cherub	32¢	$6.40	20	1/20/96	B1111-1, B1111-2, B2222-1, B2222-2	16
3049a	Yellow Rose	32¢	$6.40	20	10/24/96	S1111, S2222	12, 14 16
3071a	Tennessee	32¢	$6.40	20	5/31/96	S11111	
3089a	Iowa Statehood	32¢	$6.40	20	8/1/96	B1111	
3095a	Riverboats	32¢	$6.40	20	8/22/96	V11111	15, 21
3112a	Madonna with Child	32¢	$6.40	20	11/1/96	1111-1, 1211-1, 2212-1, 2222-1, 2323-1, 3323-1, 3333-1, 3334-1, 4444-1, 5544-1, 5555-1, 5556-1, 5556-2, 5656-2, 6656-2, 6666-1, 6666-2, 6766-1, 7887-1, 7887-2, 7888-2, 7988-2	16

Scott number	Stamp	Denomination	Total value	Number of subjects	Date of issue	Plate numbers	Notes
3116a	Family Scenes	32¢	$6.40	20	10/8/96	B1111, B2222, B3333	16
3118	Hanukkah	32¢	$6.40	20	10/22/96	V11111	15, 17
3121	Benjamin Davis	32¢	$6.40	20	1/28/97	B1111	15
3122a	Statue of Liberty	32¢	$6.40	20	2/1/97	V1111, V1211, V1311, V2122, V2222, V2311, **V2331**, V3233, V3333, V3513, V4532	13, 14 16
3122E	Statue of Liberty	32¢	$6.40	20	2/1/97	V1111, V1211, V2122, V2222	14, 16, 18
3123a	Love Swans	32¢	$6.40	20	2/4/97	B1111, B2222, B3333, B4444, B5555, B6666, B7777	16
3125	Help Children Learn	32¢	$6.40	20	2/18/97	V1111	15
3127a	Botanical Prints	32¢	$6.40	20	3/3/97	S11111, S22222, S33333	14, 16
3173	Supersonic	32¢	$6.40	20	10/14/97	B1111	15
3175	Kwanzaa	32¢	$16.00	50	10/22/97	V1111	15
3176a	Madonna with Child	32¢	$6.40	20	10/27/97	1111, 2222, 3333	14, 16
3177a	American Holly	32¢	$6.40	20	10/30/97	B1111, B2222, B3333	14, 16
3181	Madam C.J. Walker	32¢	$6.40	20	1/28/98	B111	15
3197a	Flowering Trees	32¢	$6.40	20	3/19/98	B111111, B222222	15
3203	Cinco de Mayo	32¢	$6.40	20	4/16/98	S11111	15
3206	Wisconsin	32¢	$6.40	20	5/29/98	S1111	15, 17
3227	Organ Donation	32¢	$6.40	20	8/5/98	V11111	15
3234a	Bright Eyes	32¢	$6.40	20	8/20/98	B211112, B333333, B444444	15
3243	Giving & Sharing	32¢	$6.40	20	10/7/98	V1111	15
3244a	Madonna with Child	32¢	$6.40	20	10/15/98	11111, 22222, 33333	16
3252a	Wreaths	32¢	$6.40	20	10/15/98	B111111	
3252b	Wreaths	32¢	$6.40	20	10/15/98	B111111, B222222, B333333, B444444, B555555	14, 16
3052d	Coral Rose	33¢	$6.60	20	8/13/99	S111, S222	14, 16
3052Ef	**Pink Coral Rose**	**33¢**	**$6.60**	**20**	**4/7/00**	**S111, S222, S333**	**14, 16**
3268a	H (Hat)	(33¢)	$3.30	10	11/9/98	V1111, V1211, V2211, V2222	

Scott number	Stamp	Denomination	Total value	Number of subjects	Date of issue	Plate numbers	Notes
3268b	H (Hat)	(33¢)	$6.60	20	11/9/98	V1111, V1112, V1113, V1122, V1213, V1222, V2113, V2122, V2213, V2222, V2223	16
3273	Malcolm X	33¢	$6.60	20	1/20/99	B111	15
3274a	Victorian Love	33¢	$6.60	20	1/28/99	V1111, V1112, V1117, V1118, V1211, V1212, V1213, V1233, V1313, V1314, V1333, V1334, V1335, V2123, V2221, V2222, V2223, V2324, V2424, V2425, V2426, V3123, V3124, V3125, V3133, V3134, V3323, V3327, V3333, V3334, V3336, V4529, V4549, V5650	15
3276	Hospice Care	33¢	$6.60	20	2/9/99	B1111, B2222	15
3278	City Flag	33¢	$6.60	15	2/25/99	V1111, V1211, V2222	14, 15
3278d	City Flag	33¢	$3.30	10	2/25/99	V1111, V1112, V1113, V2222, V2322, **V2324, V3433,** V3434, V3545	14
3278e	City Flag	33¢	$6.60	20	2/25/99	V1111, V1211, V2122, V2222, V2223, V3333, V4444, **V8789**	14, 16
3278Fg	City Flag	33¢	$6.60	20	2/25/99	V1111, V1131, V2222, V2223, **V2227, V2243,** V2323, V2423, V2443, V3333, V4444, **V5428,** V5445, **V5446, V5576, V5578,** V6423, V6456, V6546, V6556, **V6575,** V6576, V7567, **V7663,** V7667, **V7676, V8789**	14, 16
3297b	Fruit Berries (single sided)	33¢	$6.60	20	4/10/99	B1111, B1112, B2211, B2222, B3331, B3332, B3333, B4444, B5555	14, 16
3297d	**Fruit Berries (two sided)**	**33¢**	**$6.60**	**20**	**3/15/00**	**B1111**	
3309	Cinco de Mayo	33¢	$6.60	20	4/27/99	B111111	15
3313b	Tropical Flowers	33¢	$6.60	20	5/1/99	S11111, S22222, S22244, S22344, S22444, S22452, S22462,	19

Scott number	Stamp	Denomination	Total value	Number of subjects	Date of issue	Plate numbers	Notes
3313b	Tropical Flowers (continued)					S23222, S24222, S24224 S24242, S24244, S24422, S24442, S24444, S26462, S32323, S32333, S32444, S33333, S44444, S45552, S46654, S55452, S55552, S56462, S62544, S62562, S64452, S64544, **S65544,** S65552, S66462, S66544, S66552, S66562, S66652	
3314	John and William Bartram	33¢	$6.60	20	5/18/99	B1111, B2222	15
3315	Prostate Cancer	33¢	$6.60	20	5/28/99	V11111, V11121, V22112	15
3320a	Aquarium Fish	33¢	$6.60	20	6/24/99	B1111, B2222	15
3324a	Xtreme Sports	33¢	$6.60	20	6/25/99	V1111, V2222	15
3331	Those Who Served	33¢	$6.60	20	8/16/99	V111	15
3352	Hanukkah	33¢	$6.60	20	10/8/99	V11111	15
3355	Madonna and Child	33¢	$6.60	20	10/20/99	B1111, B2222, B3333	19
3359a	Deer	33¢	$6.60	20	10/20/99	B111111	14, 15
3363a	Deer	33¢	$6.60	20	10/20/99	B111111, B222222, B333333, B444444, B555555, B666666, **B777777, B888888, B999999, B000000, BAAAAAA, BBBBBBB**	14
3368	Kwanzaa	33¢	$6.60	20	10/29/99	V1111	15
3369	2000 New Year	33¢	$6.60	20	12/27/99	**B11111**	15
2941	Justin Morrill	55¢	$11.00	20	7/17/99	B1, **B2**	15
2960a	Love Cherub	55¢	$11.00	20	5/12/95	B1111-1, B2222-1	9, 16
3124a	Love Swans	55¢	$11.00	20	2/4/97	B1111, B2222, B3333, B4444	16
3275	Victorian Love	55¢	$11.00	20	1/28/99	B1111111, B2222222 **B3333333**	15
3330	Billy Mitchell	55¢	$11.00	20	7/30/99	B11111, B11211	15
2942	M. Breckinridge	77¢	$15.40	20	11/9/98	B1, B2	15
3036	Red Fox	$1	$20.00	20	8/14/98	B1111, **B3333**	15
3261	Shuttle Landing	$3.20	$64.00	20	11/9/98	B1111, B2222 B3333	15
3262	Shuttle Piggyback	$11.75	$235.00	20	11/19/98	**B11111, B22222, B33333**	15
3371	**Patricia R. Harris**	**33¢**	**$6.60**	**20**	**1/27/00**	**P1111, P2222, P3333, P4444**	

Scott number	Stamp	Denomi-nation	Total value	Number of subjects	Date of issue	Plate numbers	Notes
3398	Adoption	33¢	$6.60	20	5/10/00	B11111, B22222	
3408	Legends of Baseball	33¢	$6.60	20	7/6/00	P1111, P2222, P3333, P4444	
3414-17	Stampin' the Future	33¢	$6.60	20	7/13/00	P11111, P22222, P33333	
3420	General Joseph W. Stilwell	10¢	$2.00	20	8/24/00	B11-1	
3426	Claude Pepper	33¢	$6.60	20	9/7/00	B11-1	
3438	California Statehood	33¢	$6.60	20	9/8/00	V11111	
3445	White House	33¢	$6.60	20	10/18/00	P1111, P2222 P3333	
3449	Flag Over Farm	33¢	$6.60	20	12/15/00	P1111, P2222 P3333	
3451a	Statue of Liberty	34¢	$6.80	20	12/15/00	V1111, V2222	
3457e	Four Flowers	34¢	$6.80	20	12/15/00	S1111	
3461b	Four Flowers	34¢	$6.80	20	12/15/00	S1111	
3461c	Four Flowers	34¢	$6.80	20	12/15/00	S1111	
B1	Breast Cancer	(32+8¢)	$8.00	20	7/29/99	V111111, V121111	15, 20
C133	Niagara Falls	48¢	$9.60	20	5/12/00	V11111, V22111, V22222	15
C134	Rio Grande	40¢	$8.00	20	7/30/99	V11111	15
C135	Grand Canyon	60¢	$12.00	20	1/20/00	B1111	

(Note: self-adhesive panes that do not contain a plate number are excluded from this listing)

Automated teller machine (ATM) panes

Scott number	Stamp	Denomi-nation	Total value	Number of subjects	Date of issue	Plate numbers	Notes
2475a	Stylized Flag	25¢	$3.00	12	5/18/90	—	
2522a	F	(29¢)	$3.48	12	1/22/91	—	
2531Ab	Liberty Torch (revised back)	29¢ 29¢	$5.22 $5.22	18 18	6/25/91 10/??/92	— —	8
2719a	Locomotive	29¢	$5.22	18	1/28/92	V11111	
2803a	Snowman	29¢	$5.22	18	10/28/93	V11111, V2222	
2874a	Cardinal	29¢	$5.22	18	10/20/94	V11111, V2222	
2887a	G	(32¢)	$5.76	18	12/13/97	—	
2919a	Flag Over Field	32¢	$5.76	18	3/17/95	V1111, V1311, V1433, V2111, V2222, V2322	
3013a	Children Sledding	32¢	$5.76	18	10/19/95	V1111	

Scott number	Stamp	Denomination	Total value	Number of subjects	Date of issue	Plate numbers	Notes
3117a	Skaters	32¢	$5.76	18	10/8/96	V1111, V2111	
3269a	H	(33¢)	$5.94	18	11/9/98	V1111	
3283a	Classroom Flag	33¢	$5.94	18	5/13/99	V1111	
3450a	**Flag Over Farm**	**(34¢)**	**$6.80**	**20**	**12/15/00**	**V1111**	

(Note: ATM panes that do not contain a plate number are included in this listing)

Notes for self-adhesive panes

1 *Selling price was $5, which included a 50¢ surcharge. On September 7, 1990, the USPS announced it was sending 400,000 Eagle & Shield stamps to the U.S. Forces in the Persian Gulf Area. The selling price would be $4.50, thus eliminating the surcharge.*
2 *Plate numbers are in two positions, upper left and lower right.*
3 *Also available in coil format.*
4 *There are two different UPC bar codes on the back of the liner. The correct one is 16694. The other one, 16691, is the number for the African Violets booklet.*
5 *Also available in coil format with plate number.*
6 *When originally issued, the selling price was $5 (7¢ surcharge). The* Postal Bulletin *dated February 18, 1993, announced that beginning March 1, 1993, the new selling price would be $4.93, thus removing the surcharge.*
7 *The pane contains 17 stamps and one label the same size as the stamps.*
8 *Originally printed on prephosphored paper with and without a lacquer coating. When reissued with the revised back in October 1992, the panes were tagged on press (overall tagged). See* Linn's Stamp News *December 7, 1992, issue.*
9 *The Peach/Pear, Flag Over Porch, and the Pink Rose all have reorder labels in the lower right corner of the pane. To discourage the use of these labels as postage, later printings had a target and x die cut into the label. The Peach/Pear V12131, V33323 and V33333 exist both plain & die cut, while V33353 and higher numbers exist die cut only. The Flag Over Porch V23322 and V23422 exist both plain and die cut, while V12331, V13831, V13834, V13836, V23522, V34743, V34745, V36743, V42556, V45554, V56663, V56665, V56763, V57663, V65976 and V78989 exist die cut only. The Pink Rose S444 exists both plain and die cut while S555 exists die cut only. The 55¢ Love Cherub B2222-1 exists die cut only.*
10 *In 1996, to lower costs, USPS instructed printers that printing on the inside of the liners was no longer required. Several sheetlets that were originally issued with printed liners had unprinted liners on later releases. The following issues can be found with both printed and unprinted liners: 20¢ Blue Jay (S1111 and S2222 both ways); 32¢ Love Cherub (B2222-1 and B2222-2 both ways); 32¢ Pink Rose (S555 both ways); 32¢ Flag Over Porch (V23322, V23422, V42556 and V45554 both ways; V13831, V13834, V13836, V23522, V34745, V36743, V56663, V56763, V57663, V65976 and V78989 with unprinted liners only). The Flag Over Porch panes of 10 have unprinted liners on any panes with plate number V44322 or higher. The original Midnight Angel (B1111 and B2222) have printed liners while the reissue (B3333) has an unprinted liner.*
11 *In 1997 the printing on the back of the pane was changed to "NATIONAL DOMESTIC VIOLENCE HOTLINE." The original inscription was "Stamps etc." Plate V34745 exists with both backings, while 36743, V56663, V56763, V57663 and V78989 exist only with the new backing. All other plates were printed with the original "Stamps etc." inscription.*
12 *There are three different back printings: "108th Tournament of Roses Parade," "Kids! Start Stampin!" and "Delivering the Gift of Life The National Marrow Donor Program." Both S1111 and S2222 are available with all three printings.*
13 *There are two different back printings: "Stamps etc." and "NATIONAL DOMESTIC VIOLENCE HOTLINE." Plate number V3333 exists with "Stamps etc." only; V1311, V2222, V2311, V2331, V3233, V3513 and V4532 are found with "NATIONAL DOMESTIC VIOLENCE HOTLINE" only. Plate numbers V1111, V1211 and V2122 can be found with both.*
14 *Also available in a folded version for vending-machine use: Blue Jay ($2.00), Ring-Necked Pheasant ($2.00), Yellow Rose ($4.80 and $9.60), Statue of Liberty ($4.80 and*

9.60), *Botanical Prints ($4.80) and American Holly ($4.80 and $9.60) Wreaths ($4.80), City Flag ($4.95), Fruit Berries ($4.95), Coral Rose ($4.95) and Deer ($4.95).*
15 *Each pane contains four plate numbers, in selvage adjacent to corner position stamps.*
16 *The pane contains 20 stamps and one label the same size as the stamps.*
17 *The reissue has a different style die cut in the backing paper than the original.*
18 *There are two different back printings: "Stamps etc." and "National Domestic Violence Hotline." Plate numbers V1111 and V2222 exist with "National Domestic Violence Hotline" only. Plate numbers V1211 and V2122 can be found with both.*
19 *Stamps are printed on both sides of the pane (single liner between them). Plate number is only present on one of two sides. Also includes a label identifying issue and the price of the pane.*
20 *Initially, the Breast Cancer semipostal stamp was valued at 32¢ for postage and 8¢ for cancer research. Effective with the 1999 rate change, this changed to 33¢ for postage and 7¢ for cancer research.*
21 *Exists with and without a special die cut for philatelic purposes.*

Booklets with plate numbers

Scott booklet number	Booklet	Scott pane number	Denom- ination	Plate numbers	Notes
137	$3.60 Animals	2 panes 1889a	18¢	1-16	1, 2
138	$1.20 Flag	1 pane 1893a	two 6¢ & six 18¢	1	
139	$1.20 Flag	1 pane 1896a	20¢	1	3, 4
140	$2 Flag	1 pane 1896b	20¢	1, 4,	3, 4
140A	$4 Flag	2 panes 1896b	20¢	2, 3, 4	3, 4
140B	$28.05 Eagle	1 pane 1900a	$9.35	1111	2
142	$4 Sheep	2 panes 1949a	20¢	1-6, 9-12, 14-26, 28, 29	1, 2, 5
142a	$4 Sheep	2 panes 1949d	20¢	34	5
143	$4.40 D	2 panes 2113a	D (22¢)	1-4	5
144	$1.10 Flag	1 pane 2116a	22¢	1, 3	3
145	$2.20 Flag	2 panes 2116a	22¢	1, 3	
146	$4.40 Seashells	2 panes 2121a	22¢	1-3	
147	$4.40 Seashells	2 panes 2121a	22¢	1, 3, 5-8, 10	
148	$32.25 Eagle	1 pane 2122a	$10.75	11111	3
149	$32.25 Eagle	1 pane 2122a	$10.75	22222	
150	$5 London	2 panes 2182a	25¢	1, 2	6
151	$1.50 London	1 pane 2197a	25¢	1	
152	$3 London	1 pane 2197a	25¢	1	
153	$1.76 Stamp Collecting	1 pane 2201a	22¢	1	
154	$2.20 Fish	2 panes 2209a	22¢	11111, 22222	
155	$2.20 Special Occasions	1 pane 2274a	22¢	11111, 22222	
156	$4.40 Flag	1 pane 2276a	22¢	1111, 2122, 2222	6
157	$5 E	2 panes 2282a	E (25¢)	1111, 2122, 2222	
158	$5 Pheasant	2 panes 2283a	25¢	A1111	

Scott booklet number	Booklet	Scott pane number	Denomination	Plate numbers	Notes
159	$5 Pheasant	2 panes 2283c	25¢	A3111, A3222	
160	$5 Owl/Grosbeak	2 panes 2285b	25¢	1111, 1211, 2122, 2222, 1112, 1133, 1433, 1414, 1434, 1634, 1734, 2111, 2121, 2122, 2221, 2222, 2321, 2822, 3133, 3233, 3333, 3412, 3413, 3422, 3512, 3521, 4642, 4644, 4911, 4941, 5453, 5955	3
161	$3 Flag	2 panes 2285c	25¢	1111	
162	$4.40 Constitution	4 panes 2359a	22¢	1111, 1112	3
163	$4.40 Locomotive	4 panes 2366a	22¢	1, 2	6
164	$5 Classic Cars	4 panes 2385a	25¢	1	6
165	$3 Special Occasions	1 pane each 2396a/2398a	25¢	A1111	3, 6, 7
166	$5 Steamboat	4 panes 2409a	25¢	1, 2	7
167	$5 Madonna	2 panes 2427a	25¢	1	6, 7
168	$5 Sleigh	2 panes 2429a	25¢	1111, 2111	6, 7
169	$5 Love	2 panes 2441a	25¢	1211, 2111, 2211, 2222	6, 7
170	$3 Beach Umbrella	2 panes 2443a	15¢	111111, 221111	6, 7
171	$5 Lighthouse	4 panes 2474a	25¢	1, 2, 3, 4, 5	6, 7
172	$2 Bluejay	1 pane 2483a	20¢	S1111	7
173	$2.90 Wood Duck	1 pane 2484a	29¢	4444	7
174	$5.80 Wood Duck	2 panes 2484a	29¢	1111, 1211, 2222, 3221, 3222, 3331, 3333, 4444	7, 8
175	$5.80 Wood Duck	2 panes 2485a	29¢	K11111	7, 9
176	$2.95 African Violet	1 pane 2486a	29¢	K1111	7
177	$5.80 African Violet	2 panes 2486a	29¢	K1111	7
178	$6.40 Peach/Pear	2 panes 2488a	32¢	11111	6, 7
179	$5 Indian Headdress	2 panes 2505a	25¢	1, 2	7
180	$5 Madonna	2 panes 2514a	25¢	1	6, 7
181	$5 Christmas Tree	2 panes 2516a	25¢	1211	6, 7
182	$2.90 F	1 pane 2519a	F (29¢)	2222	6
183	$5.80 F	2 panes 2519a	F (29¢)	1111, 1222, 2111, 2121, 2212, 2222	6
184	$2.90 F	1 pane 2520a	F (29¢)	K1111	9
185	$5.80 Tulip	2 panes 2527a	29¢	K1111, K2222, K3333	7, 9
186	$2.90 Flag	1 pane 2528a	29¢	K11111	7, 9
186A	$2.90 Flag	1 pane 2528a	29¢	K11111	3, 9
187	$3.80 Balloon	1 pane 2530a	19¢	1111, 2222	7

Scott booklet number	Booklet	Scott pane number	Denom- ination	Plate numbers	Notes
188	$5.80 Love	1 pane 2536a	29¢	1111, 1112, 1212, 1113, 1123, 2223	6, 7
189	$5.80 Fishing Flies	4 panes 2549a	29¢	A11111, A22122, A22132, A22133, A23123, A23124, A23133, A23213, A31224, A32224, A32225, A33233 A33235, A44446, A45546, A45547	6, 7, 10
190	$5.80 Desert Storm/Shield	4 panes 2552a	29¢	A11111111, A11121111	7
191	$5.80 Comedians	2 panes 2566a	29¢	1, 2	7
192	$5.80 Space Explorations	2 panes 2577a	29¢	111111, 111112	7
193	$5.80 Madonna	2 panes 2578a	(29¢)	1	6, 7
194	$5.80 Santa Claus	4 panes 2581b-2585a	(29¢)	A11111, A12111	7
195	$2.90 Pledge	1 pane 2593a	29¢	1111, 2222	7
196	$5.80 Pledge	2 panes 2593a	29¢	1111, 1211, 2122, 2222	
197	$5.80 Pledge	2 panes 2593c	29¢	1111, 1211, 2122, 2222 2232, 2333, 3333, 4444	6, 11
198	$2.90 Pledge	1 pane 2594a	29¢	K1111	7
199	$5.80 Pledge	2 panes 2594a	29¢	K1111	
201	$5.80 Humming- birds	4 panes 2646a	29¢	A1111111, A2212112, A2212122, A2212222, A2222222	3, 7
202	$5.80 Animals	4 panes 2709a	29¢	K1111	7,9
202A	$5.80 Madonna	2 panes 2710a	29¢	1	6,7
203	$5.80 Christmas Contemporary	5 panes 2718a	29¢	A111111, A112211, A222222	7
204	$5.50 Rock 'n' Roll	2 panes 2737a & 1 pane 2737b	29¢	A11111, A13113 A22222, A44444	7
207	$5.80 Space Fantasy	4 panes 2745a	29¢	1111, 1211, 2222	7
208	$5.80 Flowers	4 panes 2746a	29¢	1, 2	6, 7
209	$5.80 Broadway Musicals	4 panes 2770a	29¢	A11111, A11121, A22222, A23232, A23233	7
210	$5.80 Country & Western	4 panes 2778a	29¢	A111111, A222222, A333323, A333333, A422222	7
211	$5.80 Madonna	5 panes 2790a	29¢	K1-11111, K1-33333, K1-44444, K2-22222, K2-55555, K2-66666	7, 10
212	$5.80 Christmas Contemporary	1 pane each 2798a, 2798b	29¢	111111, 222222	6, 7
213	$5.80 AIDS	4 panes 2806b	29¢	K111	7, 9
214	$5.80 Love	2 panes 2814a	29¢	A11111, A11311, A12111, A12112, A12211, A12212,	7

Scott booklet number	Booklet	Scott pane number	Denom-ination	Plate numbers	Notes
214	$5.80 Love (continued)			A21222, A21311, A22122, A22222, A22322	
215	$5.80 Flowers	4 panes 2833a	29¢	1, 2	6, 7
216	$5.80 Locomotives	4 panes 2847a	29¢	S11111	7
217	$5.80 Madonna	2 panes 2871b	29¢	1, 2	6, 7
218	$5.80 Stocking	1 pane 2872a	29¢	P11111, P22222, P33333, P44444	7
219	$3.20 G	1 pane 2881a	G (32¢)	1111	6
220	$3.20 G	1 pane 2883a	G (32¢)	1111, 2222	
221	$6.40 G	2 panes 2883a	G (32¢)	1111, 2222	
222	$6.40 G	2 panes 2884a	G (32¢)	A1111, A1211, A2222, A3333, A4444	3, 10
223	$6.40 G	2 panes 2885a	G (32¢)	K1111	9
225	$3.20 Flag Over Porch	1 pane 2916a	32¢	11111, 22222, 23222, 33332, 44444	6, 7
226	$6.40 Flag Over Porch	2 panes 2916a	32¢	11111, 22222, 23222, 33332, 44444	
227A	$4.80 Flag Over Porch	1 pane each 2921a, 2921b	32¢	11111	6, 7, 12
228	$6.40 Flag Over Porch	2 panes 2921a	32¢	11111, 13111, 21221, 22221, 22222, 44434, 44444, 55555, **55556**, 66666, **77777. 88788 88888, 99999**	3, 6, 7
228A	$9.60 Flag Over Porch	3 panes 2921a	32¢	11111	6, 7, 12
229	$6.40 Love	2 panes 2959a	32¢	1	6, 7
230	$6.40 Lighthouses	4 panes 2973a	32¢	S11111	7
231	$6.40 Garden Flowers	4 panes 2997a	32¢	2	6, 7
232	$6.40 Madonna	2 panes 3003b	32¢	1	6, 7
233	$6.40 Santa & Children	1 pane each 3007b & 3007c	32¢	P1111, P2222	7, 10
234	$6.40 Flowers	4 panes, 3029a	32¢	1	6, 7
237	**$2.00 Blue Jay**	**1 pane each 3048b, 3048c**	**20¢**	**S1111**	
241	**$4.80 Yellow Rose**	**1 pane each 3049b-3049d**	**32¢**	**S1111**	
242	**$9.60 Yellow Rose**	**5 panes 3049d**	**32¢**	**S1111**	
242A	**$2.00 Ringed-Neck Pheasant**	**1 pane each 3051b, 3051c**	**20¢**	**V1111**	
242B	**$4.95 Coral Pink Rose**	**1 pane each 3052a-3052c**	**33¢**	**S111**	

Scott booklet number	Booklet	Scott pane number	Denom- ination	Plate numbers	Notes
259	$4.80 Statue of Liberty	1 pane each 3122b-3122d	32¢	V1111	
260	$9.60 Statue of Liberty	5 panes of 3122d	32¢	V1111	
260A	$4.80 Statue of Liberty	5 panes of 3122Eg	32¢	V1111	
261	$4.80 Merian Botanical Plants	2 panes 3128b, 1 pane 3129b	32¢	S11111	
264	$4.80 American Holly	1 pane each 3177b-3177d	32¢	B1111	
265	$9.60 American Holly	5 panes of 3177d	32¢	B1111	
270	$4.80 Wreaths	1 pane each 3248a-3248c	32¢	B111111	
271	($6.60) H Hat	2 panes of 3267a	(33¢)	1111, 2222, 3333	
275	$4.95 City Flag	1 pane each 3278a-3278c	33¢	V1111, V1112, V1121, V1122 V1212, V2212	
276	$6.60 City Flag	2 panes of 3279a	33¢	1111, 1121	
276A	$4.95 Fruit Berries	1 pane each 3301a-3301c	33¢	B1111, B1112, B2212, B2221, B2222	
276B	$4.95 Deer	1 pane each 3367a-3367c	33¢	B111111, B222222	
280	($6.80) Statue of Liberty	2 panes each 3451b, 3451c	(34¢)	V1111	
281	($6.80) Four Flowers	1 pane each 3457c, 3457d, 2 panes of 3457b	(34¢)	S1111	

Notes for booklets with plate numbers.

1 Joint lines on some panes.
2 Electric-eye (EE) marks on tabs.
3 Cover varieties.
4 Panes available scored or unscored.
5 Plate number either on top or bottom pane.
6 Various markings on either the selvage or the panes themselves allow these panes to be plated by position.
7 Available as never-folded or never-bound panes.
8 Panes issued either overall tagged or on prephosphored paper.
9 Panes can be found with cutting lines on either stamp number 5 or 6 (vertically oriented panes) or stamp number 3 or 8 (horizontally oriented panes).
10 Each of the panes in these booklets can have different plate numbers on them.
11 Shiny and dull gum.
12 Pane 2921a has a 1997 year date.

No-hole panes

The following is a list of those panes that were officially issued by the U.S. Post Office Department and/or U.S. Postal Service as loose panes, i.e., not bound into a booklet and thus not having staple holes. Panes without staple holes can be found that aren't listed below. They aren't listed because they weren't officially issued without staple holes. The lack of staple holes can be caused by the following:

1. Staples passing through the perf holes.
2. Booklets assembled with one staple missing and the other passing through the perf holes or both staples missing.
3. Staple holes at the top of a wide tab that have been trimmed off.

Scott number	Pane	Notes
1035a	3¢ Statue of Liberty (6)	
1036a	4¢ Lincoln (6)	
1213a	5¢ Washington (5 + Slogan 1)	
1278a	1¢ Jefferson (8)	
1278b	1¢ Jefferson (4+2 Labels)	
1280a	2¢ Wright (5+1 Slogan 4 or 5)	
1280c	2¢ Wright (6)	1
1284b	6¢ Roosevelt (8)	
1393a	6¢ Eisenhower (8)	2
1393b	6¢ Eisenhower (5+1 Slogan 4 or 5)	
1395a	8¢ Eisenhower (8)	2
1395b	8¢ Eisenhower (6)	
1395c	8¢ Eisenhower (4 + 1 each Slogans 6 & 7)	2
1395d	8¢ Eisenhower (7 + 1 Slogan 4 or 5)	2
1510b	10¢ Jefferson Memorial (5 + 1 Slogan 8)	
1510c	10¢ Jefferson Memorial (8)	2
1510d	10¢ Jefferson Memorial (6)	
C39a	6¢ Plane (6)	
C51a	7¢ Jet, blue (6)	
C60a	7¢ Jet, carmine (6)	
C64b	8¢ Jet over Capitol (5 + 1 Slogan 1)	
C72b	10¢ Stars (8)	
C78a	11¢ Jet (4 + 1 each Slogans 5 & 4)	
C79a	13¢ Letters (5 + 1 Slogan 8)	

Never-bound panes

By definition, a never-bound pane is one that was never assembled into a booklet. Loose panes such as Scott 1595a-d that were in booklets have small V-notches in the edge of the tab and traces of adhesive. The other panes in this category that were in booklets will have disturbed gum in the tabs showing that they were attached to either the booklet cover or each other.

Scott number	Pane	Plate number	Notes
1595a	13¢ Liberty Bell (6)		
1595b	13¢ Liberty Bell (7 + 1 Slogan 8)		2

Scott number	Pane	Plate number	Notes
1595c	13¢ Liberty Bell (8)		2
1595d	13¢ Liberty Bell (5 + 1 Slogan 9)		
2581b	(29¢) Santa Claus (4)	A11111	
2582a	(29¢) Santa Claus (4)	A11111	
2583a	(29¢) Santa Claus (4)	A11111	
2584a	(29¢) Santa Claus (4)	A11111	
2585a	(29¢) Santa Claus (4)	A11111	
2718a	29¢ Christmas Toys (4)	A111111, A112211, A222222	
2790a	29¢ Madonna (4)	K1-11111, K1-33333, K1-44444, K2-55555	

Never-folded panes

Scott number	Pane	Plate number	Notes
2398a	25¢ Special Occasions (6)	A1111	4
2409a	25¢ Steamboats (5)	1, 2	
2427a	25¢ Madonna (10)	1	4
2429a	25¢ Sleigh (10)	1	4
2441a	25¢ Love (10)	1211	4
2443a	15¢ Beach Umbrella (10)	111111	
2474a	25¢ Lighthouses (5)	1, 2, 3, 4, 5	3, 4
2483a	20¢ Bluejay	S1111	
2484a	29¢ Wood Duck (10)	1111	
2485a	29¢ Wood Duck (10)	K1111	5
2486a	29¢ African Violets (10)	K1111	
2488a	32¢ Fruits (10)	11111	4
2505a	25¢ Indian Headdress (10)	1, 2	
2514a	25¢ Madonna (10)	1	4
2516a	25¢ Christmas Tree (10)	1211	4
2527a	29¢ Tulip (10)	K1111	5
2528a	29¢ Flag w/Olympic Rings (10)	K11111	5
2530a	19¢ Balloons (10)	1111	
2536a	29¢ Love (10)	1111, 1112	4
2549a	29¢ Fishing Flies (5)	A11111, A22122, A23124, A23133, A23213, A32225, A33213, A33233	4
2552a	29¢ Desert Shield/Storm (5)	A11121111	
2566a	29¢ Comedians (10)	1	
2577a	29¢ Space Exploration (10)	111111	
2578a	(29¢) Madonna (10)	1	4
2593a	29¢ Pledge of Allegiance (10)	1111	
2594a	29¢ Pledge of Allegiance (10)	K1111	

Scott number	Pane	Plate number	Notes
2646a	29¢ Hummingbirds (5)	A1111111, A2212112, A2212122, A2212222, A2222222	
2709a	29¢ Animals (5)	K1111	5
2710a	29¢ Madonna (10)	1	4
2737a	29¢ Rock 'n' Roll (8)	A11111, A13113, A22222	6
2737b	29¢ Rock 'n' Roll (4)	A13113, A22222	
2745a	29¢ Space Fantasy (5)	1111, 1211, 2222	
2764a	29¢ Spring Garden Flowers (5)	1	4
2770a	29¢ Broadway Musicals (4)	A11111, A11121, A22222	
2778a	29¢ Country Music (4)	A222222	
2798a	29¢ Christmas Contemporary (10)	111111	4
2798b	29¢ Christmas Contemporary (10)	111111	4
2806b	29¢ AIDS (5)	K111	5
2814a	29¢ Love (10)	A11111	
2833a	29¢ Summer Garden Flowers (5)	2	4
2847a	29¢ Locomotives (5)	S11111	
2871b	29¢ Madonna (10)	1, 2	4
2872a	29¢ Stocking (20)	P11111, P22222, P33333, P44444	
2916a	32¢ Flag Over Porch (10)	11111	4
2921a	32¢ Flag Over Porch (10)	21221, 22221, 22222	4
2921a	32¢ Flag Over Porch (10)	11111	4, 7
2921b	32¢ Flag Over Porch (5 + 1 label)	11111	4
2949a	32¢ Love (10)	1	4
2973a	32¢ Lighthouses (5)	S11111	
2997a	32¢ Fall Garden Flowers (5)	2	4
3003b	32¢ Madonna (10)	1	4
3007b	32¢ Santa and Children (10)	P1111	
3007c	32¢ Santa and Children (10)	P1111	
3029a	32¢ Garden Flowers (5)	1	4

Notes for no-hole, never-bound and never-folded panes

1 Shiny and dull gum.
2 Electric-eye (EE) marks on tabs.
3 Plate 1 panes available with and without scoring.
4 Various markings on either the selvage or the panes themselves allow these panes to be plated by position.
5 Panes can be found with cutting lines on either stamp 5 or 6 (vertically oriented panes) or stamp 3 or 8 (horizontally oriented panes).
6 Panes from A11111 have been found in 1993 Year sets only. They all had the bottom stamp removed and thus are panes of seven, not eight.
7 Has year date 1997.